P9-DEA-171

AMERICAN EVANGELISM

★ ★ ★

Its Theology and Practice

AMERICAN EVANGELISM

Its Theology and Practice

DARIUS SALTER

A Division of Baker Book House Co
Grand Rapids, Michigan 49516

Published by Baker Books
a division of Baker Book House Company
P.O. Box 6287, Grand Rapids, MI 49516-6287

Printed in the United States of America

Library of Congress Cataloging-in Publication Data

Salter, Darius, 1947–
American evangelism: its theology and practice/Darius Salter.
p. cm.
"A BridgePoint book."
Includes bibliographical references.
ISBN 0-8010-9033-4
1. Evangelistic work. 2. Evangelistic work—United States. I. Title.
BV3790.S145 1996
269'.2'0973—dc20 96-34620

Cover photographs: (Top; left to right) 1. Courtesy of the Billy Graham Center Museum 2. Tony Stone Images 3. Photo of Urbana Student Mission Convention used by permission of Inter-Varsity Christian Fellowship of the USA (Bottom; left to right) 1. Michael Hudson Photography 2. Courtesy of the Billy Graham Center Museum 3. Michael Hudson Photography 4. Michael Hudson Photography

For information about academic books, resources for Christian leaders, and all new releases available from Baker Book House, visit our web site:
http://www.bakerbooks.com/

contents

To David and Donna Salter,

the evangelists in my life

introduction

The Apostle Paul possibly would have thought it strange that anyone would attempt to write a book on evangelism. The early church did not do evangelism—it was evangelism. Evangelism as a specialized ministry separated from a plethora of other specialized ministries is not a prominent idea in the New Testament. The church was not an edifice reaching out to nonmembers, enticing and encouraging them to become members of a congregation. The church did not entice—it encompassed by enlarging its borders. Wherever a Christian journeyed the borders of the church were broadened to include that particular locale. The new locale was soon inhabited by new converts who invaded and permeated the common life of the secular community. The borders were as undefinable as the extent of the sun's light and the diffusion of salt's taste. Nevertheless, the difference between the believers' presence and absence was unquestionable.

This book on evangelism is at least partially a confession. It represents the failure of the church to be salt and light in the ordinary commerce of everyday affairs. It reveals the sad state of portable tabernacles whose windows are smudged and whose altars are dimly lit. The church's lack of conspicuousness is not due to a lack of technique, but to a lack of distinction. The demarcation between the church and the world is not due to politics and privatized rituals, but to a relationship with the Creator of the universe who became the incarnate God. When the church truly represents Him and His values, the evangelistic package becomes an easy sell. But "sell" is probably not an accurate theological term. Evangelism is more analogous to giving an unlimited supply of water to a thirsty traveler in a desert. It would be ridiculous to give a rational argument as to why the water should be given or received. The connection between supply and demand is self-evident, and so should it be with evangelism.

A book on evangelism is an admission of default, but a book on American evangelism is a double default. America is the "new Israel," "the relocation of the Garden of Eden," and "the almost chosen people." But the "quest for Paradise," to use Charles Sanford's well-chosen words, has ended in disillusionment. The city in which I now live has just broken its own record for homicides. It is far removed from John Winthrop's "city upon a Hill." Drugs, murders, abortions, broken families, and sexual abuse are among America's dubious distinctions, none of which are tantamount to paradise. We now lead all industrial nations in violent crimes. Education, social programs, and medical technology have all failed to quiet the turmoil that rages within our society.

A book on American evangelism is a statement of both dire need and limitation. The necessity is the church's conversion—the worshiping community needs to be changed by the grace of Jesus Christ so that it will, in time, change the community and the world by the power of that same grace. The church will no longer be a location, but kingdom dwellers emanating God's glory in the presence of beggars who are wasting themselves on demonic lies. Kingdom dwellers are positioned by God where they can strategically offer bread and water to those who discover that they have spent their time and money for that which does not satisfy. Until the kingdom of God invades the American church, the church will not invade America, which at the present time is a dry and thirsty land.

The admission of limitation is a statement of the obvious. But a statement of limitation is also a declaration of focus. I have no intention of severing evangelism from missiology. The evangelization of America is a component of God's total mission scope of the world. It would be imperialistic to call it the most important component. It could well be that another nation or nations will play a more important role in world evangelization than America. A failure to admit this is the result of ethnocentrism and the unwillingness or inability to assess our own desperate spiritual plight.

A concentration on America's salvation is not an issue of cultural pride; it is an issue of cultural necessity. Yes, we live in a global village, but that global village seems to become more and more pluralistic. Cultural diversity is no longer an elitist theory of anthropologists—it is now an inherent and conscious drive in both the most advanced and primitive societies. People groups flaunt their differences. These differences must be sorted through and understood by would-be third-millennium evangelists. Many of the theories and practices explored in this book are universally applicable and would easily translate into other cultures. Thus, references are easily made throughout the work to diverse people and places, past and present. However, the book is primarily about evangelism, past and present, in the United States. A widening of the scope would be beyond my ability at the present time and would necessitate a manuscript several times longer. (Most students will breathe a sigh of relief and expect to broaden their horizons in a subsequent academic course.)

Trying to present a treatise that is up to date guarantees that it will soon be out of date. Today's newspaper is news; yesterday's newspaper is history. Current facts and figures soon give way to population shifts, new technologies, and ever expanding information about ourselves and the world in which we live. Religion is by its very nature conservative, but the world to which it is offered is rapidly and continually changing. However, it is my presumption that at least parts of this book will not be outdated before a copy reaches the hands of the first reader. On the other hand, I ask forgiveness for the information that is "old hat" to the reader who is more advanced in the game than I am.

My deep appreciation goes to the many scholars and practitioners who have influenced my thinking and enabled me to sort through ideas that are critical to an understanding of the evangelistic enterprise. Ideas are thrown at a writer so fast and furiously that knowledge is always in process and never ultimately comprehended.

But there is a faith that runs deeper than a simple initiative to offer a book to those who have interests and concerns that are similar to mine. There is faith in those who have done effective evangelism down through the centuries. This faith does not presume to neglect models who have left a legacy that will continue to influence generations until the consummation of history. The story of American evangelism is as courageous and inspiring as other epochs of the Christian narrative. Attempting evangelism without first unfolding America's evangelistic story smacks of a naïveté and immediatism for which contemporary Americans have a special predilection. We need to be constantly reminded that we build on the foundation laid by other men and women.

This faith not only celebrates the church's past historical effectiveness, but is also ready to affirm God's continued use of humans as instruments for accomplishing His will. This will not automatically happen because the nation was founded by religious aspirants or because God is mentioned in our founding documents. The gospel will continue to bear fruit in the United States, not because of our religious heritage, and certainly not because we have an a priori claim on God's grace, but because grateful individuals carry out their gratitude in both deed and word. God's love will continue to transform persons in the United States and around the world until the Parousia. If we as Christians were not such clumsy transports of that love, the society that we are attempting to seduce would not be bewildered by mixed signals. An evangelism text serves best as a theological and christological treatise on social etiquette. There is always room for improvement.

Thanks to all who have covertly and overtly contributed to this endeavor. I owe deep appreciation to the administration of Western Evangelical Seminary for affording the time and money to at least begin this project. Bill Bauman, a sawmill owner from Oregon, exhibited evangelistic stewardship through a sizable financial contribution that afforded faculty research and sabbaticals. The persons with whom I taught during my eight years in Oregon have made an indelible impression on my life: Bill, Joe, Don, Stan, Tony, Susie, Albert, Allan, and Jim. Who said theological education can't be fun? An environment of mutual encouragement should never be taken for granted.

My research assistants gave invaluable help in word processing and the crafting of a readable manuscript. Meg Robertson faithfully labored with me while I was at Western Evangelical Seminary. Since arriving at Nazarene Theological Seminary, Ken Rowley and Reg Watson have endured many hours of typing, editing, and formatting this manuscript. As my research assistant, Reg stuck with me until we crafted a product worthy of submission to the publisher. As always, there are the librarians who were patient and helpful in response to my requests. Thanks to Patsy Kuhne and her staff at Western Evangelical Seminary and to William Miller and his staff at Nazarene Theological Seminary. They were always sympathetic to my grasping for that one more resource that would shed light on the knowledge gaps that are far more frequent than a writer likes to admit.

I also want to express appreciation to my editor Robert Hosack who assessed this treatise worthy of publication and offered many valuable suggestions.

The bottom line for any project is the simple maxim "No one accomplishes anything alone." The aloneness has been dispelled by hundreds of interactions with friends, not to speak of scholars, many of whom I do not personally know. For all of you I offer up heartfelt thanks to God. Ultimately it is He who makes all of our creativity possible, no matter how simple or sublime.

I

defining evangelism

Where did I first hear the word evangelism? It wasn't in the Bible, because the word does not even appear there. I can't say when the word first crossed my consciousness. I can remember when a derivative of the word became a part of my knowledge inventory: I still have many images of "evangelists" who visited our church when I was growing up. Loud! Long! Convincing! Convicting! Strict! Somber! Pious!

These men and women, for better or for worse (and I think mostly the former), made an indelible impression upon my mind. Whether they fulfilled the biblical role of an evangelist is a question that will be considered later. The word *evangelist* is used three times in the New Testament: Philip is referred to as an evangelist (Acts 21:8), Timothy is exhorted to do the work of an evangelist (2 Tim. 4:5), and we are told that some are called to be evangelists (Eph. 4:11). However, one should not assume on the basis of these limited references that there are not many other allusions to the work of evangelism in the New Testament.

Philip

Since Philip is the only person in the New Testament who is referred to as an evangelist, perhaps we can at least partially define evangelism by taking a closer look at him. The most well-known event in Philip's life occurred in Acts 8. Philip went to Samaria, where he proclaimed Christ and worked miracles. Many believed, were filled with joy, and were baptized. The apostles at Jerusalem observed that Samaria had received the word of God (v. 14). This would seem to mean that there was a great number of Samaritans who responded positively to Philip's message. We do not have sufficient reason to believe that the message of Philip received universal acclaim in the city of Samaria. At any rate, Philip was replaced by Peter and John after this initial Samaritan wave of religious awakening.

After his time in Samaria, Philip was instructed by an angel to take a certain road on his return journey. It was then that he crossed paths with a man, identified in Scripture as "an Ethiopian eunuch" (v. 27). The man was reading from the Book of Isaiah, and Philip was instructed by the Holy Spirit to join him. Philip explained the good news concerning Jesus by reference to the Book of Isaiah, from which the Ethiopian was reading. After this, the man requested baptism, to which Philip consented.

The above anecdote is not an isolated incident, but one which fits the pattern of Philip's life. Philip brought his brother, Nathanael, to meet Christ (John 1:45). Philip, along with Andrew, introduced Greeks who were visiting Jerusalem to Christ. The last statement concerning Philip's activities that we read in the New Testament is Acts 8:40: "But Philip found himself at Azotus; and as he passed through he kept preaching the gospel to all the cities, until he came to Caesarea."

EUANGELION

In order for us to understand the components of evangelism, let's list the verbs that characterized Philip's life: found, said, told, went (traveled), ran, joined, baptized, and preached. Most of these words have fairly self-evident meanings except for the last: preached. Philip preached the gospel (Acts 8:12, 40). In each case, the writer uses a derivative of the word *euangelion*, which basically means a proclamation of good news. It is Paul who champions the word in the New Testament. According to Hauck Friedrich, "For Paul the heart of the good news is the story of Jesus and His suffering, death and resurrection. Everything connected with this may be the preaching of [the] Gospel. It has the right to be so in virtue of its connection with Christ."[1]

Jesus' best known use of *euangelion* is found in Luke 4:18, where He introduces His ministry by quoting from Isaiah: "The Spirit of the Lord is upon Me, because He anointed Me to preach the gospel to the poor." Since the life of Christ was the very essence of the proclamation of good news, His birth is referred to as an *euangelion*. John the Baptist was the first in the New Testament to bring this good news to the people (Luke 3:17). The noun *euangelion* is used seventy-seven times in the New Testament and, for the most part, English translators have chosen to render the word "gospel," "glad tidings," or "good news."

Paul understood his primary task to be the preaching of the gospel: "For Christ did not send me to baptize, but to preach the gospel, not in cleverness of speech, that the cross of Christ should not be made void" (1 Cor. 1:17). It was by this means that people would believe and in turn be saved (1 Cor. 1:21). Paul carefully outlines the steps in Romans 10. Being saved is predicated upon calling on the name of the Lord. Calling on the name of the Lord must be preceded by believing on the name of the Lord. Believing on the name of the Lord cannot take place unless someone hears about the name of the Lord. Hearing will not take place without a preacher. There will not be any preachers unless they are sent by God and the church. "Just as it is written, 'How beautiful are the feet of those who bring glad tidings *[euangelizomenon]* of good things!'" (Rom. 10:15).

This bearing of good news is more than verbal proclamation. It represents the many concomitants of the gospel that find their locus in Jesus Christ. It is everything good that the kingdom entails. "And Jesus was going about in all Galilee, teaching in their synagogues, and proclaiming the gospel *[euangelion]* of the kingdom, and healing every kind of disease and every kind of sickness among the people" (Matt. 4:23). Friedrich addresses the full-orbed nature of the task.

> Euangelizesthai is not just speaking and preaching; it is

> proclamation with full authority and power. Signs and wonders accompany the evangelical message. They belong together, for the word is powerful and effective. The proclamation of the age of grace, of the rule of God, creates a healthy state in every respect. . . . It is the powerful proclamation of the good news, the impartation of soteria.[2]

The Narrow Parameters of the Message

The Word, which is life changing, is Jesus Christ. He is the content of the message. In a sense, the evangelism of which we speak is defined by narrow parameters. Jesus was quite clear about this: "Truly, truly, I say to you, he who does not enter by the door into the fold of the sheep, but climbs up some other way, he is a thief and a robber" (John 10:1). Evangelism simply as propagation, persuasion, technique, therapy, drugs, or disciplines, no matter how effective they might be in changing people, is not the thrust of this book. New Testament evangelism is more than just a process; it is a process with a specific message and goal.

I do not make the limitation above because I discount the ability of cultic commitment, psychological technique, or behavioral modification to change people. Both Jehovah's Witnesses and transactional analysis may do some good, but both are insufficient in the light of biblical evangelism and the full import of salvation. The first evangelistic message preached after the ascension of Christ was quite clear about this. Peter proclaimed, "And it shall be, that everyone who calls on the name of the Lord shall be saved" (Acts 2:21). If this prescription was not demarcated clearly enough, listen to the following words also from the mouth of Peter: "And there is salvation in no one else; for there is no other name under heaven that has been given among men, by which we must be saved" (Acts 4:12). The name to which Peter refers is the historical, incarnated Christ, with whom Peter walked and talked. Unless one believes in this same Jesus, there is no salvation. Any variation on the *sine qua non* of the message is an evangelistic miscue. Lewis Drummond writes:

> There are those who would tell us people can be saved and redeemed through the "cosmic Christ" apart from hearing the "good news" of the historical Jesus. This subtle syncretistic approach is rejected, and not because of a narrow conser-

> vatism. It is because the New Testament reveals nothing of such an approach. The Bible takes its stance because of the meaning of the historical incarnation in Christ's redemptive activity. A weak Christology based on a weak historical view of Jesus will make for a shallow experience of God. Therefore, the world needs to know all it means to call the incarnate God by His incarnational, historical name: *the Lord Jesus Christ*. The whole *kerygma* (proclamation) must be shared.[3]

William Packard introduces his book *Evangelism in America: From Tents to T.V.* by stating, "For our purposes in this book, we can use as a working definition of Evangelism any type of conversionary activity that tries to effect an authentic change in someone from one state of thinking and feeling to another."[4] Such a definition would be quite unsuitable for our purposes and would lead us far beyond the bounds of our investigation. The only conversionary activity in which this book is interested is that which facilitates a commitment to Jesus Christ through the power of the Holy Spirit.

The Broad Parameters of the Application

The exclusive claims of Christ in no way equate to a narrow focus. At His birth the angels announced the plan for His life: "Peace on earth, good will toward men." Jesus came to bring *shalom*, which may be thought of as well-being to all humankind—mentally, emotionally, physically, and spiritually. Christ addressed himself to the entire gamut of human need. Evangelism that divorces itself from the conditions that surround people is tantamount to placing the gospel in the vacuum of a bell jar. In a vacuum, sound will not travel—neither will evangelism. The evangelistic message must be transported by the particular culture and circumstances that enmesh a person or people. In fact, until evangelism begins addressing cultural barriers—economical, educational, ethnic, and so forth—it will not reach the people behind those barriers.

Atomistic evangelism attempts to address the individual before it addresses the culture. Such an evangelistic message, wrapped in the circumstances of the evangelist, fails to address the circumstances of the evangelized. The two worlds never meet. On the other hand, wholistic evangelism invades the heart by addressing immediate concerns that are often highly existential. Those of us who are part of the North American context rarely stop to think that there may be whole groups of people, perhaps billions, who do not think like us. Is it any wonder that much of our evangelism is ill-focused, widely missing the mark? Regarding the word *salvation,* which will be treated in the next chapter, Michael Green states, "It touches the whole of life: the notion of merely 'saving souls' is profoundly unbiblical."[5]

The Results of the Message

To say that the early church was evangelistically successful is to understate the case. The church exploded with great power and external manifestation: wind, fire, earthquakes, and miraculous transformations. Consider the results of Paul's healing disease and casting out demons in the city of Ephesus:

> And this became known to all, both Jews and Greeks, who lived in Ephesus; and fear fell upon them all and the name of the Lord Jesus was being magnified. Many also of those who had believed kept coming, confessing and disclosing their practices. And many of those who practiced magic brought their books together and began burning them in the sight of all; and they counted up the price of them and found it fifty thousand pieces of silver. So the word of the Lord was growing mightily and prevailing (Acts 19:17-20).

But what if signs and wonders do not accompany the proclamation of the gospel? What if no one responds positively to the message? What if there are no visible results? Can an activity that does not accomplish its intended purpose still be labeled evangelism? The attempted answers to these questions are thoroughly traced in David Barrett's *Evangelize! A Historical Survey of the Concept.* The opinions are as varied as the people and eras of interpretation, but they help us in defining evangelism. Barrett argues from the New Testament evidence that people can "be evangelized and still reject the message."[6] Quite often in the Bible we are not given the exact response to evangelistic messages (Acts 14:7). At other times, the response is quite mixed (see Paul's preaching on Mars Hill, Acts 17:22-34).

Barrett delineates necessary components of the activity of evangelism. In his view, it is an activity of Christians on behalf of non-Christians; the former communicates to the latter the good news of Jesus Christ. Beyond this, it is difficult to state absolutely further New Testament components. However, it can be logically argued that we have no reason to believe that any instance of evangelism in Scripture was without results. Just because the Bible does not state the specific results, we cannot conclude that there was ever total indifference. Perhaps this is the meaning of God's promise to Isaiah: "So shall My word be which goes forth from My mouth; it shall not return to Me empty, without accomplishing what I desire, and without succeeding in the matter for which I sent it" (Isa. 55:11).

Attempts at Definition

There are scores of synonyms for evangelism throughout the history of the English language, most of which are included in the New Testament. They include argue, speak, talk, witness, and the most common, tell. In all, 41 synonyms are used an amazing 2,468 times in the New Testament.[7] Verbal communication is a crucial process in the New Testament economy. Though these synonyms were used throughout the centuries of the church, there was little use of the word evangelism and its cognates until the seventeenth century. One use during this period is found in the work of John Milton, who wrote of the evangelism of the apostles. Another is seen in Samuel Johnson's *A Dictionary of the English Language,* where he defined evangelize: "as to instruct in the Gospel, or law of Jesus."[8]

It was in the nineteenth and twentieth centuries that the church became serious about defining evangelism, issuing the challenge to all that there had not been serious evangelism before then. Barrett points out that "the period 1886-1908 saw the heyday of the slogan 'the evangelization of the world in this generation.'"[9] No one articulated this concept more persuasively than John R. Mott, president of the Student Volunteer Movement from 1886 to 1900. Mott stated, "The evangelization of the world in this generation means the giving to all men an adequate opportunity of knowing Jesus Christ as their Savior and of becoming His real disciples."[10]

Process or Product?

Mott's definition emphasized the activity of the evangelizer rather than the response of the evangelized. The emphasis was on process rather than product. Note the contrasting emphasis on product in the following definition issued by the Church of England in 1918: "To evangelize is so to present Christ Jesus in the power of the Holy Spirit, that men shall come to put their trust in God through Him, to accept Him as their Savior, and serve Him as their King in the fellowship of His Church."[11] This definition concerns itself with effectiveness—the actual believing in Christ on the part of those who hear the message. In 1935 Mott asked, via a written survey, 200 Protestant and Anglican church leaders to define evangelism. Since the information was to be used by the International Missionary Council for its assembly at Tambaram, Madras, South India in 1938, it has become known as the "Tambaram Survey."

Barrett includes 79 out of the 125 replies in his survey. All of them emphasize either process or product. Sixty-five of the definitions emphasized the presence of the "good news" or the process of proclaiming it. E. Stanley Jones wrote, "Evangelism is the Good News of the Kingdom of God on earth, that Kingdom personalized and embodied in Christ."[12] Another wrote, "Evangelism is making known to men the message of salvation."[13] Such terseness makes no attempt at relating definition to effectiveness or the end product. From a philosophical perspective, this perspective would be much more deontological than teleological.

Contrast the above with the minority of respondents. Henry Sloane Coffin wrote, "Evangelism should be defined as the presentation of the Gospel of Christ in such wise as to win immediate loyalty to Him."[14] Archbishop William Temple defined evangelism as "the winning of men to acknowledge Christ as their Savior and King, so that they give themselves to His service in the fellowship of His Church."[15] Such descriptions add the dimension of actual change that takes place in the life of the hearers. Change is predicated upon positive acceptance of the message by the recipient.

These attempts to define evangelism leave us with a critical question that needs to be addressed. Can communication of the good news be called evangelism if it does not elicit the desired response? Martin Luther seemed to think so. He defined evangelism as "nothing other than preaching, the speaking forth of God's grace and mercy, which the Lord Jesus Christ has earned and acquired through his death."[16]

J.I. Packer gives extensive treatment to this question in his book titled *Evangelism and the Sovereignty of God.* Packer argues that our calculating, pragmatic, and rationalistic age has caused us to lose sight of God's mystery and wisdom. According to Packer, it is not our job to produce converts, but to represent a context in which converts can be produced. Hence, Packer writes:

> How then should evangelism be defined? According to the New Testament, evangelism is just preaching the gospel, the evangel. It is a work of communication in which Christians make themselves mouthpieces for God's message of mercy to sinners.[17]

In fairness to Packer, I don't think he means to limit preaching the gospel to verbal communication. But herein is the problem in basing our definition only on the New Testament. Think of the means of proclamation that Paul and the other apostles did not have at their disposal. William Abraham notes, "Every available medium is to be used: tracts, church newsletters, tape recorders, radios, telephones, televisions, photography, and the like."[18] I believe that the church must use Spirit-anointed reason to discover the most effective means for a particular time and place.

In a sense, both Martin Luther's and J.I. Packer's definitions of evangelism are defective. They leave no room for the evaluation of effectiveness. Packer has difficulty reconciling the use of human reason and giving proper credit to God's sovereign grace. It is the age-old conflict between faith and reason. There is no doubt that Christ meant for both faith and reason to be employed. How else were the disciples to know when to shake the dust off their feet? (Matt. 10:14) How else could Paul have assessed that the Bereans "were more noble-minded than those in Thessalonica, for they received the word with great eagerness, examining the Scriptures daily, to see whether these things were so"? (Acts 17:11) Of course, one may do more good than that which is immediately perceived. Many evangelists have experienced the frustration of Charles Woodmason, who on August 16, 1768, preached to a group of people in South Carolina who had never heard a minister. Woodmason recorded in his journal: "After the service, they went out to revelling, drinking, singing, dancing, and whoring, and most of the company were drunk before I quitted the spot."[19]

It could be that Woodmason had done all in his power on that particular occasion to change those people. But even a complete trust in God should not eliminate the kind of reflection that would ask, "Was I too erudite?" or "Did I say something that unnecessarily offended them?" or "Was my message bathed in the Holy Spirit?" John Wesley must have asked such questions for the purpose of refinement over the fifty years of his ministry. He was quite pragmatic in assessing both the direction and results of his ministry. His preaching was often less than easygoing. He was frequently cursed, stoned, shouted down, and verbally, if not physically, abused; he declined to preach in a yard that had too many available stones. Yet it was in these primitive circumstances, the "vileness" of field preaching, where he enjoyed almost all of his preaching success:

> I wonder at those who still talk so loud of the indecency of field preaching. The highest indecency is in St. Paul's Church, when a considerable part of the congregation are asleep, or talking, or looking about, not minding a word the preacher says. On the other hand, there is the highest decency in a churchyard or field, when the whole congregation behave and look as if they saw the judge of all, and heard Him speaking from heaven.[20]

A Working Definition of Evangelism

Are we ready to define evangelism? It is very improbable that a definition could be written that would please everyone. Here is a proposed working definition of evangelism: Evangelism is whatever the community of God does to make people new creatures in Christ Jesus. This definition assumes the following important principles:

1. "Lone Ranger" evangelism is futile. Evangelism must be done by the community of the church, the people of God. (This does not rule out one-on-one evangelism.) Unless the evangelized are placed within the context of God's people before, during, or after the evangelization effort, the results will be frustrated.

There is no way to live without connection to the body. This truth not only concerns the evangelized, but the evangelizer. For the latter, there must be accountability and spiritual support. William Abraham's stinging and astute criticism should be heeded:

> Since the middle of the nineteenth century, evangelism has, for the most part, been cut loose from local Christian communities. Given the quest for autonomy, given the cult of individualism that is everywhere around us, given the drastic changes in communication, and given the deep antipathy there is to community and tradition, it is well nigh impossible to link evangelism in an organic way with life in the body of Christ.[21]

Evangelizers will do their best to recognize these trends in society and overcome such obstacles. Evangelistic methods that foster privatization, autonomism, anonymity, and other contemporary nonbiblical values need to be aligned with values inherent to life in Christ. There is great truth in the maxim "Christianity that does not begin with the individual does not begin, but a Christianity that ends with the individual ends."

2. *"Whatever the community of God does" does not place every effort on equal footing.* There are biblical and spiritual parameters. Nevertheless, our definition allows for contemporary methods and forms that may have been completely unknown in previous centuries. The truth or substance of the message down through the ages remains the same, but the vehicles of communication change. The means of communication must do justice to the message. Much more will be said about this later on.

3. *Making new creatures in Christ Jesus is the only worthy goal of evangelism.* Anything less is a failure. As to who are new creatures and who are old creatures, only God ultimately knows. But such evaluation is not entirely beyond the scope of human observation. Jesus said, "A good tree cannot produce bad fruit, nor can a bad tree produce good fruit" (Matt. 7:18).

Even though there are defects in the truly converted, they are new creatures. A miraculous change through the supernatural grace of Jesus Christ is required. This change is self-evident to the believer and becomes increasingly evident to others. Such observation is not empirical proof but, nonetheless, is observable. This is the point of Charles R. Taber's article "God vs. Idols: A Model of Conversion." Do the evangelized continue to serve their idols or do they drop them? Idols are the ultimate source of identity and meaning to which people sacrifice large amounts of time and energy. For Westerners, they are self-indulgence, human achievement, greed, and racial pride. Taber writes:

> For persons who worship idols, whether exclusively or in combination with the worship of God, conversion entails in the words of Paul, both a radical turning from and a radical turning to. This requires that the idols be named and forsaken.[22]

4. "New creatures" is initiation language. In a sense, any message or help that enables people to move from one point on the *ordo salutis* to another can be classified as an evangelistic effort. Evangelism is closely related to discipleship and sanctification. Making disciples relates to everything that is done on behalf of the maturity of the Christian, from regeneration to sanctification. Thus, for the sake of discussion, we differentiate "evangelism" from "nurture" by including the former in the latter. John Wesley defined regeneration as sanctification begun. It is this rung in the order of salvation with which we primarily, but not solely, concern ourselves in this task.

The initiation language is best expressed by "in Christ Jesus." There is no phrase that more succinctly demarcates the Christian from the non-Christian. When Jesus told the 5,000 to whom He had just fed bread and fish, "He who eats My flesh and drinks My blood abides in Me, and I in him" (John 6:56), "many of His disciples withdrew, and were not walking with Him anymore" (v. 66). "In Christ" is symbolized by partaking of the Eucharist. But the bread and wine are more than symbols, because symbols represent something that is not there. The elements embody Christ—He is spiritually present in them and has acclaimed them as a special means of grace. Eating of the bread and wine proclaims to the world that we are living expressions of Christ's petition to His Father:

> And for their sakes I sanctify Myself, that they themselves also may be sanctified in truth. I do not ask in behalf of these alone, but for those also who believe in Me through their word; that they may all be one; even as Thou, Father, art in Me, and I in Thee, that they also may be in Us; that the world may believe that Thou didst send Me (John 17:19-21).

5. The problem with the word new *needs to be addressed.* In English, it denotes freshness and vitality that eventually gives way to staleness and lethargy. A new toy and freshly baked bread are not apt metaphors because they are static and starkly finite. "In Christ Jesus" connotes the beginning of a relationship that will develop throughout both time and eternity. When Jesus vacated His earthly ministry, He did not forsake incarnation. Now God would not dwell within only one person; He would fill every human heart that sincerely desires His indwelling presence through the divine Paraclete. Christ would be present without the limitation of human flesh. "In that day you shall know that I am in My Father, and you in Me, and I in you" (John 14:20).

Conversion is both crisis and process. God could have chosen to create the world in an instant, but, for some reason known only to the divine mind, He preferred to take six days (or for that matter 6,000 years because for God time is relative—cf. 2 Peter 3:8). It is important to note that even after the instantaneous event of the Creation there is a divine creative activity that continues to affect the universe. An overemphasis on the crisis of conversion implies a spiritual completeness that does not square with the reality of Christian nurture and discipleship. On the other hand, insistence upon process to the exclusion of crisis denies the power of the Holy Spirit and His ability to radically transform people beyond the boundaries of human limitation and behavioral modification. Biblical conversion maintains a delicate balance between thoroughness and incompleteness. It is the divine plan that the newborn Christian will continue to grow and develop—until physical death or the *Parousia*, whichever comes first.

Evangelism is aborted (or shall we say stillborn?) when it is perceived as an arrival rather than a beginning. Winning a convert and forsaking the convert is quite possibly worse than not winning one at all. It is as sad as the periodic newspaper accounts of discarded infants. One of the most apt metaphors for spiritual beginning and growth is that of the branch connected to a bush or tree. The only possibility for nurture and production is the continued rejuvenation provided by the life source. When Jesus exhorted His followers to abide, He expressed the dynamic of life found only in divine immanence—the beginning, present, and enduring God dwelling within portable tabernacles. "He who began a good work in you will perfect it until the day of Christ Jesus" (Phil. 1:6).

6. There is an intentionality to evangelism. By intentionality, I do not mean that doing is more important than being. Being the right kind of people is essential to doing the right kind of work. The message is vitally connected to the medium and vice versa. But being without doing is impossible (cf. James 2). There must be a vision for winning people to Christ and a willingness to translate that vision into workable steps. For most churches, there is ringing truth in William Hinson's words: "The church that depends on 'walk-in' prospects for its membership growth, will steadily decline."[23]

The church must plan to evangelize or evangelism will not take place to the extent that God intends. In the words of William Abraham, "We can best improve our thinking on evangelism by conceiving it as that set of intentional activities which is governed by the goal of initiating people into the kingdom of God for the first time."[24] Sovereign grace does not eliminate planning, thinking, working, and assessing the results. God's people must not only practice the presence of evangelism, but they must also accept the mandate of evangelism. The practice of evangelism happens only after a conscious decision-making process. Michael Green is correct when he defines evangelism as primarily *overflow*. He does not, however, rule out meticulous planning that channels and directs that overflow.

On the basis of the offices listed in Ephesians 4:11, we infer that some are called to the office of evangelism (i.e., give themselves primarily to the work of evangelism). This is Peter Wagner's argument in an essay titled "Every Christian Is Not a Missionary,"[25] in which he differentiates the role of witnessing from the gift of evangelism. Wagner's point is well taken, but his contention for either/or possession of the gifts may not be as biblically clear as he argues. He explains that some have a special gift of faith, such as the British orphanage promoter George Mueller, while all Christians have the fruit of faith. But it seems possible that there are many degrees of faith, just as there may be many degrees of evangelism. All Christians do not fill the office of evangelism, but it may be biblical that at some time or another every Christian is an instrument of evangelism.

CONCLUSION

In order for the scope of this investigation to be manageable, our working definition of evangelism needs to be understood as part of, yet distinct from, other arenas, such as sanctification, nurture, perfection, discipleship, and stewardship. Overdefinition causes the work of evangelism to be obscured by the total life of the church. Or, what is most often the case, the total processes of the church are collapsed into evangelism, so that the work of evangelism loses its specificity and fails to get done. Such reductionism leads Robert Coleman to state: "Many Churchmen have such an all-inclusive view of discipleship that the specific work of rescuing perishing souls from hell scarcely receives attention."[26]

I assume that when Paul told Timothy to do the work of an "evangelist," there was a mutually understood job description, though it may not have been rigidly spelled out. Indeed, if a person is to remain a new creature in Christ Jesus, he or she will have to be a part of the community of God and its enterprises. Some enterprises will be much more evangelistically oriented than others; it will not always be easy to define which are and which are not. In H.W. Gensichen's words, "Everything the Church is and does must have a missionary *dimension,* but not everything has a missionary *intention."*[27] It is of primary importance that we address intentional evangelism, while not truncating the evangelistic enterprise from the total gamut of discipleship.

Thus, the subject of intentional evangelism cannot be fully comprehended without considering the full odyssey from regeneration to glorification. Of course, there will be imperfection along the way. And the imperfections of the community may be so numerous that the pilgrim will drop out altogether. Such a scenario would not exclude the conclusion that evangelism has not taken place, even though it has fallen short of its goal. What is its ultimate goal? To prepare a bride for the bridegroom! Evangelism has failed if it does not result in the evangelized ultimately being seated at the marriage supper of the Lamb. Inception into that celebration, which begins here on earth, is what this book is all about.

II

evangelism as divine solvency

One could say that evangelism is sharing or spreading the benefits of Christ. The Bible tells the story of an evangelistic mission. Its theology is hammered out on the anvil of doing and going. Theology unfolds as Christ carries out the mission of seeking and saving the lost. In fact, it is not until Christ has been with the disciples almost three years and is on the brink of entering His passion that we receive a clear confessional statement as to the true identity of the carpenter's son. Peter exclaims that Jesus is the "Christ, the Son of the living God" (Matt. 16:16). Jesus is the long-awaited One, the hope of Israel, the coming Messiah. He is the one of whom Isaiah spoke: "But He was pierced through for our transgressions, He was crushed for our iniquities; the chastening for our well-being fell upon Him, and by His scourging we are healed" (Isa. 53:5).

Christ's response to Peter's confession indicates not only the supernatural quickening of the fisherman's critical affirmation, but that Peter expressed far more than he comprehended. Two millennia of scholarship and interpretation have not fully unraveled the mystery contained within the "Word [that] became flesh, and dwelt among us, and we beheld His glory, glory as of the only begotten from the Father, full of grace and truth" (John 1:14). There can be no doubt concerning Jesus' intimate relationship with the Father, mentioned 103 times in the Gospel of John. This Father is the God whom the Jews worshiped and claimed to serve in the Old Testament. But Yahweh was more than that. He was and is not only the Father, but the Son and the Spirit as well.

It took more than 300 years of the church's best minds (and we trust sanctified intentions) to conclude that the three persons of the Godhead are coequal, cosubstantial, and coeternal. Although the Scriptures give no such systematic treatment of Christ, they are not silent concerning His deity. The most christological book in the entire New Testament (other than the four Gospels) interprets an Old Testament text as the Father addressing the Son in the following manner: "Thy throne, O God, is forever and ever, and the righteous scepter is the scepter of His kingdom" (Heb. 1:8; cf. Col. 2:9 and 2 Peter 1:1). A close examination of Christ's references to Himself, His mighty deeds (which are ultimately punctuated by the Resurrection and Ascension), and the internal testimony of the deity of Christ in inspired Scripture led to a full wedding of phenomenology and ontology during the fifth century at the last of the seven ecumenical councils of the church. Concerning Christ, the confession of Chalcedon reads,

> One and the same Christ, Son, Lord, Only-begotten, recognized in two-natures, without confusion, without change, without division, without separation, the distinction of natures being in no way annulled by the union, but rather the characteristics of each nature being preserved and coming together to form one person and subsistence, not as parted or separated into persons, but one the same Son and only begotten God, the Word, the Lord Jesus Christ.[1]

Christological benefits do not accrue primarily via mental ascription and not even by an active conformity or obeisance to a doctrinal formula. Enveloped within the affirmation of Christ's deity is an even more mysterious message, one rooted in historical reality. The message is so unlikely and in some ways unbefitting to sovereign majesty that Paul referred to it as a stumbling block to the Jews and foolishness to the Greeks. It would make more sense if humans offered themselves as sacrifices to God. But in this case,

God offered Himself as a sacrifice for humanity. It is in this act that the salvation of humankind is found.

More than any other word in the Bible, salvation represents the benefits bestowed upon the created order by the death and resurrection of Christ. Every New Testament book uses either the noun *soteria* or the verb *sozo* except Colossians and the Epistles of John. Arland Hultgren states that "the concept of salvation has a more 'subjective' nuance to it, signifying healing, well being, peace, and eternal security which comes to the believer in consequences of faith."[2] Salvation comes to the individual by a full imbibing, through faith, of the crucified and risen Lord.

But *salvation* is not without an objective connotation. Ralph Earle argues, "The basic idea of salvation is deliverance."[3] Partaking of the death and resurrection of Christ results in both a real and judicial change within the individual. There is deliverance from the enslavement of sin and its penalty. Scripture refers to this change as conversion, a turning from a sinful past to a present and future holiness (cf. John 12:40; Acts 3:19). Paul's personal experience of such transformation led him to exclaim, "For I am not ashamed of the gospel, for it is the power of God for salvation to everyone who believes, to the Jew first and also to the Greek" (Rom. 1:16). The Scriptures are perfectly clear—spiritual health is found only in Jesus Christ. Wayne McCown, in his article "Such a Great Salvation," writes:

> It is most important for us to understand and affirm the declarative that Jesus is the source of our salvation. The Greek term rendered 'source' might also be translated as 'cause' or 'ground,' or perhaps even 'reason.' Whatever the preferred rendition, the essential point is clear. Our salvation proceeds from and is dependent upon the incarnation, suffering, and obedient death of our Lord Jesus Christ. Moreover, it avails to us only as the basis of our obedience to him.[4]

THE LIMITS OF SALVATION

The Scriptures, however, do not give us a systematic presentation of how exactly cursed creation benefits from the atonement of Jesus Christ. Isaac Watts wrote, "No more let sin and sorrow grow, nor thorns infest the ground. He comes to make his blessing flow, far as the curse is found." But the fullness of the flow of blessing is only an eschatological hope, not a present reality. Our enthusiasm for the gospel, often found in poetic expression, must not succumb to the temptation of claiming more than Scripture does.

There are three critical questions that relate to soteriology and the evangelistic enterprise. The first is the *intensive* question: "How *intensively* does the Holy Spirit transform a person through faith in Jesus Christ?" The most succinct expression is found in 2 Corinthians: "Therefore, if any man is in Christ, he is a new creature; the old things passed away; behold, new things have come" (5:17). The popular understanding of new is "without wear or taint or defect because of brief existence." While Paul undoubtedly had in mind fresh transformation, he at other times leads one to believe that he is not referring to complete metamorphosis. We know that he suffered from a "thorn in the flesh" (2 Cor. 12:7) and the general weaknesses that plague one's life (2 Cor. 12:10). Salvation does not mean that every former twist and turn of life is suddenly reversed. We are changed, but, in some sense, our identity and previous experience remains intact. Inheritors of salvation retain unpleasant memories and endure psychic phenomena such as depression and phobias that are not erased by the infusion of grace. However, one cannot say these areas are left untouched—there is no physical or psychological recess that is left unattended by the power of Christ's atonement (atonement essentially means "covering").

Every part of the human existence has been cared for in the atonement, but God's wisdom does not deem it necessary to separate Christians from non-Christians by giving the former perfect minds and bodies. Such temporal restoration would probably lead to the same kind of temptation that befell that first perfect human being. Yet, in spite of the disclaimers, there is a triangulation between spirit, body, and mind that needs to be fully Christianized. The pursuit of spiritual health as defined by soteriology yields general concomitants in both physical and emotional well-being, though not in ratioed formulas. For instance, the psychosomatic implications of the Sermon on the Mount need to be carefully explicated. If so, discerning application would no doubt release far greater healing than the Christian community has yet discovered.

The second query is the *extensive* question: "How extensive is the salvation offered by Jesus Christ?" There are those idyllic passages found in Isaiah that offer visions of utopia: the desert will blossom because of streams of water, there will be peace among carnivorous animals, and children will be protected from dangerous vipers, "for the earth will be full of the knowledge of the Lord as the waters cover the sea" (Isa. 11:9). Most of us are painfully aware that such tranquil images are found in the pages of *Childcraft* but not in real life—at least for now.

The Apostle John saw "a new heaven and a new earth" (Rev. 21:1). Do we simply accept that the redemption of Christ will be applied at a future date beyond the grave and until then, as Romans reminds us, "even we ourselves groan within ourselves, waiting eagerly for our adoption as sons, the redemption of our body"? (Rom. 8:23) Is the language above a metaphor for what God wants to accomplish in individual lives, or is the church to be actively involved in implementing the millennial reign of Christ within the chaotic elements of society? Concern for individualistic salvation and expectancy that the true church will be raptured from this cursed world before cataclysmic events destroy it lead some to believe that selfish complacency of the church has replaced societal commitments. William Dyrness, in his book *Let the Earth Rejoice,* writes,

> God is not content to change individuals. Indeed, if he were, why will he one day go to the trouble of creating a wholly new environment in which the righteousness of his people may shine? Our mission, then, must relate to these realities if it is to reflect the whole of God's purpose. And this means that our mission will include an increasingly sophisticated analysis of our socio-political situation in order to inform our obedience.[5]

Finally, there is the *expansive* question: "What should be the realistic evangelistic expectations of the church as it enters the third millennium?" The mainstream of Christians are dissatisfied with a doctrine that has God arbitrarily predetermining a number of the redeemed, which when achieved will signify the closing of the turnstile. There are also sufficient biblical references to the damnation of the lost, which casts serious doubts upon even the most effective arguments for universalism. A reference has already been made to the earnest and sincere articulation of a vision to evangelize the world in this century, if not the present generation. But such visionary eloquence has been dimmed by the seemingly impenetrable walls of other world religions, such as Islam, Buddhism, and Hinduism. Do the 100 million people whom John saw before the Lamb of God completely exclude the millions of religious people who are dying without faith in Christ? In the words of John Hick, "Is it credible that the loving Father of all [people] has decried that only those born within one particular thread of human history shall be saved?"[6]

The rest of this chapter will not be a systematic treatment of these questions because, frankly, I believe that conclusive answers are highly controversial, if not completely elusive. They are better retained as background questions as we attempt to state the clear biblical mandate for evangelism. That mandate goes only as far as the solvency that the Godhead has predicated upon and charged to the blood of Christ. A biblical map of solvency can be traced only by beginning with that which is insolvent in the human plight. These clues are readily available in the document of origins: the first three chapters of Genesis. Only by knowing what went wrong can we truly understand what God wants to make right.

LOSS OF INNOCENCE

The first temptation was to doubt God's word, as represented in the archetypical question posed by Satan: "Indeed, has God said . . . ?" (Gen. 3:1) The first sin is not about eating pleasurable fruit as opposed to self-denial. It is about eating forbidden fruit rather than being satisfied with God's provision of all the other fruit in the Garden. The clean conscience (or perhaps more correctly, "consciousness") was marred by condemnation, guilt, and shame. The clothes provided by God were a foretaste of a future covering that would be provided at Calvary. The streams flowing from the wounds of Jesus provided several solutions to the guilty verdict.

Justification

This judicial term is the explicit doctrine of Romans and was revolutionary to an Augustinian monk's theology in the sixteenth century. There is nothing humankind can do to set right the prototypical sin repeated in every life. No amends can be made, because the insult is against a holy God who perfectly loves humankind. Christ not only received the penalty for our sins, but He became sin for us. Sin is betrayal. In some sense, it is also undoubtedly a mystery: Christ is crucified for humankind's betrayal of all that is right and good. His execution in the place of a traitor and as a traitor to the interest of the Jewish nation indicates that the accusation of betrayal is more than circumstantial to the theological scheme. The man who was perfectly good was condemned for the lowest of crimes. No one has pity on a traitor—not even the Father. The Son cried out, "My God, My God, why hast Thou forsaken Me?" (Matt. 27:46) On the cross, a legal transmutation occurred: Christ's obedience took the place of our sin. Justification means that through faith in His obedience one's sin can be legally transmuted into His righteousness. His shame was so great that it reaches the deepest and most hideous part of humanity's condemnation: "Christ redeemed us from the curse of the Law, having become a curse for us—for it is written, 'Cursed is everyone who hangs on a tree'" (Gal. 3:13).

Forgiveness

Christ's prayer on Calvary was made effective by His sacrifice and applied to the whole human race: "Father, forgive them; for they do not know what they are doing" (Luke 23:34). Since "all have sinned and fall short of the glory of God" (Rom. 3:23), all stand in need of forgiveness. That forgiveness has already been pronounced on the whole human race. It cannot be experienced unless the announcement is proclaimed and then received by those who long to be freed from the ominous pointing finger of condemnation that constantly reminds them of their failures. H. Ray Dunning states, "Forgiveness is not a glib affair; it entails inward pain. In a word, the one who has been sinned against must bear that sin. But if the one sinned against is God, how much deeper the love and how much deeper the suffering."[7]

Cleansing

Innocence was replaced in the first Adam by a corruption, a spoiled consciousness. Uncleanness becomes not only a primary metaphor for refusing the cleansing stream of the blood of Christ, but an ontological reality for those confronted by the numinous holiness of God. Isaiah cried out, "Woe is me, for I am ruined! Because I am a man of unclean lips, and I live among a people of unclean lips; for my eyes have seen the King, the Lord of hosts" (Isa. 6:5). His cry was much like the one made by a person who had the despicable disease of leprosy. The lamentation, heard from the distance of one hundred yards, was an effective quarantine. Isaiah had responded to God's gracious invitation: "'Come now, and let us reason together,' says the Lord. 'Though your sins are as scarlet, they will be as white as snow; though they are red like crimson, they will be like wool'" (Isa. 1:18).

The ceremonial cleansing of the Old Testament symbolized by the washing of water and sprinkling of blood is actualized in the cleansing offered by Christ in the New Testament. This concept is represented by the Greek verb *katharizo,* from which we get "catharsis," a purging of the mind or inner being. In this step, the righteousness of God is not simply imputed, as it is in justification. It is imparted through the fulfilling of a gracious promise: "If we confess our sins, He is faithful and righteous to forgive us our sins and to cleanse us from all unrighteousness" (1 John 1:9).

LOSS OF INTIMACY

It is important to keep in mind God's first question to Adam after the primordial sin: "Where are you?" The implication is far greater than when a husband asks his wife, "Where are the keys to the car?" The latter question is one of pragmatic information, whereas the first one is a question of relationship. In fact, the first question that God asked Cain after the second sin was "Where is Abel, your brother?" Sin begins in deed, but it is ultimately a broken relationship. Thus, the primordial question that echoes throughout human history is "Adam (i.e., humankind), where are you?"

Most people would not be able to formulate the theological question, but they know the gnawing agony of wanting to be loved. Important as the desire to be loved is an innate desire to love. It doesn't take long for human beings to discover that they imperfectly love and are imperfectly loved. In all of our attempts to build bridges and form friendships there is a haunting sense of isolation. The first command is to love God; the second is similar to the first—to love our neighbor. The kingdom of God is not made up of rules, but of relationships.

The Love of God

The only way that the above yearning can be satisfied is through the cosmic and universal love of God as manifested through Jesus Christ. Most love relationships are generated in the flow of reciprocity. Kindling on one side of a fireplace ignites kindling on the other side until there is a passionate flame. But not so with God's love—it began entirely one-sided. In John Wesley's words, "No man loves God by nature any more than he does a stone, or the earth he treads upon."[8] Wesley's assertion is similar to another by the Apostle John: "In this is love, not that we loved God, but that He loved us and sent His Son to be the propitiation for our sins" (1 John 4:10). The root meaning of propitiation is "drawing near."[9] Those who do not know Christ do not know perfect love, because it is God who defines love—and His love is fully expressed in the sacrificial death of Jesus Christ. No scriptural affirmation expresses the initiating, searching, unconditional, and longing love of Christ more than the following passage from Romans: "For one will hardly die for a righteous man; though perhaps for the good man someone would dare even to die. But God demonstrates His own love toward us, in that while we were yet sinners, Christ died for us" (5:7-8).

The first thing that people need to know about God is that He loves them. God has done all that His character will allow Him to do—to say to both prince and pauper, "I love you." To go beyond the Cross would be manipulation, trickery, or sheer imposition of His power, which would in turn produce something less than reciprocating love.

Reconciliation

Outside of Jesus Christ, people grope with a sense of alienation that has an ontological root in actual estrangement from an offended God. Paul Mickey argues that God's wrath and anger are primarily theological, not psychological.[10] God's displeasure is not to be interpreted as peevish miff or emotional vindictiveness because God's pride has been wounded. Pride is inherent to humankind rather than God, because people have the tendency to think of themselves more highly than they ought. This propensity in God would be an impossibility, because of the simple fact that He is God. In Mickey's words:

> God's wrath is a holy and righteous anger. It is brought about by our willful violation of God's purpose in creation, not by a distempered spirit in God. . . . The person of God has been offended and violated not by sociological snubs, but by sin—the human predisposition to replace God with ourselves as the ruler of the universe.[11]

God endured His own wrath at Calvary in the person of Jesus Christ. This does not mean appeasement, because this term suggests that the Son had different feelings for humanity than did the Father, and that the latter was appeased by the former. The Godhead was in perfect agreement from the beginning that a Lamb would be slain to heal the breach between humankind and God. What Adam had undone, Christ would redo. The breach was healed by the ultimate gift given as a peace offering on behalf of all people who have ever inhabited the globe: "Now all these things are from God, who reconciled us to Himself through Christ, and gave us the ministry of reconciliation, namely, that God was in Christ reconciling the world to himself, not counting their trespasses against them, and He has committed to us the word of reconciliation" (2 Cor. 5:18-19).

LOSS OF IDENTITY

Adam's identity was located in the image of God. Adam did not discover who he was by looking in a mirror. He discovered who he was by looking at God. The locus of the human problem is that we desire a reflection of ourselves rather than the projection of God's image. When humankind lost the genuine image, it went into the manufacturing business of artificial images. Losing friendship with the God of the universe loosed an invasive insecurity within the souls of persons. Individuals have been trying in vain to shore up themselves ever since. "All flesh is like grass, and all its glory like the flower of the grass. The grass withers, and the flower falls off, but the word of the Lord abides forever" (1 Peter 1:24-25).

Chosen

God has chosen us. It is difficult for us to conceive of choosing as anything other than inclusion as opposed to exclusion. Finite humanity is hopelessly dualistic and possibly cannot understand anything outside of contrast. We have difficulty in comprehending how God could choose every person, because, in our minds, such a choice is no choice at all. Election that demands the arbitrary coddling of some at the expense (predetermined damnation of others) is the Calvinistic *faux de pas* ("false step"). This debilitating error often leads to a misrepresentation of the mind of God. For instance, when God said to Moses, "I will have mercy on whom I have mercy, and I will have compassion on whom I have compassion" (Rom. 9:15), He is often interpreted as exclaiming a sovereign demarcation between those He inherently loves and those He inherently hates.

Such a hermeneutic totally misses the intention of the writer. Paul is reminding the Hebrews that they have no exclusive right to God's love. Their pride in their national identity and religious heritage had almost totally eclipsed any understanding of God's unmerited favor. God has the perfect right to extend grace to anyone He desires, and that includes the whole world. Whether Israel felt snubbed or not, grace was now extended to the rest of creation. Ultimate identity, security, and esteem are for all, simply for the receiving: "I will call those who were not My people, 'My people,' and her who was not beloved, 'beloved.' And it shall be in the place where it was said to them, 'you are not my people,' there they shall be called sons of the living God" (Rom. 9:25-26).

God's choosing of Israel is the story of an obscure people rising to international prominence. At least some scholarship indicates that the designation Hebrew means "dusty ones," a name given in derision to a people who were habitually covered with the dust generated by donkeys' hooves in long caravan routes. They were constantly in motion, but with little direction.[12] In his progeny, dusty, nomadic Abraham would become a prince with God. The destination would be Canaan, a place of worship, and ultimately Zion, the city of God. It was in true worship of the one God that Israel, as well as all humankind, could find their chosenness. The phylogeny of Israel's election is meant to be repeated in every sojourner on the face of the earth:

> But you are a chosen race, a royal priesthood, a holy nation, a people for God's own possession, that you may proclaim the excellencies of Him who has called you out of darkness into His marvelous light; for you once were not a people, but

> now you are the people of God; you had not received mercy, but now you have received mercy (1 Peter 2:9-10).

Citizenship

Citizenship in the kingdom of God is a highly select privilege, but yet open to everyone. The kingdom's boundaries are confined to the human heart, yet it covers the whole earth; it is alien to the powers that rule, but at the same time recognizes their rightful authority. All the children of God find their identity in supernaturalization papers and a job description that states, "Establish the kingdom of God right where you are, moment by moment." This is not done through geographical conquest or survey instruments. It is accomplished through Christians being God's instruments. Every evangelistic invitation is a clarion call to be an instrument of kingdom spreading. We are to announce by both word and deed that Christ's kingdom has come. Walter Brueggemann asserts, "This announcement, authorized by the new government is like the announcement of a successful political coup. . . . The messenger announces that the world is now under new governance."[13]

Adoption

It was Jesus who first taught Jewish followers to call God "Abba." True, God is Yahweh and Adonai. But in terms of relationship, God is most importantly Abba (i.e., Father), and we are His children. We have security because we know that we are a part of the royal family and are no longer bondservants trying to please a stern and strict taskmaster. The Father revels in the joy, laughter, and contentment of His children. He also weeps when we bring shame to the family name. He is doing all in His power, without denying the Christian personal freedom, to see that His children make it all the way home. There is security and belonging in the Father's house. He doesn't kick us out when we goof up.

There could be cases where children of God have denied the family name, leaving home forever. However, rest assured that, for those who have received power to become the sons and daughters of God, there is a high unlikelihood that defection is often repeated in the household of faith. Adam fell because he took for granted his fellowship with the "Us" who made him. The fact of adoption means that we who were once bankrupt have become heirs to the royal inheritance:

> For you have not received a spirit of slavery leading to fear again, but you have received a spirit of adoption as sons by which we cry out "Abba, Father!" The Spirit Himself bears witness with our spirit that we are children of God, and if children, heirs also, heirs of God and fellow heirs with Christ, if indeed we suffer with Him in order that we may also be glorified with Him (Rom. 8:15-17).

THE LOSS OF LIFE

Humankind died, both spiritually and morally, in the Garden of Eden. Though God did not strike Adam and Eve physically dead on the spot, the original design of living forever was forfeited. A black veil was draped on the sunlit horizon of humanity. Having been kicked out of the Garden, humanity was without a reentry ticket that would afford access to the Tree of Life. God could not trust humankind with access to life, because that which was once an instrument of creativity had been turned into a dangerous instrument of sorcery.

Evil humanity could not be trusted to live forever. Evil, outside of Christ, had become inherent to the human condition. Therefore, human existence could not be allowed to perpetuate evil ad infinitum. God drove humanity from the Garden and placed an angelic creature to guard the gate. This action followed God's assessment: "Behold, the man has become like one of Us, knowing good and evil; and now, lest he stretch out his hand, and take also from the tree of life, and eat, and live forever" (Gen. 3:22).

It is said that Adolf Hitler aspired to become an architect. For whatever reason, this aspiration was frustrated. Instead of a constructionist, he became a destructionist. Perhaps the essence of evil is to kill rather than to make alive, to destroy rather than to create.

The New Birth/Regeneration

The terms new birth and regeneration are not often used in the New Testament—the only two instances are in John 3:3 and Titus 3:5. However, the concept that Christ has come to bring life is a major theme in the gospel narratives and the writings of Paul. No writer emphasizes this benefit of Christ's redemption more than John; he uses *zoé* approximately forty times in his gospel. He summarizes the purpose of his narrative as his readers receiving the life found in Christ: "These have been written that you may believe that Jesus is the Christ, the Son of God; and that believing you may have life in His name" (John 20:31). Jesus nowhere more succinctly expresses the purpose of His coming than in John 10:10: "I came that they might have life, and might have it abundantly."

In Christ, decay and death are eternally reversed. The dark veil that hangs over humankind is quintessentially expressed in mortality. Death is a sword with two edges—physical and spiritual. The eternal spiritual death is solved in the resurrection of Jesus Christ. Hope has been restored: "'Death is swallowed up in victory. O Death, where is your victory? O Death, where is your sting?' The sting of death is sin, and the power of sin is the law; but thanks be to God, who gives us the victory through our Lord Jesus Christ" (1 Cor. 15:54-57).

It may be that this particular act in the soul of humankind most accurately answers the condition that was incurred at the Fall. God specifically stated, "But from the tree of the knowledge of good and evil you shall not eat, for in the day that you eat from it you shall surely die" (Gen. 2:17). It is in Adam as our primordial representative that death passes down to every subsequent human being. Paul specifically stated the connection: "For if by the transgression of the one the many died, much more did the grace of God and the gift by the grace of the one Man, Jesus Christ, abound to the many" (Rom. 5:15). In Charles Wilson's words, "When he [Jesus] was incarnate and became man, he recapitulated in himself all generations of mankind making himself the center of our salvation; that what we lost in Adam, even the image and likeness of God, we might receive in Jesus Christ."[14] Outside of Christ's death and resurrection, all of the world becomes Golgotha.

In short, His death became our life. He paid our ransom and satisfied the guilty verdict. God's holiness and justice could not be neglected. The moral necessities of the universe are in keeping with the character of God—to neglect one would be to depreciate the other. Christ died in our place, covering our sin, thereby granting us life through His shed blood. The Old Testament truth has been fulfilled: "Without shedding of blood there is no forgiveness" (Heb. 9:22; cf. Lev. 17:11). Thomas Oden explicates:

> It is not the blood itself that makes atonement but the life

> or animate creation or soul in the blood that is offered as a prayer for atonement. The sacrificial victim implies not merely a death, but a death that enables life. Hence, the sacrifice is not meaningless. The offering of blood is better viewed as the offering and enabling of life, not death.[15]

LOSS OF DOMINION

In terms of the created order, humankind had governance. Even though humanity was made lower than the angels (cf. Ps. 8:5), the former's dominion is on earth, while the latter are the emissaries of heaven. At the temptation of Satan, Adam surrendered his sphere of government. In much the same manner as Esau, Adam profaned sacred space by not protecting it from the wiles of the devil. The result is that Satan is now the prince of the power of the air (Eph. 2:2). Humankind has surrendered its country, and its air space has been fully invaded. But the occupying enemy can inflict no damage outside of God's permission. However, while humanity is dominated by Satan, God is still the rightful sovereign of creation.

Victory in Gethsemane and on Calvary

Christ's death and resurrection brought the critical victory in the war against Satan and his forces. Though Christians still have skirmishes both individually and corporately, the pivotal battle was fought 2,000 years ago. The war has been won in Jesus Christ. God has yet to ban Satan to his final doom and reclaim the territory He rightfully owns. The present victory for the Christian is found in one of Paul's affirmations: "He delivered us from the domain of darkness, and transferred us to the kingdom of His beloved Son" (Col. 1:13). The transferral in no way refers to a geographical relocation; rather, God sets up domain in every consciousness that invites Him in. The casting out of demons in the New Testament served as highly visible proof that, no matter how dark the soul, the forces of evil, much like bats in a cave, cannot withstand invading light. But even after the forces of evil have been cast out, Christians should not be unmindful that Babylon, the spirit of this age, is filled with demons. In Donald Bloesch's words:

> Through his cross and resurrection victory, Jesus Christ "dis-

> armed the principalities and powers," but they still wield a modicum of power (through man's continuing sin), though now as usurpers. All their rights and privileges have been taken from them, but they continue to wage war, even though they have been defeated and dethroned.[16]

Liberty

Jesus set the agenda for His ministry by stating, "The spirit of the Lord is upon Me, because He anointed Me to preach the gospel to the poor . . . to proclaim release to the captives . . . to proclaim the favorable year of the Lord" (Luke 4:18-19). Jesus' ministry is paradigmatically set within the Old Testament instructions that formed and informed the Year of Jubilee. On this occasion, every fiftieth year, all slaves were to be set free, all debts were to be forgiven, and all indentured land was to be returned to its original owners. There is insufficient historical evidence to ascertain if this equilibrium was ever actually enforced, much less celebrated with festivity.

Rather than God bringing instant societal healing, He chose to embody liberating truth as Christ went from village to village doing good deeds and healing all manner of diseases. Christ did not choose primarily to do battle with systemic evil woven within the fabric of international politics and global economics. He chose to become a body of flesh and blood spending time in the presence of other bodies. Christians are not called to save the world, but to administer healing grace wherever they find themselves. This healing will never be fully completed—at least not in this life. But perhaps what we begin will be eternally perfected. "And whatever you shall loose on earth shall be loosed in heaven" (Matt. 16:19).

Wherever there are values that are diametrically opposed to the values of the kingdom (e.g., oppression, avarice, discrimination, economic injustice), Christians are to do all in their power to loose the social, cultural, and political bindings that ensnare their immediate world. One may become so busy fighting mythological windmills that one neglects to draw water for dying people with the means readily at hand. As William Dyrness has said, "It is in and through the created order that the human person must express his or her values, and it is in this order of things that God wills to be glorified."[17]

Christ's Intercession

The benefits above do not accrue to those who accept Christ by faith simply because a job was well done 2,000 years ago. God in Jesus Christ did not condescend to the level of humanity with the intention of simply tolerating the body of corruption for a brief period of time. True, His drinking of the cup is finished, but the continuous bearing of humanity with all of its woes is the present job of the Son as He is seated at the right hand of the Father. Because of Christ's intercession, prevenient grace issues to all of humankind. And for those who have put their trust in Christ, there is a special keeping and guiding grace that is channeled directly to them from the throne of Almighty God. The fortune of the Christian is the result of the ongoing intercession of Jesus Christ. Everything that accrues to the Christian will be good, because the child of God is held within God's wisdom. However, God's wisdom will not always be comprehended by our wisdom. Wesley taught that "all our blessings, temporal, spiritual, and eternal, depend on his intercession for us, which is one branch of his priestly office whereof therefore we have always equal need."[18]

The paradigm for every prayer that the Christian breathes is that it will be translated by the Son to the Father in a fashion that will be for the eternal good of all concerned. This may mean that Christ offers to the Father's ear not only a revision of our petitions, but a complete reversal of our pursuit of the apparent good. Or, as is often the case, Christ prays beyond our limited myopia, which is the result of life's complications being far too difficult for us to grasp. The Holy Spirit is employed by the Son to search out the supplicants' specific concerns and to direct the prayers of the saints, which are beyond human comprehension. Paul suggests this understanding in his letter to the Romans:

> In the same way the spirit also helps our weakness; for we do not know how to pray as we should, but the Spirit Himself intercedes for us with groanings too deep for words; and He who searches the hearts knows what the mind of the Spirit is, because He intercedes for the saints according to the will of God (8:26-27).

All the goodness that was purchased at Calvary is presently applied to us because of the present priesthood of Christ. Christ fully understands us because He became incarnate, experiencing all of humanity's traits, frustrations, and temptations. He has earned the right to be our priest because He offered the ultimate sacrifice—His own life. That blood is not offered at a point in time with spatial limitations, but is constantly and forever available from the throne of God because of Christ's intercession. Salvation is not primarily something that has been once and for all received, but rather is a divine solution, being applied moment by moment to the human plight. Wesley stated, "The instant He withdraws, all is darkness. They still need Christ as their King; for God does not give them a stock of holiness. But unless they receive a supply every moment, nothing but unholiness would remain."[19]

ORDER OF SALVATION

When one speaks of the *ordo salutis*, it is not to be understood as a chronological series of events, universally schemed by God to be applied to each and every person. Salvation is not a staircase by which every person ascends a regulated number of steps to spiritual maturity. Such empirical structuring is incompatible with the mysteries of godliness and with the wisdom of God that meets every person at the point of their need and, quite often, within the arena of individual knowledge and experience. An overly empirical paradigm has often led to unnecessary introspection and castigation of either the self or others. There is quite often spiritual pride on the one hand and an overly sensitive and scrupulous conscience on the other.

While the events of salvation are so ordered by God that they will be perfectly suited to the individual, they are not so mystifying that they cannot be at least partially explicated. There is at least a general expectancy that facilitates the seeking of God. Guideposts may be shared by the Christian with the non-Christian to enhance facilitation of spiritual inception and growth. The way is not universally or absolutely charted, but there are sufficient directives so that a person need not get utterly confused or lost.

Grace

Everything that God does on a person's behalf has its beginning and ending in grace. This truth finds its classical location in

Ephesians: "For by grace you have been saved through faith; and that not of yourselves, it is the gift of God; not as a result of works, that no one should boast" (2:8-9). Everything that is positive and good in regard to humanity is the result of grace. Grace is more than mercy. Mercy is not giving something justly deserved. Grace is giving something far better than what is deserved (in the case of salvation, infinitely better). Grace is more than unmerited favor; grace is God's intense desire to draw us to Himself. It is not simply that He will overlook our defects; He will one day erase all of those defects and make us perfectly whole.

The world continues to be a functional place for human existence because of what may be called common grace. The continual application of grace to all of creation, by which the world consists and exists, rules out a deistic conception of God as a watchmaker who wound the mainspring before turning to more interesting enterprises. The human species is still God's first order of business, not because there is anything inherently pleasurable about us, but because He intensely believes He can make something meaningful out of us. Anything meaningful (i.e., positive, purposeful, or good) is a result of God's prevenient and positive grace. Prevenient grace is the source of the soul's first spiritual stirrings and hunger for God. Prevenient grace differs from common grace in that the former is the dynamic intention of God to save humankind. The latter allows the world and its inhabitants to continue existence.

Awakening

The first general awakening in the soul is a vague stirring of spiritual yearning. Some may designate this yearning as the religious quest that is innate to the human condition. But it is not innate, because its primary source is completely extraneous to human origin. It is the light that lights every person that comes into the world. It is the Holy Spirit wooing human affection toward that light. There are, however, several catalysts that stimulate or enhance the nudging of the Holy Spirit. Rather, it should be said that God plays on the human condition for its own good. These catalysts include the following:

1. *The quest for origins is a quest for identity.* For some, the Genesis creation story is the most plausible explanation for the existence of the universe. Individuals need to know who they are.

They are part of the human species. The first Adam must be taken seriously.

2. *The quest for purpose or design.* Does life have any more meaning than a protoplasmic form that possesses substantive entity today and is gone tomorrow? Is there a higher value than gaining all the momentary pleasure available? Paul stated, "If the dead are not raised, let us eat and drink, for tomorrow we die" (1 Cor. 15:32).

3. *The quest for fulfillment.* There is a general anomie that exists from trying to satisfy infinite needs with the finite. Paul implies that God has made it difficult for us to settle for second best: "For the creation was subjected to futility, not of its own will, but because of Him who subjected it, in hope" (Rom. 8:20). And the preacher states, "Thus I considered all my activities which my hands had done, and the labor which I had exerted, and behold all was vanity and striving after wind and there was no profit under the sun" (Ecc. 2:11).

Conviction

This is a step beyond general awakening. Conviction is an alarm—a more defined sound—set off within human consciousness because an objective standard has been established. It is the first inkling that there may be answers to the unanswered questions of the general awakening. These objective standards are all dependent on the Holy Spirit dynamically impressing them upon the consciousness of the individual. They consist of the following:

1. *The love of God as revealed through the cross of Christ.* It is true that the law of God can be spurned and the blood of Christ trampled. However, the appeal of that love often pierces selfish values that know nothing of true love. The love of God cannot be fully discovered by simply perceiving an overwhelming cosmic affection, but rather through the preaching of the gospel.

2. *The law of God.* It has been said that one does not know how bad one is until one tries to be good. The gap between performance and the mores of society is designated as conscience. The gap between performance and God's requirements is called sin—missing the mark. Thus, the law is our schoolmaster. The Apostle Paul wrote, "I would not have come to know sin except through the Law; for I would not have known about coveting if the Law had

not said, 'You shall not covet'" (Rom. 7:7).

3. The holiness of God. God's character and all of His attributes are defined by His holiness. God is uniquely holy and holiness is uniquely God. All that God does flows from holy impulse. Faithful preaching portrays who God is in comparison with who humankind is. There is an overwhelming sense of incompleteness and undoneness; this can be referred to as "guilt." Psychologists are prone to define guilt as the gap between the realized self and the ideal self. But remember, the idealized self is ultimately defined by the image of God. God is the pattern for personhood. The analogy of faith calls for human character to always be measured by an absolute universal standard located in the holiness of God. The result of this is condemnation. But there is a promise: "There is therefore now no condemnation for those who are in Christ Jesus" (Rom. 8:1).

4. The rightness of the world. God speaks through the created order. The Holy Spirit may impress upon the individual the beauty and grandeur of one's surroundings. Rhythm, order, and the intense pleasure that comes from environmental excellence witness to a primordial intelligence. (However, there are many tragedies and perceived incongruities that subtract from this witness.)

The Faith of Reason

The faith of reason has heard enough of the gospel message to accept the grace extended and take remedial steps to draw near to God. Reason has been illuminated by the dynamic of the Holy Spirit applying the living Word by way of the written Word to the human intellect. It may properly be said that at this point conversion has begun. It may also be designated the first stirrings of repentance. There may be a high moral tone to this initial faith—the individual may read the Bible, attend church, forgo evil habits, and make specific resolutions. Overall, there will be a search for truth somewhat inhibited by honest (or possibly dishonest) doubts.

Repentance

As the pressure of the portrayal of God's character is brought to bear on human consciousness, there is a breakdown of ego defenses and sufficiencies. Individuals have been given the freedom to stop this frontal assault at any point, which the Scripture refers to as "hardening of the heart." If a person does not put up a stop sign to the invasion of holy affection, there is an overwhelming sense of inadequacy that places the past in proper perspective—failure. Repentance is an overwhelming sense of grief for not only what has been done, but for the very core of the individual's identity. There is the desire to turn away from sin, and even to make amends for past wrongs committed. These sins appear odious and repugnant as they are brought to mind by the Holy Spirit, which is the process of confession. They do not have to be painfully dredged up over a long period of time in order for this repentance to take place. God, through the Holy Spirit, can do a remarkably quick inventory. The individual finally discovers something that can be given to God: his or her sin. "The sacrifices of God are a broken spirit; a broken and a contrite heart, O God, Thou wilt not despise" (Ps. 51:17).

Faith unto Salvation

Repentance provides a stepping stone for this faith, but the entire energy to take the qualitative leap is provided by the quickening of the Holy Spirit. It is the belief that God is able to save me and desiring to save me—punctuated by the trust that He saves me now. The difference between what is called the faith of reason, the dawning of conversion, and the faith of salvation possibly correlates to what Colin Williams interprets in Wesley as the two movements of justification:

> (1) Preliminary faith, which includes the free response to God's prevenient grace and a desire to please him, but is still only the "faith of a servant." (2) Justifying faith proper, which is a sure trust and confidence in Christ bringing a conviction of forgiveness, this being "the faith of a son."[20]

The former faith believes as an ascription to truth, but the latter faith believes that the ultimate truth, Jesus Christ, is planted in the soul of the individual. Wesley stated: "Justifying faith implies, not only a divine evidence or conviction that God was in Christ, reconciling the world unto himself, but a sure trust and confidence that Christ died for my sins, that he loved me, and gave himself for me."[21]

The truth of the Reformation revelation (Rom. 1:17, "the just shall live by faith") is that the *one* requisite for justification is faith. This truth is foundational to every seeking individual's salvation. There is only one criterion by which individuals are justified—*faith.* Justification is by *faith* alone. All that goes before may clarify and fortify this faith, but faith is the one immediate necessity. It is impossible to possess true faith in the saving efficacy of Jesus Christ and not be justified. In Wesley's own words, "As on the one hand, though a man should have everything else, without faith, yet he cannot be justified; so on the other, though he be supposed to want everything else, yet if he hath faith he cannot but be justified."[22] It is at this point that the person may be said to be truly regenerated.

The Faith of Assurance

Assurance is not a condition of salvation, but rather an inward conviction that on the authority of the Word and faithfulness of God, a divine transaction has taken place. As a result of this assurance, emotion may be quite eruptive or very subdued. Whatever the emotion, there is a perception that is more mystical than empirical that forgiveness has been granted and new life planted in the soul. This new awareness is from two sources: the witness of the Holy Spirit and the witness of one's own spirit. The first witness is supernatural, an impression on the soul sent straight from God that the individual is His child. The second witness is predicated upon one's own perception as to whether one's experience validates that which one claims to have or, perhaps more properly, that which the New Testament portrays as kingdom life.

Sanctification

The human character has now taken on a divine dimension. Initial sanctification and subsequent growth in grace begins at regeneration. Through the power of the Holy Spirit humanity is enabled to produce fruit unto righteousness. This fruit is in no way a condition of our salvation, nor is it in any way a meritorious cause for us to retain our salvation. Sanctification is a moment by moment dependence on the cleansing of the blood of Christ and the energizing of the Holy Spirit. Holiness completely derived from an external source is realized only through an ongoing faith in the righteousness of Jesus Christ.

All the Reformers were adamant that the Christian life must be an inward experience that bares outward evidence. Luther stated, "Good works do not make a good man, but a good man does good works."[23] And John Calvin wrote, "Ever since the Holy Spirit dedicated us as temples of God, we must take care that God's glory shines through us, and must not permit anything to defile ourselves with the filthiness of sin."[24] Both were highly cognizant of Christ's words: "For there is no good tree which produces bad fruit; nor, on the other hand, a bad tree which produces good fruit. For each tree is known by its own fruit. For men do not gather figs from thorns, nor do they pick grapes from a briar bush" (Luke 6:43-44).

Entire Sanctification

Every human being comes into the world spiritually damaged. The infection and corruption that taint the volitional powers allow the pleasure principle to dominate human choices (and if not the pleasure principle, then at least the utilitarian principle). Even though individual acts may look perfectly legitimate when casually examined, such as disciplined study for an exam, a more scrutinizing inspection reveals that the driving force for all such activity is the simple question, "How will this benefit me?" The subtlety of this selfish motivation is normally not confronted when one is asking God to forgive his or her sins. Thus, when the Holy Spirit enters the heart at the time of the new birth, power is given to resist the temptation to break the known laws of God. The regenerated withstand overt acts of sin through the power of the Spirit. In other words, there is not a highly perceptible difference in the keeping of the law by the regenerated and the outward conformity of the entirely sanctified. But there is a distinct difference in the inward conformity: while the justified are keeping the law in order to keep their salvation intact, the entirely sanctified person is asking the ultimate question concerning all thoughts and actions: "How will this glorify God?"

Even though the justified strive to please God, the carnal mind asks, "What's in it for me?" This wars against the forward progress of the Christian. This double-mindedness sometimes causes wisdom to be warped, vision clouded, and opportunities missed because the Spirit is warring against the flesh. So much resistance has to be applied inwardly that the pressure for movement ahead is thwarted. Thus, the will is oftentimes perverted, which may not result in outward acts of sin, but in attitudes which are not in keeping with the mind of Christ. It may well be that Paul referred to this sin when he stated, "For I know that nothing good dwells in me, that is, in my flesh; for the wishing is present in me, but the doing of the good is not" (Rom. 7:18).

This is the primary question: "How can evil be defeated in one's personal life so that life is compelled by love rather than motivated by fear?" It is Christ in us that heightens this tension between seeking to please the self and glorifying Christ. Emil Brunner wrote, "Even in his worship of God, man seeks himself, his own salvation, even in his surrender to the Deity, he wants to find his own security."[25] Can there be a higher compelling interest to direct life's energies? Only the life that is filled with the holiness of God can have victory over pride, the world's values, and the general tendency to serve oneself. This wholeness by means of purification was the object of Paul's benediction to the Thessalonians: "Now may the God of peace Himself sanctify you entirely; and may your spirit and soul and body be preserved complete, without blame at the coming of our Lord Jesus Christ. Faithful is He who calls you, and He also will bring it to pass" (1 Thes. 5:23-24).

For Wesley this "bringing to pass" implied the fulfilling of the greatest commandment by the grace of God: "This implies that no wrong temper, none contrary to love, remains in the soul, and that all our thoughts, words, and actions are governed by pure love."[26] Full faith in Christ's atoning blood means that the Christian does not stop short of the belief that God is able to perform this miraculous transformation in this life. To the regenerated, Wesley wrote, "If you seek it by faith, you may expect it as you are; and if as you are, then expect it now."[27] He later gave a fuller explanation of the transition from justification to entire sanctification in his sermon titled "The Repentance of Believers":

> Though we watch and pray ever so much, we cannot wholly cleanse either our heart or hands. Most sure we cannot tell it shall please our Lord to speak to our hearts again, to speak the second time. "Be clean" and then only the leprosy is cleansed. Then only the evil root, the carnal mind is destroyed, an inbred sin subsists no more.[28]

Glorification

The curse of the Fall (death) is ultimately answered in the resurrection of Jesus Christ. Because He lives, we will also live. For the Christian, the resurrection is entered into by one of two ways—physical death or meeting the Lord when He returns to earth to reclaim His bride. We know that there will be perfect restoration because "He shall wipe away every tear from their eyes; and there shall no longer be any death; there shall no longer be any mourning, or crying, or pain; the first things have passed away" (Rev. 21:4).

Jesus said that He was going to prepare a place for us, but as for the description of this place, we have little comprehension. The language of golden streets, pearly gates, and jasper walls are figurative, representing realities that cannot be fully represented in human thought forms, much less put into words. But we are going not so much to a place as to a Person and a worship celebration that forever offers up praise to that Person. We will have a new body and mind, but not for the purpose of performing feats unrealized in this life. Rather, we will have a new body and mind because these earthen vessels have never been fully loosed to realize their ultimate purpose: to love God and enjoy Him forever. But glorification is much more than a future event—it is an ongoing relationship with God in this life, which leads to the next. Robert Wall states:

> Just as we speak of the spirit's transforming power as a process, so we must speak of the glorification process as categories, other than an eschatological punctiliar event of saving history. *Glorification must be seen as a dynamic event parallel to entire sanctification.* The body of Christ, and the individual Christian bodies therein are in process of escaping the evil world and of testifying to the glory of God in public demonstrative ways.[29]

CONCLUSION

Evangelism works between the polarities of being either overly formulative or so obtuse that the message cannot be readily grasped. Christians must discover the dialectic of retaining the mystery of Jesus Christ and at the same time clarifying His benefits to seekers. Those benefits do not neatly fit into a schematic that can be completely programmed and made available through myriad outlets by a control center. There is always the danger of mass production that forgoes the uniqueness of persons, not to mention God's ability to tailor salvation to the peculiarities of individual lives.

Evangelism is foremost a spiritual exercise. The Holy Spirit acts as the essential medium between the communicator and the recipient. Evangelism asks the recipient to know the unknowable and fathom the unfathomable—the unsearchable riches of Jesus Christ. The Holy Spirit is the difference between the message being resonant or dissonant; the means of communication being cold or hot. The benefits of Christ's life and death must be explained through the dynamic of the Holy Spirit and must in turn be proclaimed through the trust that God is the harbinger of the message.

I have argued that there are rhythms and patterns of grace that can be deciphered and applied through supernatural illumination. This supernatural illumination does not rule out the need for the evangelist to become a spiritual diagnostician through observation and analysis. God is not so capricious and the individual so atomistic that patterns of spiritual experience cannot be discovered. There are common denominators in the benefits of Christ as they are applied to universal human needs. After Pentecost the apostles affirmed, "For we cannot stop speaking what we have seen and heard" (Acts 4:20). Evangelism is God's love and power seeking effectiveness through understanding and action.

III

translating theology into evangelistic action

REALITY AND CERTITUDE

Life is a delicate balance between faith and certitude. The laws of gravity, the solidity of the earth, and my internal sense of coordination, all of which I have frequently experienced, render the assurance that I am able to place one foot ahead of the other in an experience called walking. However, it is amazing how the slightest crack in the sidewalk or the smallest patch of ice on the pavement remind me that this very elementary skill can be precarious. Nevertheless, I continue to believe that I will succeed far more often than I will fail in reaching my destination.

Walking operates within frames of reference. So does evangelism. These reference points provide ultimate meaning for living. Am I primarily a creature of time surrounded by material goods, or am I primarily a creature of eternity surrounded by spiritual values? Does creation consist essentially of life in the flesh or life in the Spirit? The Spirit world is more nebulous and mysterious; the flesh world is more describable and empirical. Most of American thought or action emphasizes the latter—the world of the tangible. This is what Tom Sine calls "inherently materialistic world views, lacking any sense of transcendence." Sine goes on to state: "In the western dream the better future has come to be seen as ever-increasing levels of economic growth, technological progress, and personal consumption."[1]

We are creatures of the flesh, but God is spirit. We perceive life from our vantage point; He perceives it from His. It would be presumptuous to believe that my natural world is more real than His supernatural one. The truth may be that the limitations of my reality are found in the infinitude of His reality. Without the reality of God's world, my reality becomes less than reality. The first perspective of reality that I need to discover is that my natural perception is very limited and finite. Evangelism will not be a high priority in a "reality" world that operates from only natural perception.

VALUE SYSTEM FOR EVANGELISM

A psychology of action is described by the following sequence: Knowledge—Values—Action. I would argue that no one ever acts outside their value system, providing they are free to do so (i.e., free from external restraints). I have had a lively discussion with my students as to whether they were free to not come to class. I challenge them with the idea that the values of conscientiousness, achievement, and responsibility to family and to God predetermine their action. They have no other choice but to come to class. Of course, someone could have failed to set the alarm, and they would have been in bondage to their sleep or to someone else's carelessness. Personal failure to set the alarm may be a sign of lethargy. Gratification of the flesh through sleep may indicate that I value rest more than I do learning. Such failures cause me to constantly question my values, but not to doubt the fact that I act within them.

KNOWLEDGE

How does a psychology of action become a theology of action? The answer is found in the word *knowledge*. Knowledge consists of accumulated facts plus experience. The theological equation goes something like this:

TOP SPHERE—Truth and experience of the Spirit world
Knowledge—Values—Action
BOTTOM SPHERE—Facts and experience of the material world

Values and action result from knowledge, which is informed by the bottom sphere or the top sphere. Evangelism will be a much higher priority for one who acts out of the top sphere than for one who acts out of the bottom sphere. When Paul operated primarily out of fact and experience, he persecuted Christians. It was on the Damascus road that he was given a new knowledge inventory from the Spirit world. Paul asked a theological question ("Who art Thou, Lord?"), and he received a theological answer: "I am Jesus whom you are persecuting, but rise, and enter the city, and it shall be told you what you must do" (Acts 9:5-6). Paul did exactly that because a new experience had entered his frame of reference. Without this new experience, his action would have remained on the same course. A factual understanding and personal experience of Christ so overwhelmingly entered his knowledge inventory that he later wrote:

> But whatever things were gain to me, those things I have counted as loss for the sake of Christ. More than that, I count all things to be loss in view of the surpassing value of knowing Christ Jesus my Lord, for whom I have suffered the loss of all things, and count them but rubbish in order that I may gain Christ (Phil. 3:7-8).

The interesting part of this passage is how Christ is the knowledge, the value, and the goal of the action.

Christ	Christ	Christ
Knowledge	Values	Goal
Knowing Christ as Lord	Suffer loss of all things	Gain Christ

How could such knowledge be so consuming? A Greek verb is the clue. When Paul wrote "I know whom I have believed," he used the verb *ideo,* from which we get "idea." An idea is a thought, opinion, or belief. Indeed, such mental conceptions provide conviction. But freedom to carry out convictions comes from something far deeper. Such freedom comes from a knowledge that is experiential as well as conceptual. An individual with an experience is never at the mercy of a person with a mere argument. When Paul spoke of knowing Christ in Philippians 3:8, he used a form of *ginosko* that implies a knowledge of experience and relationship. Thus, he could testify, "I did not prove disobedient to the heavenly vision" (Acts 26:19). The confidence needed for the work of God can only arise out of a knowledge inventory infused by the supernatural grace of God.

THE MESSAGE OF EVANGELISM

A conviction for evangelism must rest on a theology. Such a theology consists of a knowledge inventory of God and His plan for us, which is a supernatural gift of God. In understanding God's plan, we must know something about the *message, mission, means, motive,* and *model* for evangelism. These words are overlapping and are so intertwined that they are by no means mutually exclusive. We will examine each one specifically.

Unique Problem and Solution

In the midst of this coherency, there is a unique claim: God became flesh to save sinners. Any deviation from the christological message will throw the evangelistic mission off course and probably abort it altogether. There are two points of uniqueness in the message—the uniqueness of the problem and uniqueness of salvation. No one verse illustrates this more clearly than the prophecy of the angel to Joseph: "And she will bear a son; and you shall call His name Jesus, for it is He who will save His people from their sins" (Matt. 1:21).

The adequacy of Christ is centered in His deity. The Word that was God became flesh (John 1). He is addressed as God in various New Testament texts, such as Hebrews 1:8, Titus 2:13, and 2 Peter 1:1. Colossians 2:9 tells us that "in Him all the fulness of Deity dwells in bodily form." This point is so crucial that God does not leave it to our own ability to accept or even comprehend. There is an illumination by the Holy Spirit that renders a dynamic witness to the truth as we read it or hear it. Without it, human reason is unable to bridge the gap between the empirical, quantifiable variety of everyday events and the *sui generis* intervention of God into human history. The enabling of the Holy Spirit is what Danish lay theologian Søren

Kierkegaard labeled the "qualitative leap of faith."

Not only is a qualitative leap of faith needed to experience the uniqueness and adequacy of Christ, but to recognize the problem as a sin problem that can only be remedied by supernatural grace. Sin is nonquantifiable in that it is not subject to psychometrics or any other kind of empirical observation. The results of evil are observable, and Scott Peck is to be commended for arguing for evil as a category that needs to be treated and combated by psychiatry as well as other social sciences.[2] But the social sciences are not equipped to deal with the source of evil (Satan) and the root of that evil sown within persons (sin).

Environment, heredity, unique experiences, and human frailty have all served to magnify the results of sin and have wreaked havoc upon all of us to some degree. There are degrees of maladjustment, misunderstanding, and malnourishment in all of us. We are all neurotic in that we sublimate and compensate. It may well be that evangelism needs to deal with these problems. But it needs to deal with a far deeper problem—if it does not, it will be woefully inadequate.

The Godhead had a plan that brought the incarnation to directly bear upon the sin of persons. The penalty of death had been pronounced by God himself and since then has been carried out by His holy character, which cannot lie. God died in our place. He shed His blood so that humankind might realize the life found in His blood. Any euphemism at this point will depreciate the sacrifice that was made for our redemption. The full theology does not need to be completely understood, but the essentials need to be communicated for a healthy birth into the kingdom. There needs to be some comprehension of what it means to participate in the cup of the new covenant. The writer to the Hebrews wrote:

> For if the blood of goats and bulls and the ashes of a heifer sprinkling those who have been defiled, sanctify for the cleansing of the flesh, how much more will the blood of Christ, who through the eternal Spirit offered Himself without blemish to God, cleanse your conscience from dead works to serve the living God? (Heb. 9:13-14)

Contemporary analogies must not obscure the fact that Christ died to save sinners. Our sins were placed upon Him, even as the Old Testament priests laid hands upon the bullock that was slain or the scapegoat that was released to perish within the wilderness. Paul was not attempting to become an obscurantist or separatist when he wrote, "For I determined to know nothing among you except Jesus Christ, and Him crucified" (1 Cor. 2:2). He was simply testifying to the uniqueness of that message and the need for the Holy Spirit to bring the message home to the "natural" individual who "does not accept the things of the Spirit of God; for they are foolishness to him, and he cannot understand them, because they are spiritually appraised" (1 Cor. 2:14).

The coherency of the Scriptures combined with their own internal claim about themselves that they are divinely inspired (2 Tim. 3:16) make a plausible connection between a unique solution and a unique problem. However, as we have argued, God does not leave a person with only the witness of his or her own consciousness that the Scriptures are cogent, thus acceptable. The Holy Spirit who inspired them continues to witness that the salvation history they unfold is worthy of staking one's life and eternal destiny upon. Plausibility + Inspired Believability = Reliability.

The Testimony of Experience

But there is one more factor that has to be added to the authority of the message. Plausibility and spirit illumination will be insufficient without personal experience. Changed people desire to change others. Deficiency in the change means deficiency in the desire. Personally experiencing the gospel will fuel desire with passion. Without this third witness, authority will be less than authentic. Primary witness to the product leads to credibility. No one has made this point more forcefully than the English preacher Samuel Chadwick, concerning the early church:

> No one needed to ask if they had received the Holy Ghost. Fire is self-evident. So is power! Even demons know the difference between the power of inspiration and the correctness of instruction. Secondhand gospels work no miracles. Uninspired devices end in defeat and shame.[3]

The pragmatic witness of "Let me tell you how Christ worked and still works in my life" is the most enticing factor of credibility. Authority is undermined without it. Gilbert Tennent, an itinerant evangelist of the First Great Awakening, fully grasped this concept. Hear the urgency of this historic sermon as evidenced in the following questions:

> Is a blind man fit to be a Guide in a very dangerous way? Is a dead Man fit to bring others to Life? A mad Man fit to give Counsel in a Matter of Life and Death? Is a possessed Man fit to cast Devils? A Rebel, an Enemy to God, fit to be sent on an Embassy of Peace, to bring Rebels into a State of Friendship with GOD? . . . Isn't an unconverted Minister like a Man who would learn others to swim, before he has learn'd it himself, and so is drowned in the Act, and dies like a Fool?[4]

THE MISSION

An explication of the message has already shed much light on the mission. The enlightened ones are to take light to those who dwell in darkness, the full ones are to provide bread for the hungry, and the found ones are to deliver a map to the lost. The full benefits of the life of Christ are to be taken to the full gamut of human woes. The mission succinctly defined and fleshed out by those who are whole in Christ enables humankind to experience their full potential in Christ Jesus. Becoming new creatures in Christ Jesus is more than initiation into benefits of the gospel. The total process must be kept in mind or the mission will utilize some metaphors at the denial of others. Charles Finney perceived evangelism as one screaming "FIRE!" in a crowded theater engulfed with flames or as an argument for a verdict in a courtroom. Moody utilized the metaphor of a lifeboat surrounded by the drowning and perishing cries of the shipwrecked. William Booth's analogy was similar:

> And out of this dark angry ocean I saw a mighty rock that rose up with its summit towering high above the black clouds that overhung the stormy sea; and all round the base of this rock I saw a vast platform; and on this platform I saw with delight a number of the poor, struggling, drowning wretches continually climbing out of the angry ocean; and I saw that a number of those who were already safe on the platform were helping the poor creatures still in the angry waves to

reach the same place of safety.[5]

Booth did not allow himself to be caught up in the false dichotomies and unnecessary polarizations that developed in the early twentieth century. David Bosch argues that there is an ecumenical position that accents listening to the "here and now" and an evangelical position that affirms the "there and later." Rather than being stymied by such intellectual tensions, effective Christian evangelists have been able to bridge the gap between the tangible "now" and the spiritual "later." Unfortunately, some missiologists have not been able to fully agree on evangelism's proper role: "Is the church serving mankind for the purpose of making mankind more human or more spiritual?" Bosch writes concerning the present situation:

> The polarization appears to be complete: Proclamation stands over against Christian presence. Jesus as Redeemer over against Jesus the Man for others, redemption over against humanization, the salvation of the soul over against liberation and revolution.[6]

All Christians are to participate in the full scope of the mission of evangelism without the above superficial dichotomies. Does this mean that all Christians have the gift of evangelism? As we have already hinted, this question is not clearly answered in Scripture. If the gift means traveling like Paul, organizing like Wesley, or preaching like Billy Graham, then certainly not. If the gift of evangelism means fitting uniquely into the process of planting, watering, and harvesting, then the answer is "quite possibly." If the gift of evangelism means being fully cognizant that life needs to be lived so as to entice neighbors to become Christians and following up on that conviction, then the answer is "definitely yes." All Christians are to be salt, light, and leaven—conduits of grace in a world of alienation. Every Christian needs to take to heart Paul's declaration in 2 Corinthians: "He has committed to us the word of reconciliation" (5:19).

Every Christian an evangelist should mean that no one in the church should be what Tom Nees calls the new WASPS: white, affluent, separated, and protected. William Booth saw these people as "passing their time in pleasant thoughts, congratulating themselves and one another on their good fortune" while many perished all around them in the stormy deep. Tom Nees writes:

> If we are going to share the gospel, we cannot shout it from a distance. In some way it must be shared, one on one, by people who are neither afraid nor condescending, but who are willing to go to the streets and neighborhoods and hospitals, to go to the high-rise areas in the obedient example of Jesus even if it means obedience unto death, so that with Him we may be exalted and know the power of His resurrection through us.[7]

The Mission of Grace

Just as there are two uniquenesses in the message, there are two universals in the mission. All saved must vitally concern themselves with all who are lost. The mission will be blunted if the line between the lost and the found is obscured. If the Christian holds the opinion that he or she is better than the non-Christian through happenstance, inheritance, or educational opportunities, there is no need for a mission. Paul would not have endured shipwreck, beating, and imprisonment except for a clearly defined mission. He was acting as an ambassador of Christ carrying a ministry of reconciliation into an enemy territory. Whatever wounds inflicted were put into proper perspective by the trophies of grace secured for the kingdom. Redeemed persons were sufficient rewards for all he endured.

Paul, who had experienced radical grace, extended radical grace. That meant constantly seeing every person in the light of what they could become in Christ Jesus. I'm not sure if anyone ever carried out this vision more effectively than John Wesley. He preached 40,000 times to coal miners, iron smelters, copper workers, glassblowers, quarrymen, longshoremen, farm laborers, female spinners, fishermen, and barge operators. He evangelized rich and poor, educated and uneducated, upper class and lower class, proletariat and aristocrat. In "An Earnest Appeal to Men of Reason and Religion," he wrote:

> I do preach to as many as desire to hear every night and morning. You ask what I would do with them. I would make them virtuous and happy, easy in themselves and useful to others. Whither would I lead them? To heaven; to God the

> Judge, the lover of all, and to Jesus the Mediator of the new Covenant. What religion do I preach? The religion of love: the law of kindness brought to light by the Gospel.[8]

Crossing the Dichotomies

Mission operates between dichotomies: heaven and hell, lost and found, light and darkness, good and evil, death and life, the kingdom of this world and the kingdom of "our Lord and of His Christ." Any blurring of the distinction between these dichotomies will shroud the mission with hesitation and self-doubt. If the alternatives are simply a matter of personal choice and preference, mission will be viewed as an intrusion or even a cultural sin. False concepts of freedom have led to a mind-my-own-business mentality among so-called evangelicals. American rights to privatization and skewed motifs of individualization have completely undermined a proper understanding of human solidarity and our obligation to rescue the perishing. This is a serious concern. A person's dwelling in the light should not result in smugness, but in a deep desire to share the light with those who dwell in darkness.

The privilege of being an ambassador of Christ's reconciliation does not give me the right to badger, embarrass, or offend people. In fact, one must earn the right through prayer and an honest attempt to know people before invading their lives with highly intimate and personal questions. If a complete stranger is approached with the "good news," the confrontation must be done with the utmost sensitivity, discernment, and leadership of the Holy Spirit. "Frame complication and intrusion" takes place when someone who is uninvited tries to redefine someone else's time-spatial sphere. People believe that they have the right to certain preserves, such as personal space, conversational preserve, sheath or body covering, and informational preserve. In discussing Erving Goffman's "territories of the self," Larry Ingram states, "The attitude of unrestrained boldness is in direct opposition to the restraint normally expected of strangers in public places."[9] Christians must tread cautiously lest they muddy the waters with their feet. To a certain extent, the mores of culture and society must be respected lest credibility be lost.

THE MEANS OF THE TASK

A mission must be accomplished by a means. The Lausanne Covenant makes a clear statement on the relationship between means and mission.

In the church's mission of sacrificial service, evangelism is primary. World evangelization requires the whole church to take the whole Gospel to the whole world. The church is at the very center of God's cosmic purpose and is His appointed means of spreading the Gospel.[10]

Incarnational Evangelism

The purpose of this section is to explain means from God's perspective rather than ours. That God would refer to the church as His body is possibly the highest compliment that deity can give to human existence. We are to continue the incarnational ministry of Christ. Referring to the season of Pentecost that has continued from the day of the outpouring of the Holy Spirit until now, Jesus said, "In that day you shall know that I am in My Father, and you in Me, and I in you" (John 14:20). In short, we are Christ's eyes, hands, feet, and ears here on earth. David Bosch states, "The gospel takes shape concretely in the witness, in the church, and is never a general objective, immutable revelation. True evangelism is incarnational."[11] The church as a leavening factor in the world is what Herbert Kane refers to as "presence differentiated from proclamation."[12] Francis of Assisi exhorted his friars to "presence" when he told them to preach often and when necessary use words.

Dallas Willard describes the fundamental work of the church as showing those who gather in its meetings how to enter into full participation in the rule of God where they are. In this way the church will ultimately bring all nations to itself to find out how humanity can realize the universal ethical vision of righteousness and well-being.[13] The spoken message does not normally rise above the medium which speaks it. A message is always being spoken, whether it be through deed or word. The world takes careful note of ethical performance, psychological fortitude, and the courage to be in the face of overwhelming odds. Personalities embody the message of the Savior. We are "epistles read by all men," and with great scrutiny by those with whom we have close contact. Consider the exhortation of Peter to wives who have unsaved husbands: "In the same way, you wives, be submissive to your own husbands so that even if any of them are disobedient to the word, they may be won without a word by the behavior of their wives, as they observe your chaste and respectful behavior" (1 Peter 3:1-2).

One of the most crucial problems for evangelism today is the mixed signals that the church sends to the world. We preach a Christ of sacrifice, but serve the gods of materialism; we preach a commandment of love, but are preoccupied with self-serving agendas; we preach peace but are hardly able to live with those within our own household of faith. The counterproduction of the church can be controlled only through the liberation of the Holy Spirit. In the words of Reinhold Niebuhr, "Human personality is so constructed that it must be possessed if it is to escape the prison of self-possession."[14]

But because the church does not live within the full liberation of the gospel message, the world observes a church living basically the same lifestyle that it lives. It is not enough for church members not to murder, steal, or commit adultery. Most of the world does not do that, at least not blatantly so. In order to be an effective witness, the church must have an agenda that is not dictated by the surrounding culture. David Bosch states the problem in this way:

> Many evangelists, despite their spine-chilling sermons about sin, Satan, and hell, do not constitute any real threat to their listeners' life style. They are not challenging people to reorient their lives socially; they merely try to make them into good Christians who are expecting the second Advent.[15]

God's Primary Means: People

The above reason is why James Engel argues that the first evangelistic step of the church is Christian maturity. However, he is not arguing that the church has to be perfect before it can reach out to others. In fact, Christian maturity will develop as we lose ourselves in sharing the Christian message. At the heart of the gospel is the church that Christ came to redeem. If the church is tainted, the gospel that the church proclaims will be contaminated. Thus, the end of evangelism is the purification of the church. The church is not for the purpose of evangelism; rather, evangelism is for the purpose of the church. Engel says it well:

> When the church is viewed in terms of the doctrine of the kingdom, it is far more than a means of world evangelization. The establishment of the spiritual kingdom expressed through the body of Christ is an end in and of itself. In the final analysis, this is why Christ came. If the church is just viewed as evangelistic machinery, the result is a gross disservice to scriptural teachings.[16]

The Holy Spirit came so that we might carry on the ministry that Jesus began on earth. Everything Christ did was for the purpose of demonstrating that He is the polestar of all truth. The Holy Spirit is the Spirit of truth, and came to internalize that truth within portable tabernacles. The Holy Spirit turns vessels of clay into vessels of honor so that we may change falsehood into authentic existence. Christ was fully authentic, and only as the Holy Spirit aligns one with truth can one bear witness to His authenticity. Archbishop William Temple tersely stated, "The primary purpose for which the Spirit is given is that we may bear witness to Christ."[17]

Every secondary means that is used must be subservient to the primary means—the Holy Spirit energizing, liberating, and flowing out from the believer to unbelievers. There is a good possibility that the convert will rise no higher than the means used to reach him or her. Holy means will produce holy people. Holy means does not mandate outdatedness or a circle-the-wagons mentality. William Abraham has put his finger on a sore spot when he says, "Sociologically, modern evangelism is deeply infected by secularism. Decisions are generally made on a technical and pragmatic basis."[18]

Power of the Spirit

The evangelist will tarry for the infilling and empowering of Pentecost. Every man and woman in the church will ask God to make them clean vessels through which God flows, not only on special occasions, but in the everyday course of events. The lack of the Holy Spirit's power in the life of the believer is the single greatest barrier to effective evangelism. Lack of the Holy Spirit comes through either outright disobedience or lack of utilizing the means of grace. Dallas Willard calls these means of grace "disciplines of the Spirit," categorizing them into disciplines of abstinence (such as solitude, silence, and fasting) and disciplines of engagement (such as studying the Word and worship). Only then can our relationship with the Holy Spirit be nurtured. Such nurture of the Spirit's glow in our lives will dispel the world's indifference to our witness. In Samuel Chadwick's words:

> The ministry energized by the Holy Ghost is marked by aggressive evangelism, social revolution, and persecution. Holy Ghost preaching led to the burning of the books of the magic art, and it stirred up the opposition of those who trafficked in the ruin of the people. Indifference to religion is impossible where the preacher is a flame of fire. To the Church, Pentecost brought light, power, joy. There came to each illumination of mind, assurance of heart, intensity of love, fullness of power, exuberance of joy.[19]

Evangelism cannot be done without the gifts of the Spirit. Rather than thinking in terms of a theological catalog of gifts, God's enabling is as varied and timely as the situation in which people find themselves. There are sundry opinions as to the interface between supernaturally bestowed gifts and natural aptitude. Suffice it to say that whatever abilities a person has, they are gifts from God, especially if they have been consecrated to the work of the kingdom. Not many vocations would have more inroads into the lives of others than would a Spirit-filled auto mechanic. Every vocation needs to be fitted for bearing fruit. This will normally not be in terms of spectacular gifts, but by praying that every deed, no matter how technical or simple, be saturated by God's grace.

THE MASTER MOTIVE

There is one master motive in doing the work of evangelism: to bring glory to God. God's glory was the ultimate reason for which Jesus gave His life as a ransom for sinners. Bringing glory to God meant glorifying both the Father and the Son. Just before Jesus went to the cross, He said to His disciples: "Now is the Son of Man glorified, and God is glorified in Him; if God is glorified in Him, God will also glorify Him in Himself, and will glorify Him immediately" (John 13:31-32).

Glory comes to God by extending His kingdom both quantitatively and qualitatively. The first petition of the Lord's Prayer is "Thy kingdom come, thy will be done on earth, as it is in heaven." Extension of the kingdom may not necessarily be extension of the church, which was the essence of Walter Rauschenbush's argument. In Rauschenbush's view, evangelism correctly conceived will bring a radically different state of affairs, a revolution of kingdom principles. At the heart of spreading the kingdom is attacking sin at both the individual and corporate levels by spreading the religious ethic of Jesus. Rauschenbush believed that Christ "was sent by God, with his Father's thoughts and his Father's will in his heart, to make those thoughts known on earth and secure obedience to that will."[20]

The elements of obedience, sacrifice, ethical maturity, openness to outcasts, and sovereign allegiance were all part of Christ's bringing glory to His Father. These qualities are to be repeated in our lives just as they were evident in the life of Christ. Without these elements, evangelism becomes unworthy of the glory of God. The same relationship of intimacy and fidelity that Christ had with the Father, we are to have with the Son. Christ prayed that the apostles would be sanctified so that they might be effective instruments of evangelism: "As Thou didst send Me into the world, I also have sent them into the world" (John 17:18).

We can do no better in evangelism than to make sure that we are witnesses to the holiness of God, wearing the spotless wedding garment. No one has ever said it better than Bishop Stephen Neill, as he stood before the World Council of Churches in 1939:

> Most educated men in the world today have some knowledge of the Gospels, and some mental picture of the character of Jesus. They realize, perhaps better than many professing Christians, that the only true criterion of Christianity is likeness to Christ. The heart of their complaint, though perhaps they would be hard put to it to frame it in words, is that they do not see in Christianity and in the Church that likeness to Christ which they have a right to expect. Real holiness is impressive and attractive; if the Church has failed to hold the respect of the ordinary man, may the cause not be, in part at

least, that the children of the Church have failed to set before the world the challenge of unmistakable holiness after the manner of Christ?[21]

Secondary Motives

Beneath the master motive of bringing glory to God are three derivative motives for doing the work of evangelism. We have already touched on the motive of obedience. Evangelism is a Christian's duty. Obedience is the opportunity that Christians have to say to Jesus, "I love You. I not only love You, but I trust You." This is the best use of my time and energy, because God commands me to Pray! Go! Tell! Free! Give! so that people will become a part of His kingdom. These biblical commands are not to be taken lightly. In fact, a high regard for the authority of the Scriptures is vitally linked to evangelism.

Immersion in the Word of God is directly proportionate to evangelistic zeal. Overarching themes of compassion, confrontation, and sharing the way of salvation become obvious throughout the Scriptures. The apostle's willingness to endure hardships for the sake of gaining new converts calls the church to confession and repentance, and then boldness. When the Sanhedrin commanded Peter and John to speak no more in the name of Christ, they responded, "Whether it is right in the sight of God to give heed to you rather than to God, you be the judge; for we cannot stop speaking what we have seen and heard" (Acts 4:19-20). Wayne Detzler challenges us to integrate the Bible into our behavior so that we might powerfully impact the world with our witness: "As a result, people are saved, and the church accomplishes the purpose for which she was born: the evangelization of the lost."[22]

The second penultimate motive is that people are important. People are inherently important. They are ends in themselves, not a means for institutional growth, statistical advancement, or the evangelist's self-aggrandizement. They are in no way to be manipulated or used in any way that would subtract from divine-human potential. The goal is to maximize the welfare of all with whom we come in contact. True, the importance of people is derived from the creatorship (creative ability) of God, as is all creaturely existence. But it should be remembered that people are the highest form of all creaturely existence. Dietrich Bonhoeffer stated:

> To give bread to the hungry man is not the same as to proclaim the grace of God and justification to him, and to have received bread is not the same as to have faith. Yet for him who does these things for the sake of the ultimate, and in the knowledge of the ultimate, this penultimate does bear a relation to the ultimate.[23]

People are of ultimate importance to God, and they should be to us. No matter how ugly, disgusting, draining, nauseating, or depressing a person may seem, he or she has been made in the image of God. That image is tarnished, and it is our job to renew and polish. Renewing and polishing touches people physically, spiritually, and psychologically. The old dichotomy of body and soul is moot. Evangelism expresses concern for the whole person. True religion will affect a better way of life. Security and discipline, as well as many other virtues, are affected when Christ lives within a person. In no place and era was this more evident than in the Wesleyan revival of the eighteenth century, as indicated by the following incident. A wagonload of Lincolnshire Methodists had been arrested because of their newfound religion and were brought before a justice of the peace. When the justice asked for the accusation, this was the reply:

> "Why they pretended to be better than other people, and besides, they prayed from morning to night." The Justice asked, "But have they done nothing besides?" "Yes, sir, ain't please, your worship, they have converted my wife. Till she went among them; she had such a tongue! And now she's as quiet as a lamb." "Carry them back" ordered the Judge "and let them convert all the scolds in town."[24]

But it must be constantly kept in mind that people have an eternal, as well as a temporal, existence. It is this fact that makes evangelism qualitatively unique among all other ministries, whether they be performed by the church or other agencies. There cannot be evangelism without an eschatology. Yes, there is a certain aspect of eschatology that is realized. We experience the kingdom now and attempt to expand it to as many places and in as many ways as possible.

But interpreting eschatology as only a present realization betrays the etymology of the word. Eschatology is the principle or study of last things. It is true that the last days begin with the first coming of Christ, but He is the beginning of the end, the One who will bring history as we know it to completion. *Eschatos* is also used in the context of the expectation of the coming last day, the last plagues, the overcoming of the last enemy (death), the resurrection of the dead, and the final judgment.[25] In a sense, the present moment is a last thing or moment, but that should not preclude the knowledge that Christ is going to return and set up a new heaven and a new earth. This earth as we know it is going to be refined with a fervent heat, and its inhabitants are going to dwell with either the eternally blessed or the eternally damned. Such knowledge does not necessitate predicting dates or pinpointing the Antichrist. The figurative and symbolic language used throughout the Scriptures concerning last things is in keeping with the mysteries of godliness. Bosch states, "To wait for the end never implies passivity, but rather intense activity in the here and now. Involvement in the world is one of the chief ways of preparing ourselves for the *parousia*."[26]

Without a deep appreciation for eschatology—an understanding that people are either eternally saved or eternally lost—the church will not do the work of evangelism. If evangelism essentially means political liberation, material fulfillment, or psychological healing, the brunt of evangelism will be passed off to humanistic activism, with little foundation in biblical reality. The reality is that we need to get ready to die so that we will be ready to live. There will be a generation alive when Jesus returns to earth. That people are lost and that Christians will be judged for not doing something about their lostness is a powerful incentive for one to redeem the time. In the words of the Lausanne Covenant, "This promise of his coming is not a piece of unpractical theologizing. On the contrary, Christ and his apostles never spoke of it to satisfy idle curiosity, but always to stimulate practical action."[27]

Holistic Evangelism

Practical action means that I will do all the good I can to make this world the best possible world. This can best be done by taking the whole gospel to the whole world. The whole gospel knows no tension between being heavenly minded and doing earthly good. Speaking and applying the whole gospel means not only having a worldview that includes the belief that people are eternally lost, but an eye for doing the minuscule details that will further the gospel within a sphere of influence. William Blake was reported to have said that "the common good readily becomes the topic of the scoundrel, the hypocrite and the flatterer, but he who would do some good must do so in minuscule particulars." This is the exact sentiment that Albert Schweitzer expressed when he decided to leave his professional post and enter medical training for missionary service in Africa:

> Only a person who can find a value in every sort of activity and devote himself to each one with full consciousness of duty has the inward right to take as his object some extraordinary activity instead of that which falls naturally to his lot. Only a person who feels his preference to be a matter of course, not something out of the ordinary, and who has no thought of heroism, but just recognizes a duty undertaken with sober enthusiasm, is capable of becoming a spiritual adventurer such as the world needs. There are no heroes of action: only heroes of renunciation and suffering. Of such there are plenty. But few of them are known, and even these not to the crowd, but to the few.[28]

A tension exists between those who believe that they are going to set up a utopia here on earth and those who are going to wait for God to zap the world and take them home. Hands are best kept holy by using them for God's glory, not by sitting on them. Our stewardship is to present the world and its people as holistically as possible to Christ when He appears in His glory. But even with the help of the Holy Spirit, Christians will not be able to return the earth or its people to the pristine condition of the Garden of Eden. The final restoration will take place only at His appearing. In the meantime, we must remember that God is Lord of the cosmos as well as the church. It is true that Satan is the prince of the power of the air, and most people are on his frequency. However, his frequency is subordinated to God's regulation. John Calvin was correct when he said, "Only God is sufficient for my ruin." If this is not so, then Satan is a logical polarity to God. The triumph of evangelism is based on the absolute falsehood of this dualism.

Eternal Reward

In all likelihood, a church will not be evangelistic if it believes only in temporal restoration, without eternal reward or punishment. Jesus consistently spoke of the damnation of the lost in terms of outer darkness, unquenchable fire, and the wrath of God. It is highly improbable that those who do not believe in a lake of fire, of which Jesus spoke, will gather together on a weeknight to go out and share the plan of salvation with the lost. There is no deep-seated incentive to find people if we do not believe they are lost. Improving only their temporal state is not worth the necessary time and energy, especially if the people we are attempting to reach are among the privileged in society. Robert Coleman prophetically writes:

> I am afraid, however, that the sense of impending doom and desire to flee from the wrath to come, so characteristic of our forefathers, does not seem of great concern today. Martin E. Marty, eminent church historian at the University of Chicago, has keenly observed that "the passing of hell from modern consciousness is one of the major, if still undocumented major trends of our time." After all, a generation preoccupied with immediate sensual gratification is not likely to think much about the eternal consequences of sin.[29]

Perhaps it is a fair question to ask how a loving God could send people to hell. Believing that God assigns people to everlasting torment is an underestimation of evil and its consequences. It could be that the next life is simply a logical extension of earthly existence. Christ bore the hell of sin's wrath on the cross so that my hell-bent nature might be forgiven and changed. If I choose to go my own way, God's just love will not be indifferent to my decision. Indifference would allow me to go to a place (i.e., heaven) for which I am totally unfit. Sin in the midst of God's holiness would possibly be as great a punishment as sin in the midst of its just consequences. However, God will not allow that kind of incongruity to take place. God's wrath on sin will be carried out. In John Stott's words, "Redeeming love and retributive justice joined hands at Calvary."[30] Humanity is free by way of prevenient grace to choose either. Whether one speaks of heaven or hell, the choice begins now as a vision for the future. Eschatology is best understood in terms of continuity between the "now" and the "later."

THE EVANGELISM OF CHRIST: THE ULTIMATE MODEL

There is more material being produced today on how to do the work of evangelism than ever in the history of the church. Our main problem is not "how to," but rather the "power to" or "want to." Nevertheless, we do need a model, and Christ remains the quintessential evangelist. The definitive statement of Christ as the prototype evangelist has been given by Robert Coleman in his *The Master Plan of Evangelism.*[31] Coleman's central argument is that Christ did not give the greater part of His energy to reaching the masses. Rather, He selected a small group of men and trained them for the work of evangelism. Wherever He went they went, when He taught they listened and observed, when He performed a miracle they were amazed, and when He reached a loving hand across a cultural, sexual, or racial barrier they were almost in a state of shock. By spending quality time with a group of men, disclosing Himself to them, Jesus reproduced Himself in them. Through the power of Pentecost, they would reproduce themselves in others.

In a follow-up book, *They Meet the Master,*[32] Coleman, through inductive Bible study, demonstrates that Jesus utilized specific principles that can be implemented today. He reached people through felt need (e.g., the woman at the well); He reversed social order by inviting Himself into someone else's home (e.g., Zacchaeus'); He told stories of common interest from which a critical truth could be inducted (e.g., when a lawyer asked for his neighbor to be identified); He demonstrated a willingness to interrupt His own agenda to reward persistence and faith (e.g., the man let down through the roof by his friends); and He rewarded faith over and over again, whether it was found in Gentiles, women, or slaves.

Coleman lists many practical things Jesus did that His followers need to notice. They include responding to ministry needs in everyday situations, looking for evidences of spiritual interest, observing common courtesies, listening as much as talking, asking probing questions, using human interest stories, confronting sin through loving grace, and believing the best about the possibilities of grace in the worst of scoundrels. Above all, Jesus never manipulated anyone, but offered them alternatives of response to a very clear invitation. Christ offered the message of salvation in season and out of season.

In considering Christ as a model for evangelism, there are several overarching themes that should be considered. Jesus was a person of compassion. He acted with passion. He was not an ivory-tower theorist implementing a sociological experiment in the city for the sake of His students. Jesus was emotionally moved by the plight of the people whom He encountered. A central theme of His parables is compassion for others: a father's everlasting love for a lost son, a stranger's willingness to befriend a dying man wounded on a dangerous road, and a manager's willingness to forgive a steward who was deeply indebted to him.

Christ's compassion exhibited itself in the face of poverty, physical infirmity, demonic possession, and enslaving sin. At no point was it more apparent than when a father brought his demon-possessed son to Christ (Mark 9). The deaf and dumb boy's situation was so desperate that he had often attempted suicide. He periodically exhibited epileptic convulsions that violently threw him to the ground, caused him to foam at the mouth and grind his teeth, and eventually brought on a complete rigor mortis of the muscle system. The scene was sickening, and the interruption of Christ's schedule by the father was both a breach of social etiquette and an embarrassment to the disciples. The father pleaded with Jesus, "If You can do anything, take pity on us and help us!" The emotional plea flowed into a river of infinite love, the heart of a caring Christ. Mark tells us, "And when Jesus saw that a crowd was rapidly gathering, He rebuked the unclean spirit, saying to it, 'You deaf and dumb spirit, I command you, come out of him and do not enter him again'" (9:22, 25).

The compassion of Christ was universal and inclusive. Yes, He came to the lost sheep of the house of Israel, but He never assumed that those sheep would automatically follow Him. He was constantly looking for sheep beyond His historically defined fold. The gospel was open to a Samaritan, a Syrophoenecian, a Roman centurion—even to a lunatic who lived in the tombs. The cemetery dweller was the scourge of the town, a proverb of madness and a horror to any who would dare pass his way. Christ cast the demons out of him and presented him clothed with civility to people who thought a madman to be worth far less than the pigs, which had just drowned before their eyes (Mark 5:13). Jesus' compassion made the statement time and time again that people are worth far more than possessions.

Experiencing the Rhythm of Christ

The compassion of Christ cannot be experienced without knowing the Christ of compassion. Jesus demonstrated an intimacy with the Father that is to be replicated by our intimacy with Jesus. Jesus taught His disciples to pray by spending quality time with the Father. Christ prayed much more than He talked about prayer. Persistent, confident, fellowshipping prayer puts God's children on His wavelength. Getting to know God means adopting His values. The only way we will be able to "transform the rhythm of our lives" is to spend extended time with our Lord. Tom Sine explains Christ's rhythm in the following manner:

> In the New Testament we typically find Jesus in one of two places. He is either with the people, visiting, teaching, healing, and celebrating, or he is with God alone. He appears to have had little time for anything else, and yet he never seemed hurried.[33]

The desire and know-how for evangelism is found in having the mind of Christ. There has to be a meeting and agreement of the minds. The impetus for evangelism is found in thinking His thoughts and following His ways. The more Christians focus on Christ and see life and people from His perspective, the more desire we have to fulfill His plan: "The Son of Man did not come to be served, but to serve, and to give His life a ransom for many" (Matt. 20:28).

Evangelism will be miscued if it is founded on technique rather than deep spirituality. Admittedly, legalism, ritualism, pietistic externalism, and an unrealistic mysticism can all be substituted for true spirituality. But true spirituality that comes from the heart of Christ will be modeled in an earthly pilgrimage that involves itself in the social order as well as the individual lives of people. Genuine spirituality will realize that the natural order has been entrusted to supernatural power flowing through people who have put themselves at the disposal of God's concern for the entire order of existence. Again, to quote Bosch's words, "This summons to faith does not issue from the heights of superiority but from the depths of solidarity."[34]

Solidarity with God means greater solidarity with His creatures, especially people. Individual sanctification makes Christians key links in the process of corporate sanctification. Holiness brings glory to God, and this is best exemplified by increasing the sanctity of one's surrounding world. Any false or superficial ideas of separateness will thwart evangelism. Evangelism always works within the tension of drawing close to the heart of God while yet sensing the heartbeat of those around us. The Christian needs to tarry as He tarried and go as He went. The last statement is critical for evangelism. There must be a going after the gathering. For most churches, there is only the latter. Christ did not assume that people were going to come to the synagogue or temple looking for a spiritual guru. In Donald McGavran's words, "No true shepherd will ever say, 'Only such sheep as care to follow me will I shepherd.'"[35] It is more necessary to seek out sheep today than ever in the history of the church. There are less people coming out of curiosity and welfare needs than in past generations. There are too many other entertainment values and self-help institutions that obscure the visibility of the church. We must get the message out.

Getting the Message Out

Jesus was itinerant in His mode of operation. A wedding, a cemetery, a community well, and a dinner party all provided opportunities to exchange ideas and confront people with spiritual truth. Strangely enough, in the New Testament no one ever finds salvation within the walls of a religious institution. This is not to say that Christ did not sow seed in the temple, but most of His seed sowing was done on the highways and byways of life.

Harry Stout argues that Whitefield's success resided in the fact that he was able to utilize *secular* space and time. In the rapid rise of eighteenth-century consumerism, there was a religious void within the public sphere. "Before religion could become a marketplace phenomenon, it required an entrepreneur, a Wedgewood or Garrick who could offer it in public settings during the week for the general public."[36] It was this necessity that George Whitefield readily understood. He preached up and down the east coast of the colonies with such a reputation that, within a few hours of the announcement that he could be heard at a particular location, thousands would gather by the time he arrived.

It was Whitefield who counseled Wesley to preach wherever he could find a convenient spot. This was especially crucial for Wesley since he was excluded from the churches because of his newfound faith in God. In 1740 he was enjoying about the same popularity in Anglicanism as Jesus enjoyed in the synagogues. Thus, Wesley's statement "I determined to be more vile" (in reference to his entering the fields and marketplaces clothed in clerical garb) became a watershed in his ministry, if not in all of Christendom. Concerning this strange methodology, he said, "What marvel the devil does not love field preaching! Neither do I: I love a commodious room, a soft cushion, a handsome pulpit. But where is my zeal, if I do not trample all these underfoot in order to save one more soul?"[37] Wesley was derided by his peers and reprimanded by his superiors, to whom he replied, "Churches are not reclaiming sinners because they never come into a church, perhaps not once in a twelfth month, perhaps not for many years together."[38] Francis of Assisi, George Fox, George Whitefield, John Wesley, Billy Graham, Salvation Army street bands, Evangelism Explosion teams, and small group home Bible studies have all followed the model of Christ. The gospel must be taken beyond the walls of the church.

CONCLUSION

Doing evangelism is not the simple result of a decision to do evangelism. The decision must flow from an ideology, a comprehensive worldview that includes a personal God who desires to make Himself intimately known to His Creation. Unfortunately, many churches and denominations often make decisions to reach out without a plausibility structure, a cosmic construction according to God's purpose and design. Evangelism that tries to operate in a vacuum is like a flickering candle that has the God-given oxygen sucked from around it. It is short-lived. It can only burn as it operates within the reality paradigm for burning.

What has been discussed in this chapter is the theological energy required for evangelism. The forward energy is a combined thrust of reliability, plausibility, personal experience, and transcendent images that preempt earthly pursuits. This combined energy is best described as certitude—a firm belief system that depends on Spirit-anointed means to exalt Jesus Christ. A biblical theology for evangelism finds both its means and ends in exalting the Savior. Evangelism finds its fullest expression in worshiping Jesus and enabling others to join the celebration.

Such evangelism always brings us back to the first evangelistic text spoken by an itinerant preacher in the New Testament: "Behold, the Lamb of God who takes away the sin of the world!" (John 1:29) Evangelism outside of this theological context is not worthy of the name. What is worse than not doing evangelism is not doing it when one *thinks* that he or she *is* doing it.

Progress cannot be assessed until the starting point is located and the direction of the compass is charted. Every would-be evangelist or evangelistic group must first set their eyes upon Jesus, the author and perfecter of their faith, the preeminent one who is the force and focus of every evangelistic effort. Jesus operated out of Himself under the anointing of the Holy Spirit and at the direction of the Father. We too must operate out of Him, He in us, anointed by the Holy Spirit. This is incarnational ministry. "When the Helper comes, whom I will send to you from the Father, that is the Spirit of truth, who proceeds from the Father, He will bear witness of Me, and you will bear witness also, because you have been with Me from the beginning" (John 15:26-27).

IV

the narrative of american evangelism

At the heart of America's religious experience is the story of evangelism. There is a thread of evangelistic enterprise that weaves its way from John Winthrop's "City on a Hill" declaration to the recycled yellow school buses that transport children to Sunday School all across America. There has been a consistent enterprise of ingathering by America's churches. When old methods have become outmoded, more workable means have been adopted. Pragmatism has meant the unceasing effort to search for methodologies that will be numerically efficient in the great harvest of souls.[1]

One must tread very cautiously when identifying historical methodologies that have been prevalent in winning people to Christ. Most often, what superficially appears to be a dominant and immediate influence in initiating persons into the kingdom is really only a catalyst in a long line of influences. There are those people who have overwhelmingly mystical experiences, such as seeing a blinding light that sweeps them into the kingdom while reading the Scriptures. But even those people must realize that, in all probability, their subconsciousnesses are more than likely filled with past religious experiences and gospel references that suddenly burst upon their consciousnesses. The long and intricate formation of attitudes, values, and psychological traits are critical in choices that are made for or against Christ.

Sharp demarcations concerning methodologies are not only implausible, they are impossible. Almost any era that can be described probably represents to some degree all the systematic procedures for winning people to the cause of the gospel. But the thesis of this chapter is that some systems fit particular people and churches more than others. The situation in life plus gifts of leadership have dictated procedures for doing the work of the kingdom. Where the fit between the person or persons and field of service has been most compatible, evangelistic success has been most imminent. The promise of power from the Holy Spirit does not disallow time-spatial elements. "But you shall receive power when the Holy Spirit has come upon you; and you shall be My witnesses both in Jerusalem, and in all Judea and Samaria, and even to the remotest part of the earth" (Acts 1:8).

It should also be noted that people, for the most part, do not become members of churches in highly esoteric ways. Granted, people are only born into the kingdom by the Holy Spirit. But whether we are talking about new life in Christ or new membership in the church, the greatest influences are family and friends. The largest avenue into the church is heritage. It is the general (but far short of universal) rule that Christian parents produce Christian children. The lineage of family and friends has far greater appeal than any improvisational technique.

However, Christians have improvised ever since Noah counted the animals and loaded them onto the ark along with his family. And no doubt part of that evangelistic impromptu has been much more biblical and Spirit-led than other parts. However, most of it has been with good faith that God blesses human ingenuity when the goals are worthy and noble. In Charles Ferguson's words, the church has indeed gone about "organizing to beat the devil."

The following history attempts to identify both historical eras of evangelism and persons who have played key roles. All categorization begs for disclaimers and qualifications. Some of the personages are unique to their time and place, but others would have found a way to be evangelistically successful whatever their time-spatial placement. The following men and women have shaped history according to what they believed to be a transcendent design. But transcendent design does not prevent evangelism from being inextricably bound by a sociological context. Being overly categorical about such historical analysis would be more difficult than Lewis and Clark finding the source of the Columbia River, a rushing mass of water fed by thousands of tributaries. But such complexity, and at times even bewilderment, add to the joy and excitement of historical exploration.

EXPANSIONISTS

The expansionists' story of evangelism takes place from the founding of the English colonies on America's eastern shores to the massacre of Marcus Whitman and his family in what is now Walla Walla, Washington in 1847. Whitman's trek as a pioneer Methodist medical missionary along the Oregon Trail across the Continental Divide was one of tremendous courage and sacrifice. As Americans moved west, they were followed by rough-hewn circuit riders, camp meetings, church planters, and missionary explorers such as Whitman. Sometimes it was difficult for observers to make a clear demarcation between unadulterated evangelistic zeal and the quest for personal gain. Even Christopher Columbus stated that his contact with the North American natives was for the purpose of discovering "the manner in which may be undertaken their conversion to our Holy Faith."[2]

The story of the Catholic missionary enterprise to the West and Southwest has not been sufficiently told. Miguel Jose Serra (1713–1784), whose statue stands in the U.S. Capitol, witnessed thousands of conversions to Christianity as he established twenty-one missions throughout California. He taught the Native Americans agricultural methods and protected them whenever they were abused by encroaching soldiers and colonists. From 1769 to 1845, 146 Franciscans baptized nearly 100,000 Indians.[3] As early as 1630, there were 25 mission stations in the New Mexico region and 35,000 Indian converts.

One of the most courageous stories of missionary exploration concerns Jacques Marquette, a Jesuit who founded a mission on the northern tip of Michigan in 1672. He then went southwest, ministering to the Indians in Illinois. His final endeavor was to traverse the Mississippi River as far south as Arkansas, a 2,500-mile round trip by canoe. He died from fever and dysentery just before his thirty-eighth birthday, after having established a mission near present-day Utica, Illinois in 1674.

Two other names have become legendary in terms of evangelism among the Indians: John Elliot and David Brainerd. Elliot completed a translation of the New Testament for the Algonquin Indians in 1661 and the Old Testament in 1663. He established Christian Indian villages and taught them to govern themselves after the pattern of Exodus 18. Elliot certainly gained the respect of the Native Americans, but it is not clear how Christian they actually became. Nevertheless, Elliot's actions argued for the inherent worth of the "red man" and awakened the conscience of the early colonial churches.

David Brainerd (1718–1747) envisioned a Christian influence on the Indians of western Massachusetts that would be accomplished through prayer and living a holy life. Before he died at the age of 29, Brainerd witnessed an outbreak of revival among people who had previously been quite indifferent to his message. Brainerd died in the home of Jonathan Edwards, who later published his journal. Brainerd's account remains a monument of perseverance in prayer and devotion to the lost.

All of the early denominations exhibited evangelistic zeal, some much more than others. The Congregationalists and Unitarians lagged behind the Presbyterians, Baptists, and Methodists. But even the Congregationalists could boast of Asahel Nettleton and Charles G. Finney, men of different eras but the same indefatigable labors. The Presbyterians were probably more chagrined than boastful of James McGready, the rough and tough Kentucky evangelist. A contemporary stated,

> His person was not prepossessing nor his appearance interesting, except his remarkable gravity, and small piercing eyes. His coarse, tremulous voice excited in me the idea of something unearthly. His gestures were the reverse of elegance. Everything appeared by him forgotten, but the salvation of souls.[4]

This frontiersman denounced the sinners of Rogues Harbor in Logan County, Kentucky in no uncertain terms. McGready was an impassioned evangelist who often witnessed people shouting, swooning, and falling prostrate under his preaching.

Between 1800 and 1830, Baptists, Presbyterians, and Congregationalists all showed significant growth through revivalistic methods. The Baptists in 1790 had 872 churches with 64,975 members, but in 1836 had 7,299 churches with 517,525 members.[5] As an aftermath of Presbyterian James McGready's revivalism, the Cumberland Presbytery became a separate entity in 1806, and by 1829 "had presbyteries in Kentucky, Tennessee, Alabama, Mississippi, Arkansas, Indiana, Illinois, and Missouri, and missionaries from Pennsylvania to Texas."[6]

Baptists

The Baptists were as suited as, if not more than, the other denominations to take advantage of the westward expansion. Their hard preaching, emotional atmosphere, and democratic church government appealed to the free-spirited frontiersmen. The uneducated preachers and informal worship reflected frontier conditions. Representative of the frontier preachers was William Hickman, who arrived in Garrard County, Kentucky in 1784. His preaching was said to have been like thunder in the distance, and John Taylor, another Baptist preacher, wrote that no man in Kentucky baptized as many people as Hickman. During his years in Kentucky, he organized some twenty churches.

But Baptists did not wait until they got to the western side of Appalachia to evangelize. Isaac Backus averaged 1,200 miles a year on horseback as an itinerant evangelist throughout New England. From 1740 to 1800, Baptist churches in New England increased from half a dozen to 325.[7] In the South, Shubael Stearns was founding the Sandy Creek Baptist Church in Guilford County, North Carolina in 1755. By 1758, the little group had grown to over 600, at which time the Sandy Creek Association was founded. In a 1765 letter, Stearns wrote:

> The Lord carries on this work gloriously in sundry places in this province, and in Virginia, and in South Carolina. About seven hundred souls attended the meeting, which held six days. We received twenty-four persons by a satisfactory declaration of grace, and eighteen of them were baptized. The power of God was wonderful.[8]

Methodists

No denomination outdid the Methodists on the frontiers of American life. Though Methodism had almost been wiped out by the Revolutionary War, it became the fastest growing antebellum denomination. By 1800, there were 64,894 Methodists; by 1815, 200,000; and by 1850, 1,259,906. In fact, from 1800 to 1810, Methodism's membership increased 168 percent, while America's population increased 36 percent. In *Organizing to Beat the Devil,* Charles Ferguson argues that the Methodist enterprise was the American enterprise. He states in his prologue:

> The combination of exuberance and statistics that belongs to the national scene, of idealism and bureaucracy, of ponderous effort and quick wit, of grandiose plans and infinite detail—all may arise out of forces of which Methodist churches in their various branches are a part, if not indeed, the chief exemplar.[9]

Frederick Norwood, in pointing out that in most cases the Methodist Conference of a territory preceded the actual status of a state, generalizes:

> These exercises in the relationship of space and time, provide a new method of placing the westward expansion of Methodism in proper context. . . . We are reminded that in this case, as in so many others, the history of Methodism is inextricably bound with the history of the United States.[10]

After reading several hundred pages from Francis Asbury's *Journal* and evaluating his work from a dozen or so church historians, one finds it almost impossible to exaggerate his imprint upon the early Methodist church. He rode 270,000 miles, crossed the Alleghenies over 60 times, preached 16,500 times, and ordained 4,000 men. When he came to America in 1771 there were 600 Methodists; when he died in 1816, there were over 200,000. His *Journal,* giving close account of his Herculean efforts, furnishes the best and most complete travelogue written in America before the Civil War. He penned, "You must have a stomach for every man's table and a back for every man's bed." His lot was rough terrain, creeks, fever, pain, darkness, and often a "crowded log cabin, twelve feet by ten, agreeable; without are cold and rain, and within six adults and as many children, one of which is all motion, the dogs, too, must sometimes be admitted." He lamented sometimes that filth could be shoveled from the floor with a spade. "O, for a clean board to sleep on!" At the end of some days all he could recall in his journal were the words "Pain, Pain, Pain."[11]

The story of early Methodism, contrary to popular opinion, is not one of eloquent, flamboyant preachers and phenomenal camp meetings. Even if the stories of Jesse Lee, Peter Cartwright, and William McKendree were not exaggerated, they would still be only a few of the hundreds of class leaders, lay preachers, and itinerants whose great labors and popularity with the frontiersmen planted the gospel message. The early Methodist heritage is a story of men and women in love with Christ and His gospel. The lay preachers had risen through the ranks, were educated at "Brush College," and had informally taken the vow of chastity, poverty, and obedience. It is not within our scope to discuss the psychology of high expectations, severity, and even martyrdom, but it worked.

Ivan Howard, in a meticulous study, reminds us that nearly half of the itinerants who had died by 1847 were less than 30 years of age.[12] James Finley wrote, "There was nothing in those days to render an itinerant life in the least degree enticing." Able Stevens later evaluated, "The system speedily killed off such as were weak of body, and drove off such as were feeble in character."[13] By 1800, 650 ministers had agreed to the itinerant system, which meant possibly going to a circuit half the size of Michigan, four or five hundred miles from the closest Methodist, simply at the suggestion of Asbury. However, the Methodists were not alone in an ideology that propelled them to spread the gospel with great sacrifice against tremendous odds.

REVIVALISTS—THE AWAKENERS

Periodically there have been outbursts of the Holy Spirit that have orbited churches into rapid growth. This is not to say that the Holy Spirit is not doing a mighty work in other evangelistic measures. And, admittedly, it is difficult to draw a qualitative demarcation between vast awakenings and smaller explosions of the Holy Spirit. The difference is often quantitative, having to do with extent of both time and geography. According to William McLoughlin, religious awakenings or revival movements sometimes grip whole communities or nations for many years.[14] They are normally not marked by a single prophet, but rather by many evangelists. These evangelists deemphasize the institutional side of religion in favor of God's personal authority and initiative in individual lives. McLoughlin argues that there have been five great awakenings in the history of America, "periods of fundamental ideological transformation necessary to the dynamic growth of the nation in adapting to basic social, biological, psychological, and economic changes."[15]

It should be noted that these societal transformations have not been limited to America. Of particular note is the simultaneous and, in many ways, similar work which God was doing on both sides of the Atlantic during the days of Jonathan Edwards and John Wesley. While the Arminian Wesley was preaching free grace responded to by a free will, Edwards was staunchly defending God's sovereignty and the utter helplessness of persons. Edwards was not the pathetic preacher that some have pictured him to be, but graphically depicted the insecurity of life in the face of an awesome God. Metaphors, similes, hyperboles, analogies, and imagination were abundant. In Perry Miller's words, "Edwards' sermons are immense and concentrated efforts to get across, in the simplest language, the meaning of the religious life."[16] Edwards depicted the misery of humankind as over against the remedy of a glorious and sufficient God.

It was Edwards who more than any other person validated the work of George Whitefield, the Tennent Brothers, Theodore Frelinghuysen, and others who romped through the New England states carrying with them the Spirit that had transformed Northhampton. There was consistent moral transformation and, at times, emotional outbursts. Edwards explained in his defense of the revival that transformation and emotional displays were compatible.[17] Indeed, many were quick to label Edwards' followers as overly enthusiastic fanatics because rational behavior did not always prevail in public. Edwards responded, "There are false affections and there are true. A man's having much affection doesn't prove that he has any true religion; but if he has no affection, it proves that he has no true religion."[18]

Camp Meetings

Robert Handy states, "Throughout the nineteenth century, revivalism in its changing phases and many different strands was the most conspicuous, though often highly controversial, source of renewal in Protestant life."[19] But yet in spite of the above continuity between the two centuries, there seems to be a distinct revivalistic watershed at the beginning of the nineteenth. The 1801 Cane Ridge camp meeting serves as a demarcation because of its first annum date, its chronological relationship to the second Great Awakening, it being the first religious explosion west of the Alleghenies, and it being the first to use the most characteristic revival methodology in the nineteenth century, the camp meeting. The camp meeting, whose time had come, would provide entertainment, accessibility, socialization, ecumenicity, and a scheduled stopping point for the itinerant preacher. William McLoughlin states, "Without the time or money to establish churches in the early years of settlement, the frontier dwellers had nowhere else to get their children baptized, to pray and sing together, to have weddings performed by ministers, or to give vent to pent-up feelings."[20]

Sydney Ahlstrom points out that "the most important fact about Cane Ridge is that it was an unforgettable revival of revivalism, at a strategic time and a place where it could become both symbol and impetus for the century-long process by which the greater part of American evangelical Protestantism became 'revivalized.'"[21] The event was the brainchild of a Presbyterian minister named Barton Stone, who had been influenced by the revivalistic measures of James McGready. Approximately twenty-five miles north of Lexington, Kentucky, the beautiful expanse of ground can be found where 15,000 to 25,000 people met, now made a shrine by the Christian Church denomination. Stone's vision for an ideal nonsectarian church prompted him to send invitations to the August gathering. James Finley, a Methodist preacher and historian, described the scene:

> The noise was like the roar of Niagara. The vast sea of human beings seemed to be agitated as if by a storm. I counted seven ministers, all preaching at one time, some on stumps, others in wagons, and one was standing on a tree which had, in falling lodged against another. . . . Some of the people were singing, others praying, some crying for mercy in the most

> piteous accents, while others were shouting most vociferously. While witnessing these scenes, a peculiarly-strange sensation, such as I had never felt before, came over me. My heart beat tumultuously, my knees trembled, my lips quivered, and I felt as though I must fall to the ground. A strange supernatural power seemed to pervade the entire mass of mind there collected. . . . I stepped up on to a log, where I could have a better view of the surging sea of humanity. The scene that then presented itself to my mind was indescribable. At one time I saw at least five hundred swept down in a moment, as if a battery of a thousand guns had been opened upon them and then immediately followed shrieks and shouts that rent the very heavens.[22]

The temptation is to jump immediately from Cane Ridge to the revivalistic measures of Charles Finney, but to do so is to do an injustice to the revivalistic continuity of the nineteenth century. Mendel Taylor states that, between 1801 and 1804, the camp meeting spread like wildfire through Kentucky, Tennessee, Ohio, western New York, Pennsylvania, the old South, and western New England, and that by 1811, 400 to 500 were being held annually in the United States. Taylor further observes that by 1820 there were 1,000 camp meetings in operation, and, during the years 1802–1811, Methodists added 100,000 members to their ranks.[23] Two of the more famous, yet typical frontier Methodist camp-meeting preachers of that period were Peter Cartwright and William McKendree. Charles Ferguson recounts Nathan Bangs' impressions of McKendree at the Methodist General Conference in 1808:

> Bangs could hardly believe his ears when he heard that McKendree had been asked to preach or his eyes when he saw the man enter the pulpit and stand up to address a house that was full to the overflowing. McKendree was sunburned and dressed in ordinary clothes, "with a red flannel shirt which showed a very large space between his vest and his small-clothes." He appeared "more like a backwoodsman than a minister of the Gospel," Bangs observed. "I was mortified," he added, "that such a looking man should have been appointed to preach on such an important occasion." Bangs was all the more mortified when McKendree stam-

> mered through his prayer and then stood before the congregation, at first almost at a loss for words. Then a magnetism seemed to emanate from him to all parts of the house. "He was absorbed in the interest of his subject; his voice rose gradually until it sounded like a trumpet. The effect was overwhelming. . . . The house rang with irrepressible responses; many hearers fell prostrate to the floor. An athletic man sitting by my side fell as if shot by a cannonball. . . . Such as astonishing effect, so sudden and overpowering, I seldom or never saw before."[24]

Charles Finney

Gilbert Barnes states that "at the turn of the decade, in 1830, the revival burst all bounds and spread over the whole nation, the greatest of all modern revivals."[25] This mushrooming of revivalistic fire has been largely credited to the work and preaching of one man, Charles Grandison Finney (1792–1875), perhaps the most influential personage in regard to revivalistic methodology in the last two centuries. In 1821 Finney claimed to have experienced an intense baptism of the Holy Spirit which he described as

> a wave of electricity, going through and through me. Indeed it seemed to come in waves and waves of liquid love; for I could not express it any other way. It seemed like the very breath of God. I can recollect distinctly that it seemed to fan me like immense wings.[26]

Within the next ten years, Finney was catapulted into national prominence as an evangelist, during which time he held successful meetings in Philadelphia and New York, while also concentrating many of his meetings in upper New York state, which came to be known as the "burnt-over district." His most famous meeting was a six-month revival from September 10, 1830, to March 6, 1831, in Rochester, New York, in which the city was literally captivated. During his first year as pastor of the Broadway Tabernacle in New York City, Mr. Leavitt, editor of the *New York Evangelist,* recorded a series of messages preached by Finney, which were immediately compiled under the title *Lectures on Revivals of Religion.* In it, Finney stated that "the connection between the right use of means for a revival and a revival, is as philosophically sure as between the right use of means to raise grain and a crop of wheat. I believe, in fact, it is more certain and that there are fewer instances of failure."[27]

Among those means instituted (or at least formalized) by Finney were a series for a determined period of time called protracted meetings; an "anxious seat" where worshipers could sit in order to indicate their determination to seek the Lord; prayer preparation before and during the revival; and inquirer meetings for conversation with seekers. But yet to say that this "doctrine led logically to a new conception of revivals, one that denied their miraculous nature, mysterious showers of blessings from heaven,"[28] as McLoughlin claims, is somewhat of a misleading oversimplification. "Supernatural power" was a very real part of Finney's philosophy, demonstrated by his always having someone to pray as he preached and his magnetic, personal influence attributed to his "second blessing experience." In terms of logical, persuasive preaching and a spirited aura, Charles Finney was second to none among the nineteenth-century revivalists.

The Miracle Year

Although revival outbursts during the last century were usually historically defined in terms of dominant personalities, the religious fervor from 1857 to 1860 proves to be an exception. Timothy Smith calls 1858 the "Annus Mirabilis." Whatever the cause for the religious awakening—whether the slavery conflict or the financial crisis of 1857—revival swept the major cities of New York, Philadelphia, and Chicago. Newspapers reported noon prayer meetings with as many as 2,000 in Chicago, and a religious periodical gave report of a public school in Cleveland where all but two boys had professed conversion.[29] Smith quotes from William C. Conants, whose compilation revealed that "88 towns in Maine, 40 in New Hampshire, 39 in Vermont, and 147 in Massachusetts experienced unusual awakenings."[30]

J. Edwin Orr has devoted an entire book to this awakening titled *The Fervent Prayer,* in which he tabulates such figures as 6,110 people meeting daily in New York City in 1858 for prayer.[31] He reports that for a period of two years there were 10,000 additions to church membership weekly and, at one point, conversions reached 50,000 a week.

REVISIONISTS OR RESTORATIONISTS

Revisionists believe that they have a clearer perception of the truth than does the establishment. Usually, their perspective on the church to which they are joined is that it has grown cold because of an institutionalism that has clouded its vision. Revisionists esteem fresh illumination more highly than institutional authority. The extraordinary call of God takes precedent over the ordinary call and sanction of humanity. The call is to return to Scripture in order to restore New Testament character to the present-day church.

The revisionist evangelist is motivated by a compulsion to take fresh illumination to the people. This illumination may include a new interpretation of Scripture (e.g., John Nelson Darby), a new perception of the gifts of the Spirit (e.g., Charles Parham), or a conviction that people are being neglected (e.g., Benjamin Titus Roberts). Such newly discovered convictions normally lead to new sects, which later evolve into denominations. The sects may at first be branded as heresies, but if they are biblically sound, they normally bring fresh life to the church and result in new people being reached with the gospel, people who quite possibly would not have been reached by the existing institutions.

At certain historical periods, restoration is no doubt a necessary law for new life and thus new converts. Such were the ideas of Barton Stone, who wanted a unified church open to everyone, and of Thomas Campbell, who wanted to return to a pristine church modeled after the New Testament example. Their idealism spawned generations of Disciples of Christ and their many offshoots— United Church of Christ, Church of Christ, the Christian Church, plus the smaller denominations almost too numerous to trace. Just as Martin Luther, these men did not believe God had added anything to the canon, but they were convinced that the church had neglected a portion of the truth entrusted to it.

The Holiness Movement

A sectarian movement was the impetus for a tremendous evangelistic thrust in the latter half of the nineteenth century. The Civil War had left mainline denominations fragmented and exhausted, with little evangelistic fervor. The church would have to get its own house in order before it could rectify the woes of the nation and bring healing to the millions of disillusioned. Many in America's largest denomination, Methodism, turned to a reemphasis of John Wesley's doctrine of entire sanctification, an ideology that had produced great evangelistic results on both sides of the Atlantic in the late eighteenth and early nineteenth centuries.

On June 13, 1867 a group of men met in Philadelphia and issued the following invitation: "We affectionately invite all, irrespective of denominational ties, interested in the subject of the higher Christian life, to come together and spend a week in God's great temple of nature; to realize together a Pentecostal baptism of the Holy Ghost, and all with a view to increase usefulness in the churches of which we are members." With that invitation was born the National Campmeeting Association for the Promotion of Holiness, then the National Holiness Association, and, finally, the Christian Holiness Association. John Inskip was elected as its first president. He was a well-known Methodist minister who, before going into full-time evangelism, had seen over 4,000 people converted in his pastoral ministry. Before he died in 1894, he had personally led and conducted forty-eight of the first fifty-two camp meetings.

The vision and impetus for a national camp meeting that would be devoted primarily to the teaching and preaching of holiness belonged to W.B. Osborn. Osborn, a New Jersey pastor, carried a heavy burden for his own denomination, the Methodist Episcopal Church, which had been split by slavery and left in spiritual barrenness and confusion by the Civil War. The most vivid physical monument left by Osborn is the Ocean Grove community on the coast of New Jersey. Osborn was the leader of a group of proprietors who bought the land for the development of a spiritual retreat. Its tabernacle, which seats 7,200 people, reminds those who step inside of its holiness heritage. Large lighted signs on each side of the majestic pipe organ read: "So Be Ye Holy" and "Holiness unto the Lord." Visiting Ocean Grove may be the closest one can come to actually taking a time machine back and stepping into a nineteenth-century American community.

From 1867 to 1883, the National Campmeeting Association for the Promotion of Holiness conducted fifty-two national camp meetings, some of them exceeding 20,000 in attendance. The following is a description of the camp at Manheim, Pennsylvania, in

1867, at which the well-known Methodist Bishop Matthew Simpson was present:

> The writer left the stand in the midst of the scene, and went up along the left-hand outside aisle. Such a sight he had never seen before. Thousands were in the attitude of prayer. An awful presence seemed to rest upon the multitude. There were suppressed sobs, and praises, too.
>
> There were those who insisted that at one time they heard sound, a strange sound, as of a rushing mighty wind, and yet as if subdued and held in check over that prayerful congregation. The writer went to his tent, far back from the circle, but God was everywhere. It was an awful season. Souls were wrestling with God, who was unrolling to many the long, long list of their sins. Unfaithful church members were looking and shuddering over the dreadful past. The people were face to face with God.[32]

In the camp meeting above, there were probably 25,000 in attendance, including 300 ministers. Melvin Dieter calls the camp at Manheim "one of the largest convocations in American nineteenth century religious history, perhaps the greatest in number of attendants at a single meeting until the Moody-Sankey revivals, which followed it by a decade."[33] Robert and Hannah Smith, who were present at and influenced by the camp at Manheim, held what may have been the largest gatherings in England during the nineteenth century, which resulted in the ongoing Keswick Conventions with their own nuance of Christian perfectionism. The meetings at Brighton and Oxford, with overflow crowds of 6,000, were endorsed by Moody and caused even the theologically opposed and highly Calvinistic B.B. Warfield to admit that "there is nothing more dramatic in the history of modern Christianity than the record of this 'Higher Life Movement.' "[34]

Probably the most influential person in holiness revivalism was Phoebe Palmer, a Methodist laywoman who for thirty-seven years held a Tuesday meeting in her home for the promotion of holiness. She and her husband held large evangelistic campaigns in the United States, Canada, and England. J. Edwin Orr credits them with being a mainstay of the 1858 Awakening, with one of their greatest campaigns taking place in Hamilton, Ontario, with crowds from 5,000 to 6,000.

After Palmer died in 1874, Dewitt Talmadge wrote:

> It was no rare thing, in her evangelistic meetings in the United States and Europe, to have ministers of the Presbyterian Church, and the Baptist Church, and the Methodist Church, and the Episcopal Church, and all the churches, coming and kneeling down at the altar, bemoaning their unbelief and their coldness, and then rising up saying, "I have got it—the blessing." . . . Twenty-five thousand souls saved under the instrumentality of Phoebe Palmer! What a record for earth and heaven! The Methodist Church cannot monopolize her name. She belonged to that church, she lived in it, she died in it, she loved it, but you cannot build any denominational wall high enough to shut out that light from our souls.[35]

ORGANIZING PROCLAIMERS

Finney was a transitional person between Jonathan Edwards and evangelists of the late nineteenth century. Between 1730 and 1830 there was a gradual erosion of dependence on God's sovereign power and an increasing use of pragmatic measures. Edwards was surprised by God; however, Finney believed that correct formulas brought certain results. In other words, God's revivals could be prognosticated. However, there were already signs of pragmatic organization by the time of the first Great Awakening's waning days. Harry Stout argues that by 1750 revival had disappeared as an awakening phenomenon that dominated communal consciousness:

> Defined by the traditional criteria of communal awakening, mass enthusiasm, obsession with religion in public discussions, and heated controversy, the revival had died. But defined more functionally as a mass event in an open setting orchestrated by a skilled performer and geared to raising individual experience and passion, "revivals" persisted as strongly as ever.[36]

Dwight L. Moody

But there are still several changes that need to be observed before we come to the evangelistic campaigns of the late nineteenth century. Finney knew little of the vast organizational machinery, extensive voluntary enlistment, sophisticated raising of finances, and enormous publicity of Moody and those that followed. However, Moody also knew little of the sweeping emotional energy generated by outpourings of the Holy Spirit. Winthrop Hudson states, "Whereas Finney's great successes were won in communities where the population rarely exceeded ten thousand, Moody was to achieve fame by galvanizing into action the forces of cities with a million or more inhabitants."[37]

Moody was the prototype of a new breed of professional evangelist. He gave himself to the "business of conducting revivals."[38] Everything was carefully planned in advance. Nothing was left to chance.[39] But the difference was far greater than organizational: whereas Finney had concentrated on the theology of revival, Moody and his successors concentrated on the technology of revival. In fact, Moody said that he didn't even know he had a theology. Right or wrong, Finney carefully explained in his "Revival Lectures" how God's power related to human planning. Moody was too busy getting souls into the lifeboat to worry about theological nuances. He majored in implementing a practical idea that brought an immediate result. "I suppose they say of me 'He is a radical; he is a fanatic; he only has one idea.' Well, it is a glorious idea. I would rather have that said of me than be a man of ten thousand ideas and do nothing with them."[40]

The love of God was the theme of Moody's evangelistic campaigns. Love was more than a byword for Moody. If a person truly loved, it would be demonstrated in ardent devotion to God and boundless energy spent in the salvation of souls. From the moment of his conversion in a Boston shoe store, love issued in doing: filling up pews with street urchins; carrying tracts to the bordellos, saloons, and city shanties; establishing his own Sunday School in Chicago; organizational work for the YMCA; and rising at 4 A.M. to study the Scriptures. Evangelism was not something learned in the classroom, but spurs won through hard and long hours of labor. Bernard A. Weisberger states, "His own schedule during a revival was a fearful thing to contemplate: up before dawn for study, two or three prayer meetings, lectures, or training sessions with workers, the large evening meeting, and often as not, a talk in the inquiry room afterwards."[41]

Even though Moody majored in technique, he did not believe that the above could be accomplished by human power. Success could come only through full consecration to God and endowment with power from the Holy Spirit. After hearing preacher Henry Varley state that "the world has yet to see what God can do with a man fully consecrated to him," Moody vowed, "By the grace of God, I'll be that man."[42] While he was in New York raising money after the Chicago fire in 1871, Moody received the baptism of the Holy Spirit that he had been seeking. "God revealed Himself to me, and I had such an experience of His love, that I had to ask Him to stay His hand."[43]

Billy Sunday

No one had more influence on the technique of city-wide revival campaigns than D.L. Moody. Billy Sunday continued in Moody's technique of mass evangelism, but with a much different kind of message. The nation needed healing after the Civil War, so Moody's message of love was infinitely marketable with the popular mind. After entering the twentieth century the nation was casting a wary eye toward ever increasing threats on the other side of the Atlantic. America needed an archetype of patriotism and manifest destiny to sound a clarion call to a nation entering the "Christian century." Billy Sunday was God's American prizefighter squaring off against Germany and everything else that threatened God, mother, and domestic tranquility. Sunday didn't come to the pulpit to love people; he came to "duke it out" with the same fierce competition that had characterized his spikes-first slide into home plate as a professional baseball player. Concerning Sunday's New York campaign, Weisberger states, "On the evening of the appointed day for registration, he announced his own purchase of 25,000 liberty bonds, and told the world that 'if hell could be turned upside down, you would find stamped on its bottom, Made in Germany.'"[44]

If one were to accuse Sunday of getting sidetracked from the pure gospel, of confusing Christ's cross with America's cause, of being a tool of the privileged upper class, of using grossly exaggerated sensationalism as communication, there would be at least an element of truth in the indictment. It was also true that his preaching caused thousands to "hit the sawdust trail," a phrase that he coined. In one New York meeting alone, 98,264 people had come forward. The revivals—which consisted of careful planning, thousands of prayer meetings, the building of large wooden tabernacles, Sunday's two-fisted confrontational preaching, and Homer Rhodeaver's melodic gospel songs—averaged 40,000 conversions in cities of 500,000 or more. Sunday's macho preaching was for the purpose of converting "hog-jawled, weasel-eyed, sponge-columned, mush-fisted, jelly-spined, pussy-footing, flour-flushing, Charlotte-russe Christians" into men of God.[45] The invitation appealed to the courage of manhood. Sydney Ahlstrom explains:

> The "altar call" was, of course, the climax and goal of the revival service. Professional evangelists had made the decision increasingly easier, so that by Sunday's time any "decent American" could painlessly respond. The burden was easy and the sawdust trail was wide. His invitation on the twelfth day of his New York campaign was typical. "Do you want God's blessing on you, your home, your church, your nation, on New York? If you do, raise your hands. . . . How many of you men and women will jump to your feet and come down and say, 'Bill, here's my hand for God, for home, my native land, to live and conquer for Christ?'" Then Rody and the choir began their musical accompaniment, and a sea of humanity surged forward—one out of every ten in that audience of twenty-thousand.[46]

It must not be forgotten that there were a host of lesser-known but equally competent evangelists who traipsed the U.S. and circled the globe during the years of Moody and Sunday: A.B. Earle, Wilbur Chapman, R.A. Torrey, and the unique and irrepressible Southerner, Sam Jones. These men were probably better preachers than their nationally recognized counterparts. Finely tuned nuances of theology limited the popularity of some speakers. Nevertheless, flaming-dart throwers such as Sam Jones were certainly popular enough. A riverboat captain built Jones a 5,000-seat tabernacle in Nashville, Tennessee to accommodate the crowds, a building that later served for three decades as the home of the Grand Ole Opry.

Billy Graham

No evangelist has enjoyed more popularity than Billy Graham. In fact, his wide acceptance is a conundrum that confounds those who believe that evangelism should have some prophetical thunder or perhaps the shock effect of a Jonathan Edwards. How can a true man of God have such little polarizing effect between the forces of righteousness and echelons of power in an evil world? Nonetheless, Billy Graham's "the Bible says" preaching brought so many people forward that in one service when the swell of penitents was about to topple the platform on which he was standing, he cried out, "Stop, ladies and gentlemen; there is no more room! If you want to give your life to Christ, go home and drop me a letter in the mail and we will send you the follow-up literature."[47]

Graham went two steps further than Moody or Sunday. While Graham's predecessors were befriended by big business, no evangelist has ever enticed the world's power brokers like Graham. He has been the personal friend of every U.S. President since Eisenhower. Most have found it expedient to be seen with him at the proper time while running for office. Even though Graham, for the most part, has not given public endorsement to political hopefuls, well-publicized golf outings, private luncheons, and personal appearances at political conventions have served the purpose of enhancing a politician's image in the popular mind. Secondly, from the very beginning of his ministry, Graham slipped into the age of visual electronics. In 1950, he made a film featuring his Portland crusade for distribution around the world. It was also in Portland that Graham improvised a media center with lights, cameras, and recorders. He also provided a fully equipped press room so that his revival effort would be duly covered. Graham preached to millions around the world, and the effect was multiplied through *Decision Magazine,* the "Hour of Decision" radio program, and Hollywood-style movies that showed fictionalized fragmented families coming to Christ through a Graham crusade.

Advancements in communication and data processing brought Graham into an arena unknown to evangelists of other ages. People were not simply reached with a gospel message—they were tabulated, stored in memory banks, appealed to for financial resources, and made to feel that they were an ongoing and crucial link in the success of the Billy Graham Evangelistic Association. "Selling effectively" became the operative phrase for going forward, because, after all, "the association was dispensing the world's greatest number of product with the greatest economy to the greatest number of people as fast as possible."[48] With IBM efficiency, Graham's 500 employees in his central Minneapolis administrative center send out 100 million pieces of mail a year and annually receive 2.5 million letters.[49] Staying in contact has never been done on a more massive scale.

Graham has been peerless as a mass evangelist over the last half of the century. His simple, narrative-style messages, guileless personality, integrity beyond reproach, and down-home demeanor have endeared him to the American public and thousands of others around the world. In fact, when Graham was asked, "For what do you want to be best remembered?" he quickly responded, "Integrity." In an age when the popular mind links evangelists with moral scandal, Graham has lived beyond reproof and question even by his most ardent detractors. In his *A Prophet With Honor,* William Martin states, "From the outset, for reasons that defy facile explanation, Billy's preaching demonstrated a phenomenal characteristic that it never lost. When he gave the invitation at the conclusion of his sermons, people responded, usually in numbers far exceeding what anyone would have predicted."[50]

MIRACLE WORKERS

The uniqueness of religion is found in the supernatural. The uniqueness of Christianity is found in Christ and His revelation through the written historical record and the dynamic witness of the Spirit. Though all evangelists would be in agreement with the above, they do not agree as to how and how often Christ makes His presence evident in an empirical manner. Most would agree that Christ works in a providential way by His protection and direction in the everyday lives of Christians. But concerning the claim that Christ is in the business of frequently or infrequently stopping us in our tracks with astonishment by intervening in our lives in an extraordinary manner, there is not full agreement.

The incarnated Christ worked in an extraordinary manner by healing those such as the blind, the lame, the leprous. Though there certainly must have been thousands in Judea who did not feel the healing touch of Christ, there is no record in the New Testament of a sick person coming in contact with Jesus and failing to find healing. There were groups of people, such as residents of Nazareth and religious leaders, who did not discover miraculous intervention in their lives. But we are told that this was because of their unbelief.

The signs and wonders that Jesus performed were a definite boon to His evangelistic efforts. Jesus' extrasensory perception in revealing a woman's past caused her to win many converts by telling her neighbors, "Come, see a man who told me all the things that I have done" (John 4:29). Indeed, the miracles of Christ attracted huge crowds: "And a great multitude was following Him, because they were seeing the signs which He was performing on those who were sick" (John 6:2). But even after Christ fed the 5,000 by multiplying the loaves and fishes (maybe they did not know of His meager source), they were still asking for a sign in order to believe on Him.

Not only did Jesus Christ work miracles, but He gave His disciples authority to do the same. After a missionary journey, they rejoiced that this authority was effective in their own individual ministries (Luke 10:17). However, we are not told anything of the actual evangelistic results of such miracles. In fact, after three years of Christ performing what must have been hundreds of miracles witnessed by thousands of people, there was evidence of only 120 people who maintained anything close to a coherent belief in His messiahship even after the Resurrection. It would require the promised coming of the Holy Spirit to seal Christ's authenticity for the early disciples. The Holy Spirit would have to convince the world of "sin, righteousness, and judgment," because they did not believe in spite of the miraculous signs and wonders that Christ performed. Christ Himself said, "If they do not listen to Moses and the Prophets, neither will they be persuaded if someone rises from the dead" (Luke 16:31).

If Christ did not doubt the efficacy of miraculous signs to bolster faith, He at least expressed ambivalence concerning their significance in making disciples. It is one thing to gather a crowd; it is quite another to radically change self-loving narcissists into followers of the Cross. Thus, there has been a wide range of belief concerning the importance of demonstrating the immediate observable intervention of God for the purposes of evangelism. Sincere Christians have been sharply divided as to how God desires to demonstrate His power in a way that will arrest the attention of Western society's hedonistic pursuits.

Historical Trends

Just as in the case of Cane Ridge, camp meetings throughout the nineteenth century were scenes of barking, prostration, shouting, leaping, and other forms of psychosomatic manifestations. But these were not unique to the American scene. John Wesley reported such incidents in his revivals, and Martin Luther had such a personal encounter with Satan that he threw an inkwell at him. Luther's fit in the choir and being overwhelmed with God's "tremendum" and "mysterium" when he served his first Communion quickened his responsibility to God and society. But it is not evident that such displays of God's power were a regular part of his ministry. Also, in Wesley's evangelism, the emotional outbursts and falling out under the power of the Holy Spirit almost totally disappeared within two years of his Aldersgate experience.

Throughout the nineteenth century there was a steady erosion of events and reports that smacked of the unusual in the realms of the spiritual. One must keep in mind that America is a nation founded after Nicholas Copernicus and Galileo established with reasonable certitude that the planets revolve around the sun and Sir Isaac Newton hypothesized and demonstrated that there are very predictable laws that govern the universe. In other words, Americans had learned that every action consists of a cause and an effect. After the Civil War, American ingenuity began to harness these causes and effects in a great industrial revolution. Americans more than ever were masters of their own fate. Future blessing could now be mass-produced with steam-driven pistons and internal combustion chambers ignited by refined oil. God was no longer needed to work miracles. A tacit blessing obtained through a once-a-week church attendance was sufficient divine aid. The utilization of scientific principles and inroads of evolution made American churchgoers doubt that God had ever been in the miraculous creation business in the first place. If God did not need to miraculously intervene in creating the universe, why was His wonder-working power needed now?

But the increased adoption of scientific determinism escaped a growing number of urban poor who were neglected by "gilded-age" Christianity. Not only did the churches neglect them, but so did the big-time evangelists. The divorce was by mutual consent. The disinherited cared for neither the sophisticated intellectualism of new-fangled theology nor the strutting of spat-shoed preachers. The down-and-outers needed spiritual, emotional, economic, and physical relief. They sought for healing that went far beyond formal worship or even ritualistic altar calls.

Pentecostalism

It was among the disinherited of society that the Pentecostal movement arose at the turn of the century. Everything the Pentecostal preachers espoused (speaking in tongues, instantaneous healing, and exuberant psychosomatic worship) had been experienced earlier in American religious history. But the new Pentecostal proponents taught that what was once considered an aberration was to be expected as normal worship. Pentecostal preachers such as Charles Parham and William J. Seymour promised immediate intervention by a supernatural God, a solace not to be found at increasingly deistic mainline churches.

The best-known Pentecostal evangelist of the twentieth century is Oral Roberts. Born in poverty as a son of an Oklahoma preacher, Roberts experienced a miraculous healing from tuberculosis when he was eighteen. As a result, he set out on the evangelistic trail the next year. By the time the evangelist was thirty-nine, it was boasted by his organization that in 147 campaigns he "stood before (on his own platform) an aggregate of more than 8.5 million people, preached over 78,000 sermons on radio, and 31,200 on television, and 'led to Christ for salvation' nearly 3 million."[51] Even if such boasts were exaggerated, Roberts was one of the most popular religious personages in America, playing second fiddle only to Billy Graham.

Roberts has been a capable enough preacher, but the crowds gathered mostly because of his gift of healing. It was after a mystical experience with God in 1947 that Roberts heard a divine message: "From this hour, your ministry of healing will begin. You will have my power to pray for the sick and to cast out devils."[52] Roberts became convinced that most illnesses are caused by demon affliction. Casting out demons became a mainstay of his evangelistic campaigns.

As Robert's ministry matured, there seemed to be more recognition that diseases had natural causes or even psychological sources. Nevertheless, throughout the 1950s, he continued to pray for and lay his right hand (which he believed the power of God flowed through, serving as a "point of contact") upon as many as 2,000 on a given night. The poor and lower middle class flocked to his 10,000-seat tent to find miraculous healing from a loving God. Roberts constantly denied that he had any inherent power to heal. And there is probably some truth in his statement to a reporter that the fundamental difference between him and Billy Graham was his ministry to the unchurched, who needed a God of love and compassion.

In the 1960s, Roberts' attention was increasingly focused on his university; in the 1970s it was his newly established medical center that captured his energies; and he spent the 1980s fund raising to keep it all afloat. By the early 1960s, Roberts had seized television for the purpose of mass-marketing the gospel message and empirically demonstrating to millions that God is still in the healing business. As the crusades stopped and Roberts' energies were channeled into new enterprises, he still believed that his main business was to win souls. At the height of his healing ministry, he explained to reporters, "If a man's soul is right, he'll go to heaven, whether he's sick or well."[53]

Though Roberts has made some seemingly serious blunders through the years from the perspective of a secular worldview and has been equally criticized within the church, his ministry has consisted of passionate, sincere preaching that offers an application of supernatural power to present ills, as well as a glorious hope for the future. He has exhibited this certitude in the face of enormous criticism by the media and sneers from Americans who found the meaning of life in more "respectable" ways. Roberts wasn't concerned about being fashionable, but rather about meeting the needs of hungry people who sought "Bible deliverance as God's answer."[54]

Assemblies of God

The Pentecostal movement gained ascendancy in America during the 1960s. No denomination grew faster than the Assemblies of God, a Pentecostal sect founded in 1914. The Assemblies of God, which now has more than 2 million members in the United States, fits the anti-institutionalism and free-expression characteristics of the sixties and seventies. More importantly, the Assemblies of God meets the hunger of thousands of people who were nauseated by the liberalism and dead formality of their mainline denominations. The swelling of Pentecostal denominations, as well as the groups of Christians who espoused a baptism of the Spirit yet remained in their own denominations, became known as the "charismatic" movement. Charismatics emphasize exuberant forms of worship and visible displays of the gifts of the Spirit, such as speaking in tongues, words of knowledge, and miraculous healing.

John Wimber

No one has gained faster prominence in the charismatic movement than John Wimber, pastor of Vineyard Fellowship in Anaheim, California. Wimber founded the church in 1978, and it was averaging approximately 4,000 on Sunday morning in 1985. Across the United States, there were also 140 congregations with 40,000 members under the Vineyard Fellowship umbrella. Wimber believes that evangelism is, and will be, greatly retarded without visible signs and wonders. According to him, "power evangelism" gets the job done because it is rational, but at the same time transcends the rational. Wimber argues that conversion needs to be confirmed beyond logic and intellectual assent to the Scriptures. "Signs and wonders were the proof of Jesus' Messiahship, the calling card of the Kingdom of God. Their presence in the early church demonstrates that Jesus intended them to be an integral part of the disciples' ministry."[55]

Needless to say, this methodology of evangelism is very controversial among evangelical Christians. William Abraham, writing in *The Logic of Evangelism,* affirms Wimber's accent on eschatology, discipleship, and the subordination of rational means to the Holy Spirit's power:

> What is striking and original is the refreshingly casual style of his ministry, the honesty and candor that confronts the skeptical observer of his activity, the way in which he has been able to avoid the sectarianism and sensationalism of much modern Protestantism, and the extent to which he has earned the respect of the established churches.[56]

But Wimber's approach is far too sensational for others. For example, Wimber reported an incident in which he saw a complete stranger on a plane. Wimber saw "adultery" written across the man's face, and after moments of staring at the man, he revealed the name of the woman with whom he was having an affair. Before the plane landed, the man and his wife confessed their sin and accepted Christ as their Savior. Wimber states:

> This might seem like an unusual, if not bizarre event, yet I could write hundreds of other accounts like it; both from my own experience and from that of others I know. I call this type of encounter power evangelism, and I believe it was one of the most effective means of evangelism in the early church.[57]

Another question deserves to be asked about John Wimber's methodology: Is it an aberration from or extension of the church growth school of which he has been a part? The answer is both. At first glance, there is an incongruity between the statistical rationalism of church growth exponents and the spiritual intuitiveness of Wimber. Yet both provide an observable empiricism that rules out ambiguities and mitigates the mysteries of godliness. The worldview of both is quite simplistic: God is predictable. God's transcendence and immanence have been fused together in ways that are palatable to the nontheological minds of twentieth-century Americans. But this is nothing new. In Reinhold Niebuhr's observation of American history, experience has always triumphed over dogma.

John Wimber's signs and wonders and the snake handlers of Appalachia represent the extreme forms of experiential certainty in opposite cultures. Nevertheless, there is a continuum of passion, empiricism, and security that unites them and all Pentecostals together. Freud's *Future of an Illusion* has caused secular scientists and sociologists to misread the craving for passionate religious experience that shows no signs of abatement. Pentecostals have indeed come to live in Harvey Cox's secular city and will not only increasingly demand more space, but will provide a good bit of the energy source for confronting it.

THE EVANGELISTIC PASTORS

Most pastors would consider themselves evangelistic, but some have been considerably more successful at it than others. This does not necessarily mean that from eternity's perspective their work has been more meaningful or lasting. In fact, their many converts may be less Christian than someone else's few converts. I have thoroughly discussed the ins and outs of this question in another book, *What Really Matters in Ministry.* In that book I discuss personal qualities that are likely to dictate evangelistic success: God-oriented ideology, charisma, self-initiative, long-term commitment, authoritative vision, inclusiveness, energetic optimism, and meaningful communication. Pastors must definitely dwell in this world, but must also possess an ideology that puts them in contact with the transcendent world. Pastors who are able to convert truth into life are able to draw the mundane and supermundane together. The following pastors have brought the gospel to bear on the exigencies of life. They have overcome the obstacles of their time and place.

Russell Conwell

According to Arthur M. Schlesinger, Sr., from 1875 to 1900 the church had more than its fair share of obstacles to advancement. Urban immigrant laborers found themselves in despicable circumstances in the untried frontiers of the industrial revolution. Schlesinger states that "the working class commonly regarded the church—with its fine upholstery, stained-glassed windows and expensive chairs—as an institution, where ill-clad worshippers were unwelcome and where the Nazarene himself would have been snubbed."[58] The church was too immersed in its own theological quagmire (caused by inroads of evolutionism and higher criticism) to be about the business of rescuing people from the humdrum of sweaty, dirty, mundane existence. Doubts about the origins of humankind had raised further doubts about where humankind needed to go.

This morass of doubt and anomie was met by the institutional church, best typified by Russell Conwell's Baptist Temple in Philadelphia. The church began in the 1880s "to provide reading rooms, gymnasiums, social clubs, day nurseries, sewing classes, and manual-training, causes which, along with religious instruction, were available throughout the week to all comers."[59] Conwell had trained to be a lawyer, but entered the ministry when he was thirty-seven with almost no formal theological education. He had the uncanny knack of relating the entire existence of the church to the minuscule particulars of life. In his view, everything should be done for the purpose of "saving souls." Conwell stated:

> The Church of Christ should be so conducted always as to save the largest number of souls. It matters little what your theories are or what mine are—God, in His providence, is moving His Church onward and upward at the same time; adjusting it to new situations; fitting it to new conditions; advancing civilization and requiring us to see the new instrumentalities which He has placed in our hands for the purpose of saving the greatest number of human souls.[60]

Conwell involved his people in an enormous display of concern for those both inside and outside the church. Concerning his ministry at Baptist Temple, he could boast: "And yet through twenty-five years, there was not known to be a single member of that church out of work a month who desired a position."[61] His chief means of inspiration were practical homespun messages that explored the heights of human potential through divine grace. It was theological humanitarianism buttressed by positive thinking:

> He who can give to this people better streets, better homes, better schools, better churches, more religion, more of happiness, more of God, he that can be a blessing to the community in which he lives tonight, will be great anywhere, but he who cannot be a blessing where he now lives will never be great anywhere on the face of God's earth.[62]

As his "Acres of Diamonds" message exhorted, greatness consists of mining the precious gems that exist all around, blooming where one is, and taking advantage of the God-given opportunities that abound for everyone.

Conwell's term "institutional church" meant that the church should touch every facet of life. His sensitivity to the educational needs of the poor was the beginning of Temple University. Also, he felt that the church should not only offer education, but entertainment as well. He began an annual church fair with food, costumes, and games. It was his goal to put secular entertainment out of business "because the churches will hold the best classes and for divine and humane purposes, will conduct the best entertainments."[63] In response to critics who said that he had sold himself over to the world, Conwell replied, "The old hermits went away and hid themselves in the rocks and caves and lived on the scantiest food and kept away from the world."[64] Conwell's going over to the world allowed him to fill his 3,000-seat sanctuary several times per Sunday. The following quote summarizes his ministry: "We must know what the world needs first and then invest ourselves to supply that need, and success is almost certain."[65]

George Truett

In 1897 George Truett became the pastor of First Baptist Church of Dallas, Texas and remained at that post for over forty years. During that tenure, he built a 4,000-seat sanctuary and received 15,789 members into the church.[66] Truett was probably not as innovative as Conwell, but he was an excellent pulpit communicator and civic leader. He had a political intuition that enabled the church to always be at the center of community affairs. Truett had a passion for evangelism, and instilled this zeal into the lives of his listeners. In an appeal to his parishioners, he said:

> O my fellow Christians of this church, a church dearer to me than my heart's blood. . . . I summon you anew today to give your best to Christ; to be done with all playing at your religion; to be done with all lukewarmness. I summon you to come with the red, rich blood of human sympathy for all mankind, for good and bad, for high and low, for rich and poor, and give your best to win this city and state and world to Jesus, so that you hear that plaudit which it were worth worlds at last to hear, "Well done, thou good and faithful servant."[67]

Truett's preaching not only brought about evangelistic ardor, but encouraged his people to be involved in social causes. Christians were to shape secular policy toward sacred good. Stewardship was to be practiced in all areas of life. These emphases defeated horse-track betting and caused firemen to change their minds about striking against the city. The *Dallas News* of September 12, 1932 stated concerning Truett, "All manner of distress has known his comforting; all sorts of happiness have acknowledged his influence, all kinds of personality have found strength from his caring and sympathy."[68]

Truett demonstrated the importance of being an evangelist in order to inspire evangelism. Once a year, for much of his ministry, he traveled to western Texas and held a "cowboy roundup." The gospel became the common denominator for a man and a people who, for the most part, lived in two different worlds. Truett was one of the great evangelistic preaching pastors of the early twentieth century. He had a greater emphasis on preaching than any other enterprise of the pastorate. A love for study, a memory like a steel trap, a strong voice, and a vigorous physique rendered every moment under his preaching highly worthwhile. Several testified to the range of his voice, the passion of his delivery, and the unique cadence of his speech. He was constantly jotting down notes that would serve as ideas for his sermons. He wrote,

> We do not go forth on our God-appointed mission as preachers to be ranters and lambasters and snickering caterers, with an endless succession of grotesque, spectacular, bizarre, barn-storming methods; but we are to go as true prophets of God, as faithful, compassionate shepherds of souls, hiding ourselves ever behind the cross of Christ.[69]

Gordon Cosby

As a teenager Gordon Cosby had an unusual zeal for evangelism. In fact, he and his brother were so serious that they made an agreement that each would have to pay the other a dollar if they failed to witness during the course of a day. On more than one night this meant that Gordon, upon remembering his negligence, would have to crawl out of bed to find a suitable target. The only person available at this time of night was the motorman for the trolley at the end of the line. Even though Gordon was completely sincere, such evangelistic endeavors brought little results. There must be a better way, he thought.

Throughout college, seminary, and Army chaplaincy, Gordon Cosby dreamed of evangelism that would be more spontaneous and relational than his past endeavors and the efforts of the many churches with which he had been associated. His ministry was officially born as the Church of the Savior with the 1947 purchase of a gray stone building at 1707 19th Street in Washington, D.C. The "headquarters" of the church was moved to a Victorian mansion at 2025 Massachusetts Avenue on February 2, 1950. The evangelistic emphasis was definitely not on numbers. The message emphasized a high level of commitment to both members of the body and the outside world. Membership vows consisted of the following:

> I recognize that the function of the church is to glorify God in adoration and sacrificial service and to be God's missionary to the world, bearing witness to God's redeeming grace in Jesus Christ. . . . I unreservedly and with abandon commit my life and destiny to Christ, promising to give Him a practical priority in all the affairs of life. I will seek first the Kingdom of God and His Righteousness.[70]

There were no official programs of evangelism as such. Rather, members were to exercise their gifts in their everyday occupations in order to attract people to Christ. Elizabeth O'Conner wrote, "The medium of evangelism would be our common life. We would seek to embody the gospel; to be the forgiven community, the community which knows how to accept, knows how to love."[71]

The church was so serious about the sanctity of vocation and the employment of spiritual gifts that they instituted a service of ordination for laypersons who wished to make each day's work a sacrament. The ordinance was presented before the congregation with the following statement: "Today, (name) has come to acknowledge to God and to us that the work he does each day takes place on holy ground. He comes to ask God's blessing on his work and for guidance in making each act he performs pleasing in God's sight."[72] Gordon Cosby stated, "I believe the primary task of the professional minister to be that of training non-professional ministers for the ministry."[73]

The most ostensible expression of the sanctity of everyday work as a means of evangelism was the "potter's house." It was here that "artists, writers, beatniks, scientists, businessmen, politicians" and people from all walks of life discovered how their expertise related to Christian discipleship. In the potter's house, a retreat center named Day Spring, in homes, and at the headquarters, the church made extensive use of small groups in order to bring people into the kingdom and disciple them. The groups were given to Bible study, prayer, self-discovery, spiritual accountability, and expressions of love. In O'Conner's words: "The joy of involvement was interwoven with the pain of it. . . . Raw edges rubbed against raw edges."[74]

The Church of the Savior has majored in evangelism through servanthood. Servanthood is learned within the Christian community and is exemplified within the nuclear family and beyond. The world needs saints—Christians who will "throw themselves into the breach between the peace and healing of God and the loneliness, anguish, and terror of the world's lost."[75] Cosby believes that evangelism is best accomplished by members of the community making a deep commitment to Christ. New creatures in Christ will produce new creation in the world around them. O'Conner explains that the evangelistic mission of the Church of the Savior is best expressed by the commandment "Thou shalt love."[76]

> We are called first of all to belong to Jesus Christ as Savior and Lord, and to keep our lives warmed at the hearth of His life. It is there the fire will be lit which will create new structures and programs of service that will draw others into the circle to dream dreams and have visions.[77]

Harold Ockenga

Harold Ockenga was so identified as a leader and thinker for evangelicalism in the quarter of a century that followed World War II that many forgot he was a very evangelistic pastor at the famed Park Street Church in Boston. He was one of the leading lights in the founding of such evangelical institutions as *Christianity Today*, the National Association of Evangelicals, Gordon-Conwell Theological Seminary, and Fuller Theological Seminary. But it was before and during the war that Ockenga swelled the numbers at Park Street Church with his sound biblical preaching and creative outreach.

In 1936, at the young age of thirty-one, Ockenga became pastor of Park Street's 1,500 members, many of them lingering deadwood. Some would have thought that his highly intellectual and expository sermons would have had no appeal to the masses, but they were wrong. On summer evenings, Ockenga moved his services to the outdoors adjacent to Boston Commons. As he stood on an oak table to proclaim the gospel, the crowds became so large that the city canceled his permit. He then moved to a hotel window next to the church, delivering his Sunday evening sermons. The remarkable conversions that occurred encouraged him to begin a radio ministry over a 50,000-watt station that would cover all of New England.

Ockenga was not satisfied with reaching only New England—he wanted the whole world to hear the gospel. He instituted a missionary conference and saw his missionary budget become five times greater during the 1940s. But missionary outreach did not depreciate his evangelistic zeal for his own city. He risked his reputation by inviting a little-known Youth for Christ evangelist to his pulpit in 1950. The meetings were so successful that the services had to be moved to Boston Garden. Next Ockenga toured New England, introducing Billy Graham and holding services. Auditoriums were filled with thousands wherever they went, and hundreds made commitments to Christ. Ockenga's validation of Graham's evangelism was no small part of the latter's success.

Conwell, Truett, Ockenga, and Cosby all demonstrate an essential fact about church evangelism: the evangelistic tide of churches will not rise higher than the pastor's gravitational pull for the lost. These men were unalike in so many ways—scholarly and folksy, oratorical and organizational. But what did they have in common? A burning desire to see people come to know Christ. The focus was so intense that they were willing to step beyond the traditional way of doing things. Each stepped in the direction that was right for their time and place. They were convinced that if the motivation was prompted by the heart of Christ and love for people, God would honor their efforts.

THE INNOVATORS

When it comes to harvesting souls, Americans have been no less enterprising than in other endeavors—perhaps more so. The array of evangelistic plans, especially over the last fifty years, has been dizzying: Ambassadors for Christ, Project Philip, Youth for Christ, Navigators, InterVarsity Christian Fellowship, Campus Crusade for Christ, Athletes in Action, Fellowship of Christian Athletes, Here's Life America, Young Life, Prison Fellowship Ministries, Teen Challenge, Jews for Jesus, and many other endeavors that are sponsored by individual denominations. If "different strokes for different folks" fits anybody, it applies to "they who would win souls." Nathan Hatch notes:

> The range of evangelical belief and practice is so broad that few conceivable interest groups are left unattended. One

> can join an evangelical church of thousands or a house church; enjoy music that ranges from Andre Crouch to Bob Dylan to Bill Gaither to J.S. Bach; take social ethics from John Howard Yoder or Harold Criswell; learn psychology from Robert Schuller, Jay Adams, or Paul Vitz; learn about the role of women from Phyllis Schlafly, Elisabeth Elliot, or Virginia Mollenkott; imitate the lifestyle of the Fellowship of Christian Athletes or the Sojourners Community; vote with the politics of Jesse Helms, Mark Hatfield, or Jesse Jackson. Such radical pluralism involves a healthy measure of entrepreneurial activity and is especially adapted to the task of spreading a movement across class and cultural boundaries. This enables evangelicals to meet a broad range of ideological, psychological, and social needs and to draw adherents from the widest possible backgrounds.[78]

Even though many of the above have not given themselves explicitly to evangelism, they have served as evangelistic doors through which people could enter the kingdom. This vast array of efforts gave rise to the neologism parachurch, from the Greek word *para* ("alongside of"). The relationship between the various parachurch groups and the church has at times been tenuous and other times outright competitive and covetous. J. Alan Youngren argues that the parachurch has been fostered by the peculiarities of the American frontier spirit: (1) less respect for tradition and traditional social structures, (2) communalism—an attitude favoring the autonomy of one's own community or group, (3) self-reliance and an independent spirit, and (4) infatuation with almost anything new.[79]

Youth for Christ

No group was more successful in reaching America's teenagers during the 1940s and 1950s than Youth for Christ (YFC). Pep rallies, entertainments, lively music, and celebrity testimonials gathered thousands together to hear a simple gospel message. Youth for Christ was officially founded in 1945. Torrey Johnson was elected as its first president and Billy Graham as its first full-time evangelist. Youth for Christ began to specialize in Bible quizzing, talent contests, campus life clubs, and family seminars. The organization grew to over 1,100 full-time and 3,800 part-time staff and volunteer workers in the United States, with work in six other countries. Joel Heck summarizes the work of YFC campus ministry:

> In its Campus Life Operation Manual, Youth for Christ spells out its understanding of evangelism, rejecting both the buttonholing style of evangelism and the present style of "evangelism" that fails to speak the Gospel. Disciple-making is a large part of YFC's understanding of evangelism, for when a Campus Life club comes to a high school campus, it comes there for the long term. The focus is not on getting decisions, but on developing relationships with kids, speaking the Gospel to them in a way that shows how the Gospel fills their deepest needs, and following through in order that the fruit of the Gospel may remain (John 15:16).[80]

Youth for Christ rallies made evangelism synonymous with fun—the organization sponsored wild goose chases, pillow fights, race cars pushed by their owners, world's largest banana splits, and the "electric shock seat." Special teams materialized who could give their testimony while doing everything from playing basketball to playing banjos. During the 1960s, YFC sent out thirty-seven teams to seventy countries, traveling over a million miles and reaching almost 3 million people with the gospel. James C. Hefley states that the varied methods used by YFC "may shock some tradition-bound adults accustomed to finding God only in the quiet sanctuary of a church. The hard truth is that these methods are/were reaching thousands for Christ who might never enter a church and probably wouldn't relate to what went on there if they did."[81]

Young Life

Though not as expansive as YFC, Young Life has made a tremendous impact among high school students. In 1940, Jim Rayburn brought together a board of directors for an organization that would minister to teenagers. The emphasis was a bit different than Youth for Christ, which majored in rallies. Young Life emphasized spending time and forming relationships with teenagers on their turf. Area clubs then drew the kids together in homes for a weekly meeting. Emile Cailliet states:

> The common ground of the club is simply wholesome fun and entertainment, including spontaneous discussion of teen-

> age concerns. The lack of pressure and the deference shown to individual belief and decision (even at times when this is against religion), and the honesty with which they are expressed, have a large part in members' respect for the club, its leader, and each other.[82]

During the 1980s, there were over 1,100 Young Life clubs in the United States and 100 foreign countries with a weekly attendance of more than 70,000 young people. In addition, they hosted nearly 70,000 teenagers a year in seven major campsites. This work was carried out by 800 paid staff members and 6,000 volunteers.

Campus Crusade for Christ

No one has been more innovative than the founder of Campus Crusade for Christ, Bill Bright. Bright gave us Here's Life America, Athletes in Action, and the "four spiritual laws." In 1976, Here's Life America introduced to the Christian community a campaign of lapel buttons and bumper stickers bearing the words "I found it!" When a curious person would ask the bearer, "Found what?" the Christian responded with a verbal witness about Christ. Needless to say, many were critical of Bright's shotgun style and hit-or-miss approach. For some, it was more like hit-and-run with little follow-up by the church.

Bright's incessant personal witnessing and creative evangelizing is a put-up-or-shut-up methodology. Anyone with the proper training should be able to give a verbal witness to the essentials of the gospel. Having begun on the campus of UCLA in 1951, Bright moved his staff of over a hundred into a fabulous hotel resort in San Bernardino, California in 1962. Thus, people could come for serious and extensive training in evangelism. People cannot win and disciple others without being first discipled. Disciples must become disciplers by learning the following "transferable" concepts:

1. *How to experience God's love and forgiveness*
2. *How to be filled with the Holy Spirit*
3. *How to work in the control and power of the Holy Spirit*
4. *How to witness for Christ effectively in the power of the Holy Spirit*
5. *How to live by faith*
6. *How to pray*
7. *How to study the Bible*

8. How to grow in faith
9. How to worship God
10. How to know God's will for your life[83]
Bright states:

> Campus Crusade for Christ is committed to aggressive evangelism. By aggressive evangelism I mean going to men with the good news of our living Christ and His love and forgiveness, not in argumentative tones nor with high pressure techniques, but taking the initiative to tell (as the Apostle Paul wrote) all men everywhere about Christ. We realize that this can best be accomplished by multiplication rather than through addition. This is the reason of this ministry. Each week on hundreds of campuses the leadership training classes are held in which thousands of students learn how to experience and share the abundant life in Christ.[84]

Universalization through Particularization

There has quite possibly been a program of evangelism for every subgroup in America: motorcyclers, longshoremen, truckers, hot-rodders, mothers with preschoolers, the deaf, and countless others. Thus, the gospel is particularized and universalized at the same time. Targeting subgroups with common interests has been called contextualization: changing form while maintaining substance. It is the communication of essential Christian truths in ways that make sense to people held together by unique common denominators. The communication components (i.e., illustrations, applications, arguments, and explanations) must be attractive to the listeners. People are unlikely to respond to communication with which they have little in common or which does not include elements that are related and suited to their particular culture.

MINISTRY TO THE WHOLE PERSON

Though they may not have always been able to articulate the concept, evangelicals have recognized that people will not normally respond to the gospel message outside of felt need. Indeed, there have been times when churches have neglected to feed the hungry and clothe the naked. These churches have atrophied while upstart groups of socially conscious crusaders have fulfilled the words of Christ: "To the extent that you did it to one of these brothers of Mine, even the least of them, you did it to Me" (Matt. 25:40). The benevolent empire found diverse expression in Samuel Hopkins' theologically informed abolitionism and in Jerry McCauley's experientially informed prohibitionism. There is a consistent humanitarian impulse of evangelism at its best that flows from Roger Williams to Chuck Colson. In Timothy Smith's words, "Religious doctrines which Paine in his book, *The Age of Reason,* had discarded as the tattered vestment of an outworn aristocracy, became the wedding garb of a democratized church bent on preparing men and institutions for a kind of proletarian marriage supper of the lamb."[85]

Millenarian Optimism

No one believed that the marriage supper was coming sooner than did Charles Finney. When he observed the reform that the revival brought to Rochester, he exclaimed that the millennium might be ushered in within the next three months. In Finney's mind, God's purposes included human cooperation. Finney's optimism was no less than that of the Wesleys, who on another continent had clothed the poor and visited the prisoners. Gilbert Barnes traced a direct correlation between Finney's revivalism and Theodore Weld's ardent attempts to raise America's antislavery consciousness.[86] Timothy Smith documented the antebellum church's programs for immigrants, antislavery activism, temperance, Sabbath schools, public education, economic relief for the poor, and ministry to the deaf, delinquent, and orphaned. The church took seriously the words of John: "But whoever has the world's goods, and beholds his brother in need and closes his heart against him, how does the love of God abide in him? Little children, let us not love with word or with tongue, but in deed and truth" (1 John 3:17-18).

The Salvation Army

Just when evangelicalism was becoming ingrown after the Civil War, the Salvation Army forged ahead. It provided an institution whereby the American tendency toward volunteerism and activism could be put to good use. Arriving on American shores over a century ago, the Army sought to implement the radical social ethics of its founder, William Booth. Booth was a nonconformist, Wesleyan perfectionist who refused to be institutionalized. He saw ministry to the poor as a means to an end: the salvation of souls. Booth sent the first arrivals equipped with holiness theology and a commission to make holy war on sin and poverty. George Scott Railton landed in early spring of 1880, and by the fall there were twelve corps and 1,500 Army converts.[87]

From the very first days until now, the Salvation Army has been the epitome of general assistance to the poor and a first-hand knowledge of what slum life is really like. They began rescue missions, thrift stores, soup lines, lodging facilities for alcoholics, coal provision in the winter, ice provision in the summer, housing for unwed mothers, shelters for prostitutes, holiday dinners, parties for the underprivileged, medical care, farm colonies, country camps for inner-city children, work opportunities in their own factories, and even a poor man's bank. The list seems endless. The Army gained international attention during the First World War. By the time the first Salvation Army chaplains sailed for Europe, Salvationists were already hosting 300,000 soldiers and sailors weekly in more than 400 facilities in France and Britain.[88]

It is a misconception to picture Salvationists as naive do-gooders with no overall social philosophy. William Booth began with sharp criticism of established religion and other institutions such as industry, and endorsed reformers and their programs. The *War Cry* continued Booth's attack on the American front by calling for compulsory jurisdiction in labor, rebuking the power of the rich, and criticizing the unjust distribution of wealth. It heartily supported a statement by President Woodrow Wilson that called "for the humanizing of industry through legislation providing reduced hours, the right to organize unions, and protection against industrial accidents."[89] In 1897, the Labor Day issue of the *War Cry* carried a commendation of the work of the Salvation Army by the Secretary of the United Mine Workers of America and the Socialist Party leader, Eugene Debs.[90]

Army assistance continued to escalate at the turn of the century. Early in 1903, the American Salvation Army reported a monthly average of 137,000 lodgings and 365,000 meals.[91] From 1905 to 1910, over 300,000 Christmas dinners were fed to the poor each year.[92] But the immense work of the Army should not obscure the fine work of other parachurch organizations that operated on a smaller basis. The Army was paradigmatic of the many associations, independent missions, and individual churches that not only affected social concern, but actually broke away from established religion because of its aversion to the lower classes.

Inner-City Missions

Inner-city missions multiplied during the late nineteenth century. In 1872, Jeremiah McAuley opened his famous Water Street Mission in New York. "Three years later he wrote that a 'gospel service' had taken place every evening from that time, with 'hundreds of souls' converted and 'as many as twenty-five or thirty' crowding the front aisle at one time."[93] One of its most famous converts was Samuel Hadley, whose ardent labors and death inspired the founding of the National Federation of Gospel Missions. Space does not allow to give accounts of the many who followed him, such as Louis Klopsch, Stephen Merritt, George Hilton, John C. Appel, Sarah Wray, and John Hallimond.

Varied Enterprises

Also gaining national recognition were Emma Whittemore's "Door of Hope" for fallen girls (started in 1890), Florence Crittendon homes for unwed mothers (1883), the volunteer prison league (1896), Hope Hall for released prisoners (1879), and the Herculean efforts of the *Christian Herald,* which raised and distributed $3.5 million for relief work during the years 1865–1920.[94] The work of the Salvation Army has often overshadowed the equally earnest efforts of its sister organization, the Volunteers of America. Splitting away from the parent body in 1896 under the leadership of Ballington Booth, the volunteers gradually "developed a diversified program of social service, including dinners and fresh air outings for children, orphanages, homes for women, and shelters and 'hotels' of several varieties."[95]

One of the greatest concerns for almost all relief organizations was unemployment. An unemployed person, or even an employed person in improper conditions or working for insubstantial wages, spelled trouble. The Whosoever Gospel Mission of Germantown, Pennsylvania maintained a $75,000 plant at the turn of the century that employed 125 persons daily on a "work-for-what-you-can-get-plan."[96]

Christian Missionary and Alliance

One should not get the idea that slum work around 1900 was shouldered solely by parachurch groups. For example, Norris Magnusun points to the Christian Missionary and Alliance Church, having begun in 1882 "for the especial purpose of Gospel work, particularly among the neglected classes, both at home and abroad."[97] Its first converts were among the poor, and within the first five years of its existence it had a rescue house for women; a "rest and healing" home; a training college for missionaries, evangelists, and rescue workers; an orphanage; a ministry to immigrants from Germany; and several rescue missions.[98]

Church of the Nazarene

In 1895, Phineas Bresee left the Methodist church to found the Church of the Nazarene as a downtown mission to the poor. Bresee, one of the most prominent clergymen in all of California and chairman of the board of the college which was to eventually become Southern California University, felt that the poor would not join the institutional church because of the rich and wealthy who sat in its pews. In 1898, when Bresee explained the rationale for his break with the Methodists, he wrote:

> We were convinced that houses of worship should be plain and cheap, to save from financial burdens, and that everything should say welcome to the poor. We went feeling that food and clothing and shelter were the open doors to the hearts of the unsaved poor, and that through these doors we could bear to them the life of God. We went in poverty, to give ourselves—and what God might give us—determined to forego provision for the future and old age, in order to see the salvation of God while we were yet here. God has not disappointed us. While we should be glad to do much more, yet hundreds of dollars have gone to the poor, with loving ministry of every kind, and with it a way has been opened up to the hearts of men and women, that has been unutterable joy. The gospel comes to a multitude without money and without price, and the poorest of the poor are entitled to a front seat at the Church

> of the Nazarene, the only condition being that they come early enough to get there.[99]

Free Methodists

Founded much earlier than the Church of the Nazarene, the Free Methodists also began with the strong imperative that the gospel needs to be preached to the poor. Breaking away from the Methodists in 1860 under the leadership of B.T. Roberts, it continued its strong social commitment into the twentieth century. Documents from 1875 to 1915 show clear statements against both industry and labor union abuses, secret societies, alcohol, racial discrimination. The documents also contain Roberts' rebukes against the evils of riches, a position that was the original cause for the beginning of the denomination. Roberts, referring back to the period of slavery, preached, "Holiness is not indifference. One who is truly holy does not feel that he has done his duty by simply abstaining from sin. . . . You might have attended the 'holiness meeting' week after week, without hearing one prayer offered for the liberation of the slave, or one testimony borne against the 'sum of all villainies.'"[100] Shortly after Roberts' death, the Free Methodist Church declared, "It is encouraging to observe that the wisdom of the founder of our Zion, with respect to reformative principles, is confirmed by the development of the times. We now, as from the inception of our church, stand in the front rank of America's reformative organizations."[101]

Church of God (Anderson, Indiana)

Most of the groups above would have prided themselves for their stance against racial discrimination and ministry to nonwhites. Because of its conceptual understanding of what the church should be, the Church of God (Anderson, Indiana), founded in 1880, had little to be ashamed of in its efforts to cross racial barriers. By the 1890s, it had begun to plant black churches in the South. In 1897, a camp meeting in Hartselle, Alabama was attacked by a mob because blacks and whites knelt at the altar together after a sermon on tearing down the "middle wall of partition."[102] In 1890, when Daniel Warner preached uncompromisingly for "Justice to the Negro," clubs and several pieces of brick came crashing through the window.[103] Concerning that period, Charles E. Brown observed, "The Church of God preachers and leaders probably suffered more for their friendship with colored people in the south than the leaders of any other religious work who ever operated there."[104]

The Church of God also made very early advances among German, Scandinavian, Slovak, and Greek immigrants. By 1899, the church was publishing its periodical, *The Gospel Trumpet,* in both German and Danish in addition to English. Many of the Church of God meetings in larger cities around 1900 were held in two languages. By 1929, the Church of God had printed a hymnal in Slovak, and soon were printing "monthly periodical tracts, Sunday School lessons, pamphlets, mottos, and Bible stationery for work among Slovak immigrants."[105]

Lifestyle and Themes of Sanctification

Many of these reform-oriented groups accented the fact that their social involvement was not condescending or moralistic, but actually identified with the downtrodden. Their ministry went beyond philosophizing about humanity's problems and empathized with the poor's actual conditions. Thus, "the members of the Salvation Army's slum brigade took apartments in the tenement" and, in the case of ethnic ministry, "wore their style of clothing."[106] Magnusun states, "What ultimately gave gospel welfare organizations their strongest insight and motivation for service . . . was the continuing close contact of their field workers with the poor."[107]

Donald Dayton argues that evangelical social ethics have been largely grounded in themes of sanctification. Such themes usually lead to dichotomous thinking and are not slowed down by the ambiguities of moral issues. Absolutes are the framework for operation rather than compromises. An idealistic operationalism takes precedence over the institutionalized process of the establishment. A quick perusal of Dayton's *Discovering an Evangelical Heritage,* Timothy Smith's *Revivalism and Social Reform,* and Norris Magnusun's *Salvation in the Slums* all point to the influence of Wesleyan holiness. It is no accident that the Wesleyan Methodist Church was the first church to form due to the issue of slavery. Though the mantle had now fallen somewhat on different groups, Smith's statement in regard to the middle of the century remained relevant fifty years later:

> All of the socially potent doctrines of revivalism reached white heat in the Oberlin and Wesleyan experience of sanc-

> tification—ethical seriousness, the call to full personal consecration, the belief in God's immanence, in his readiness to transform the present world through the outpoured Holy Ghost, and the exaltation of Christian love.[108]

CONCLUSION

One important theme ties all of the above together: evangelism was accomplished by people who were willing to place reason at the service of a faith that was expressed in doing. Human ingenuity did not mean a lessened dependence on the Holy Spirit, but often a reliance on God's resources that allowed persons to realize evangelistic results while facing tremendous odds. This was often accomplished at the price of great personal sacrifice in terms of time, money, energy, and a renunciation of normal parameters of comfort and success. For many the demarcation between professionalism and privatism was almost completely erased. The cause for which they existed defined the totality of their lives. They comprehended Paul's simple evangelistic paradigm: "Be ready in season and out of season" (2 Tim. 4:2). Perhaps that's the only way to fulfill his subsequent imperative: "Do the work of an evangelist" (2 Tim. 4:5). Do we need to remind ourselves that evangelism is work?

As one stands on the brink of the third millennium, he or she may long for the glory days of the late-nineteenth-century evangelists or even stand in awe of the Herculean tasks of those frontier blazers such as the Jesuits in the Southwest or the Methodist circuit riders who crossed the Alleghenies. But do any of us need to be reminded that today's frontiers are no less demanding and the present opportunities no less abundant? Will there be current trailblazers to AIDS victims, to teenage runaways, to forgotten elderly, and to dysfunctional families? Will there be an evangelism that possesses sufficient truth and contemporary relevance to preempt the economic and technological assumptions of modernity? The wake-up call to evangelism begins with realization that every generation is entrusted with unique opportunities to fulfill the Great Commission. That commission must reach almost four times as many people on this globe at the beginning of the next century as it did at the beginning of this century. The soon-to-be 6 billion earthly inhabitants are living embodiments of Christ's perennial observation: "The harvest is plentiful, but the workers are few" (Matt. 9:37). May their silent screams not be an eternal testimony to the church's failure to respond to Christ's very clear command: "Therefore beseech the Lord of the harvest to send out workers into His harvest" (Matt. 9:38).

V

testing the soil: a psychology of evangelism

Once upon a time, theology informed psychology. The understanding of how people act and think was derived mostly from Scripture and pastoral care. Psychology was a subspecies of a comprehensive interpretation of God's relationship to His creation. Two events vastly changed that interpretation for Western civilization. Charles Darwin argued that people had evolved from apes in his *Origin of Species,* and Sigmund Freud predicted that religion would one day become a piece of attic furniture, a collection of myths replaced by the facts of science. Both thinkers served to loosen psychology from its theological moorings. Cure of the soul became cure of the mind when humans no longer had souls.

But people have been psychologists since Adam asked himself, "Why did she do that to me?" Such answers are not easy to come by. And if life's questions confounded Adam in his pristine condition, it is immeasurably more difficult to wade through the complexities of character formation constituted of heredity, environment, physiology, and circumstantial stimuli. R.S. Peters states:

> Objectors to psychology often muddle prediction with prophe-

> cy and ridicule psychologists because they cannot prophesy whether a boy will choose an academic career or whether a politician will break a promise. But such objectors seldom realize that astronomy is almost the only science which can make such long term, unconditional predictions, and that this possibility is connected with the special nature of the solar system as a relatively closed system.[1]

It is with Peters' caution that we approach the relationship between psychology and evangelism. Evangelism is a spiritual exercise carried on under the canopy of God's sovereignty. People are not mice and are far less predictable than Pavlov's dog. One must always bear in mind the words of Paul: "Oh, the depth of the riches both of the wisdom and knowledge of God! How unsearchable are His judgments and unfathomable His ways! For who has known the mind of the Lord, or who became His counselor?" (Rom. 11:33-34)

One of the chief motives today for people exploring the principles of Christianity is the pursuit of wholeness and mental health. Augustine taught that happiness and health are vitally linked together, a link that can come only through a relationship with Christ. Everyone desires happiness—even he who steals, lies, or murders—but happiness is realized through "God's medicine which is the medicine of the mind including two things: restraint and instruction. Restraint is accomplished by fear, instruction by love."[2] Absence of fear and peace of mind are prerequisites to meaningful achievement in this life. Both can only come from knowing God and are requisites for the communicators who would preach the love of Christ.

Space does not permit the opportunity to delve into the many psychological insights of spiritual leaders throughout the history of the church. Notable examples would be the "Twelve Steps to Humility" by Bernard of Clairvaux and the "Spiritual Disciplines" of the Jesuit founder, Ignatius of Loyola. It is sufficient to say that anyone who would be faithful to evangelistic ministry must understand people. The great leaders of the church were able to exegete people as well as texts. Richard Baxter, a Reformed pastor of the sixteenth century, wrote, "We ought to study how to convince, and how to get inside people, and how to leave the truth to the quick—not to leave it in the air."[3] He challenged pastors to spend time in the homes of their people so they might become acquainted with their spiritual difficulties as well as their general needs. He further wrote, "As those in the audience have understanding and affection, so we must use ours to communicate with theirs."[4]

EARLY AMERICAN PSYCHOLOGY

Whether one speaks of Peter Cartwright on the frontier or Henry Ward Beecher in his Brooklyn church, American evangelists have been astute observers of human behavior. Most college-trained persons throughout the nineteenth century would have had a course in mental and moral philosophy. There was clear teaching on the decision-making process as it related to conversion, namely in terms of faculty psychology: if the appeal was made to the intellect and if the desires weighed the presented alternatives, then the will would act accordingly. A person could be distinctly conscious of the steps within the process as he or she came to a decision.

Jonathan Edwards argued that, for conversion to take place, there would have to be a complete regeneration of the affections. Without this conversion by grace, people would act on behalf of themselves rather than a supreme love for God. Edwards' *Treatise of Religious Affections,* written to defend the emotional manifestations of the first Great Awakening, was not only the first psychological treatment of revivalistic evangelism, but some may even claim it as the first full-length psychological text produced in the New World. Edwards' main premise was that true religion would produce affections if the emotions would be influenced: "He who has no religious affection is in a state of spiritual death, wholly destitute of the powerful, quenching, saving influence of the Spirit of God upon his heart."[5] However, an awareness of a change in the affections or an emotional manifestation does not guarantee conversion. A person may be emotionally deluded: "That which they call the witness of the Spirit, is nothing more than an immediate suggestion by which they are assured of their being converted, or made the children of God, and from which they derive the persuasion that their sins are pardoned, and that God has given them a title to heaven."[6]

Thomas Upham (1799–1872), whose text in mental and moral philosophy stayed in print for over half a century, believed in radical religious conversion, but did not perceive the original condition of persons to be quite as bleak as did Edwards. He argued that there is an innate love in the category of benevolent affection for God. People are created in the image of God, with a disposition to love His creation, since God loves, from the very perfection of His nature, what is worthy to be loved. This affection is not fully operative because people are fallen creatures and have had their intellectual and moral glory greatly obscured. This supreme law, if restored by a spiritual regeneration, will keep the other desires in proper perspective because conscience and will without divine help are insufficient to do so. As long as the principle of love for God is predominant, it is impossible for inferior principles to become excessive and morally evil in their actions.

From Edwards to Upham, mental philosophers were interested in explaining how God through regeneration could break humankind's vicious preoccupation with self. Upham's insights are helpful:

> It is not self-love, but the perversion of self-love, which is properly called selfishness; and while self-love is always innocent, and, under proper regulation, is morally commendable, as being the attribute of a rational nature, and as being approved by God himself, selfishness, on the contrary, is always sinful, as existing in violation of what is due to others, and at variance with the will of God. It is due to the cause of morals and religion as well as of sound philosophy, to make this important distinction. Self-love is the principle which a holy God has given; selfishness is the loathsome superstructure which man, in the moments of his rebellion and sin, has erected upon it.[7]

SEPARATION OF PSYCHOLOGY AND THEOLOGY

At the end of the nineteenth century, psychology began to lose its theological bearings. Therapy, counseling, and behavioral prediction were for the purpose of relating the person to his or her self rather than to God. Psychology, increasingly defined by Sigmund Freud's psychoanalysis, allowed people to escape from a God who was nothing more than a wish fulfillment. According to Freud, there was no such thing as ontological guilt that demands forgiveness and redemption. Freud taught that people instead experience a sense of guilt caused by the superego, which is comprised of parental restrictions and cultural inhibitions. Consciousness, morality, religion, and civilization resulted from a phylogenetic event—the killing of the primal father.

The above thought is the genesis of three of Freud's books: *Civilization and Its Discontents, Totem and Taboo,* and *Moses and Monotheism.* These are the basic thoughts: The first social unit of humanity was a tribe headed by one man, called the patriarchal hoard. The one male or father excluded the other males from sexual fulfillment, keeping all the females for himself. The penalty for intruding into the forbidden garden of sexual pleasure was death or, more specifically, castration. The sons rebelled in anger, killing the father and eating him. But in eating him, they preserved infinite identification with him.

Mutual protection from the aggressiveness above can only come through laws. However, in the Freudian scheme, even though the aggressive nature is thwarted, it does not simply vanish. Repression causes the aggression to be turned inward, which is masochism. For Freud, the masochistic feeling is a "sense of guilt." Religion only serves to aggravate the sense of guilt. Freud wrote:

> I have never doubted that religious phenomena are to be understood only on the model of the neurotic symptoms of the individual which are so familiar to us, as a return of long forgotten, important happenings in the primeval history of the human family, that they owe their obsessive character to that very origin and therefore, drive their effect on mankind from the historical truth they contain.[8]

For Freud, the self could be discovered through dream analysis and free association. Psychoanalysis made its way into the church, and the old rubrics of sin and salvation became passé. The self did not need to be converted, but rather needed to be asserted by the analysis of psychotherapy. E. Brooks Holifield traces this change in Protestant ministry in his carefully researched *A History of Pastoral Care in America: From Salvation to Self-Realization.* Instead of salvation, people now needed self-discovery. Sin was defined as an interruption of natural development. The church increasingly turned to client-centered counseling rather than Christ-centered preaching. For mainline Christianity, which did not know whether the human crisis was sin or maladjustment, evangelism lost its edge. Even in the church, theology had been dethroned by psychology as the queen of the sciences. Even where the coup d'etat was incomplete, it was difficult to discern which dogma defined the evangelistic effort of the church. Daniel Day Williams stated the confusion: "Psychologists speak of anxiety, egocentricity, acceptance, integration, freedom, love; the Christian faith speaks of anxiety, sin, forgiveness, faith, freedom, love; sometimes the words are the same, sometimes not."[9] The problem was more than semantical.

INADVERTENT PSYCHOLOGICAL CONTRIBUTIONS TO EVANGELISM

Two of Freud's disciples, while retaining some of his ideas concerning the unconscious and the ego, were not so adamantly opposed to religion. Carl Jung and Erik Erikson continued to explore the purpose and place of the ego in human development. At the core of Jung's psychology is a maturation process known as individuation, a move toward wholeness. Jung defines this as the "process by which a person becomes a psychological individual, that is separate, indivisible unity or whole."[10] Jung was in no sense an evangelical Christian, and it is not even clear that he was a theist. He believed that because of the collections stored in the mental attics he called the "unconscious," there needs to be an ongoing drive toward wholeness. Those who believe in instantaneous Christian conversion should keep this point in mind. Even Christians sometimes behave out of character, act absurd, or demonstrate vacillation, which Jung would credit to the "shadow side" of the individual. The Jungian interpreter Edward Whitmont writes, "Only when we realize part of ourselves which we have not hitherto seen or preferred to see, can we proceed to question and find the sources from which it feeds and the basis on which it rests" can wholeness and integration within take place.[11]

Jung's most important contribution to evangelism was his description of psychological types. According to him, there are basically two types of people: extroverted and introverted. Whitmont states, "The extrovert is a person whose consciousness is predominantly directed toward external objects—toward the outside world. The introvert is predominantly oriented toward the inner world of the psyche."[12] Both will exist in the same person, but an individual will predominantly be one or the other. Each type will process information in one of two ways: thinking or feeling. Thinking relates observed facts to one another and places them in an orderly arrangement; feeling places a value judgment on the perception. However, some will make a judgment before the relationships are adequately processed by thinking. Hence, thinking and feeling are quite often opposed to one another, and one, for the most part, expels the other. People often tend to make judgments before all the facts are in.

Sensation and intuition are means by which we receive the information that we process. Sensation observes through the five senses; intuition is a perception beyond the five senses, allowing us to visualize potential or possibilities beyond immediate sensation. Whitmont offers a word picture to explain the distinction:

> The defendant is brought in and the judge notes that he is tall, well-built, blond and blue-eyed, is dressed in a dark pinstripe suit and has certain specific nervous mannerisms. This judge is using his sensation function. Or he may see the defendant for the first time and have a sense that the man is innocent, in which case he may be using his intuition (or his bias—in which case his "hunch" will have a self-righteous emotional tone). Ask him afterwards what color the suit was and he probably will not know. Or he may hear the case and conclude that, from the evidence presented, it may reasonably be deduced that the man is probably guilty. Then he has been thinking and has possibly excluded some intangibles which may speak a quite different language. Or if the man reminds the judge too much of his detestable brother-in-law he may angrily say, "Six months in jail!" He would hardly be an impartial judge if his emotions intruded in this manner.[13]

Jung's explanation of types supplies sufficient reasons for the evangelist to be sensitive to different kinds of personalities. Not only do people need to be approached differently, but their individual personalities need to be affirmed and protected even after conversion. Mass evangelism often serves to submerge and obliterate the individual, but the Christian community exists to heighten the meaning of individuality. Community can only take place when the persons within it assume individual responsibility for its direction and outcome; but in the mass, humans become depersonalized entities. Victor Frankl puts it succinctly: "Man begins to be human only where he has the freedom to oppose bondage to a type. . . . The more standardized a machine is, the better it is; but the more standardized a person is—the more inferior is he from the ethical standpoint."[14]

All this is to say that different kinds of people will respond to different kinds of messages. A feeling type will tend to respond emotionally; a sensing type will respond anxiously; a thinking type will respond rationally; an intuitive type will respond quickly, but without reasons as to why he or she did so other than it "just felt like the right thing to do." The following pardigm places hearers of the gospel into different types. However, keep in mind that a person will often bear the characteristics of several types:

1. *Extroverted thinking type:* Would need to make sure that all the facts of the gospel make sense. Upon accepting them, they would tend to be dogmatic, legalistic, and pedantic in implementing their newly found faith.

2. *Extroverted feeling type:* This person would likely accept the evangelist's message from a sense of propriety and concern for the approval of others. This person tends to be conformist and would have a difficult time becoming a Christian in opposition to conventional wisdom. Fellowship rather than a crusader spirit are high on this person's priority list.

3. *Extroverted intuitive type:* This person is intrigued by new ideas and may enter into the precepts of the gospel much like a soldier of fortune taking on a new assignment. This person is easily bored, and it is difficult for him or her to put down deep and stable roots. Infatuation, rather than conviction, leads to a restless pursuit of whatever meets the need of the moment.

4. *Extroverted sensing type:* The individual will be more conscious about responding to an event of symbolism and aesthetics than a message of dogma. This person needs to experience religion from the standpoint of stimulation and excitement. He or she will be

attracted to Christianity via a spectacular event rather than a well-reasoned argument.

5. Introverted thinking type: Just the opposite of the extroverted feeling type, this person will need to perceive that Christianity is a cogent philosophy for life. The individual will more than likely adopt a life system with the least cracks in the plausibility structure. These people are imaginative thinkers and will demand patience of the evangelist who wants the convert to immediately ascribe to every dogma of the church, especially those that smack of logical contradictions.

6. Introverted feeling type: This person will find it difficult to make a clear decision for Christ because of oversensitivity to the thoughts and feelings of others. Excessive introspection and preoccupation with inner feelings will be difficult to separate from Christian experience. Because of psychological moods, it will be difficult for this person to come to a full and joyful assurance of faith.

7. Introverted intuitive type: This individual will be most difficult for the evangelist to read and is most likely to respond to the gospel out of unconscious needs that he or she doesn't understand. The convert will not be able to articulate what has happened, since the medium of the inner world is far more important than the logic of the outer. This type is not prone to find Christ through the normal methodologies of evangelism. He or she is more likely to have a vision or hear a voice quite independent of normal avenues offered by institutional religion.

8. Introverted sensation type: This person is also unlikely to be converted by rationalistic appeals. High individual creativity makes this person highly suspicious of the organized church. The relationship is mutual, because the introverted sensation type is normally too abstract for "normal" people. Their off-the-wall, detached approach to life would more likely be drawn to Gordon Cosby's "potter's house" than the colonial church in the town square.

Jung believed that the preceding types are shaped not only by the events which lodge within the individual, but by a collective unconsciousness that is the shared experience of all humanity. This means that there are archetypes and symbols that are common to all of us but, at the same time, most people will exhibit a "highly-developed function as his functional type."[15] It is important for the communicator not only to perceive these tendencies in others, but to have some clue as to how he or she is perceived by others. Two opposite types should not be surprised when they are not able to communicate with one another. Whitmont states, "All too often each will feel misunderstood by the other and will feel that the other is reaching in an irresponsible, immature, irrational way, and this argument can be played back and forth *ad infinitum.*"[16]

Dialogue is important in all communication—especially in evangelism. Evangelists must know who they are evangelizing. Carl Jung's type descriptions help us to understand that presentations of the gospel need to be diverse—tailored to various kinds of listeners. They also give us clues as to why some people join particular denominations. Would an extroverted sensation type more likely be an Episcopalian? Are Quaker meeting houses filled with introverted feeling types? Simple answers to such questions border on foolishness and defy the miraculous superintending grace of God. Yet churches do seem to take on different personalities not unlike the psychic makeup of their individual members.

ERIK ERIKSON

Erik Erikson has given us a much clearer picture as to why people develop the way they do. After studying at Freud's Vienna Psychoanalytic Institute, he came to the United States at the age of thirty-one. Erikson did not see personality development in the light of Freud's "Oedipus complex" or Jung's "collective consciousness." In his view, personality is shaped throughout the totality of life as the ego negotiates the transitions of maturation. Thus, the personality of an individual is an "epigenetic" structure built through successive ego adaptations.

For Erikson, the ego is much more than a neutral arbitrator between the id and the superego. The ego adapts itself to the crises of life in the best interests of the individual and, thus, is a powerful force for wholeness. It strives for trust in the face of mistrust, for autonomy under the threat of shame, for initiative when inhibited by guilt, and for industry though being hindered by feelings of inferiority. These negotiations are never perfect, but rather make their way through eight stages of life with various degrees of success or failure (see p. 141).

Psychosocial Crises

Old Age VIII								Integrity vs. Despair, Disgust. WISDOM
Adulthood VII							Generativity vs. Stagnation. CARE	
Young Adulthood VI						Intimacy vs. Isolation. LOVE		
Adolescence V					Identity vs. Identity Confusion. FIDELITY			
School Age IV				Industry vs. Inferiority. COMPETENCE				
Play Age III			Initiative vs. Guilt. PURPOSE					
Early Childhood II		Autonomy vs. Shame, Doubt. WILL						
Infancy I	Basic Trust vs. Basic Mistrust. HOPE							
	1	**2**	**3**	**4**	**5**	**6**	**7**	**8**

Erikson's "Life Cycle" needs to be applied to the ministry of evangelism. The more difficulty the ego has had in negotiating successive stages, the more likely the person will form a weak identity (i.e., an identity assaulted by insecurity and role confusion). Religion may well be the source of faith to transcend failure, a source which Erikson calls the oldest and "most lasting institution to serve the ritual restoration of a sense of trust in the form of faith while offering tangible formula for a sense of evil against which it promises to arm and defend man."[17] Yet even after conversion, lack of identity formation may lead to excessive defense mechanisms. The church or sect with which one surrounds him- or herself may simply be a security blanket to keep the world and its evil adherents out. Such exclusiveness Erikson calls totalism, an exclusiveness that draws rigid boundaries between the self and others. Such isolation is devastating to evangelism, a process that requires developing spiritual intimacy with others. Erikson states:

> The counterpart of the intimacy is "distantiation": the readiness to repudiate, isolate, and, if necessary, destroy those forces and people whose essence seems dangerous to one's own. Thus, the lasting consequence of the need for distantiation is the readiness to fortify one's territory of intimacy and solidarity and view all outsiders with a fanatic "overvaluation of small differences" between the familiar and the foreign.[18]

When the ego successively adapts to the crises of life, there is a readiness to make a meaningful contribution to the surrounding world. Erikson calls this ego quality generativity, "the concern in establishing and guiding the next generation."[19] Generativity means accepting at least partial responsibility for the welfare and destiny of others. The acceptance of destiny normally comes through those who can instill the hope of destiny in others. Erikson accents religion as a source for discovering destiny:

> The disinherited (disinherited in earthly goods and in social identity) above all desire to hear and rehear those words which made their inner world, long stagnant, and dead, reverberate with forgotten echoes; this desire made them believe that God from somewhere in the outer spaces, spoke through a chosen man on a definable historical occasion.[20]

There is no greater expression of generativity than the great traditions of caring evangelism that have passed from generation to generation. This single God-given generational concern is the greatest single evangelistic process.

Erikson's fifth stage, identity versus role confusion, which takes place during adolescence, has important implications for reaching young people with the gospel. Adolescents, in their concern with what they appear to be in the eyes of others as compared with what they feel they are, are obsessed with being accepted by their peers. This will quite often mean accepting the ideology of the immediate surroundings—an ideology that will provide a sameness and continuity between the inner world of the self and the outer world of cliques and clans. But if the person is rejected by the "friends" he or she was seeking out, or if the values of the so-called "friends" fail to satisfy, the adolescent may seek a deeper ideology.

Christianity provides a coherent worldview when the false securities of adolescence are shattered by the normal failures and vicissitudes of everyday life. The identity crisis of adolescence leads to a search for coherency among conflicting truth claims. Ambivalent relationships with both parents and peers make it all the more important that a stable role model be available at this time, such as a youth director, pastor, or coach. This is especially critical for a teenager who has experienced bad parenting or extended parental absence—and who may consequently search for a spiritual father. Erikson states:

> If the earliest stage bequeathed to the identity crisis an important need for trust in oneself and in others, then clearly the adolescent looks most fervently for men and ideas to have faith in, which also means men and ideas in whose service it would seem worth while to prove oneself trustworthy.[21]

FURTHER APPLICATION OF THE LIFE-CYCLE

Adaptations of Erikson's Life Cycle abound, but none has been more popular than Daniel J. Levinson's *The Seasons of a Man's Life.* Levinson observed through extensive interviewing that most lives evolve through a somewhat orderly sequence of transitions. Each transition phase involves questions concerning realizing potential or assessing contributions that have already been made to family and society. Levinson writes, "The primary tasks of every transitional period are to question and reappraise the existing structure, to explore various possibilities for change in self and world, and to move toward commitment to the crucial choices that form the bases for a new life structure in the ensuing stable period."[22]

Levinson argued for three major transitions in adult life: early adult transition (ages 17–22), midlife transition (40–45), and late adult transition (60–65). Each transition is a time for modification, excluding uncomplimentary characteristics or including new elements perceived as necessary for the task ahead. Transition is a time for serious reflection on the events that occurred in the antecedent years or events that the person fears might occur in the not-so-distant future. No change is more traumatic than midlife transition:

> The life structure again comes into question: What have I done with my life? What do I really get from and give to my wife, children, friends, work community and self? What is it I truly want for myself and others? A man yearns for a life in which his actual desires, values, talents, and aspirations can be expressed.[23]

It is easy to relate evangelism to this serious reflection regarding the vital questions of life. Christian communication needs to direct these felt needs to the real need of life—a relationship with Jesus Christ. As a person moves through the Life Cycle, there is less attention to the noise and opinion of the throng and more turning to personal creativity and realization of inherent gifts. During the early transitions, a person may adopt a mentor for the realization of dreams and goals. If this mentor is a Christian, he or she will serve as a powerful catalyst in evangelizing the non-Christian. Eventually, the mentor will probably drop by the wayside, allowing the individual to become one's "own person," less tyrannized by the mentor ideal and earlier illusions of grandeur.

As an individual moves through the transitional stages, there is an intensified sense of mortality, especially as physical strength abates. There is an ever-increasing sense of lost causes and irreversible losses. Success and its accruements are questioned or, worse yet, bitterness and cynicism arises about dreams never realized. Such pain directs thinking toward mortality and a sense of impending death. Levinson states:

> Immortality is one of the strongest and least malleable of human motives . . . fundamental for our love of life, our value, our wish to be involved in the world, and experience really what it offers us. It is reflected in the trauma that accompanies every advance towards acknowledging our short-lived existence in the world.[24]

Levinson is correct in that immortality is the primary motive behind grabbing all the gusto. Such grabbing normally ends in disillusionment, or what Levinson calls de-illusionment, the process of readdressing illusions, which is far more beneficial.

Gail Sheehy based her book *Passages* on Daniel Levinson's research, and James Engel has adapted both in order to theorize when a person is most likely to come to Christ. For Engel, key points on the Life Cycle are "pulling up roots" and "mid-life transition." These are stages when people are open to change because of anxiety, loneliness, lack of self-acceptance, and a search for a more stable belief system. Engel argues that there is little interest in spiritual change when a person is building the dream and putting down roots during early adulthood. At this point, people are too busy striving to get ahead, but in later transition "old beliefs are, in effect, 'up for grabs,' and the church has a great opportunity if it can demonstrate that Christian values indeed will provide a more satisfying direction for life."[25]

One of Engel's most controversial points is his claim that at particular stages in life people are relatively satisfied and would not, as some claim, accept Christ if they only knew how.[26] If people maintain a balance between expectations and achievements, they are relatively happy. Happiness is often relative to ignorance of life's options, absence of personal disturbance, and minimum tension between present circumstances and the ideal state. "Most people in the western world, then, are not just 'waiting for someone to accept Christ,' and it is best to recognize that fact. In reality, witness to the 'satisfied' is the toughest challenge we face."[27] All of the above guides us in asking the questions that are unique to the various stages of life in order to penetrate veneers of satisfaction.

The Complete Spiritual Decision Process Model Showing the Stages of Spiritual Growth			
GOD'S ROLE	COMMUNICATOR'S ROLE		MAN'S RESPONSE
General Revelation		–8	Awareness of Supreme Being
Conviction ↓	Proclamation ↓	–7	Some Knowledge of Gospel
		–6	Knowledge of Fundamentals of Gospel
		–5	Grasp of Personal Implications of Gospel
		–4	Positive Attitude toward Act of Becoming a Christian
	Call for Decision ↓	–3	Problem Recognition and Intention to Act
		–2	Decision to Act
		–1	Repentance and Faith in Christ
Regeneration			*New Creature*
Sanctification ↓	Follow Up ↓	+1	Post-Decision Evaluation
		+2	Incorporation into Church
	Cultivation ↓	+3 • • •	Conceptual and Behavioral Growth • Communion with God • Stewardship • Internal Reproduction • External Reproduction
E T E R N I T Y			

EVANGELISM AND A PSYCHOLOGY OF ETHICS

Another stage theory that needs to be discussed is that of Lawrence Kohlberg (1927–1987). He developed a six-stage cognitive understanding of ethical maturity. Even though atheistic, Kohlberg's principles of human welfare and justice give insights into the relationships between conversion and moral implementation. There are also inferences that certain kinds of evangelism would produce more mature Christians than would others. For instance, excessive preaching on heaven and hell produces a Christian who considers rewards and punishment to be the chief considerations regarding the wrongness or rightness of action. Or constantly presenting God as a judge who requires obedience and maintains a fixed order may influence the new Christian to give more heed to the kingdom than the King—an institutionalism with a tendency toward a legalism that is aimed at making society function as ethically as it should.

The Kohlbergian premise involves a Socratic approach to learning. According to Kohlberg, indoctrination, conditioning, behavioral modification, and modeling of virtues are all poor methods of teaching ethical concepts. He would replace a recitation of facts with a stimulation of thinking through the presentation of ethical problems. The evangelist would do well to note that not only did Socrates ask questions, but Jesus Himself often asked incisive questions that called for serious reflection and decisive action.

The second group of Kohlberg's premises is based on the Piagetian cognitive structure of development, an invariant stage sequence that is irreversible and universal. As for the stages themselves, each stage presupposes a prior stage. On the basis of years of observation, Kohlberg claims that there are six stages and no others. A person advances through invariant sequential stages and has tremendous difficulty grasping a stage that is higher than the one above his or her present intellectual level. Each stage represents advanced logical operations and the ability to imagine a perspective other than one's own.

Stage 6, the highest level of ethical advancement, consists of justice: the inviolability of human life and the equal distribution of rights, privileges, and duties. Kohlberg argues that if we define our morality in terms of virtues and vices, we will vacillate among popular opinions, conventional beliefs, and the praise and blame of others. Justice is the only principle that can adequately solve moral conflicts because it is transcendent above consensual, contractual, or conventional morality. According to Kohlberg, Christ, Socrates, and Martin Luther King are among the few people who have ever reached this level of ethical implementation. They were moral leaders in that their civil disobedience flowed from principles of justice, and they were willing to bear the consequences of their protest against human indignities.

Kohlberg's theory enables the evangelist to examine his or her motives and message. Is the message utilitarian or manipulative rather than truly aiming at the enhancement of the welfare of the recipient? Does the message allow the listener to operate out of freedom and illumination rather than entrapment and propaganda? Kohlberg has made us more keenly aware that acting out of self-conviction is more beneficial and satisfying than acting out of fear or compulsive conformity.

Theological critique abounds in the face of Kohlberg's moral development theory. Before we subject Kohlberg to a religious critique, it needs to be made clear that he makes no religious claim for his theory. In fact, one of his main purposes has been to demonstrate that religion does not need to inform ethics: if his system keeps the two mutually exclusive, it will be more palatable for American public school officials who fear Judeo-Christian dominance. According to Kohlberg, religious education and moral education can be completely separated.

However, Kohlberg is not entirely negative about religion. According to him, religion serves not as a source for moral prescription, but as a support for moral judgment and action. Religion can encourage the self, which is staggered by the injustices of the world. It can renew one's sense of moral purpose and commitment and can heighten one's moral sensitivity. In Kohlberg's view, moral support—rather than moral answers—comes from a belief in God. "Religious faith as necessary but not a sufficient condition for ethical reasoning" is the phrase most often used by those who seriously attempt to adopt Kohlberg's scheme to the area of faith development.

FAITH DEVELOPMENT AND EVANGELISM

No one has done more to relate cognitive development to faith discovery and maturity than James Fowler. He has listed six levels of faith development and paralleled each of them to the corresponding cognitive level of moral reasoning.[28] For instance, Stage 3 is a conformist stage both for religious and ethical decision-making because the people do not have a sure enough grasp on their own identities and judgment to construct and maintain an independent perspective.[29] Fowler clarifies that "this is not to claim that cognitive operations are paramount in our understanding of human faith. It simply indicates that we have not found the other structural characteristics of a given faith stage in the absence of the correlated level of cognitive development."[30]

Fowler's insights are informative for the Christian evangelist. He first of all declares that the desire to have and exercise faith is a universal human trait. Secondly, he demonstrates the immaturity of a faith that is simply inherited from another or adopted from one's environment. Synthetic conventional faith is conformist in that it is keenly attuned to the expectations and judgments of significant others rather than maintaining an independent perspective. Fowler writes:

> This is the central meaning behind the terms synthetic and conventional. The Stage-3 individual's faith system is conventional in that it is seen as being everybody's faith system or the faith system of the entire community. And it is synthetic in that it is non-analytical, it comes as a sort of unified, global wholeness.[31]

Faith maturity comes as one moves beyond value systems that have been handed down by parents or other mentors. There is increased questioning concerning the meaning of inherited rituals and symbols. Detachment calls for a separation from meanings dictated by others and a move toward the reality of truth, in spite of loss of self-esteem or security. Reality is defined by openness, paradox, complexity, and vulnerability to further conversion to a truth that seems to better represent reality than the worldview that is already held. These people have normally experienced a good deal of suffering and are able to identify with a large part of the human community. The highest stage is when the person's faith has been universalized to the extent that it transcends commonly held mores and often acts in extraordinary and unpredictable ways. Fowler states:

> It is my conviction that persons who come to entirely universalizing faith are drawn into those patterns of commitment and leadership by the providence of God and the exigencies of history. It is as though they are selected by the great Blacksmith of history, heated in the fires of turmoil and trouble and then hammered into usable shape on the hard anvil of conflict and struggle.[32]

Fowler helps us to understand different degrees of faith and why some people may be much more committed at the beginning of their Christian walk than others are after years of discipleship. A magnanimous faith attempts to get the whole picture, exercising charity whenever possible. However, Fowler's magnanimous spirit turns into a latitudinarian spirit—a live-and-let-live philosophy. According to Fowler, the worth of faith is judged by its tenacity, implementation in the common life, and openness to others rather than its object. Faith is an absolute within the human experience, while its content remains relative. If the object to which we devote ourselves confers value on us and has intrinsic value, the faith that we are exercising is worthwhile. "Faith, classically understood, is not a separate dimension of life, a compartmentalized specialty. Faith is an orientation of the total person giving purpose and goal to one's hopes and strivings, thoughts, and actions."[33]

We may want to ask Fowler, "How does one know when something has intrinsic value? How is one assured his or her values are being enhanced? How does one know when he or she has arrived at the highest values?" Christians readily answer these questions by the witness of the Spirit to the truth of Christ as the only way. Yes, there are various degrees of faith, but faith has no intrinsic value outside of the object to which it is devoted. Fowler fails to show that my faith in the chair in which I am sitting is only as good as the chair itself. The Christian faith is ultimately validated by its object, Christ.

The above validation is quite different from the faith of Miss

T., which Fowler designates as a Stage 5: a relatively mature faith. Miss T states that "it doesn't matter what you call it. Whether you call it God or Jesus or Cosmic Flow or Reality or Love, it doesn't matter what you call it. It is there. And what you learn directly from that source will not tie you in creeds. . . that separate you from your fellow man."[34] Many theologians would call Miss T's faith an illusion. It fails to be grounded in an objective reality that will provide a firm faith through the vicissitudes of life. Is it not possible that this so-called faith might mistake a mirage for the water of life that flows from the throne of God?

In a curious sort of way, all of the stage theories above, especially Levinson's, Kohlberg's, and Fowler's, in spite of their universal claims, are uniquely American: autonomous, optimistic, pragmatic, individualistic, democratic, and egalitarian. For Fowler, the validity of conversion, faith, and moral integrity do not rest on an outside transcendent authority, but the perceived congruence between the believer and faith object. Lesslie Newbigin asks, "And is faith the proper name for something that is merely a psychological condition and has no cognitive element, has no object about which ontological claims can be made?"[35] Newbigin places this subjective religion in what he designates as the operative plausibility structure of our modern world, "the public world of what our culture calls facts, in distinction from the private world of beliefs, opinions, and values."[36] In the words of William Gladstone, "Subjective religion has again lost its God-given hold upon objective reality."[37]

THREE PRINCIPLES IN THE PSYCHOLOGY OF EVANGELISM

Unconditional Positive Regard

Most personal relationships are formed on the basis of mutual benefit. Part of this motivation is due to the reality of life itself. It seems that we are thrown into a multitude of relationships: car pools, service organizations, athletic teams, classroom groups, office bureaucracies. The list is so endless and complex that we may choose at times to shut each other out as do subway riders in New York City. Thus, relationships are picked up and discarded with little thought. We feel that other people need to be a part of our lives only as long as they have something that will enhance our present welfare. Since most people are perceived as contributing very little to our well-being, we tend to treat them as insignificant, rather than significant. Robert Ornstein and Paul Ehrlich describe the contrast between today's world and ancient societies:

> Today things are very different. Even small societies are usually composed of hundreds of thousands or millions of people. In a nation like the United States, a city dweller might see about 1,000 people in a single day, many more than hunter-gatherers would see in a lifetime. Moreover, the number of potential relationships increases much more quickly than does the number of people one person might encounter. It is impossible for one person to keep track of the 12 million possible relationships between 5,000 people—but many high schools in large cities have that many students. A small town of only 15,000 people has 112 million possible relationships. Understanding that many is simply inconceivable, yet much of humanity lives in cities of ten times that population or more.[38]

Even if we do not ignore the people all around us, the awareness of others will often be one of pity or condescension. True, people have problems: poverty, sickness, and deformities of both mind and body. At first glance, certain individuals may be ugly to the point of repulsion. The ability to perceive people as a meaningful part of one's existence whatever their circumstances in life is due to divine grace. Individuals are not important simply because they enhance our own meaning and allow us to discover a destiny of benevolence and service. They are significant because God meant for them to discover meaning and arrive at a purposeful destiny. Unconditional positive regard is recognizing that God has a design and purpose for every single individual. Every human being has a right, not to the pursuit of happiness, but in Lesslie Newbigin's words, "to the pursuit of the end for which humans, as a matter of fact exist."[39] No creed states it as concisely as the Westminster Standards: "Man's chief and highest end is to glorify God and fully enjoy Him forever" (The Larger Catechism, answer 1).

Thomas Oden's comments concerning unconditional positive regard are applicable to evangelism (though he is primarily referring to a counseling relationship): "Therapeutic acceptance must happen in a living relationship in which another person actually mediates to him such unconditional positive regard that its import comes through to keen awareness."[40] Even though the author uses acceptance and unconditional positive regard somewhat interchangeably here, he concludes that the latter is a much more active affirmation of love than is acceptance, which is a passive openness to another's consciousness. But the important point is that both allow the evangelized to value themselves so that they will value others more—to love one's self so that one may love others and to accept one's self for who and what one is, so one may become who and what one needs to be. This covenant of unconditional love has been modeled by God through Jesus Christ and is communicated nonverbally and unconsciously, as well as overtly.

Justification by faith through grace alone is foundational to an accurate understanding of the helping process. Knowing that we have been redeemed by grace in spite of our bankruptcy and ugliness is key to our response to others: If God can reconstitute my humanity, He can do it for anyone. A theology of acceptance and unconditional positive regard through Christ is crucial to the work of evangelism. Adding innate goodness, merit, works, or achievements that win approval and positive regard by the evangelizer is anathema. We are not trying to get people to please us, but rather to find the affirmation of God that will provide them ultimate meaning and fulfillment.

This poses critical questions for the evangelist regarding the place of prophetical pronouncement and repentance. How can the evangelist call sinners to repentance and at the same time communicate unconditional positive regard? One answer is that acceptance and psychological affirmation do not represent a scientific determinism that waters down the concept of sin, but actually frees a person to take further responsibility for his or her actions. One insight provided by Oden (and underscored in his books *Game Free*[41] and *TAG*[42]) is that if people are to feel accepted and open themselves up, they must sense that their counselor, pastor, or evangelist accepts him- or herself and is being open. We are to disclose ourselves to those we love as Christ disclosed Himself to the world in His full humanity. If we want to know others, we must let them know us. Christ fully accepted Himself and the Father's design for Him. His crucifixion was the prototypical disclosure of personhood.

Empathetic Listening

One of the ways that unconditional positive regard is displayed is through empathetic listening. Many evangelistic agendas and programs are seen as ends in themselves. The canned approach is so busy verbalizing formulas that the evangelist seems to be detached from genuine concern for persons. Listening implicitly says to the other person, "Who you are and what you say is important." The idea of the "I" can speak to the idea of the "thou" only if the "I" listens long enough to find out what the "thou" has to say. All communication demands a meeting of the minds. Most minds never meet because they are preoccupied with their own agendas.

Empathy means to have feeling, passion, or affection for someone else. Empathy is listening so intently that one begins to feel the same emotion as the other person. It may be that one could become so fully involved in the other person's plight that it is almost as if one has experienced the same hurts that the other person has suffered. It is possible to understand Christ's passion as His empathetic listening to the needs of humanity. This insight into the cross of Christ is extremely necessary if the evangelist is to be an intercessor before the throne of God. Jesus Himself fulfilled the listening criterion: "For we do not have a high priest who cannot sympathize with our weaknesses, but one who has been tempted in all things as we are, yet without sin" (Heb. 4:15). Frank Lake's commentary on Christ's suffering is worth quoting:

> By His cross and passion, God in Christ His Son shares man's passive and innocent identification with injustice, loss of rights, mockery, shame, ruthless cruelty, the curse, rejection by the Beloved source, thirst, hunger, emptiness, exhaustion, weakness, the taste of death, paradox, contradiction to the point of confusion, and the suffering of the serpent's curse.[43]

Listening is part of the transpersonal covenant.

Communication is much more than words—it is involvement in another person's life. Involvement earns the right to speak to another's condition. George Fox, the founding father of the

Quakers, often penned in his journal, "I spoke to their condition." He understood the plight of the poor because most of his life, at least before marriage, he lived in poverty. He was in prison for over six years of his life in conditions so filthy and abominable that people were converted just by seeing the conditions to which George Fox committed himself. Fox's 55,000 converts are a testimony to his listening through a life of suffering and sacrifice. Even though the evangelist will normally not be imprisoned, listening states a willingness to "walk in the other's shoes," even if one has never been where the other has been.

Empathetic listening in evangelism risks closeness to others. There is vulnerability in absorbing the hurts and problems of those who are seeking answers to life's complexities. Catharsis—a cleansing, a self-emptying—must be in process before Christ can overcome the obstacles that are blocking faith. The evangelist, who may be a pastor, teacher, parent, or some other trusted individual, will often serve as a catalyst for confession of sin or expression of grief and remorse. As an agent of Christ, the listener will offer absolution and forgiveness in a nonjudgmental response to those seeking acceptance. Thus, the evangelist represents God's ears and mouth on earth. Forgiveness most often comes through the body of Christ in the power of the Holy Spirit. The words of Christ must be heeded carefully if believers are going to be redemptive agents: "Receive the Holy Spirit. If you forgive the sins of any, their sins have been forgiven them; if you retain the sins of any, they have been retained" (John 20:22-23).

Empathetic listening requires far more than sentimental acquiescence to another's condition of guilt. Acceptance does not mean a stamp of approval on someone's past, but rather an offering of Christ's power to change and forgive. Evangelists must constantly bear in mind that "all have sinned," including themselves, thus avoiding the infliction of paternalistic condescension. The evangelist's job is to offer the optimum atmosphere in which penitents can express their guilt to an individual waiting and willing to extend Christ's mercy. People should be freed to express their guilt, wrongdoing, or negated values instead of secretly covering them up and risking symptoms of pathological disorder. Above all, people seeking salvation will come to understand that they are unconditionally valued by Jesus Christ in spite of their value negations.

Listening provides the opportunity for the evangelist or pastor to show interest in the totality of the other person, rather than simply trying to attain some preconceived goal. Techniques without relationships are quite often dehumanizing. It is through open ears and an open mind that the evangelist has the greatest opportunity to demonstrate a gospel of grace and acceptance. In a process of listening, the evangelist must resist the temptation of being repulsed by sins that penitents reveal, no matter how dark they may be. Listening by the evangelist will enable counselees to properly distance themselves from the wretched crisis or crises that are bearing down on them at the moment by giving them a perspective on the series of events that have led up to the moment. Understanding of their own situation will often come through articulation and self-expression. Listening will guard the evangelist from giving inadequate advice based on inadequate information. Such carefulness and time in the evangelistic-therapeutic relationship is based on Frank Lake's premise:

> To some extent every depressed person is a sick man within a sick family, within a sick society. . . . Pastoral care is an interpersonal relationship in the name of a personal God. Though at times, it is true, God acts through non-verbal communication such as the laying on of hands, it is as a personal word and through a personal fellowship and incorporation that He deals with our personal problems.[44]

Loving Care

A family was driving down an interstate highway. Seeing a car broken down, they stopped to offer assistance. They were gratefully greeted by a thirty-year-old woman and her six-year-old daughter. The car was beyond immediate repair, so the stranded twosome climbed into the good Samaritans' automobile. Betty had made a start with Christ some months before, but was now falling back into her old ways of drugs and alcohol. Her problems were far greater than a broken-down automobile. The Christians who stopped took the penniless Betty and her daughter home with them to spend the night. That one night was extended to eleven months of spiritual and emotional nurture. Betty desperately needed to be surrounded by supportive and understanding people who would nurture her back to health and hope. Little did the Christian family realize that a stop to offer assistance would provide the complex healing that Betty desperately needed. Today, she is a strong Christian developing wonderful gifts of speech and drama that are totally consecrated to Christ. Her redemption from a life of sin would not have happened had not someone cared for her.

James Engel states that the key to evangelism is "to touch people where they are with Biblical truth in a loving and empathetic manner."[45] People will not respond to the gospel in a vacuum. The question "Does anyone care for my soul?" is surrounded by a multitude of other questions: "Does anyone care about my finances, my divorce, my children, my addiction?" In fact, the spiritual question is normally preempted, or at least obscured, by a host of more immediate and practical questions. James Engel calls these immediate questions of life "felt needs." If the felt needs become intensive enough, a person will look for a change. Betty had desperate needs. One of the most pressing was an escape from the haunting dreams and twisted thinking of her past drug culture. Thus, she was an active seeker for a better lifestyle, but the church had provided only a partial answer. She needed loving care provided within the context of encouragement, confrontation, enablement, and other biblical principles of Christian nurture.

Abraham Maslow theorized that people progress through a hierarchy of needs. He argued that individuals exist at one level or another, and will not find communication meaningful if it is targeted at a need above and beyond their present condition. People concerned about physiological needs will not be giving much thought to self-esteem gained through achievement and recognition. The same message that plays in Peoria will probably not play well in Bangladesh or even in a small isolated town in Appalachia. The U.S. Army's advertisement, "Be all you can be," works somewhat in middle-class America, but would not work well at all in Ethiopia. "Eat all you can eat" would best appeal to people who do not know how they will get their next meal.

It could probably be argued that Betty had needs on every level of Maslow's hierarchy. She had the immediate need of security and safety. It is a frightening experience for anyone to be broken down on an interstate highway in the middle of the night. Once when I lived in another state, a woman and her small children had been stranded in a van on an interstate highway. Even though thousands of cars passed by, no one stopped to help or even inquire about her situation for twelve hours. This neglect made front-page headlines and served as a shameful indictment of all of us who are part of a frantic pace, attempting to fulfill our self-serving agendas. Love is when someone else's needs become more important than our own.

Betty's most overwhelming need was probably in the area of "belongingness and love." Perhaps her life had been a series of disappointments and betrayals—an abusive father, fickle friends, and numerous men who had used and mistreated her. If the gospel is presented without a caring and loving attitude, it seems hollow and irrelevant. Estrangement and fragmentation are predominant characteristics of our urban society. Loneliness and alienation stalk urban dwellers even though they are surrounded by thousands of people. Human beings once lived in sparsely populated areas, but now are lost in a vast human sea of expressionless faces and nameless entities. It is no wonder that small support groups have been one of the chief means of post-World War II evangelism. The most desperate needs for most Americans are relationships, intimacy, acceptance, and affirmation.

Charles Sheldon, a pastor in Topeka, Kansas, wrote a fictionalized account of a church that took the love ethic of Jesus seriously. This 1896 novel suggested that our decisions regarding life and certainly evangelism can be informed by a simple question: "What would Jesus do?" In this light, evangelism can be categorically absolute and situational at the same time. Christ's agape love dictates to every situation, but evangelism must be in the context of concern for a person's specific circumstances. Evangelism demands investment of resources in the lives of others. Cheap evangelism is a contradiction in terms.

Rollo May defines agape as "esteem for the other, the concern for the other's welfare beyond any gain that one can get out of it; disinterested love, typically the love of God for man."[46] Caring evangelism must be free from hedonistic goals and an orientation to success. Love with no strings attached is the categorical imperative for sharing Christ with the lost. Authentic evangelism is motivated by the mind of Christ, an attitude of servanthood, humility, and freedom from self-promotion. Such attitudes will cause the world to drop its defenses and be receptive to the church's message.

CONCLUSION

A comprehensive view of the psychology of evangelism has yet to be written. Evangelism needs to fully discover this truth: If souls are worth saving, people are worth understanding. Evangelism has sometimes failed because passion has displaced perception. Evangelism will not only pray for wisdom-filled passion, but will attempt to provide a fresh evangelistic edge that has been sharpened by the best of psychological discovery. The application of grace can be enhanced by investigating the complexities of human formation.

Evangelism has often suffered from subjectivity and the imposition of the evangelist's inner experience upon another. Legitimization of true religion has often been sameness of experience and conformity to sectarian expectations—while plaguing incongruities between inner realities and the group ethos are suppressed. It may be that psychology could at least partially serve to save us from wholesale evangelistic packaging—teaching us that universal grace does not mean assembly-line production. Every human being that has ever been in existence was no less handcrafted than Adam. A healthy psychology of evangelism will give close scrutiny to the complexities of the Creator's craft. An evangelism that lacks such appreciation or that would run roughshod over those intricacies is a legalistic evangelism. It is more interested in capturing than it is in captivating. An evangelism led by the Holy Spirit will seek to use whatever tools are available to explore captivation at the point of the person's most perplexing inner problems. If psychology can be sanctified to the end of evangelistic finesse, every endeavor should be made to do so.

VI

applying grace to society: a sociology of evangelism

Referring to the 1960s, Allan Bloom, in his best-selling *The Closing of the American Mind,* states that "the social sciences were of interest to everyone who had a program, who might care about prosperity, peace or war, equality, racial or sexual discrimination."[1] He could have added evangelism to his list. While firmly holding to the belief that people are converted to Christ one by one rather than en masse, Christians have increasingly turned to social data for insights into the evangelism. If evangelism is to be relevant, certain relevancy cues must be gathered. Society can be understood by microscoping its parts, and the individuals can be better comprehended by telescoping the whole. General principles are inferred from extensive data gathering and statistical analysis. Statistically speaking, we know more about each other than we ever have before.

THE PROBLEM OF REDUCTIONISM AND PREDICTIONISM

Sociology has not only been employed by present-day evangelism, but it is being used to investigate evangelistic methods and motives of the past. Such revisiting of bygone evangelistic enterprises has frequently led to methodological reductionism. Methodological reductionism seeks to reduce supernatural phenomena to psychological causes and economic motives. This reductionism is consistently applied to religion because, in Allan Bloom's words, "pursuit of salvation would, for example, need to be reduced to another kind of cause, like repressed sexuality, whereas pursuit of money would not. Search for material causes and reduction of higher or more complex phenomena to lower or simpler ones, are generally accepted procedures."[2]

A case in point is Paul Johnson's *A Shopkeeper's Millennium,* which hypothesizes and argues that "Charles Finney's revival provided a solution to the social disorder and moral confusion that attended the creation of a free labor economy."[3] The industrial revolution was causing the old system of apprenticeship and guild patronage to break down. The distancing of employer and employee caused increased problems of alcoholism, absenteeism, and insubordination. According to Johnson, business owners called Finney to Rochester in order to regulate the membership of their own class and to ensure the subordination of laborers to the ruling elite entrepreneurs. For merchants, "their livelihood hinged not only on cunning and business acumen, but a reputation for honesty and reliability, and a conformity to the cultural and behavioral norms of rural western New York. Among such men, ungoverned ambition was a fatal liability."[4]

According to Johnson, Finney's incessant prayer meetings, magnetic preaching, and methodical measures served to tame the autonomous working-class social life and to keep it subject to the older lines of authority. Such an economic interpretation of Finney's evangelism at first glance appears highly incompatible with giving God all the glory. But one must remember that God's glory does not preclude "[leading] the blind by a way they do not know" (Isa. 42:16) or working through their wills by motives they do not understand. Natural motives do not eliminate supernatural causes any more than secondary causes eliminate primary causes. God is the primary mover behind good deeds that are prompted by less than the purest of human desires. Just because a person is led to an object because of compensation, sublimation, fear, greed, or other unconscious motives, the actual finding of the object is not invalidated. Methodological reductionism is faulty when it invalidates beliefs or tenets of faith because there are underlying psychological impetuses.

Not only does sociology suffer from reductionism, but it proffers predictionism in ways that are untenable for spiritual endeavors. Trends regarding the sizes of suits that men have purchased at an elite men's store are helpful in ordering the new spring collections. But the number of odd sizes left when the fall collection is ordered indicates a certain degree of failure. If patterns of behavior do not live up to airtight prognostication in the kingdoms of this world, it is much more so in the kingdom of our Lord.

THE MYSTERY OF GRACE

Grace is that supernatural gift of God that allows all who will receive it to overcome the curse of sin with its many attending effects. It does not promise that everything will be all right in this life. It does promise to overcome the odds in ways that not only counter a fragmenting society, but also go beyond the best help that the social sciences can offer. This is evangelism's secret. People need something beyond the tenets of educational psychology and sociological analysis, and even our best welfare programs. Their needs are much deeper than those that can be met by the Ways and Means Committee of the U.S. Congress. People need to know that there is another world beyond this world, a transcendent world waiting to break in upon mundane affairs in the form of positive grace.

The church often loses sight of the truth that grace is marketed much differently than laundry detergent. This is the criticism of sociologist James Hunter in his book *American Evangelicalism: Conservative Religion and the Quandary of Modernity.* He describes trends of contamination caused by evangelicalism's use of mass marketing techniques. The message is tainted by the elimination of gospel stigma, superiority in benefits rather than the truth, depreciation of mystery, self-orientation, and denial of suffering. The cognitive style of rationalization, domestication, and cooperation cannot escape modernity having a pronounced influence on the worldview of American evangelicalism. The contemporary worldview is attenuating the supernatural while turning to means prescribed by marketing technique. Sovereignty and providential direction have been traded for rational authority and efficient administration. Hunter states, "To the pressures of cultural pluralism, Evangelical belief avoids the abandonment of its exclusiveness by becoming tempered and civilized."[5]

LEARNING ABOUT THE WORLD

In spite of the problems of reductionism, predictionism, and naturalism, those who are serious about evangelism must learn as much about the human situation as possible. Richard Perkins, who has explored the connection between Christianity and sociology, states that the "major rationale for Christians studying sociology centers on the hope that the more Christians know about how the cosmos operates . . . the more likely they will be able to influence, alter, or avoid its snares."[6] To simultaneously influence the world and avoid its snares is an almost impossible task, quite possibly the greatest tension that the evangelist faces. Hunter argues that accommodation is inevitable; cooperation necessitates compromise. Yet it is this very tension that Christians are to bear—solidarity with the world and separation from it. This was the end to which Christ prayed: "I do not ask Thee to take them out of the world, but to keep them from the evil one" (John 17:15).

THE GALLUP POLL ON THE UNCHURCHED

For almost the last half century George Gallup of the Princeton Religion Research Center has done sociological analysis of the church by polling the churched as well as unchurched.[7] He concludes that: women are more religious than men; Southerners are more religious than Northerners or Westerners; marrieds are more likely to be in church than singles; the uneducated are more religious than the educated; and blacks are more spiritually attuned than whites. There were a couple of changes over the ten years since Gallup had last conducted his religious quotient poll. There was an increase in those who said they believed Jesus Christ to be God or the Son of God (75 percent to 84 percent). Sixty-six percent of the people polled claimed to have made a commitment to Christ. Eighty-eight percent said that they prayed at least once a week and 71 percent reported to believe in life after death.

Overall, there is still a high degree of religious inclination in America, and that interest has risen over the last several years. What Peter Berger called a "rumor of angels"[8] has now become a fanning of wings that can be felt on the face of America's religious landscape. But the landscape has jagged edges and potholes that make evangelistic charting difficult. America's intensified pilgrimage is not without its confusion and contradiction. In spite of 66 percent of Americans being members of a church, 76 percent of the respondents believed that a person can be a good Christian without attending church. These people demonstrate the lack of relating everyday Christian lifestyle to the need for community and the spiritual provision of *koinonia.* Such attitudes reflect low institutional commitment and the increasing privatization of values characteristic of contemporary society.

Deinstitutionalization means that religion is increasingly relegated to private spheres and that less and less attention is given to the traditional symbols that have marked corporate identification. The prediction made by John Naisbitt in *Megatrends* that institutions would carry decreasing authority has proven true and continues to wreak havoc on the mainline churches.[9] The pigeons of America's individualism have come home to roost in the rafters of the church, and the droppings are forcing the "worshipers" out into the great outdoors to do their own thing. For many, reciting a mantra around a campfire on Sunday morning is as sacred as meeting with the *ecclesia* at a specific time and place. Unless the church begins to give clear and precise teaching on corporate sanctification, *koinonia* will continue to disintegrate into more individualistic enterprises.

Another irony and somewhat unsettling discovery in Gallup's poll is that while two-thirds declared that they had made a commitment to Christ, only one-third claimed to have ever had "a religious insight or awakening." One might ask if the word "commitment" has lost the life and meaning that it once carried. Or possibly the respondents overly associated experience with ecstatic behavior claimed by some charismatics, or trancelike characteristics found in Eastern mystery religions. More than likely, the disjuncture between commitment and experience is due to the view of religious conversion as only cognitive assent, without an encompassing emotional upheaval. Becoming new creatures in

Christ Jesus has been traded for a rationalistic acceptance of a domesticated God who has our best interests in mind. The transcendent God whose ways are not our ways and who brings radical transformation to human lives has somehow vanished. James Hunter states, "Insofar as the image of God has become redefined in this way, God has become domesticated in the consciousness of Evangelicals. His image is less capable of stirring the thoughts and emotions."[10]

In spite of the above contradiction, there were some encouraging trends with important evangelistic implications. Over three-fourths of those polled held the Bible in high esteem. Belief in its authority was substantiated by confidence that it is the inspired Word of God. Fourteen percent of the unchurched indicated that they would be willing to attend a Bible study sponsored by a church or synagogue. Eighty-two percent had received religious training as a child, and 86 percent expressed desire for their own children to be involved in religious instruction. Of all programs that the church conducts, the unchurched demonstrated the greatest interest in summer activities for children and youth. The overall picture: churches that expect to reach twenty-first-century families ought to create quality programs and facilities for children and youth.

Single parents face the greatest obstacles, such as lack of time, energy, and money, in providing religious education for their children. The church that is serious about evangelizing society needs to institute a total program designed for the ever increasing fragmentation of families. Loving and helping hands need to reach out to working, single parents with children. Many mothers and fathers have no decent place to leave their children while at work, and school-age children have no suitable place to go after school. Care will have to be provided beyond the traditional Sunday School approach. It could be that Americans will increasingly feel that they need the church on Sunday less than any other time.

We live in a highly transient society—on average, people change residences once every five years. One of the chief reasons indicated by those in their twenties for not going to church was that they moved to a new community and simply failed to find a new church. Thirty-one percent of college graduates gave relocation as the key reason for church truancy. Denominations will need to pay much closer attention to the uprootedness of their own members, and individual churches will need to pay much closer attention to the new residents in their community. On an encouraging note, 58 percent of the unchurched indicated that there was a possibility that they would sometime again become active in a church. Only 38 percent indicated that they had been invited to church at least once over the previous twelve months.[11]

SECULARISM

As I will later argue, there is a *spiritual* revival taking place in America. But increased attention to the supernatural does not mean that Americans have changed their naturalistic, rationalistic, and materialistic presuppositions about life. Secularism is a process that profanes life, because it ropes off less and less of it for sacred purposes. For many, the only entity left protected is the eleven o'clock hour on Sunday morning—and that itself may be a sacrifice to civil religion, social standing, or business advantage, even though traditional forms are maintained. Even those who maintain the facade of religion think sensately and scientifically rather than sacredly. The sacred has been marginalized to the point that "ignostics" are so ignorant of the Christian faith that George Hunter states, "Their assumptions, vocabularies, decision making and life style reflect no Christian agenda."[12]

Hunter lists several essential characteristics of secular people that need to be taken seriously if the church is going to be evangelistically effective in the present age. Secular people, unlike medieval people or even colonial Americans, are more concerned with life than they are death. Even though there is a general sense of guilt, contemporary persons seem to be plagued more by doubt. People are more in search of a controlling purpose than they are absolution. Secular persons see the church as irrelevant because of the reactionary stance that the church has often taken to science, civil rights, and the arts.

The church needs to know that secularism has infected society with a deep malaise of loneliness and alienation. There is a pervasive dysfunctionalism that results in a deep distrust of both institutions and individuals. The last resort for many secular people is to hide in an addiction to work, money, sex, and codependent relationships. Their attempt to control life results in millions of lives out of control. In Bruce Larson's words, "We all came out of dysfunctional families, just as those described in the Bible; Joseph who was adored, Jacob who was abhorred, or Joseph's brothers who were ignored."[13] Hunter gives specific suggestions as to how the message of the church can become relevant to a dysfunctional people awash in a sea of secularism.

ETHNICITY

America has always been a land of immigrants. At the turn of the century they were essentially European, arriving through one gate: Ellis Island in New York City. Thousands arrived every day, found menial jobs, blended into society, and virtually severed all communication with their native land by the second generation. The goal was to become as American as possible in as short a time as possible. Most of them were already highly religious when they arrived, affiliating with a Protestant, Orthodox, or Catholic church, or Jewish synagogue. This is not to say that they did not face many crucial problems such as language and poverty that tended to bar them from the religious mainstream. In Timothy Smith's words, "The social cultural changes which occurred among immigrant groups in America seem to have been more a consequence of their urbanization than the result of conflicts with the 'host' culture."[14]

Today, the host culture is not so friendly. America is no longer the land of plenty, but the land of fierce competition. Those who are already trying to get a bigger piece of the pie are no longer saying "give me your tired, your poor, your huddled masses" through a carefully managed gate on the Eastern shore. Immigrants are coming in through every conceivable crevice and are often perceived as a threat, especially in industrial jobs that have already been numerically attenuated by computers, robots, and foreign imports. Fifty thousand Asians from the Philippines alone arrive every year to the West Coast. *Time* reports, "In San Jose, bearers of the Vietnamese surname Nguyen outnumber the Joneses in the telephone directory 14 columns to 8."[15]

Even as they strike their claims to the American West, Asians are encountering problems: racism, the ambivalence of assimilation, the perils of prosperity, ethnic jealousies, and the sometimes dire inequalities of a laissez-faire society. Asians, in general, are still strangers in the Western paradise, and they are keenly aware of their status.[16]

Time predicts that whites will be outnumbered by nonwhites in the U.S. by the middle of the twenty-first century. Ethnic minorities already form 40 percent of the school population in New York City, and they are far more committed to their ethnic identity than they are to absorbing the cultural religion of Thanksgiving turkeys and Norman Rockwell paintings. The church has been ill-equipped to deal with a multiracial society. Seminaries train pastors to read Greek and Hebrew, but not to speak Cambodian. The 2 million Hispanics in Los Angeles and 700,000 Cubans in Miami are far more interested in jobs and survival than they are in Christian theology. Missiologist J.T. Seamands writes:

> It is a sad but true fact that few of our church members here in the homeland are prepared for this new confrontation and thus they are unable to seize the evangelistic opportunities all about them. Since many are not fully committed to Christ themselves, they have nothing to offer people of other faiths. Others know little or nothing of these other religions and don't know how to witness intelligently to Hindus, Moslems, Buddhists, etc.[17]

In an astute and challenging address to the National Convocation on Evangelizing Ethnic America held in Houston, Texas in May 1985, C. Peter Wagner reminded his audience that Americans are not a "melting pot," but, rather, they are a "stew pot." Ethnic diversity is here to stay. Wagner claims that minorities are now the majority in at least twenty-five major U.S. cities and that Anglos now form only about 30 percent of the U.S. culture. The rapidly increasing minorities are under-evangelized, especially in comparison to Anglos and blacks. Wagner estimates that only 10 percent of Los Angeles' 4 million Hispanics are practicing Catholics, and only 4 percent are practicing Protestants. If Los Angeles is a microcosm of the rest of the country, the following statistical analysis by Wagner should be startling to the church:

> For the past eight years I have been collecting and updating facts concerning the ethnic makeup of the Los Angeles area. Here are the known groups with the best estimate of population: Hispanics (4 million), blacks (972,000), Germans

> (450,000), Italians (350,000), Koreans (270,000), Armenians (225,000), Iranians (200,000), Japanese (175,000), Arabs (160,000), Yugoslavs (150,000, divided sharply between Serbians and Croatians), Chinese (150,000), Filipinos (150,000), Vietnamese (100,000), American Indians (95,000), Russians (90,000), Israelis (90,000), Dutch (75,000), Hungarians (60,000), Samoans (60,000), French (75,000), Thai (50,000), Greek (50,000), British (50,000), Asian Indian (30,000), Dutch Indonesian (30,000), Egyptian Copts (10,000), Romanian (10,000), Turks (5,000), and Gypsies (5,000). I fully expect information on other groups to surface as time goes by. One television station, KSCI, has programs in English, Spanish, Arabic, Farsi, Armenian, Vietnamese, Korean, Japanese, Cantonese, and Mandarin.[18]

Wagner commends certain groups that are effectively evangelizing ethnic minorities. Southern Baptists worship in eighty-seven languages in 4,600 language-culture congregations every Sunday and 35 to 40 percent of new Assemblies of God churches each year are ethnic. Non-Anglo churches are most effectively planted by ethnics who have a burden for the people of their own race. Examples are the multithousand-member congregation of Kwang Shi Kim in Norwalk, California, and a similar endeavor by Non Soo Kim on West 33rd Street in New York City. But the task cannot be left solely to the nationals, because often the Anglo congregations are the people with money and resources. Wagner calls for a mobilization of prayer and church planting, while being especially sensitive to ethnics when they first arrive in the U.S. Evangelism must be done in power and love and without paternalism. There will have to be particular attention paid to the problems of alienation, estrangement, job skills, poverty, and language barriers. Wagner states:

> We need to realize that not all ethnics are the same. Some are nuclear ethnics, and they require language churches. Some are fellow-traveler or marginal ethnics, and they need bilingual churches or English-speaking churches. A few are alienated ethnics, and they will be very happy in Anglo churches. If we are evangelizing ethnics, we must not major in telling them what we think they need, but rather, we must minister to them on their own terms.[19]

The Refugees Among Us, a provocative 1983 volume in the *Unreached People* series, challenged the church to locate, evaluate, and become engaged with immigrants. Urban missions expert Raymond Bakke calculates that during the 1970s, 8.8 million people immigrated to America—a number equal to the immigration of the century's first decade. Bakke recommends Christians volunteering for immigration social work, providing refugee worship space in already existing churches, and providing support services for internationals who settle in low-cost housing areas. He provides an extensive bibliography that will help Christians better understand how to evangelize ethnics.[20] Another article titled "Finding Ministry through Families," by James A. Edgren, provides case histories about American families who have adopted refugee families and churches who have multiplied their ministries to newly arrived ethnics. (More information can be obtained from the Advanced Research and Communication Center [founded and headed by Edward R. Dayton], located at 919 West Huntington Drive, Monrovia, CA 91016.)

Evangelism scholars have devoted much of their time and energy to bridging ethnic boundaries. One such scholar is missiologist Ralph Winter, who approaches evangelism with global sensitivity. He delineates the evangelistic enterprise by the following strata: E-1 evangelism is not having to cross a cultural barrier in order to share the gospel with someone else. If an Anglo witnesses to a Hispanic who speaks broken English, the Anglo will be practicing E-2 evangelism. E-3 evangelism would consist of the Anglo going to Mexico and preaching the gospel through an interpreter to persons who can speak only Spanish. Ralph Winter argues that E-2 and E-3 witnessing, which he terms cross-cultural evangelism, are critical to the success of the evangelism enterprise. According to Winter:

> In summary, the master pattern of the expansion of the Christian movement is first for special E-2 and E-3 efforts to cross cultural barriers into new communities and to establish strong, on-going, vigorously evangelizing local churches and denominations, and then for that new "national" church to carry the work forward on the really high-powered E-1 level.[21]

URBAN MINISTRY

The single greatest evangelistic need in the United States today is for the church to take E-2 evangelism to the urban areas of our nation. Fifty percent of the world's population lives in cities. In light of this fact, Roger Greenway states, "The urban poor constitute the largest unclaimed frontier Christian missions has ever encountered."[22] John Naisbitt notes, "In the United States for the first time in 200 years, more people are moving to rural areas than urban—many more."[23] If that is true, the problem for evangelizing the inner city is even more acute because the well-to-do are moving out of both the urban and suburban areas, leaving the not-so-well-to-do to fend for themselves. As the inner core of the city expands, the church moves farther out and thus neglects the mission field on its front doorstep. As Thomas Oden explains, there is a law of nearness that is often neglected by today's church. Historically speaking, Oden argues, "Rather than plan vast programs for persons at great distances away, the essential energy of Christian care has been the parish itself where some live in need, others in relative abundance."[24]

Today, the "yuppies" who move back to the heart of the city are often more interested in investing in mammon rather than salvation enterprises. Ministerial candidates learn very little about how to minister to the homeless, prostitutes, runaways, and illiterate families on welfare. Young ministers with four years of college, and for some three years of advanced professional training, often owing thousands in guaranteed student loans, hardly feel enticed to move their families to areas where the pay is low and the stench is high. Such a ministry demands patient seed sowing with little immediate return. Success will have to be measured on different terms than are normally sought by those attempting to make their mark in the ecclesiastical world. The goals that many ministers have are often incompatible with inner-city work. Present-day theological education needs to be carefully reconsidered in the light of faithfulness to God's call. Roger Greenway indicts current seminary curriculums with the following:

> Most of America's evangelical schools are located in suburbs and small towns. Many have intentionally relocated

> their campuses away from ethnic neighborhoods and urban congestion. Is it any wonder, then, that the Bible is read and theology is discussed in ways that filter out the city with its pressing social issues, poverty, suffering, and maze of people? Does it surprise us that we find it difficult to address the city's problems from well-developed theological perspectives?[25]

Greenway, writing in *Cities: Missions New Frontier,* offers suggestions for training men and women to minister beyond white middle-class churches: a biblical theology for the inner city, regular chapel speakers and lecturers that are laboring in the inner city, faculty involvement in urban areas, fieldwork assignments to the inner city, required courses in urban ministry, and the establishment of seminaries in urban areas (or at least classes by extension).

The suburban church will have to be willing to expend money in the inner city in ways that will not bring immediate growth in membership or financial return. Downtown missions will have to be established and largely facilitated by volunteer personnel; day care centers will need to be funded for single parents who can afford to pay very little; English classes will need to be offered for newly arrived immigrants; financial assistance and volunteer help has to be given by suburban Christians to already existing inner-city ethnic churches.

Denominations will need to take a careful look at which churches and groups are the most successful in converting the urban dwellers to Christ. Sects that stress the experiential dimension of the Christian faith as well as the cognitive seem to be more appealing. The Assemblies of God, which emphasizes speaking in tongues, laying on of hands, public prophecy, and the immediacy of vision and dreams, are making inroads as fast as anyone. Margaret Poloma and Brian Pendleton argue for a direct correlation between a higher experiential and personal faith and a high incidence of evangelistic contact. They conclude, "Evangelism, essentially an act of 'selling' a person's religious beliefs and church is undoubtedly facilitated by satisfaction with the product, by a structure that supports this salesmanship, and by a personality that is effervescent and outgoing."[26]

MAINLINE RELIGION'S LOSS OF EVANGELISTIC URGENCY

The reasons above as to why sectarian movements prosper are the very reasons why the mainline churches have lost their evangelistic fervor. The clear ideologies of the founding fathers were eroded by pluralistic liberalism. Historical denominations such as Methodism, Presbyterianism, and Episcopalianism could no longer offer definitive value choices and coherent worldviews to religious consumers. The synthesis of religion and cultural faith was eroded in the sixties and seventies by events that shook faith in the utilitarian God who had brought post-World War II prosperity: Vietnam, civil rights, and Watergate. With the ensuing battles over abortion, family rights, and public education, the pluralistic mainline has tried to be everything to everyone. But some have felt that they were nothing to anyone. Smaller denominations took more definitive, vocal stands and offered more absolutistic worldviews and thus appeared to be more viable alternatives for millions of Americans looking for answers in a culture becoming increasingly complex. Wade Roof and William McKinney state, "Overall, the evidence seems irrefutable: the liberal branches of Protestantism are shrinking both as a proportion of Protestantism and of the general public."[27]

Dean Kelly argued in 1974 that conservative churches were growing because they could "explain life in ultimate terms to their members so that it makes sense."[28] Ultimate terms and absolutistic values are able to evoke energy and time from members in ways that liberal denominations cannot. A pastor who teaches clear biblical imperatives concerning the importance of saving the lost from eternal damnation is much more likely to enlist a lay member to give Saturday and Sunday to a bus route that transports unchurched children. Kelly writes that any organization that can enlist virtually all the time and energy of its members—even though they be few in number and limited in ability in a single-minded, meaning-motivated venture, has harnessed an engine that is in a category of magnitude as much beyond our ordinary vehicles of collective effort as the jet plane is beyond the horse-drawn carriage.[29]

Leonard Sweet argued the same essential thesis as did Kelly.

Denominations that are going to be evangelistic must offer definitive sources of authority. The identity crises of Vietnam vets, question-all-authority hippies, and discovering-our-place minorities were compounded by the identity crisis of the church. In order for identity formation to be secured, there must be the discovery of coherence, commitment, and continuity. Conversion loses its spiritual dimension, and probably will not take place at all, unless it is founded on this three-legged pedestal. The evangelism of liberation was emaciated because tradition was replaced with an endless string of "hows and fads." "For the first time in America's history, its people were without a sense of the transcendent, certain demonstrable truths that gave purpose to the nation's history as well as shared meaning and confidence to its citizens."[30]

THE GROWTH OF EVANGELICALISM

Thus, in the late seventies and eighties, the old-time religion became the new-time religion. Baby boomers had now matured sufficiently to have children and see the need for stabilizing influences that would ward off the evil influences of drugs, alcohol, and adolescent anarchy. Americans began to search for a religion that would remind them of a friendlier, more unified society. Conservatives came out of the closets, becoming active in electronic evangelism and right-wing politics. These efforts were largely without denominational trappings; "community" churches benefited the most from evangelicalism's increased visibility. Baby boomers no longer went back to the churches that their ancestors had attended for several generations. Rather, they were enticed by independent movements or upstart denominations that offered practical answers to life's problems.

But the continued expansion of conservative religious opportunities was not without its problems. Evangelism was somewhat cut off from historical orthodoxy. The churches' creeds were bypassed in favor of interpreting biblical passages either in light of the problems of the day or in the framework of imported, nineteenth-century theologies such as dispensationalism. People who had watched "nuclear test explosions, civil rights demonstrations, the assassination of a president, and other popular leaders, the sexual revolution, the Vietnam War—all in the 'security' of their own living rooms"[31] needed a God who would love them and help them to achieve the meaning and values of a middle-class society. But much of evangelism does not take into account that these American values may not be the values of a transcendent, holy God as revealed in the Bible and interpreted by the seven councils of the church. Benefits replaced truth claims and self-discovery preempted Christ-discovery (at least the Christ who had been crucified and asks His followers to submit to the same). In Sweet's words, both liberals and conservatives were prone to miss "the answer to the question that substantively engages issues of authority and identity: Why should I become a Christian? Because it is true."[32]

Consumer-oriented evangelism continues to be a threat to the faith handed down by the Christian tradition. God has become a lapel button and bumper sticker advocating that a good time was had by all. Civility and domestication have replaced God's sovereignty and transcendence. Humanity playing by God's rules is religion at its best, but God playing by humanity's rules is religion at its worst. If one listens closely enough at the choral introits of some worship services, the popular but modified Burger King jingle might be heard: "Hold the wrath, hold the justice, special orders don't upset us; we serve it your way!" The disestablished church of mainline Protestantism is gradually being replaced by a popular evangelical church that is very much a part of the middle-class establishment. The following parody by Jack Cashill is both amusing and tragic:

> My strategy is to consolidate the various name brands, even the strong flagship brands like Southern Baptist into one identifiable, Exxon-like entity. The target audience here is Mom, Dad, Butch and Sis—solid suburban Americans who want a little God in their life and a place to go before brunch. And after test-marketing various possibilities, I have decided upon the name Middle American Christian Church, or MacChurch for ad purposes. I will not be sure of MacChurch's theology until focus groups are run, but I plan on following the promotional path blazed so successfully by Holiday Inn. In other words, this will be your "no surprises" church. When Dad brings the family here, he can be sure that they will not be asked to speak in tongues, handle snakes, or give money to the Sandinistas.[33]

SIGNIFICANT SOCIOLOGICAL SHIFTS

Secular to Spiritual

The materialistic greed of the eighties created the spiritual hunger of the nineties. The old-fashioned glutton has taken all the vacations, driven all the BMWs, and experienced all the sights and sounds that the human psyche can absorb. The failure of major security firms on Wall Street, the Savings and Loan disaster, the Housing and Urban Development debacle, and the increasing national debt has begun to unsettle those who are willing to admit that there is a reckoning day for the sins of avarice. People will always be materialistic, but there is a limit to how many skiers a yacht can pull and how many yachts a person can own. All of the Donald Trumps sooner or later get "out-trumped" by either Father Time or their megalust.

With the fading of materialism, there is the increasing attention given to self-improvement and life extension. A recent 850-page tome titled *Life Extension: A Practical Scientific Approach* sold 1 million copies by offering corporate up-and-comers a biochemical guide that ensures longevity if readers take megadoses of vitamins, nutrients, and exercise. Increased leisure time not only means an accent on the physical, but a search for the metaphysical. According to the National Opinion Research Council of the University of Chicago, a full two-thirds of Americans say they have had an ESP experience, and 42 percent say they have had contact with the dead.[34] The religious picture will become more complex with the importation of Eastern mystery religions and the continual spreading of new cults.

New Age religion is the case in point for the increasingly amorphous religious picture and the continual confusion between the subjective and objective elements of theology. There are an ever increasing number of New Age books, some 400 members of the New Age Publishing and Retailing Alliance, and around 4,000 New Age bookstores across the country. The *New Age Journal* increased its circulation from 50,000 in 1983 to 165,000 in 1989. The magazine claims to chronicle "the way thousands are trying to create a more harmonious world by seeking spiritual fulfillment, by demanding the best of themselves and others, by using their talents to help others, by looking for new ways to improve and protect their health, and by developing more satisfying relationships at home and at work."[35]

Evangelicalism will be simply another option on the religious smorgasbord of numerous spiritual entrées. Terry Muck points to the rise in the number of Muslims, Hindus, and Buddhists in the United States.[36] If Christianity is to be more than an optional dessert, its adherents will have to be aggressive and convinced that Christ is the only way. Pastors and teachers will need to effectively explain biblical doctrine and see that their laypeople are versed in apologetics. The church, with all of its fascination with psychology, will need to once again realize that it should offer a radically different means for self-discovery (i.e., self-crucifixion). It must give careful attention to the sociological critique of Robert Bellah and his associates: "We believe that much of the thinking about the self of educated Americans, thinking that has become almost hegemonic in our universities, and much of the middle class, is based on inadequate social science, impoverished philosophy and vacuous theology."[37]

Relative to the Absolute

Could it be that the philosophy of relativism that has dominated this century because of John Stuart Mill's pragmatism, B.F. Skinner's behavioralism, and Joseph Fletcher's situational ethics has played itself out? Could it be that Americans will look for more permanent handles to grip and will be less satisfied with Rogerian inner direction to discover life's meaning? There may be evidence that Americans are regaining a renewed sense of right and wrong. A February 1995 issue of *Newsweek* stated, "But just when change seems dead as Cotton Mather, red faces have begun to shove themselves back into our late twentieth century consciousness."[38]

During the 1950s, an Oxford literature professor delivered a series of radio messages over the BBC in London. He argued in terms that could be understood on the most elementary levels that there are universal standards of right and wrong. These universal standards are accountable to an absolute standard that is found in God and revealed in Jesus Christ. If this is not so, we have no reason to expect certain kinds of behavior from our fellow human beings. C.S. Lewis has become increasingly popular not only among Christian readers, but also with secular society, especially through his *Chronicles of Narnia,* which include *The Lion, the Witch, and the Wardrobe.*

Robert Bellah's best-selling *Habits of the Heart* explains that contemporary psychology does not offer an autonomous standard of good and evil that survives outside the needs of individual psyches for growth. Bellah warns the church concerning the fragility of community based on an orientation toward needs rather than more absolutistic categories of sin and redemption. American religion is divided between two great poles—radically individualistic religion that serves a cosmic selfhood and conservative religion that serves a God who confronts man from outside the universe.[39] The result is that Christian communities suffer from either "a therapeutic thinning out of belief and practice (or) a withdrawal into the narrow boundaries of the religious community itself or both."[40] Without becoming exclusivistic, the church needs to hear Scripture and become a community that sets standards, adopts values, captures consciences, and becomes authoritative in the life of human beings. While Bellah in no way argues for a homogenization of society and an abandonment of the constitutional pluralism of the First Amendment, he does advocate "bringing the concerns of biblical religion into the common discussion about the nature and future of our society."[41] The American obsession with fulfilling individual tastes will have to be curbed in honor of commitment to communities that hold to authoritative standards.

Allan Bloom was equally explicit about the ability of religion to provide absolute norms for both moral behavior and intellectual endeavor. In his view, the closing of the American mind has resulted from the most distinguishing intellectual fact of our society: "Almost every student entering the university believes, or says he believes, that truth is relative."[42] This presupposition has led to confusion about not only what a liberal education should be, but also about how we should conduct ourselves in the practical areas of life. Bloom condemns the intellectual banality of rock music and its antinomianism that advocates free sexual expression, anarchism, and mining of the irrational unconscious.[43] The family has also suffered from America's adopted relativism, as high divorce rates and continued fragmentation attest. Solving the divorce problem, which Bloom calls America's most urgent social problem, "is equivalent to squaring the circle, because everyone loves himself most but wants others to love him more than they love themselves."[44]

The divorce index indicates the unwillingness of Americans to sacrifice individual desires for the common good. If secular sociology continues to call attention to this problem, it may be the prophet that the church so desperately needs. Evangelism begins with getting one's own act together, and marriage failure is currently the single greatest travesty in the church. The mutual intimacy of two persons committed to one another provides the ideal testing ground for implementing Christian personhood. The wedding ceremony continues to remain, even for many non-Christians, a uniquely Christian event. The failure of its symbolism to carry through to reality is a betrayal of biblical truth at its most basic level. The possibility for marriage to work in the face of secular bombardment and commercial hedonism is one of the greatest witnesses that the church can give. The world has the right to ask, "If Christianity cannot make marriage work, what can it do?" If a husband's love for a wife is the most visible symbol of Christ's love for the church that Christians have to offer, it becomes the quintessential witness of the church to the world.

One of the first evangelistic tasks that the church has to face is the recovery of biblical family values. Groups like James Dobson's Focus on the Family and Bill Gothard's Institute in Basic Youth Conflicts continue to be important evangelistic tools. Dobson is now heard weekly on 450 radio stations, receives 200,000 letters each month, 1,200 phone calls per day, ships out 52 million pieces of literature and 1 million cassettes annually and employs a staff of 700 people on an annual budget of 60 million dollars.[45] There is an increasing number of groups picking up the battle cry over the last decade: Coalition for Better Television, Christian Family Renewal, United Families of America, and many publications pleading for better families.

The church's rediscovery that there is both evil and good will lead to a recommitment to convert people from one to the other. The acceptance of "I'm OK, you're OK" and "Live and let live" as life philosophies has quenched evangelistic fire. Evangelists need to do battle with evil without projecting evil and without becoming overly enamored or contaminated with it. The church must evaluate society and its individuals in the light of Christian principles without condemning the present cosmos. When evil is found,

Christians will absorb that evil through the love of Christ and, in turn, will overcome it. Responding in kind will allow evil to triumph, which is why Paul wrote, "Do not be overcome by evil, but overcome evil with good" (Rom. 12:21). Scott Peck writes:

> I do not know how this occurs. But I know that it does. I know that good people can deliberately allow themselves to be pierced by the evil of others—to be broken thereby yet somehow not broken—to ever be killed in some sense and yet still survive and not succumb. Whenever this happens, there is a slight shift in the balance of power in the world.[46]

From East to West

Americans are not finished with the exhortation "Go West, young man." However, at the beginning of the third millennium there is a unique twist. History has come full circle (i.e., has circled the globe). Going west is now going east—to the Far East. Some of the hottest economies in the world are in Japan, Taiwan, and Korea. The breakdown of communism in Asia and the opening up of China will continue to increase trade between the U.S. and the Oriental world. This will economically benefit all of America, but especially the West Coast.

The Pacific Rim states (California, Oregon, and Washington) will be three of the fastest growing states in the U.S. heading into the twenty-first century. West Coast cities provide the closest ports of call for Asian markets. The natural resources of Washington and Oregon, coupled with fast-growing technology, will continue to provide jobs almost as fast as they can be filled by those from other states. The shipping of airplane parts, preassembled log homes, and many other exports will bring economic boom. At the present time more than 300,000 Americans work for Japanese companies; 100,000 Japanese work for American ventures in Japan. These disproportions will continue to grow as the Japanese run out of people and space—and the Western states will become the chief beneficiaries.

California will continue to be America's fastest-growing state, with an estimated population of 33 million by the year 2000. By then Los Angeles will be the largest city in the U.S. Immigrants from Asia will continue to fill the Los Angeles basin, an area that already boasts the greatest concentration of mathematicians, scientists, engineers, and skilled technicians in the country. The population centers around and within the Silicon Valley; San Francisco, Oakland, and San Jose (already near 6 million in population) will continue to grow at alarming rates. The margins of discomfort caused by traffic, pollution, and out-of-sight prices for real estate will keep a steady flow of people moving into Oregon, Washington, Idaho, and Nevada.

Portland, Oregon will continue to become the second Silicon Valley, and its population will increase by 50 percent over the next twenty years. Seattle is already the nation's fourth largest apparel market, and Boeing has multibillion dollar contracts with both domestic firms and foreign countries that will keep the company busy for the next quarter of a century. In 1992 Seattle was voted the urban area most conducive to the entrance of new corporations out of all urban areas in America. At the present time, Portland and Seattle are two of the hottest housing markets in America, with real estate prices that are quickly escalating. Technology will continue to become more complex, and the West Coast inhabitants will place a higher premium on education and specialized training than any other location in the U.S.

There are a host of churches demonstrating evangelistic effectiveness on the West Coast: John Wimber's Vineyard Fellowship, Jack Hayford's Church on the Way, Chuck Smith's Calvary Chapel, Ron Mehl's Beaverton Foursquare, and Dale Galloway's New Hope. All of these men are capable pulpit communicators and interpret evangelism in the light of their personalities and biblical convictions. They have capitalized on the high-tech/high-touch society that Naisbitt defined and predicted a decade ago. The more depersonalization that takes place because of automation and computerized information processing, the more that people look for the highly personal touch in other areas, especially religion. Churches, in order to be evangelistic, will have to offer the loving care and horizontal fellowship that is missing at the workplace. They will have to offer the values that the scientific world divorces from its agenda. Clear, contemporary, biblical preaching followed up by warm, personal concern is the mandate for the West Coast.

Young to Old

Experts predict that by the year 2000 there will be 35 million people in the United States sixty-five years or older. By the year 2050, this number will grow to 67 million. In the next sixty years, the percentage of our population that is eighty-five and older will rise from .5 percent to 5.2 percent. Americans are living longer and are more healthy in the later years than ever before. Even though the elderly have more stamina, many are retiring earlier. Rarely does a person work beyond sixty-five and, quite often, individuals opt for "early retirement," which puts them out of the workforce while they are still in their fifties. It remains to be seen whether the great American experiment of Social Security will last, but at the present it seems here to stay.

Retirement is usually eagerly anticipated, but when it arrives it often brings despair, depression, and even anomie. It will be more and more common for people to face a quarter of a century of retirement. But what to do with those years can be a painfully difficult choice. Enthusiastic Christians who have worked within a purposeful life design need to perceive retirement as the opportunity to redirect energy into a more full-time Christian ministry. The couple who serves in the "food pantry" ministry in the local church and the individual who turns the golden years into a series of short-term missionary appointments are prime examples. However, such meaningful existence is not the lot for millions of Americans. Many come to despise the compulsory unemployment and discover, as did one retiree, "the difference between not having to do anything and not having anything to do."

This trend has two critical applications for evangelism. First of all, the "elderly" will need to be mobilized for the great task of sharing the Good News. All of us need to understand that there is no such thing as Social Security in the kingdom of God. The idea of spiritual retirement needs to be countered by biblical types who found meaningful existence in the late stages of life: Noah, Sarah, Abraham, and Moses. Everyone has something to contribute other than simply filling three feet of real estate on a church pew. More time and money than ever before translates into volunteer help in the inner-city mission, being a member of the greeter team in the church foyer, and delivering friendship baskets to church newcomers. Carl Bostrom has written:

> Retirement is not a one-time irrevocable and irreversible set-

> in-concrete decision and action, after which a variety of options are ruled out. It is a decision/action, often which may well need continuous re-examination based upon changing circumstances, and new perception of one's role in the light of one's personal goals and objectives. Retirement may well mean extraordinary new possibilities and undreamed of potentials as doors continue to open and health and income factors make other and preferable options available.[47]

Extraordinary new possibilities include reaching the elderly by the elderly. For every parachurch organized to evangelize the elderly, there are ten that cater to adolescents. But it is now being demonstrated that a sexagenarian faces an identity crisis as traumatic as the teenage years. T.R. Cole has stated that it has been observed that the enormous gains in longevity through medical and technological progress have been accompanied "by widespread spiritual malaise . . . and confusion over the meaning and purpose of life—particularly in old age."[48] Such need activation is fertile ground for the message that there is a place for everyone in the kingdom of God. Is there a greater place in the kingdom of God than to be actively involved in perservering intercessory prayer for the lost? Could this be God's special call to the elderly?

Old age enters a paradigm of loss marked by decreased physical abilities, leaving home and neighborhood, and depreciated status and prestige. Many new decisions concerning lifestyle, residence, occupation, and transportation have to be made. Transition is a key time to reach people with a message of security, especially when the greatest transition of life—death—seems so imminent. A person who has filled an important place both at work and at home is suddenly prone to ask life's most existential question: "Who needs me?" The church needs to be the first to answer, "God needs you and has just the place for you to fill."

In the midst of disequilibrium, God can offer adaptability and hope in the face of a society that wants to shelve and forget the elderly. An eschatology for the elderly includes actualization of present worth as well as the vision for a better world where there will be no more death or tears. In James Field's words, the most helpful ministry that we have to offer the elderly is an increased understanding of the redemptive love of Christ, which engenders "a vital faith in the living God, a faith which will bring them into immediate contact with the only one who can help them navigate all the treacherous seas of life with its inevitable losses and pressures to abandon all hope."[49]

Second to Third Millennium

Baby boomers will cross the most significant time line of the last 1,000 years. Those who believe that history has been broken up into seven one-thousand-year periods (i.e., that the creation week is a microcosm of the historical macrocosm) will deem the entrance of the third millennium as the chronological event of the ages. Evangelism over the next twenty years will be increasingly couched in eschatological terms. The years immediately before and after the year 2000 will mark the heyday of premillennialism—an emphasis on the sudden return of Christ and the ushering in of the kingdom of God on earth.

Timothy Weber has traced the rise of premillennialism in the American religious consciousness over the last one hundred years. There is a growing interest among evangelicals in the future, which is not entirely unrelated to the present fascination with astrology, the occult, and New Age religion. Hal Lindsey's *The Late Great Planet Earth* has sold close to 20 million copies, many of them in drugstores and supermarkets "right along side of gothic romances, cheap westerns, and books on the latest fads: dieting, organic gardening, the personal lives and loves of Hollywood celebrities, and UFO's."[50] Indeed, the apocalyptic literature of the Bible is novel, and it is difficult to protect an honest search for truth from being tainted by sensationalism and idle curiosity. Much of prophetical teaching ironically falls victim to a biblical prophecy: "For the time will come when they will not endure sound doctrine; but wanting to have their ears tickled, they will accumulate for themselves teachers in accordance to their own desires" (2 Tim. 4:3).

A recent publication predicted that Jesus would return in September of 1989. There were churches that doubled their attendance on the Sunday that preceded the day for the predicted rapture. Any Christian who is a serious thinker would tend to question the depth of commitment gained by evangelistic appeals motivated by emergency rapture preparation. Nonetheless, some claimed conversion, which probably demonstrates that well-intentioned prediction gone amiss can somehow bring good ends. But Christians will have to maintain a cautious stance without being overly skeptical or cynical regarding the proliferation of apocalyptic teaching. There will have to be a delicate balance between discovering the signs of the times and Jesus' reminder that "The kingdom of God is not coming with signs to be observed" (Luke 17:20).

Doomsdayers will abound—with persuasive arguments and plausible evidence. The ecological problems of population explosion, accumulating waste, a disappearing ozone layer, and acid rain seem to indicate the beginning of the end of life as we know it. Of the six hottest recorded years that planet Earth has endured, all six have been in the 1980s. With the breakdown of communism and the reunification of the European Common Market, Revelation has already been reinterpreted to support new conspiracy theories and Antichrist interpretations.

Evangelistic preaching will be packaged in the jeremiads that marked the Puritan covenant sermons and national day admonitions that were so popular at the turns of previous centuries. Both secular and religious sources will increasingly argue that America is in a state of decline and has already lost its political and moral clout through a selfish philosophy of materialistic extravagance. Our government spends 200 billion dollars per year more than it collects, and Americans more than tripled their outstanding balance on credit cards during the 1980s to 175 billion dollars. What has seemed like economic boom has really been the facade of economic bust. Judgment day predictions will picture an emaciated America crippled by AIDS and a staggering debt engendered by an international marriage to the whore of Babylon, the ultimate symbol of lust and greed.

The world will change so rapidly in the next twenty years that for many it will seem a violent rush toward a cataclysmic end. It will not be difficult to interpret evangelism as escapism. Survivalist literature will abound, as exemplified by Jim McKeever's 1978 *Christians Will Go through the Tribulation: And How to Prepare for It*. Timothy Weber calls McKeever's book "a veritable handbook for physical and spiritual survival." "McKeever tells readers how to build bomb shelters, store food and water, manage without access to public utilities, water or sewer service, and get in touch with various 'survivalist' organizations."[51] Most evangelism will not be snared by such extremist measures; yet it will be hard-pressed to give biblical interpretation to a world seemingly spinning out of control.

Robert Ornstein and Paul Ehrlich argue that our world has changed in more critical ways since World War II than it changed between the birth of Christ and that War.[52] Few would argue with that assessment. Neither would they disagree with Albert Einstein's telegram sent to President Roosevelt on May 23, 1946: "The unleashed power of the atom has changed everything save our modes of thinking, and thus we drift towards unparalleled catastrophe."[53] Evangelism will increasingly carry an apocalyptic vision. It remains to be seen whether third millennium evangelism will produce a strident militant minority or a wimpish apathetic majority.

More to Less

The close of World War II unleashed an explosion of material goods in the U.S. that surpassed any previous production by a single nation: houses, automobiles, electrical appliances, apparel, and endless commodities. The ignorance of doing without could no longer be bliss because TV and radio now reminded people of needs they didn't even know they had. There was an upward spiral of consumerism that only the most negative gainsayer would foresee as a collapsed slinky worn out by false expectations and a lack of economic foresight. The postwar economic ascendancy reached its peak during the 1980s, and this apex marked the beginning of the turning of the American dream into a fleeting mirage.

Since the 1929 stock market collapse, Americans have used the terms recession and depression as if there were automatic laws built into the American economy that determined that for every valley, there will be a mountaintop of economic revival. But only the most naive would believe that capitalistic theory can continue to upright itself with little regard for the national debt, regular fiscal crises, and the hostile international trade market. In an electronic age, the U.S. now produces just 3 percent of the consumer electronic devices that its own people utilize. Reibstein states that "more Americans than ever are pessimistic about the future: they fear they will never live as well as their parents and worry that their children may have it even worse."[54] He goes on to argue that there has been an erosion of buying power, especially in the middle class. The economic pie has grown less rapidly than the number and appetites of Americans attempting to get their share.

Those who are experiencing the greatest financial pinch have been traditionally known as the middle class. In a meticulous study of economic trends during the 1980s, Donald Barlett and James Steele argue that those who are defined as middle class are shrinking, while at the same time shouldering a greater share of the tax burden. At the same time, the number of millionaires increased 985 percent from 1980 to 1989 and from 1986 to 1989 enjoyed a 53 percent tax cut.[55] Barlett and Steele paint a picture of tens of thousands of American workers losing their jobs through the greed of corporate takeovers and mismanagement: "In interviews across America, reporters heard constant refrain . . . over and over, blue collar and white collar workers, mid-level managers, middle class all—talked of businesses that once were, but are no more."[56]

Economic disillusionment will provide an impetus, at least for some, to search for more meaningful purposes. Economic welfare has been inextricably tied to the church, for better or for worse, throughout most of its history. In the medieval period, the church was part of the problem rather than the solution. A healthy evangelistic foray ought to be in the form of providing stewardship stability in shaky times. Think of Elisha, who restored to a laborer his lost axe head in 2 Kings 6, allowing the man to continue his livelihood. If financial woes are going to be a need felt more and more by the American populace, the church should be an active player in the creation, conservation, and consumption of resources. The church that is most evangelistically successful will be the body of believers who are committed to bringing a balm to the pinch of everyday existence. Present indicators point to a pinch that is more than just irritating—it will leave a deep bruise on American economic life, especially as it has been interpreted over the last half of the century.

From Consensus to Fragmentation

No one would argue that America is philosophically and theologically homogeneous. In his seminal work *A Christian America:*

Protestant Hopes and Historical Realities,[57] Robert Handy announced that the official funeral for the Protestant coalition took place at the Scopes trial in Dayton, Tennessee in 1925. Not only did a reactionary Protestantism embarrass itself as it attempted to deal with encroaching scientific theory in light of the First Amendment, but it also suffered a fission into repelling and mutually disdaining components (i.e., fundamentalism and modernism). The breach was created by the battering ram of a new scientific paradigm that established religion was ill-equipped to defend itself against, much less encompass within its own worldview. For the last seventy-five years, much of conservative religion has retreated to new structures rather than examining what went wrong in the old ones and dialoguing with its "enemies"—who are really its neighbors and here to stay.

These neighbors (information elitists, computer analysts, and various types of technocrats) are almost as likely to be Hindu, Buddhist, or Islamic in the third millennium as they are Christian. The ideology that "Jesus saves" will not only be unacceptable currency in the religious market, but will make the same kind of impression as the latest trite bumper sticker: "In case of the Rapture this car will be out of control." Such verbiage may increasingly become the inside language of a cultural antiquity—the language of people who are unable to effectively present their faith in an age of pluralism. To use George Hunter's metaphor, we have lost the home court advantage. Evangelical Christians need to realize that we no longer make the rules simply because we have been here since the days of George Whitefield. Evangelism can no longer assume a common language in a community that is an amalgam of the global village. As our already pluralistic society becomes ever more fragmented, evangelism will need to incorporate an apologetic model of evangelism that is not only crystal clear about its own truth claims, but is also aware of the basic tenets of other claims to truth.

Could it be that present evangelistic models only primarily reach those who already possess the basic worldview of the evangelist? If one examined the list of individuals converted through the use of "spiritual laws" or a mass crusade, would we discover that the evangelized were at least tangentially, if not forthrightly, already nurtured in the existing paradigm of the evangelist? An ever expanding pluralism means that an increasing number of people will live outside of the monotheistic Christocentric equation that "real" Christians have used to reach "nominal" Christians with the gospel. Thus, if evangelism does not make an extreme effort to widen its market base through loving dialogue and increased knowledge inventory, its evangelistic business will be markedly attenuated. It may be like the general store in a small town that never dusted off its shelves or paved its parking lot, and eventually succumbed to the invasion of Wal-Mart. Wal-Mart simply offers more options. American evangelicalism cannot assume that its product is on the front shelf or even on the shopping list. That assumption developed when Christianity was the culturally accepted (and sometimes only) option.

From Forward to Backward

"Invest in Cracker Barrel," a friend of mine tells me. It's probably good advice. For the past several years, the restaurant chain's stock has been splitting about every eighteen months. Cracker Barrel packages nostalgia—that down-home feeling of "y'all come on in." The restaurant decorates its huge front porch with rocking chairs and church pews. Before sitting down to a home-cooked meal of heavily seasoned green beans, mashed potatoes, and roast beef, one waits in the "general store" area, which is filled with jars and cans that look like they came straight off Grandma's shelf. The entire motif hearkens back to a simpler, quieter time.

Most people's lives are filled with a daily routine of automation, computerization, and impersonalization sandwiched between morning and evening rush hour traffic. Life looks toward the weekend, which offers escape from the hustle and bustle of the daily grind. Thus, the church is faced with the dilemma of how to move its operation into the age of technology and at the same time avoid the complexity that marks everyday existence. Many churches serve to complicate life, rather than to simplify its complexities. After attending a local church for a couple of years, a person may be serving as a member of the board, involved in a committee or two, playing on the church's athletic teams, and attending a myriad of church events, while also being expected to be at the church's several weekly services. If not completely burned out, he or she is likely to at least be frustrated because of a hectic lifestyle that has been unexpectedly imposed. Suddenly the person reevaluates:

"Why complicate my life when it is already complicated enough?"

Evangelistically effective churches are doing two things. They are simplifying their organization, while at the same time emphasizing the high touch that offsets a high-tech society. Though they may not actually place a rocker on the front porch, there is an attempt to offer retreat from the dehumanizing pace that characterizes American life. In *The User Friendly Church,* George Barna commends churches that stress people over programs. In these churches, a visitor is not overwhelmed with brochures, programs, and introductions on the first visit.[58] Instead of being singled out in the worship service as a newcomer (which can be embarrassing), the visitor is befriended by a family and taken home or to a restaurant for dinner. Being the church is defined by authentic hospitality. It is an attitude by the totality of the congregation that Christianity means highly personal service in an age that devalues personhood.

Doug Murren pastors the Eastside Four Square Church, located north of Seattle. The church averages over 4,000 people each weekend in its multiple worship services. The facility is high-tech—praise songs and typed announcements are flashed on a huge video screen, and music is to the beat of amplified guitar and synthesizers. Murren emphasizes a combination of electronic and personalized ministry designed to reach baby boomers. Sermons speak to the practical areas of life: "If they can't use it on Monday, don't say it on Sunday." Seminars take their cues from TV shows which emphasize relationships. The multiple worship services offer young families attendance options, which implicitly communicates, "We are here to serve, not to be served." Murren notes that baby boomers distrust authority and want to be treated as individuals. Though Eastside has approximately 1,400 members, membership is not pushed. The Four Square denomination is characterized by a loosely knit denominational system that deemphasizes ecclesiastical structure. The *Seattle Times* has reported that "the overriding comment from those who attend Eastside Church is that it is just plain friendly."[59]

Branson, Missouri may one day be the entertainment capital of the United States. Motels and theaters are springing up overnight as top-name entertainers relocate their base of operation. The Ozarks offer a respite from the urban blight and the suburban pressure of coping with life's oncoming blitzes. "The pace down here is just slower" is the oft-quoted refrain. Rather than seeing itself in constant competition with ever more recreational America, the church needs to begin to take some cues from Cracker Barrel and the southern hills of Missouri. Nobody is suggesting that we replace pews with rocking chairs; then again, no one should have to travel to hillbilly country to enjoy the "common touch" that dispels the complexities of life. There ought to be at least a little of that in every church.

CONCLUSION

Grace has never placed a premium on ignorance. Evangelism in the twenty-first century will seek to know as much about people as possible. A Christian sociological paradigm does not claim that evangelizing people is as simplistic and formalistic as selling soap powder. But it does contend that evangelism should be no less informed than McDonald's when it plants a new store or GM when it designs a new model. There is always the danger that dependence on social science may preempt dependence on the Holy Spirit. But there is no law of logic stating that an increased degree of one results in a lesser degree of the other. If Christ loved the world, then we at least need to learn it. Someone once said, "If we want to talk with God we had better find out something about the world because that is the only subject in which God is interested."

Evangelistic churches must not ignore secular voices when they charge that worship services are irrelevant and boring and that the institutional church is more interested in money than people. After listening to the critique, church leadership can cue relevancy through drama and music with a contemporary flavor. Every culture is idiomatic, and one must learn its idioms in order to speak its language. But appealing to the taste buds of the evangelistic market, while at the same time not allowing the triumph of popular culture, is one of evangelicalism's greatest dilemmas. Even performers of classical music and drama are bemoaning the death of the serious arts that demand years of training.

Many evangelists believe they have the answer, claiming that theological content can remain while form is changed. But if form can change while substance remains constant, one might just as well serve wine in Styrofoam cups rather than crystal at state dinners. Knowing just what the public wants still does not diminish what they must have: a two-thousand-year-old story about a man who was crucified and then rose from the dead. The vintage just doesn't suit the taste buds of many who are invited to partake. Even if we offer them accompanying music in agreeable rhythm and beat, the lyrics aren't all that soothing. The final verse is always about taking up a cross.

There is the continuing need to explore the interface between theology and the social sciences. Evangelism must seek to place psychometrics, demographics, statistical data, and the various research theories at its service. Such investigation should not be for the purpose of depreciating sovereign prevenient grace. With all of our sociological understanding, we are probably no closer to the whys of human meaning than those who lived in the days of Solomon, Plato, and Christ. Some seek religious meaning, while others do not. Understanding the demarcation is not an easy task. If imbibing from the social sciences can throw illumination on the decisive factors that move people toward God or perhaps serve to position people in the flow of God's redemptive purpose, it will be worth the effort. Effective evangelism in the twenty-first century will be fortified by information processing as never before. Even Paul could have used a good laptop computer to store some demographics on Ephesus or Colossae or to keep track of the many correspondents from his missionary journeys.

VII

contemporary american methodologies

Most evangelistic techniques are normally variations of broader methodologies. It will be the purpose of this chapter to explore and evaluate those outreach themes as they are practiced in today's church. Some churches will emphasize one or two of these methodologies at the exclusion of others. Others practice all of them. Everything that a church does in a user friendly manner serves to improve its evangelistic thrust. For example, if there are friendly ushers and greeters at the door, a visitor is more likely to return to that particular church. However, this chapter is about overall programs that have been formulated and defined with the expressed purpose of evangelism.

SMALL GROUPS

Psychological Underpinnings

The 1988 Gallup survey *The Unchurched* forecast that "small groups" will be the key evangelistic methodology of the nineties. The present proliferation of small group ministries within the church has not happened in a philosophical and cultural vacuum. Psychology has taught us the importance of verbally sharing with one another, making sense out of life through articulation, and healing through catharsis. Freud taught the law of psychoanalysis: there is meaning to whatever the mind produces, and listeners can assume associations that are coherent if they lend an ear again and again. Carl Rogers popularized this part of depth psychology for modern-day pastoral counselors by stressing the mind's inner drive to work out its own problems. What people need most is someone else to give gentle, nondirective guidance, and small groups provide this therapeutic counseling on a collective basis.

There has been a proliferation of small groups in the church, stimulated by pastoral writers emphasizing an interpersonal psychology of reciprocal participation.[1] Americans have continued to depend on small groups to address a wide range of dysfunctional problems—alcoholism to anorexia, overeaters to overachievers. *Newsweek* reported that, in a given week, 15 million Americans attend 500,000 support groups for their afflictions and addictions.

> All of a sudden, people are pouring back into churches and synagogues with a fervor that hasn't been seen since the 50's. It appears that a great religious revival is sweeping the land—until you examine the situation a little more closely. Then you'll notice the biggest crowds today often arrive in mid-week. And instead of filing into the pews, these people head for the basement where they immediately sit down and begin talking about their deepest secrets, darkest flaws and strongest cravings.[2]

The Pietistic Tradition

But small groups are not simply a psychological trend or an emergency procedure adopted by a church in the midst of a fragmenting society. The Pietistic branch of the Reformation, which called for audible reflection on inner religious experience, proliferated small groups throughout eighteenth-century Europe. Moravian communities such as Hernhut emphasized small groups as a means of confession, bolstering of religious assurance, and participation in the common life. It was through visiting Hernhut and also noting Peter Bohler's use of groups in the evangelism and nurturing of students that John Wesley envisioned religious societies broken into bands that would meet weekly. The members of the bands joined together for spiritual accountability through confession, praise, prayer, and sharing mutual concerns. Wesley remembered the encouragement and inspiration that the "Holy Club" had afforded him while a student at Oxford. The "methodism" with which he had been derisively dubbed by scoffing students served him well in preserving 70,000 converts through societies, classes, and bands. Wesley has served as a model to those who have been serious about evangelism and discipleship through small groups.

A New Testament Emphasis

The New Testament does not leave us in the dark concerning the importance of spiritual nurture through Christians being together. Togetherness and significant spiritual events are inextricably bound together. "They were all together in one place" (Acts 2:1). Paul reminds the Ephesian elders, "I did not shrink from declaring to you anything that was profitable, and teaching you publicly and from house to house" (Acts 20:20). The New Testament offers plenty of other examples of Christians being assimilated and nurtured in intimate contexts. The house ministry of the early church is reflective of many of the New Testament exhortations to minister to one another through comfort, confession, encouragement, prayer, edification, admonishment, and restoration. Early Christians were no doubt continuing in the model of Jesus, who organized the first small group (or was it John the Baptist?). Neal McBride states, "Jesus' ministry to large groups was preceded and proceeded out of this small group context. . . . Relationships, not organizations, were central in Jesus' method. . . . Jesus used the small group context to teach and model spiritual knowledge, attitudes and behavior."[3]

The Evangelistic Small Group

An evangelistic small group focuses on a specific goal. Its goal is to bring people who are outside of the Christian fold into a personal relationship with Christ. The group will serve as a point of encounter for the non-Christian who is actively searching for religious authenticity. If the encounter is to properly function, there must be certain operative rules. Theological and technical jargon must be eliminated.

The group leader will guard against controversy and contention, especially disagreement that arises from discussion of such nonessentials as ecclesiastical and denominational issues. The newcomer will be made to feel welcomed and appreciated. Those who are group insiders are to avoid airs of spiritual superiority and exclusiveness. All members of a group must remember that any newcomer will have a secondary agenda to work through before he or she can address the group's primary agenda: "Am I dressed all right? Will these people like someone who has the last name Salter? What's a nonchurch-going pagan like me doing in a place like this?" Only warm acceptance and affirmation by the group will dispel second-guessing and suspicion of the insiders by the invited. Joe Aldrich offers the following suggestions for creating a wholesome atmosphere in an evangelistic home Bible study:

> First the purpose of the study is evangelism. Second, the non-Christian must feel comfortable and welcome. Third, most of the discussion should involve non-Christians. As a general rule, the Christian should avoid active participation in discussion. Fourth, religious cliches should be avoided. Fifth, discussion of various churches and denominations should be avoided. Sixth, Christians should resist the temptation to "straighten out" doctrinal views of the participants which are not central to the issue of salvation. The issue is Jesus Christ, not infant baptism, total immersion, the inspiration of Scripture, pretribulationalism, or Post Toasties. Seventh, the Christian should refrain from bringing up all kinds of parallel passages. As a general rule the study should confine itself to one passage. Anyone can make significant observations on five or six verses. However, once the "resident experts" start spouting off other passages, the non-Christian realizes he is outgunned and out of place. Eighth, as a general rule, the Christian participants should avoid giving advice or sharing pious platitudes and spiritual band-aids. If they share, it should focus on their personal experience of the truth, not an untested list from some seminar or textbook. Ninth, the Christian must avoid the temptation to press for "holy huddle" syndrome. Some of your best friends may be there, but your mission is to reach out in love to the non-Christian. He must be made to feel special. He is![4]

Dale Galloway of New Hope Community Church in Portland, Oregon, boasts of over 2,000 Christians that meet in small groups each week. His book *20-20 Vision* predicates New Hope's small group outreach program on Acts 20:20.[5] Galloway has structured the entire organization of his church around a small group ministry. Paid staff members designated as district pastors have jurisdiction over a zip code suffix of the Portland metropolitan area. The district pastors give direction to volunteer lay pastors who are in charge of "Tender-Loving-Care (T.L.C.)" groups. The lay pastor is responsible for securing a home or other meeting place, building a prospect list, coordinating the hospitality and activities with the host/hostess, and keeping a meticulous record of ministry contacts through the small group ministry.

Sam Shoemaker stated, "Before the average person comes into a vital Christian experience, he usually needs a period of exposure to the experience of others."[6] Small groups promote an entrance point that is different from stereotyped measures, such as ranting preachers and sawdust trails. Galloway's church, while continually developing a network of home Bible studies, offers a plethora of special interest groups that meet at the church site at various times during the week. These groups address drug abuse, child abuse, single parents, and any other issue that may hold the slightest collective interest. Homogeneity and honesty are provided by the existential needs of the group and the willingness to be transparent about the issue that has brought the group together. Richard Peace writes, "This is the nature of an authentic Christian group—a holy people who have faced their dark sides, found forgiveness in Christ and from one another, and are able therefore to live transparently honest lives. A non-Christian entering such a group finds the experience virtually irresistible."[7]

There are many items that can be used for stimulating group discussion besides Bible study. (However, the group should not try to camouflage its spiritual overtone.) The group definitely needs to have a program informed by a specific topic. Lack of direction and purpose will spell dissipation. Peace states, "When informed attention is paid to group processing, the chances increase that a group will be able to reach maturity and fulfill its potentialities."[8] The group should not become a sensitivity session designed to elicit emotions and tap unconscious reservoirs in order to provide therapy. Such objectives need to be left to professionals who work with refined skills in formally defined structures. Neither should the group members stifle emotional response because the conversation has touched a sensitive nerve. The emotive outlet may cause a certain amount of group discomfort, but will be necessary for healing and growth. The group will serve as a sounding board in ways that everyday structures of life are unable to provide. Galloway states (concerning the Tender-Loving-Care group), "It is a place where people are known in an impersonal society. It is a place where people are loved in an unloving society. It's a place where people find acceptance and a loving, prayerful response to their personal needs."[9]

Not only do small groups offer entrance points for people to a congregation, but as the church grows, cells maintain critical ecclesial qualities that may otherwise be lost. Churches are quite often stifled when they reach 200 members because they lose the friendship, intimacy, and personal care that once marked the church when it was smaller. As a church grows, pastoral care must be increasingly rendered by laity, even in a church that has a multiple staff. Carl George makes an extensive argument that the church must make this adjustment if it is to continue to grow. A "meta-church" (change church) will consist of three specific gatherings: (1) a celebration (several hundred) that consists of corporate worship akin to a festival full of praise and excitement, including the proclamation of the Word, (2) a congregation (50–100) that contains ingredients of Bible teaching, acquaintance networking, ministering to one another through gifts of the Spirit, and providing fellowship activities beyond Sunday, and (3) the cell group (about 10) for the purpose of providing intimacy, loving support, accountability, crisis ministry, and an attraction point for newcomers. George states, "I believe with Peter Wagner, that churches that offer people a variety of group-size choices will better retain growth than fellowships that offer fewer options. More important, I'm convinced that the kind of group that does the best job of "keeping" people is the mouse-size home cell-group."[10]

Critique

Strength: Small groups meet head-on many of the diseases of our age (such as loneliness, alienation, and impersonal existence in a highly technical society). They provide a nonthreatening entrance into the church, a church that is currently burdened with a reputation for institutional irrelevancy and monetary greed. The group process enables the participant to place a topic within a Christian context, and then extend the ensuing conversation to friends and relatives beyond the group. Above all, evangelistic groups provide an open, caring fellowship where one is identified by his or her first name in contrast to a dehumanizing society far more interested in production than personal development. Small groups provide high touch in a world rushing to reduce people to entities serialized by numbers rather than personified by names and faces. Every newcomer is made welcome by the group code-phrase, "We want to enter into your life because you are important."

Weakness: Small groups sometimes play into the hands of the same cultural tendencies that Christianity attempts to combat: narcissism, preoccupation with self, and affirmation of the group's lifestyle (which may be sub-Christian). Theological truths may be subverted by psychological technique. What in the group experience will enable the individual to move beyond a benefits threshold to a greater sphere of self-transcendency via a relationship with a Holy God? Sometimes the transition from the *koinonia* of coffee and doughnuts to the self-denial of the bread and wine is never made. Bible study does not guarantee that the feeling orientation of the evangelistic group will become something more than the current enthrallment with self-improvement in American culture. How-to's and practical principles drawn from Scripture often stop short of a reformation that leads to holy living and certitude that we are ready to face God because we are like Him. Mutual horizontal sharing that taps human potential can often be far removed from Charles Wesley's petition: "Adam's likeness now efface, stamp thine image in its place" (from "Hark the Herald Angels Sing").

ONE-ON-ONE

However one describes American evangelicals, it is a given that they assess a personal relationship with Jesus Christ as far more important than institutional attachment. Such was the legacy of Martin Luther, John Wesley, and our Puritan forefathers. In fact, the first crucial theological test that our Pilgrim ancestors faced had to do with the political and ecclesiastical status of the nonbelieving second and third generation of the Massachusetts Bay Colony. The emphasis on individual conversion, sometimes at the expense of corporate sanctification and covenant grace, led to most evangelicals adapting the Anabaptist perspective on baptism. Baptism was to be a postconversion witness to justifying grace. After conducting a survey among evangelical churches, David Hubbard and Clinton McLemore concluded that "the evangelicals studied are notably appreciative of spiritual ministry that proceeds from a personal faith commitment and that they are notably unappreciative of a ministry grounded in sacradotal-sacramental belief and practice."[11]

Thus, for most evangelicals, personal faith that results from conversion is a prerequisite to becoming a member of a local body of believers and a part of the universal church. Most pastors and denominational leadership emphasize the necessity of reproduction—individual instrumentality in enabling others to come into the same Christian experience. Pastors and evangelists who have modeled personal witnessing such as Charles Spurgeon and Dwight Moody have become ecclesiastical heroes. In fact, the ability to effectively share the gospel in one-on-one encounters has often been reputed as the mark of authentic Christian vitality. Pastors of growing churches both practice and teach the importance of personal witnessing.[12] Denominational leaders believe that evangelism programs filtered down to the grass roots constituency are perhaps the only thing that will prevent their ecclesiastical structure from becoming an archeological fossil.

Harry Denman

Consider the case of Harry Denman, who for many years served as secretary for the Board of Evangelism in the Methodist church. This somewhat eccentric individual modeled what he taught by giving most of his salary away, spending his vacations with prison inmates in Nashville or Birmingham, never owning more than one suit at a time, and turning every conversation that he could in the direction of Jesus Christ. The following extract from his own testimony serves as an impetus to be a personal witness whenever possible:

> I was staying in a hotel. The day clerk was very kind to me. The Lord put it on my heart to speak to him about being a Christian. I did not know whether or not he was a Christian. I told the Lord I would do it, but not at that time because there were many people in the lobby.
>
> Two mornings later I came down to the dining room for breakfast. The night clerk was on duty. The day clerk was supposed to be there. After breakfast the night clerk was still on duty. I inquired about the day clerk. He said, "We found him dead in his room this morning. He used a gun." I went to my room and begged God for forgiveness. I was trying to have a revival, and I failed God and this man who had been gracious to me.[13]

Dawson Trotman

In 1956, Dawson Trotman lost his life while attempting to rescue a drowning person at Schroon Lake, N.Y. His final act was a fitting symbol to his lifelong thrust—training Christians to reproduce themselves. While still in the U.S. Navy, Trotman began discipling sailors for the purpose of equipping them to win others to Christ. Largely through personal testimony, 125 men were converted on one ship. Out of the 125, missionaries were sent to four different continents. Trotman believed Scripture memorization to be the key to personal growth and evangelistic effectiveness. His organization, the Navigators, spread discipleship courses far beyond the armed services and was adopted as the nurturing program by the Billy Graham Evangelistic Association. The Navigators stressed a high accountability for Christians to share their faith with unbelievers. The everyone-wins-one emphasis was explained by Trotman in his short and very pointed booklet *Born to Reproduce:*

> So this first man at the end of six months has another man. Each man starts teaching another in the following six months. At the end of the year, there are just four of them. Perhaps each one teaches a Bible class or helps in a street meeting, but at the same time his main interest is in his man and how he is doing. So at the end of the year the four of them get together and have a prayer meeting and determine, "Now let's not allow anything to sidetrack us. Let's give the Gospel out to

> a lot of people, but let's check up on at least one man and see him through."
>
> So the four of them in the next six months each get a man. That makes eight at the end of a year and a half. They all go out after another and at the end of two years there are 16 men. At the end of three years there are 64; the 16 have doubled twice. At the end of five years there are 1,024. At the end of fifteen and a half years there are approximately 2,147,500,000. That is the present population of the world of persons over three years of age.[14]

Though Trotman's construct was highly theoretical, nevertheless he emphasized the importance of each Christian discovering another person willing to be discipled into the Christian faith.

Bill Bright

Bill Bright's emphasis is somewhat different than Dawson Trotman's. He developed a thesis that insists that every Christian needs to always be prepared to give a verbal witness. This does not mean that Bright calls for insensitivity to the setting or the target persons. Bright teaches Christians to develop circumstances and conversations that would be fruitful for the gospel. Almost any setting will do—a restaurant, an airplane, or a ball game. The essence of the gospel, which for him consists of four spiritual laws, can be shared in five minutes or less. Bright writes:

> As the name suggests, there are four basic truths to the Four Spiritual Laws: (1) God loves you and has a wonderful plan for your life. (2) Man is sinful and separated from God, thus he cannot know and experience God's love and plan for his life. (3) Jesus Christ is God's only provision for man's sin. Through Him you can know and experience God's love and plan for your life. (4) We must individually receive Jesus Christ as Savior and Lord; then we can know and experience God's love and plan for our lives.[15]

Bright's plan provides Christians with a concise formula by which the gospel can be shared with unbelievers. Literally thousands of witnesses armed with the "four spiritual laws" have been deployed to campuses, beaches, shopping malls, busy pedestrian thoroughfares, and sundry large gatherings. Much seed has been planted and thousands have made initial commitments to Jesus Christ. But with this type of evangelism there is hardly any way to evaluate the depth and permanency of these commitments.

James Kennedy

No one has exceeded James Kennedy's efforts in providing Christians with a formula by which their faith can be shared, plus the follow-up tools that attempt to ensure that the new Christian does not quickly fall by the wayside. Not only has Kennedy built a multithousand member church in Fort Lauderdale, Florida, but his model for winning new converts, Evangelism Explosion, has been emulated perhaps more than any other single church program for saving the lost. Each week hundreds of lay evangelists spread out to the surrounding community in groups of three. Normally these people visit homes that have already shown interest in the church by way of attendance. They may be new in the community, or may have simply visited Coral Ridge Presbyterian Church for the first time.

After a few minutes of getting acquainted, the prospects are asked two diagnostic questions so that the evangelists are able to ascertain both their spiritual certitude and understanding of the gospel: (1) "Have you come to a place in your spiritual life where you know for certain that if you were to die today you would go to heaven?" (2) "Suppose that you were to die today and stand before God and He were to say to you, 'Why should I let you into my heaven?' What would you say?"[16] Quite often the question serves to highlight either the works-righteousness orientation or spiritual anxiety of the prospect.

If the prospect indicates a willingness for the evangelist to continue, the gospel is presented in the form of five statements supported with illustrations and Scripture:

1. *Grace*—Heaven is a free gift. It is not earned or deserved.

2. *Man*—Everyone falling within the species of humanity has sinned. Man has made a colossal mess out of everything and, according to God's word, cannot save himself. "Martin Luther said that the most damnable and pernicious heresy that has ever plagued the mind of man was the idea that somehow he could make himself good enough to live with an all-holy God."[17]

3. *God*—He is loving and merciful but at the same time just;

therefore, He must punish sin. God loves us and doesn't want to punish us but yet He must keep His word that sin must and will be punished.

4. *Jesus Christ*—"God in His infinite wisdom devised a marvelous solution. Jesus Christ is God's answer to our predicament. He sent Him into the world and as you know, we celebrate His birth every Christmas."[18] Christ paid our debt with His death on Calvary. People don't have to pay for it. Jesus has already paid the price, and sinners can have eternal life as a gift.

5. *Faith*—It is not mere intellectual assent, but a trusting in Christ alone for salvation. Throughout the presentation, the emphasis is placed on salvation being a free gift and the impossibility of anyone earning it.

After these five truths of the gospel have been presented, the listener is asked a simple straightforward question: "Do you want to receive this gift of eternal life?" If the answer is yes, a sinner's prayer, which covers four petitions, is repeated by the convert after the evangelist. These petitions involve receiving Christ as Savior, trusting Him as Lord, forgiveness of sins, and the assurance of pardon. After the prayer is concluded, the new Christian is offered Scripture that bolsters assurance. Before leaving the house, the evangelists offer a brief instruction concerning growth in grace through witness, worship, reading the Word, prayer, and perseverance.

The strength of the Coral Ridge program is its emphasis on converts becoming mature Christians through fellowship in a local church. A series of follow-up contacts are planned, including phone calls, letters, cassette tapes, socials, Bible studies, and classes for new believers. Follow-up calls aid the new Christian in reviewing a checklist of prayer, Scripture reading, and questions concerning continued assurance of salvation. Evangelism Explosion has conducted leadership clinics for churches across the U.S. and around the world with the goal of mobilizing a million full-time lay evangelists. Kennedy claims that the program rests on two important principles. The church is a body under orders by Christ to share the gospel with the whole world, and evangelism is more caught than taught.[19] Kennedy writes:

> This emphasis on spiritual multiplication, looking past the first generation to the second, third, and fourth, is the secret of an expanding and multiplying evangelistic ministry. In just a few

> years this has produced instances of great-great-great-great-great-great-great-great grandchildren in the faith. The acid test of any follow-up procedure will ultimately be, "Is it producing spiritual grandchildren and great grandchildren? If not, something is amiss, and somewhere the process is breaking down."[20]

The process starts with the pastor. It is highly unlikely that the sheep will spawn other sheep if the shepherd does not model personal evangelism.

Critique

Strength: People are often challenged to witness but are never shown how. On-the-job training allows the trainee to observe evangelism in action. The memorization of an outline gives the would-be witness a definite course of action. Without the basic steps to lead someone to Christ, attempts at giving an explanation of the way to salvation often founder or get sidetracked by the prospect's objections or flimsy excuses. Every salesman begins with a canned pitch, however many impromptu insights or spontaneous comments develop from it. Every person has to begin somewhere, and that somewhere is the fundamentals of the gospel. Unless these fundamentals are so absorbed by the Christian that they become an automatic part of his or her verbal skills, witnessing becomes extremely difficult and is left only for those highly articulate in the areas of theology and apologetics. Even ministerial professionals may so obscure the message with theological jargon and esoteric language that the unconverted fail to grasp its simplistic immediacy.

The absorption of biblical essentials and the constant sharing of them serves to mature and strengthen the Christian. Instead of Christians being involved with vicious cycles of preoccupation, they are absorbed in the spiritual welfare of others. There always needs to be that delicate balance between introspection of self and circumspection of the lost. These programs of witnessing normally call for high commitment and accountability. Many Christians are hesitant to give an evening a week to leave the warm confines of their home and step on someone else's turf. There is probably no greater indication of spiritual maturity than a burden for the lost and the willingness to do something about it.

Without Christ as their personal Savior, middle-class Americans who live behind brick facades and manicured lawns are as lost as the Masai in Kenya.

Personal evangelism calls for a tremendous dependence on the Holy Spirit. He enables the Christian to face and handle the same kind of rejection that Christ encountered. Those who persevere allow God to replace their fragile egos with a willingness to be an ambassador for Christ, whatever the cost. It will normally cost very little—just a little time and energy, which are commodities that many professing Christians are unwilling to give. But to those who are willing, there is probably no greater joy that we can experience than to be a part of the Great Commission: Go! Teach! Make disciples!

Weakness: The call of the gospel is more fittingly described as a wooing of the prince to the princess than it is the selling of a prospectus by a stockbroker to a client. The mysteries of the gospel are not easily translated into calculated formulas. American rationalism, formulated to accomplish a purpose, has invaded both the public sermon and the private witness. The American sage and folk theologian Benjamin Franklin noted the pervasive swing to pragmatic rationalism when he stated, "What a convenient thing it is to be reasonable since it enables one to find or make a reason for everything one has a mind to do."[21] Pascal wrote, "The heart has reasons that the mind knows not of." Christianity is an appeal to the affection as well as the intellect. The affection cannot be transformed by cognitive consent, but needs a radical upheaval by the grace of God.

People cannot simply make up their minds to be Christian. They need a heart warmed by God's Spirit, which will in turn direct the volitions. The warm heart is a gift of God and is not easily measured. People can comply to institutions, but only God can effect inward righteousness, a circumcision of the heart rather than of the flesh. There is a timing of sovereign grace that cannot be turned on and off at will. People are brought into the kingdom by the influx of the Holy Spirit and not by a simple affirmative nod of the head. James Hunter criticizes the dominant impulse in present-day evangelism to systematize, codify, and methodize the gospel.[22] Evangelicals may be far too eager to erase the unruly elements of the conversion process, while packaging the gospel for easy, rapid, and strain-free consumption. Such cognitive reductionism means that the "spiritual" aspects of evangelical life are increasingly approached by means of and interpreted in terms of principles, rules, steps, laws, codes, guidelines, and so forth.

A uniformity of process quite often aims at a uniformity of product, while ignoring the uniqueness of the individual and the varieties of religious experiences. One training manual insists on the importance of presenting the gospel within every home at each call. Such insistence sometimes obscures the foremost reason to call on anyone—to minister to them at the point of their need. The discernment of the Holy Spirit may indicate to the evangelist that a prescribed formula is inappropriate, at least at the present time. The prospect may not have sufficient awareness of the implications of the gospel to make a well-informed and serious commitment, even after hearing an hour-long presentation.

The Kennedy plan seems to be best suited to someone who has been attending a mainline church, living a moral life, yet with a poor concept of what it means to have a personal assurance of salvation. While the church has historically taught the importance of the witness of the written Word as external evidence, the internal witness of the Spirit has been recognized as having equal impact, if not greater. A profession of faith based on a cognitive perception of the promises of Scripture presents an epistemological problem. People can never ultimately know that Christ has saved them unless the Word is quickened to their heart and the Spirit bears witness with their spirit that they are children of God. Most evangelism training manuals do not deal with this important doctrine. The biblical promise that God does not leave us to our own perception or interpretation is both a caution and a confidence. It is God who ultimately validates true spirituality. Evangelism Explosion does well to call the evangelist to humility: "Do be conservative in your estimation of what happens on your visit. You may see a profession of faith. Only time will tell if your prospect was born again, accepted the Lord and was converted."[23]

REVIVALS

When one hundred pastors whose congregations have an average attendance of 1,650 on Sunday morning were asked if they have a regularly scheduled revival at least once a year, 69 percent of them answered yes.[24] It would be difficult to make any correlation between "revival" efforts and the causes of growth in these large churches. The pastors did not define their understanding of revival or their intentions and goals for special services. Cause and effect are further complicated when one considers that a high percentage of small nongrowing churches plan revival efforts once or twice a year, but with little evangelistic results. To relate evangelism to revivalism, three exploratory questions need to be asked: (1) What is the theology of revival? (2) How does one plan for revival? (3) What are the evangelistic implications of a revival?

A Revival Theology

Revival throughout Scripture is a quickening of spiritual life that leads to renewed hope and increased activity for the realization of God's purposes. Nehemiah experienced renewal as the king's cupbearer in the winter palace of the Persian monarch; Isaiah was spiritually renewed as he was in the temple at Jerusalem; Peter, James, and John were in the biggest revival of all on the Day of Pentecost. Each incident reveals consistent revival characteristics:

1. *Complicity with the problem.* Nehemiah stated, "I and my father's house have sinned" (Neh. 1:6). Isaiah exclaimed that not only did he live among unclean people, but that he himself was unclean (Isa. 6:5). The disciples must have had plenty of time during the ten days secluded in the Upper Room to rehearse their failures in being totally committed to Christ and His cause while He was still on earth. People who experience revival do not consider themselves to be aloof to the condition of their church or community. In fact, they are likely to perceive that they are the church in minuscule by asking, "If everyone in this church was as committed to Christ as I am, what kind of church would this be?" People who experience revival not only desire individual sanctification, but have a keen sense of social evil and corporate righteousness. They both implicitly and explicitly say through prayer and preachment, "We are in this thing together."

2. *Confession of the problem.* Both Isaiah and Nehemiah confessed their sin without gloss or excuse. Nehemiah bluntly stated, "We have acted very corruptly against Thee and have not kept the commandments, nor the statutes, nor the ordinances which Thou didst

command Thy servant Moses" (Neh. 1:7). After Isaiah had his life-transforming experience, he proclaimed, "Be broken, O peoples, and be shattered" (Isa. 8:9). After his horrendous sin, David prayed, "The sacrifices of God are a broken spirit; a broken and a contrite heart, O God, Thou wilt not despise" (Ps. 51:17). Proverbs 28:13 states, "He who conceals his transgressions will not prosper, but he who confesses and forsakes them will find compassion." It is always proper for Christians to confess their sins to God. A corporate atmosphere of mutual confession shaped by the direction of the Holy Spirit is the cultivated ground in which renewal can take place.

3. Commitment to the problem. Revival does not take place in the absence of problems that need to be remedied. There are walls that need to be rebuilt and people who need to be evangelized. Nehemiah did not pray in a vacuum. He asked his brother to report to him the exact condition of Jerusalem. Upon learning that the walls of Jerusalem were broken down and its gates were burned with fire, Nehemiah wept, mourned, fasted, and prayed for days (Neh. 1:4). But Nehemiah didn't stop there. He left the comfortable confines of the king's winter palace and went to Jerusalem. There he toiled with a sword in one hand and a trowel in the other as an equal among his native brothers and sisters. Revival leads to personal sacrifice.

All of the above take place in the context of a holy God. Revival cannot take place without a display of God's majesty. The problem with American churches is not so much an ignorance of the promises of God as an ignorance of the God behind the promises. When John on the Isle of Patmos saw the Christ, whose eyes were like a "flame of fire" and whose face was like "the sun shining in its strength," he "fell at His feet as a dead man" (Rev. 1:14, 16, 17). Revival is synonymous with the holy awesome God breaking in upon humanity. Such prospects are not enticing to religious professionals, ossified laity, and a public largely guided by Freud's pleasure principle. Revival is a manifestation of God's supernatural grace and power. It is a law of spiritual life. All of us have gates that have been broken down, or at least a few doors that need rehinging, and need to cry out as did Nehemiah: "I beseech Thee, O Lord God of heaven, the great and awesome God, who preserves the covenant and lovingkindness for those who love Him and keep His commandments" (Neh. 1:5).

The Sovereign Nature of Revival

One may legitimately ask, "Can the church or an individual prepare for revival?" There is certainly something very sovereign about the overwhelming afflatus of the Holy Spirit. It should be noted that the Holy Spirit chose to come on the Day of Pentecost, a date determined by the triune Godhead rather than scheduled by the committee of the apostolate.

In 1970 I was a senior at Asbury College in Wilmore, Kentucky. The chapel on February 3 for the over 1,000 students was devoted to individual testimonies. The first student who stood to give his witness was known as a campus cutup. He reported to the entire congregation how God had radically transformed his life over the prior three days. That first testimony was the beginning of hundreds that would be given almost without intermission for the next eight days. All classes were canceled as God's Spirit enveloped the campus in love and reconciliation.

Television and newspaper reporters visited Wilmore to find out what was happening in the small community. As the world got the news, requests came from churches and other colleges to report the events by sending student representation. As the students vacated the campus, going to places far and near, people from the surrounding area and beyond replaced them in Hughes Auditorium. Immediately upon stepping on the campus, the visitors could sense an atmosphere that was unmistakably of God. And wherever the story was told, people emptied out of their pews, coming forward in contrition, expectancy, and dependency upon God to change the status quo of their own lives and the life of their church.

My own recollection does not tell me that people were praying any more than usual at Asbury. I'm confident that there were always saints praying for revival in Wilmore. The prayer for revival is one of those universal and automatic petitions of people who are on God's frequency. In fact, there had already been similar Asbury campus visitations by the Holy Spirit in 1930 and 1950. It seemed that God was simply keeping His own timetable. His timing is always perfect and He doesn't need the perfect setting. The Asbury campus was not that different from other Christian colleges and was not that far removed from the general unrest and antiauthoritarianism that characterized collegiate life in the late sixties and early seventies. There was plenty of conflict concerning long hair for the men and short skirts for the women—between questioning students and Asbury institutional authority. God delights in bringing coherency out of chaos in His own time and way.

Preparation for Revival

But it does seem from Scripture that God's timing is not independent of humanity's spiritual comprehension and response to that comprehension. Scripture leads us to believe that within God's unchanging character there is a flexibility that is in accord with human concern. Such was the case when Abraham interceded for Lot and when Moses stood between God and an unruly mob of complaining people. God has willed that we touch His heart with desires that are within the divine plan. God desires that we seek Him, find Him, and discover the fullness of His presence. But He has predicated that discovery upon Jeremiah 29:13 ("You will seek Me and find Me, when you search for Me with all your heart"). There is a high correlation between genuine desire for revival and the event of revival. The kindling of desire for revival by the Holy Spirit is revival already begun.

Preparation for revival will consist of the following steps:

1. *Envision what would happen if God did bring a revival to your environment.* Quite often the prayer for revival is prayed within a vague nostalgia for the good old days or in the broad sentiment that things ought to be better than they are. The genuine revival prayer asks God, "What exactly do You want to do in my life and in the life of our local congregation?" The true pre-revival petition presumes that God wants to begin with the petitioner. If God began a revival in me, I would be more loving, gossip less, give more, and gripe less. My value structure would change and the total stewardship of my life would be more Christlike. God would effect a change in my life so definitive that it would be immediately noticeable to my family, if not the whole church and neighborhood. "God wants to change me" is the preface to revival and the caption over revival efforts.

2. *Carry a burden for revival.* Ask God to make His desires your desires. A burden may include primarily praying about this one concern, fasting as a means of grace, and keeping a journal as to what God is presently saying and doing about revival at a specific location among a specific group of people. A prayer burden does not

mean that one has to adopt a solemn deportment that increases psychological stress, but rather a joyful anticipation that aligns itself with God's expectations for His church. Wesley L. Duewel writes:

> Prayer burden is God-given. Its source is not natural sympathy, emotion, or predilection. It is not something worked up by long or hard praying. It is not the result of psychological manipulation or mass psychology. While it may spread from one person to another, it does so primarily among those deeply spiritual, deeply committed, and deeply involved in intercession. A burden that is primarily emotional will be superficial and will yield no lasting spiritual results. It is a burden born in the heart of God which indicates it is a valid part of Christ's intercession, and it is conveyed to you by the Spirit's guidance and touch.[25]

3. *If the "revival" is a planned event with dates and visiting professionals, state the purpose of the time set aside for spiritual emphasis.* Is the primary purpose increased knowledge of God's Word? Deeper prayer life? Winning the lost? Reconciliation of church members? Reaching out into the community? Confusion of purpose means diffusion of results. If the purpose is not stated clearly and specifically, the expectations will be shallow and myopic. Praying for God to do a specific thing during a revival effort should be as pointed as praying for rain in a time of drought. Most revival efforts accomplish very little because prayers and expectations are very indefinite.

4. *Covenant with others.* Leadership will enlist others to pray, give, and attend. This needs to be done six weeks to two months ahead of time by way of sign-up lists or even written covenants handed out to the entire congregation. The covenants will be returned to the pastor or a special committee indicating that the respondents are willing to be "stewards of revival" by giving of their time, energy, and material means. The covenants should be clear about the length of time and amount of resources that are sought from each individual. A covenant should be entered into willingly, in the absence of pressure tactics by the pastor or any other leadership.

5. *Preach and teach on the principles of revival in the Scripture.* What were the activities of people on whom God poured out His Spirit? What was their perception of God? What conditions does

God lay down for revival of His church? Are there any specific church situations in Bible times that would parallel our own situation? A good place to begin would be the three great revivals in the Book of Acts: the Jewish revival in Acts 2, the Samaritan revival in Acts 8, and the Gentile revival in Acts 10. Such preaching will exalt the majesty of God and accent the gap between the abundant life and listless Christian experience. There is a vital connection between clear, dynamic biblical preaching that exalts God and the promised pouring out of the Holy Spirit. Lewis Drummond writes:

> Liberal, rationalistic, speculative theology dies. That kind of thought system never brings about awakening. This does not mean revivals spawn anti-intellectualism. That too is a perversion of the Spirit's work. This has surely been made crystal clear in the pietistic movement. But an empirical, purely rationalistic, liberal theology that downgrades the transcendent elements of Christianity are laid to rest in awakening. People are made vividly alive to the fact that this transcendental miracle-working God is among them—and breaking in on the causal continuity of history.[26]

6. Plan! Plan! Plan! Preparation is a law for anything that is to be done efficiently. Planning includes finances, personnel, publicity, and structuring of specific events during the days devoted to spiritual emphasis. Be clear and specific concerning obligations to workers both within and outside of the church. It is best to communicate to invited professionals just what will be expected of them and the accommodations, expenses, and honorarium that will be provided for their services. The church must bear in mind that there are very few full-time evangelists in service today because remuneration is seldom sufficient to meet expenses and fund retirement, Social Security, housing costs, and a lifestyle anywhere close to that of the average pastor. Because of the scarcity of committed revival workers, planning at least a year ahead of time is highly recommended. The "Revival Countdown Calendar" (see p. 216) should prove helpful to those who are serious about conscientious planning. In all of our planning we should expect to be surprised by God. He will use our planning and preparation, but not always in ways we anticipate.

Revival Countdown Calendar

I. Basic Information about Scheduled Revival

Person Responsible

______ 1. Evangelist ______________

______ 2. Song evangelist ______________

______ 3. Advertising—refer to Revival Services or Evangelistic Meeting

______ 4. Time of services— Weeknights_____ Sunday_____

______ 5. Service—Saturday night ❑ Yes ❑ No

______ 6. Order visual art advertising leaflets or cards ❑ Yes ❑ No

______ 7. Order visual art banner ❑ Yes ❑ No

______ 8. Do newspaper advertisement ❑ Yes ❑ No

______ 9. Do newspaper story ❑ Yes ❑ No

______ 10. Do radio spots ❑ Yes ❑ No

______ 11. Special events:
Men's Breakfast ❑ Yes ❑ No
Ladies' luncheon ❑ Yes ❑ No

______ 12. Special emphasis:
Tuesday and Friday—Sunday School nights, social after, recognize ❑ Yes ❑ No

Wednesday and Thursday—Links nights, social after, recognize ❑ Yes ❑ No

______ 13. Baby-sitting provided ❑ Yes ❑ No

______ 14. Music:
Choir ❑ Yes ❑ No
Special groups ❑ Yes ❑ No
Accompanists: ______________
Other: ______________

______ 15. Finance decisions by board:

Projected Expenses

a. Evangelist/song evangelist honoraria $ ______________

b. Evangelist/song evangelist travel, housing, and entertainment $ ______________

c. Advertising $ ______________

d. Letters to congregation $ ______________

e. Training materials $ ______________

f. Follow-through materials $ ______________

g. Special costs ____ $ ______________

______________ $ ______________

Total $ ______________

Sources of Revenue

a. Church budget $ ______________

b. Offerings during revival $ ______________

c. Designated gifts $ ______________

d. Pre-revival banquet and pledges $ ______________

e. Other__________ $ ______________

______________ $ ______________

Total $ ______________

______ 16. Cancel Caravan Wednesday night of revival ❑ Yes ❑ No

______ 17. Cancel choir practice Wednesday night of revival ❑ Yes ❑ No

______ 18. Secretary refuse calendar reservations during revival ❑ Yes ❑ No

______ 19. Ushers nightly ❑ Yes ❑ No

______ 20. Greeters nightly ❑ Yes ❑ No

______ 21. New greeters ❑ Yes ❑ No

______ 22. Friendship in worship cards nightly ❑ Yes ❑ No

______ 23. Remind commitee chairpersons on countdown ❑ Yes ❑ No

______ 24. Correspondence with evangelist ❑ Yes ❑ No

______ 25. Correspondence with song evengelist ❑ Yes ❑ No

______ 26. Plan schedule for Sunday A.M. service to provide adequate time for message and invitational

Revivals and Evangelism

More often than not, revival efforts are planned with little consideration of the lost. The emphasis is on renewing the commitment and passion of believers rather than reaching unbelievers. One should not disdain holy convocations that are set aside for the sanctification of believers. But such planning should not be done by the evangelism committee if the objective will not be the converting of the unsaved. This is not to say that a genuine renewal will not have long-term evangelistic effects. Live coals serve to ignite their surroundings. Passion that has been inflamed will spread. Those who have been involved in the spiritual intensity of revival begin to see lost humanity as God sees it. Sanctified motivation with God-given goals does not get sidetracked from the mission of Christ to redeem the lost. It is amazing how genuine revival can loosen the tongue and tap hidden reservoirs of spiritual energy.

It is reported that a student at Asbury College was going home on a Greyhound bus to share what God was doing during the 1970 revival. She began to share with her seat partner. As her fellow traveler listened intently, the person in the seat behind them leaned forward to hear what was being shared. The person in the seat in front of them turned around and the individual across the aisle leaned toward the young lady, who had an unusual tale of God's transforming power. This college student now had a small congregation. When the bus pulled into the Cincinnati station, the bus driver, who had partially heard this young lady's witness to the transforming grace of God, requested that she briefly repeat what she had shared with the others. He also invited the rest of the travelers to tarry a few minutes if they would like to learn more about this unusual event at an obscure college campus.

There is little doubt that true revival will result in evangelism. It is difficult to keep a good thing secret, but quite often revival efforts are removed from the unbeliever. With the advent of television and the proliferation of the media world, church has lost much of its entertainment value. Seldom do the unconverted simply wander into church. They will not come to church unless deeply concerned friends pray for them and invite them to an event open to outsiders. If the special services are for the purpose of reaching beyond the walls of the church, several practical suggestions need to be followed:

1. *A prayer list of five to ten unsaved people needs to be composed.* These people will no doubt be friends, relatives, and family members of those already attending the church. Specific intercession should be offered on behalf of these people at least three months ahead of time. Sensitive efforts should be made to reach out to them.

2. *These people for whom prayer is being offered should be invited on a specific night of the special services.* This special evangelistic service will have an upbeat tempo and exclude as much theological jargon as possible. Some humorous moments could be included in the service by means of drama, ventriloquism, or pantomime so that newcomers will not think they are in a morgue. On that evening, do not ask the congregation to sing choruses from memory. The message should be simplistic, concrete, positive, and geared toward someone searching for alternate answers to the world's enticements. Above all, the service should exalt Christ. It may be helpful to have the specific evening at an off-site facility such as a hotel or restaurant. The service needs to be as nonthreatening as possible, while yet maintaining its singular purpose—salvation of the lost.

3. *Visitation with both the above targeted persons and also periphery persons within the church needs to be made.* There are always those used-to-come marginal people on every church's membership rolls. Planning ahead will allow the pastor, visiting evangelist, and other leadership to use their time visiting and contacting prospects throughout the week. James Kennedy recounts being called as an evangelist to conduct a revival effort at a local church. What happened during those days was to change his ministry forever.

> When I arrived the pastor told me that I would be preaching each night, but more important, he said, we would be visiting in the homes each day—morning, noon, and night—to present the gospel to people individually. I was petrified, for I knew that I had no ability whatsoever to do this. However, the next morning we went out. After about a half-hour of my stumbling attempts at evangelism, the pastor took over the conversation and in about fifteen or twenty minutes led the man to Christ. I was astonished but did not realize even then the impact this was to have on my life. For ten days I watched this pastor lead one person after another to Christ for a total of fifty-four individuals during those ten days. I went

> back to Fort Lauderdale a new man and began to do just what I had seen done. People responded. Soon dozens, scores, and then hundreds accepted Christ. This principle of "on-the-job-training" had been applied to my life and had produced its results.[27]

4. Advertisement should be used in publicizing the revival effort. One newspaper ad should be purchased and as much free media as is available needs to be secured. Newspapers in small towns are eager for human interest stories, and the visiting evangelist may well serve as a great resource. Guest spots on local television and radio will raise community awareness.

The best advertisement, of course, is church members. A personal invitation is much more effective than impersonal media. Part of the covenant for the revival effort should be to set goals for contacting people. It would not be too much to ask laypersons to make at least ten phone calls apiece during the course of a week. One thousand personal invitations to attend the services should serve to put at least a dozen people in touch with the gospel—people who otherwise would not have been confronted concerning their spiritual condition. If evangelistic services are to reach the unconverted, laity must be mobilized to make contact with acquaintances. While distributing flyers and making spot radio announcements may have contributing effectiveness, people will not normally come to church unless invited by a friend. James Engel explains:

> The general principle emerging from decades of communications research is that the mass media generally do not play a decisive role in any type of major decision. Rather, their primary effect is contributory through the stimulation of awareness and interest and subsequent attitude change. . . . Some form of personal witness, on the other hand, usually is the dominant decisive influence, although there are many exceptions to any generalization of this type.[28]

Critique

Strength: Evangelism that erupts out of the heat of revivalism bears the authenticity of New Testament outreach. Spontaneity of joyous sharing that comes from a recent renewal of spiritual life will normally be more effective than a canned pitch or a calculated effort. Revival means a renewal of love for Christ and for fellow individuals. Pentecost brought a burning love for surrounding lost humanity. Renewed acquaintance with the love found in Christ produces an inherent desire to introduce others to that same love. This passion cannot be produced through seminars, persuasion from the pulpit, or even long-term training. In the enthusiasm of revival, sharing the good news becomes second nature rather than a contrived or calculated effort. In contrast to all of the evangelistic techniques that have been developed, nothing will ever surpass one person saying to another, "Let me tell you what Christ has done for me."

A revival brought by the Holy Spirit brings an air of joyous celebration. To many outsiders, churches have the atmosphere of a funeral dirge. The solemn assemblies are too sedate and sober to attract Americans attempting to grab all the gusto they can on the weekends. Christians need something that will fill them with exuberance and joy that overcomes the stresses of everyday life. Victorious living will stimulate inquiries as to the source of the inner strength of Christians. They will be able to respond, "Come and see a community of people who have experienced the same thing that I have." Evangelism has to be much more than volition; it needs to be an affectionate invitation to someone to meet the King of kings. If people are invited to a royal banquet, they are normally not at a loss to share the good news with their neighbors. So it is for those who have a renewed vision of the marriage supper of the Lamb.

Weakness: Even though God seems to honor certain conditions for renewal, revival is not something that can be secured through calculation. But that isn't the real problem. In most revival efforts, very little spiritual preparation is made. The services amount to little more than the congregation gathered together to hear an exciting preacher. The attendants gain new scriptural insights and are nurtured in the faith. This accomplishment is not to be minimized, but there is little degree of revival and rarely any evangelism. Since the church is unsure whether it is targeting revival for the believer or evangelism for the lost, it usually accomplishes neither.

Throughout the nineteenth century, nurture was juxtaposed with revival. The dichotomy is superficial because revival needs to be a periodic part of nurturing spiritual growth. But quite often revivalistic thinking preempts the daily discipline of the means of grace. God intends us to have continuous growth rather than halting stops and spurting accelerations. Quite often revivalistic Christians view spiritual health as taking quantum leaps during the fall and spring revival efforts. Dallas Willard writes:

> The approach to wholeness is for human kind a process of great length and difficulty that engages all our own powers to their fullest extent over a long course of experience. But we don't like to hear this. We are somewhat misled by the reports of experiences by many great spiritual leaders and we assign their greatness to these great moments they were given, neglecting the years of slow progress they endured before them.[29]

Periodic revival efforts are often a means of avoiding real issues in a church. "Evangelistic services" are planned, but no one is doing the work of evangelism. Revival is not a substitute for evangelism—it is the power to do evangelism. Instead of working, confronting, and reaching out, revival efforts are quite often perceived as short-term solutions to long-term problems. There is much to do before and after revival, and the pouring out of the Holy Spirit does not lessen, but rather increases, those responsibilities. In his essay "Revitalizing a Dying Church," Harry Reeder writes:

> The dying church is like a person sick with cancer. Last minute cures are possible and God can do all things. But if the patient is to recover, the normal course is going to require building the spiritual blocks of the church layer by layer beginning with the foundation. Many of the spiritually sensitive and discerning members probably have left the church. Therefore cultivation of spiritual growth and biblical expectations in the lives of God's people is one of the first challenges facing the revitalization pastor. As much as the members want an "instant" cure, a "quick fix", they must learn to go back to the basics, cultivating a biblical faith, walking with God and thinking His thoughts, loving Jesus Christ and obeying His commands, depending on His grace and Spirit and the power of the gospel.[30]

The sons of Korah wrote and sang, "Wilt Thou not Thyself

revive us again, that Thy people may rejoice in Thee?" (Ps. 85:6) I praise God that He has often answered that prayer throughout the history of the church. It should be the hope of every Christian that God is willing to pour Himself out on all who sincerely seek Him.

CHURCH PLANTING

Church planting is considered to be one of the foremost methods of reaching new people for Jesus Christ. As the frontier moved west in the eighteenth and nineteenth centuries, circuit riding preachers followed it. They preached in brush arbors, schoolhouses, camp meetings, and any suitable spot where a crowd could be gathered. If sufficient interest was demonstrated by the populace and there were numerous converts, the evangelist chartered a church. If the church was under denominational auspices, a pastor would be sent in due time to care for that congregation and possibly two or three other fledgling churches in the nearby area. The exceptional independent work would be left to fend for itself by either calling a pastor or depending on local leadership. Even throughout the twentieth century, churches often began because of successful revivals that were held in storefronts, school auditoriums, and portable tents. But today revivalistic effort is probably one of the least used means for planting churches.

Why Plant New Churches?

Before we examine church planting methodology one may legitimately ask, "Why plant new churches?" There are almost 400,000 church buildings in America, and only a small percentage of those are filled on Sunday morning. The 1996 *Yearbook of American and Canadian Churches* indicates 335,156 churches belonging to 224 denominations. This number does not include the many nonaffiliated independent churches throughout the U.S.[31] Those that are filled to capacity normally make a transition to multiple worship services or build a larger sanctuary. It seems to the casual observer that many areas are already overchurched. Small communities of a thousand people often boast of a half dozen or more churches, all of which are only partially filled on a given Sunday. So why don't we simply cooperate and work together in filling established churches rather than creating more options?

The answers given by church planting proponents normally include the following:

1. *It is the New Testament pattern to evangelize through planting churches.* Paul and Barnabas were ordained to travel the Gentile world and plant churches (Acts 13:2). The evangelistic enterprise would have failed if churches had not been established and general directions (such as those found in the pastoral epistles) had not been implemented.

2. *Two churches will attract more people than one church.* Additional points of light flickering in neighborhoods, on freeways, in ghettos, on rural hillsides, and in suburbs will serve as additional beacons for soul-sick travelers.

3. *Demographic change.* Populations tend to move from the country to the city, from the city to the suburbs, from the suburbs to the country, and then yuppie children move back to the inner city. The church must follow people if it is going to reach people.

4. *It is easier to start a new church than to revitalize an old one to the extent that it can be evangelistically effective.* Old churches that have been shrinking in numbers are almost impossible to reverse. It is difficult to change the image of a church fellowship after it has been decaying for several decades. The leadership is in a conserving, maintaining mode of existence, not to mention extremely set in their ways. Facilities are often old and unattractive and do not entice younger families, who are accustomed to something much better throughout the week.

5. *There is an enthusiasm created by newness.* People are excited about being on the ground floor of a beginning enterprise. There is much greater opportunity for leadership and ownership in a new church than in an older institution. Quite often it is difficult and awkward for newcomers to be assimilated into an older congregation that is composed of friendships and families that are not open to outsiders. Newness provides opportunities for Spirit-led, enterprising ministers to develop their own styles and forms of ministry, which are frequently very contemporary in format.

6. *The very existence of new churches depends on evangelism.* If new prospects are not discovered and enticed to be a part of the new endeavor, the launch will be aborted. New church pastors and leadership realize that their success depends on aggressive evangelism and are much more cognizant of how to go about it.

Methodology for Planting Churches

What are the methods by which a church is planted? Elmer Towns argues that there are six: First, a mother church establishes a daughter church and nurtures it until it is able to function on its own. Second, a church establishes a Sunday School in a given area and, when the church school becomes a suitable size, begins holding a worship service rather than commuting to a central location. Third, a church begins with a Bible study group and at some point of development begins to function as an incorporated church. Fourth, a denomination sends a person or group of people to a given area to establish a church. Fifth, the denomination provides the personnel and resources from headquarters until the church is self-supporting. Sixth, an independent church planter goes to a particular area to establish a new congregation. It is likely that the planter will be bivocational until the congregation is of sufficient size to support him and his family.[32]

My perception is that there is only one form of church planting, and all six represent the one to a greater or lesser degree. *All beginning churches should be sponsored by another local church that is compatible with the church's vision and theological beliefs.* The planters from the sponsoring church may utilize means such as Bible studies, Sunday Schools, and so forth, but every new church should be supported by and accountable to a local church. Even if a denominational headquarters decides to plant a church in a certain area, it should not be done without the consultation and enlisted support of a healthy congregation in the vicinity. If there are no churches of that denomination in the vicinity, a church from another locale should be asked to assume a sponsoring role, even if it is removed by several states.

What about individuals with no denominational backing who have a vision to begin a community church? First, a test of their call should be the approval of the local church of which they are a member. Secondly, they should seek the sponsorship of a local denominational church in the vicinity. If a supporting congregation cannot be found within close proximity, a church somewhere in the U.S. must be located that will offer to serve as a guide and support base for the new church. If a would-be founding pastor cannot procure such an arrangement, he or she needs to reevaluate this calling and perhaps redefine the original vision. (See my discussion in chapter 3 of "rugged individualists" who begin churches out of theological conviction. Rugged individualists should be an extremely rare exception today.)

Sponsorship of a church plant assumes various forms. Support may be in terms of prayer, encouragement, and accountability. The sponsoring church may offer various types and degrees of material support—paying salaries, loaning equipment, renting a site, or even buying property. All or part of the personnel may come from the older congregation. A group of people may volunteer to leave the established church to form the nucleus of the new fellowship. In the early days, the sponsoring community (which normally has more talent than can be utilized) may provide song leaders, pianists, organists, secretaries, and other gifted people to the new church (which normally does not have a very large pool of talent from which to choose). Above all, there must be clear communication as to the exact arrangement between the old church and those who are beginning the new plant. Joseph James, an experienced church planter, writes:

> Strained relationships between the mother and daughter churches are likely to result if no guidelines are established for how the "daughter families" will be selected. The pastor of the mother church might assume that only families in the newly targeted area of ministry would be eligible for the new work. At the same time, the church-planting pastor might think it is all right to canvass all the church members aggressively to gain as many seed families as possible.[33]

James has highlighted only one of many areas of possible conflict if there is not careful planning and clear understanding between the primary parties taking responsibility for the new work.

Normally some particular person will assume the leadership in planting a new church. Even if a team has responsibility, an individual will emerge as the charismatic, if not official, leader. The characteristics of the successful church planter are essentially those of the effective pastor, which I have outlined in *What Really Matters in Ministry*. However, it will be more critical that the qualities be possessed and demonstrated by a church planter than a settled pastor, because inherited church characteristics may serve to partially compensate for inabilities. A pastor may rely on built-in factors of lay leadership, a conducive facility, and a great music program to maintain the status quo over a number of years. It is possible for an inadequate pastor to inherit a gifted church, but an inadequate church planter will almost never succeed in his or her efforts.

The Charles E. Fuller Institute of Evangelism and Church Growth has developed a "Church Planter Performance Profile."[34] The profile lists thirteen qualities of the successful church planter:

1. *Visionizing capacity.*
2. *Intrinsically motivated.*
3. *Creates ownership of ministry.*
4. *Relates to the unchurched.*
5. *Spousal cooperation.*
6. *Effectively builds relationships.*
7. *Committed to church growth.*
8. *Responsive to community.*
9. *Utilizes giftedness of others.*
10. *Flexible and adaptable.*
11. *Builds group cohesiveness.*
12. *Resilience.*
13. *Exercises faith.*

People with these qualities must face the unique challenge of having to chart a course rather than follow a path that has already been set. Above all, a church plant pastor needs to have a vision and the ability to be flexible and patient when the vision does not go as preconceived. The conviction to follow through in spite of temporary roadblocks needs to be exhibited by both pastor and spouse.

Practical Steps

The practical steps for beginning a new church consist of the following:

1. *Envision a new church and accept ownership of the vision until it becomes a fully functioning local body of believers.* You should already be a part of a sponsoring church, or find one. Define what will be the relationship between the old and new congregations.

2. *Have someone do very careful demographic research.* Feed the information to the appropriate planning committee.

3. *Write a mission statement for the new church.* Compatibility between the mission statement and the envisioned demographic

profile of the church should be assessed. Whether a church is going to locate in the inner city or the economically upscale suburbs should be reflected in the mission statement.

4. *The organizational plan and ecclesiastical structure of the church should be charted.* If the church is a part of a highly organized denomination, the church discipline will serve as an operational manual. If the church is nondenominational or a member of a loose confederation of churches, attention will need to be given to church structure. How the church governs itself is one of the first orders of business. It will be helpful to examine organizational charts of existing churches. Elmer Towns states, "The two major reasons for failure are lack of spiritual maturity and lack of ecclesiology. When the church planter does not know the role that a new pastor should assume, nor the biblical role of a church planter, it is a lack of ecclesiology that will harm his church."[35] Organizational planning with statements of brief job descriptions will serve to define roles and increase efficiency.

5. *Incorporate a nonprofit organization.* Every state has different incorporation laws, not to mention various bonding requirements for the clergy. It will be necessary to consult an attorney and to obtain necessary information from the county court clerk.

6. *Construct a time line for the first three years.* Target the date when the church will become an official entity for the reception of charter members. Other events or achievements that need to be planned are the date of the first morning worship service, the dates of other services that will be scheduled, the purchase of property, the hiring of an architect, and financial independence.

7. *Adopt a specific plan for evangelizing the surrounding area.* In a sense, planting a church is a recapitulation of the various methodologies delineated in this book. The church may rely completely on friendship networking or door-to-door visitation. The unique concept of phone marketing (described below) may be implemented in order to produce an immediate congregation. Unless specific means for evangelizing are planned and implemented, the church will probably not take root. Evangelism Explosion and Campus Crusade both offer examples of religious surveys that can be used not only to introduce neighborhood people to a specific church, but to the plan of salvation as well. The following (see p. 228) is a spiritual questionnaire developed by Evangelism Explosion.[36]

SIDE ONE

Assurance Questionnaire Form

ASSURANCE QUESTIONNAIRE [7][0][1] (1 2 3)

I am ____________ of ________________
We're trying to determine people's religious thinking and assist anyone looking for a faith.

I. Will you help us by giving your thoughts in response to five brief questions? (1) Yes (2) No — [ ] 4

II. Of what religious group or church are you a member? — [ ] 5 [ ] 6

(01) Baptist	**(08) Lutheran**
(02) Catholic	**(09) Mormon**
(03) Christian Church	**(10) Methodist**
(04) Christian Science	**(11) Presbyterian**
(05) Congregational	**(12) None**
(06) Episcopal	**(13) Other**
(07) Jewish	

____
(Please print name of "other" group.)

III. What local church do you attend? — [ ] 7

(1) ____________________________
(Please print name of local church.)
(2) None

IV. How often do you attend? — [ ] 8
(1) Weekly (2) Often (3) Seldom (4) Never

V. Have you come to the place in your spiritual life where you know that you have eternal life—that is, do you know for certain that if you died today you would go to heaven? **(1) Yes (2) Hope So (3) No** — [ ] 9

VI. If you were to die today and stand before God and he said to you, "Why should I let you into my heaven?" what would you say? — [ ] 10

(Print person's actual words)

(1) Faith (2) Works (3) Unclear (4) No answer

This completes the questionnaire. Your answers are interesting. Thank you for your help.

Gospel & Testimony?
(1) Yes (2) No (3) Didn't Ask

May I have a few more minutes of your time to share with you how I came to know I have eternal life and how you can know it too? — [ ] 11

(After presenting gospel, check address and note day and time for follow-up appointment.)

SIDE TWO

Address: (1) Yes (2) No (3) Didn't ask — [ ] 12
Name (please print) ____________
Street Address ____________ Apt. ____
City ____________ State ____ ZIP ____
Phone ____________ (1) Local (2) Other

FOLLOW-UP APPT. (1) Yes (2) No (3) Didn't ask — [ ] 13
Day ____________ **Time** ____________ — [ ] 14

Future Visits: (1) Yes (2) No (3) Didn't ask — [ ] 15
May I visit you with some friends when we have more time and share how I came to know I have eternal life and how you can know it, too? — **Check Address**
Day ____________ **Time** ____________

Letter: (1) Yes (2) No (3) Didn't ask — [ ] 16 **Check Address**
May I send you a letter which explains how a person can know for certain that he has eternal life?

Future Phone Call: (1) Yes (2) No (3) Didn't ask — [ ] 17
May I phone you in a day or so and share how I came to know I have eternal life and how you can know it, too?
(Get at least first name and phone number.)

Invitation to Worship: (1) Yes (2) No (3) Didn't ask — [ ] 18
We would like to have you worship with us any time you can.
(Give day, time, place of worship)

LITERATURE: (1) Yes (2) No (3) Didn't Offer — [ ] 19
(Print Title) ____________________

ATTEMPTED CONTACTS	DAY OF WEEK	Time of Day: MORNING	AFTERNOON	EVENING	NOT HOME*	
						Contacted (1) At home (2) In public (3) By phone — [ ] 20
						Admitted in home (1) Before survey (2) Before gospel (3) No — [ ] 21
						Results: (1) Profession (2) Rejec. (3) No decision (4) Assurance — [ ] 22
						Age: (1) Jr. H. (2) Sr. H. (3) 18–21 (4) 25–40 (5) 40+ — [ ] 23
						Sex (1) Male (2) Female — [ ] 24
					Date	Comments ____________

*** Put "T" Telephone.**
"V" Personal Visit

8. Because the church is newly formed, visibility is important. Radio, TV, mailers, and handout brochures can all be utilized. At least one newspaper ad needs to be placed concerning the time and place of the first service. Of course, finances will be limited, but whatever is done needs to be done well. Quality is much more important than quantity. First impressions are crucial—the church's image will be represented by the advertising utilized by the planters.

Electronic Marketing Using the Telephone

The Southwest Yearly Meeting of Friends experimented in church planting through telephone blitzing. During the telephone contact, several questions were asked: "Do you presently attend a church? If not, would you mind if we sent you a piece of literature about our church? If you were to attend a church, what kind of church would it be?" Upon receiving answers to these questions, the caller informs the prospect of the new church, its location, and the time of the first service. Several phone calls and letters follow if a person shows interest. Phone marketing works on the law of averages. Several denominations have discovered that for every one hundred phone calls placed, ten individuals will indicate interest in the new project. Out of every ten that indicate interest, one will actually attend the first service. If the church planter expects to have 200 people on the first Sunday, there must be 20,000 phone calls placed by a volunteer core of dedicated workers over several weeks. The key to the whole process is very careful planning and record keeping by the leadership. It should be noted that this method can also be used for the evangelistic outreach of an established church. It is best to target a specific group, such as those who have moved into an area of a precise telephone prefix within the last six months. Often, helpful information can be obtained from the telephone company, a gas or electric utility, or a company that specializes in demographic data.

God's Leadership in Church Planting

Every step of church planting needs to be bathed in prayer. Obviously the demarcation between success and failure is much sharper for the individual who sets out to plant a church than for the pastor who accepts responsibility for the maintenance of a mature ministry. High risk is an impetus for total dependency on the Holy Spirit. Church planters do not have to be any more sure of their calling than ministers who accept the call of an older church. Both need to hear God say, "This is the way, walk ye in it." But there is a unique timing for the church planter. God's plan calls for striking while the iron is hot. The formation of a new body of believers must be done with sensitive submission to the Head of the body, Jesus Christ.

Critique

Strength: We have already stated the major arguments for starting new churches. Lyle Schaller states the following correlations:

> While denominational statistics are not fully comparable on a year-to-year basis nor across denominational lines, there are four statements that can be derived from statistical reports which deserve the careful attention of anyone interested in developing a denominational strategy for church growth. Every denomination reporting an increase in membership reports an increase in the number of congregations. Every denomination reporting an increase in the total number of congregations reports an increase in members. Every denomination reporting a decrease in membership reports a decrease in congregations. Every denomination reporting a decrease in congregations report a decrease in numbers. While this does not prove a cause and effect relationship, it does introduce the first component of a denominational strategy for church growth.
>
> The first step in developing a denominational strategy for church growth should be to organize new congregations.[37]

Every time a new church is planted, the church broadens its spiritual base. People who normally would not assume a role in the older congregation are called on to be leaders and to accept responsibility for the growth of the new body. Responsibility matures the believer and, in turn, both broadens and deepens the church's influence. When individuals have to work and sacrifice to make something happen, there is far greater appreciation of the end result than when the situation is simply inherited. Those who are second- and third-generation members have difficulty in maintaining the momentum of a congregation's founders. Church planting inspires the vision and momentum that is unique to the pioneer spirit. Earl Parvin writes:

> Suburban America's greatest need is for church planting. The larger segment of American society (45 percent) is concentrated around shopping centers; therefore church planting mission organizations are giving priority to establishing local churches in the suburbs, which can in turn evangelize those complexes by means of normal in-house evangelistic programs. Effective, growing suburban churches, which are training congregations of active discipling Christians, are the key to efficient world evangelization. From this base should emerge the vision, manpower, and funds to minister to the spiritual needs of rural America, central city America, and even to the uttermost parts of the earth.[38]

Weakness: There is a high incident of failure among church planters. Failures are not a reason to quit, but they are a reason to examine the causes for failure and to proceed cautiously. Over the span of a couple of years, one denomination saturated a state with approximately fifty church plants, most of which failed. Quite often, the planters were fresh out of a Bible college with little to no pastoral experience. There was a lot of enthusiasm, but little preparation. Deep hurts and scars were left in the wake of disillusionment. Many dropped out of ministry before they had hardly begun. It is paramount that experienced people be in the leadership of church planting. One denomination of approximately 1,000 churches has planned to double that number in the U.S. over a fifteen-year span. One wonders if a small denomination can provide the mature leadership for that many church plants.

Every year Americans raise their "need" threshold. Expectancy levels for churches, schools, and government continue to rise. The search is on for a religion that can satisfy on several fronts. There has to be suitable accommodation for the children, aerobics for the young marrieds, *a cappella* music for the middle-aged, and arts and crafts for the elderly. Most people pass a dozen churches before they get to the church of their choice. Quite often a large church of a thousand members outgrows ten churches with a hundred members each because the latter are not in a position to offer complete programs. The goal should not be to plant churches, but to provide as many entrances into the kingdom as possible. Whether this can be done at a centralized location or through numerous satellites in the area depends on the cultural context, quality of leadership, and the type of person that the church is attempting to entice. This decision can be made only through careful research, planning, and dependence on the leadership of the Holy Spirit.

GOING OUT IN ORDER TO BRING THEM IN

A recent assessment of evangelism for the 1990s stated, "The days of going door-to-door with only a Bible in hand and good intentions in the heart are over."[39] While it is true that gathering demographic and sociological data is necessary for the complex task of evangelism, nothing will replace face-to-face contact. Many churches grow without doing door-to-door evangelism, while many who practice it do not grow. But every church needs to consider the commission to make contact with those homes in the immediate neighborhood. When done methodically and correctly, door-to-door evangelism will be an important component in a comprehensive evangelism program.

The Unpopularity of Door-to-Door Evangelism

There are two reasons that overshadow whatever excuse churches give for their lack of house-to-house calling. First, the pastoral leadership is not engaged in "shoe leather evangelism." Out of all the clerical duties, going door to door is considered one of the most demeaning. The pastor has to step out of the realm of people by whom he is called and into the world of people by whom he is not called and even possibly shunned. The reproach of going outside the camp is too great for some ministers to bear. The books that surround them in their study are friendlier than the faces at the door. Visiting a parishioner in the hospital garners hearty appreciation, while stepping up on a stranger's porch places the pastor in the same class as the magazine salesperson. There just isn't enough instant gratitude or long-term rewards to keep most pastors out there ringing doorbells with the good news of salvation.

Second, the low priority given house visitation by the clergy is compounded in the laity. Unless there is a leader with sufficient clout to inspire by example, most laity will not assume the adequate self-initiation to leave the warm confines of their home. Most churches are not able to provide the energy to move their members beyond their comfort zone into a neighborhood that does not necessarily welcome a smiling Christian on its doorsteps. There is the risk of being embarrassed by not knowing what to say or, worse yet, having a door slammed in one's face. "Don't these people know what a nice person I am or what an important position I hold at work?" Being reduced to a nameless entity by strangers who cannot identify with the Great Commission is too much for most church members to emotionally process.

The Implicit Message of Door-to-Door Evangelism

Door-to-door evangelism will make several strong theological statements. First, it recognizes the domain of mission. While it is true that the world is our parish and that we need to be world Christians, every church has a geographical sphere for which it is responsible. Robert Schuller states, "We act as if we are the only church in Orange County." While that statement is quite ambitious, it still asserts a "domain of mission," a domain which for the Crystal Cathedral may be realistic, but for other smaller churches this goal may be self-defeating. However large the domain of mission that a church adopts, it still needs to reach the homes in its immediate neighborhood. Specific definitions as to "immediate" neighborhood would be arbitrary, but is it too much to expect every church to knock on the doors of every home in a half-mile radius at least once a year?

Second, there is a message of concern demonstrated by a house call that can not be accomplished in any other way. Most people are impressed by a church's willingness to make a personal call. If they weren't, politicians would rely only on television, newspaper, and other kinds of impersonal media. There are a wide range of responses to ringing doorbells: indifference, hostility, surprise, acceptance, and even amazement. When most people move into a new neighborhood, they are never called on by any church. The response to a smiling, alert person who represents a local church is more often positive than negative.

Third, door-to-door visitation enhances the identity of the evangelistic church. For most of us, the glistening steeples of white clapboard churches spiraling above New England villages is reserved only for history books or a Christmas card. The identity of most churches will have to be earned rather than assumed. Personal outreach into the surrounding neighborhood not only invites people to church, but also says, "We just want to let you know that we are here whenever you need us."

How to Do Door-to-Door Evangelism

Door-to-door visitation must not be done haphazardly. Rather, it must be carried out with careful planning. One of the staff members should enlist several laypersons to make door-to-door visits on a certain date. Saturday morning between 10 A.M. and 12 noon is an ideal time. If the houses are close together, ten people can call on 500–700 homes during that time frame. The leader should carefully chart out the area before the calling date. Each person will have a map of his or her specific streets. A brochure needs to be prepared for the occasion. If the people are not home, the brochure should be left in the door. The rules for calling are the following:

1. *Take courage.*
2. *Be positive.*
3. *Do not intrude or leave a brochure if a person doesn't want one.*
4. *Give a brief invitation to attend your church.*
5. *If the person already has a church, commend them. If they are members of a cult, say nothing.*
6. *Do not engage in any kind of argument or controversy.*
7. *Remember that you are sowing seed for the most part, and rarely will a visit become an extended theological discussion. Surveys and gospel presentations should be left to those with more advanced training, such as participants in Evangelism Explosion.*
8. *Don't act as if you are doing the people a favor by calling on them. Avoid condescending attitudes. Express genuine gratitude for the person who accepts your brochure and entertains your invitation.*
9. *Confidence exemplified by a smile should be the demeanor for every call. A doomsday countenance will only serve to drive people away, rather than invite them to a joyous celebration of the King of kings.*

Providing Transportation

The majority of Americans are able to provide their own transportation to church. But the church that is serious about the Great

Commission is ready to provide transportation to anyone who sincerely confesses, "I do not have a way to get there." If there is any such thing as unalienable rights, included among them is the opportunity to worship with a local body of believers. It is up to the church to provide that right for those who are dependent upon others for their travel.

Church bus routes became popular in post–World War II America. When GIs returned from the war, American manufacturing could hardly keep up with the demand for goods and services. It was sometimes difficult for young families to buy a car even if they had the money. Churches began to catch the vision of reaching apartment complexes and tract housing that mushroomed around new industrial plants built by General Motors, General Electric, Republic Steel, Liby-Owens-Ford, IBM, and the dozens of other blue-chip stock companies. Urban sprawl and the prolific birth of children brought church buses out on Sunday morning to catapult the church into the heyday of the American Sunday School.

The baby boomers have now grown up and maintain two or three cars. But there are still plenty of people who cannot provide their own transportation to church. "We will come and get you" is the logical extension of an invitation to church. Jack Hyles, who claims to have the largest Sunday School in America (30,000), suggests suitable areas for a bus ministry: apartment house complexes, trailer courts, isolated areas cut off from neighborhoods by freeways or county lines, low-cost housing developments, and institutions with dormitory arrangements (such as colleges, convalescent homes, juvenile centers, migrant areas, and military installations). Hyles writes:

> Every church has in its area widows who have no car, children with unsaved parents, poor people who would not have private transportation or the finances to use public transportation, elderly people who cannot drive, and wives of unchurched husbands. This does not even include the deaf, the blind, the handicapped, the retarded, and countless others to whom the church has been brought as near as their front curbs because of the bus ministry.[40]

Bus ministry is so demanding in time and energy that no amount of exhortation and cajoling by the pastor will sufficiently motivate. The inspiration to give long hours on both Saturday and Sunday will come only from an ideology that sees a clear demarcation between the saved and the lost. Bus ministry proponents not only believe in "no salvation outside of the church," but they quite often are committed to the creed that "there is no salvation outside of my particular church." The perishing need to be rescued, and a resurrected school bus serves as a lifeboat.

Bus ministry is not successful without proper training and organization. The first step in envisioning evangelistic outreach via a bus ministry is to identify the personnel. The following individuals are essential for every bus route:

1. *The bus captain will work the territory on Saturday and find out who is willing to ride the bus.* He or she will clearly communicate the church's identity and exact time the bus will pick up and return the riders home. Any misunderstanding can be disastrous, because this is the primary person to whom unchurched parents are entrusting their children. The success of the individual route is predicated upon the bus captain more than anything or anyone else. The bus captain rides the bus on Sunday morning, giving directions to the driver and going to the door of the home if need be.

2. *The bus captain assistant is responsible for ministry to and activities for the bus passengers.* This is extremely important if there are large numbers of children. The list of recreation possibilities are almost limitless: car counting, balloon blowing, cookie relaying, toilet paper passing, and bubble gum blowing, all with appropriate prizes to the winners. The bus captain and assistant should be skilled in making appropriate spiritual application and gospel presentations to the unconverted. The ride on the bus is often an evangelistic service in itself.

3. *The bus driver is a highly responsible person who not only meets state requirements, but is also aware of essential safety rules.*

4. *Another crucial team member is the bus mechanic, who sees that every bus is in proper working order.* He or she regularly checks the bus on Saturdays to insure that safety features are functioning. The mechanic should also be present on Sunday mornings to take care of any emergencies.

5. *A secretary needs to keep careful records concerning the routes and riders.* If there are several buses out, it is good to have this individual near a phone, ready to receive emergency calls or provide wake-

up calls to riders who request them.

Bus workers will need to be encouraged, equipped, and rewarded on a constant basis. The worth of the ministry will need to be highlighted in worship services, workshops, and celebration banquets. The workers and the congregation will need to be constantly reminded of the benefits of bus ministry: increase in conversions and attendance, the opportunity for the church to live beyond itself, the training of evangelistic workers, the expanding of church leadership, the training of pastors, and the touching of lives outside of the church's social sphere by providing food, clothing, and a response to a broad array of human needs.

A church should carefully count the cost before launching a bus program. Are there particular groups of people or places to which the church needs to increase its ministry? Church growth is an insufficient motive to start a bus program and nurture it as a meaningful component of evangelistic outreach. There may not be suitable prospect areas in upper-middle-class neighborhoods. And if the church goes to socioeconomically removed neighborhoods, is the ministering church able and willing to absorb people who are culturally different? Has the church leadership thought through the anticipated problems of attempting to impose values on people who do not have a biblical worldview? In all of our evangelistic busyness of transporting people to church, we should not neglect those who are unable to attend services, even if transportation is provided. Aggressive evangelistic ministry must be taken to shut-ins, whether they be found at home or in an institution.

If only negative obstacles are envisioned, opportunities will be lost to reach people who otherwise would remain outside the kingdom. Transformed lives are the only legitimate goals for bussing. Testimonies of those who have been touched because someone cared enough to reach out are a sufficient reward. A young boy from a non-Christian home was picked up from the streets of Detroit and taken to Sunday School. There he met Christ as his Savior and by God's grace transcended his heritage and environment. From those inauspicious beginnings he went on to earn a Ph.D. from a noted university and served as the president of a seminary.

Critique

Strength: The willingness of church members to knock on doors and offer disadvantaged people transportation to church demonstrates a commitment not exhibited by nominal Christians and, for the most part, mainline churches. This ministry serves as a case in point for the thesis of Dean Kelly's seminal work *Why Conservative Churches Are Growing*. Kelly states, "There is about any serious meaning venture a certain irreducible fierce asperity, insistence, exclusiveness, rigor—a fanaticism that brushes everything else aside."[41] People who leave the comfortable confines of their homes and spend long hours cultivating a bus route sometimes exhibit a greater courage than those who travel to more exotic places to spread the gospel.

Bus ministry stomps on the myth that "God helps those who help themselves." We should not assume that everyone can get to church. Bus ministry is a very legitimate way for the church to break out of its self-serving mode, cross social barriers, and minister to the less fortunate. Children especially have the right to hear the good news during their developmental years. Equally important, a child can be placed under the influence of a positive role model through bus workers who invade homes and neighborhoods where few inspirational individuals exist. The opportunity for a child to be around smiling, self-sacrificing people who demonstrate a high degree of generous love and concern leaves an indelible impression that will last forever.

Weakness: Many bus routes have been started out of improper motives—with more desire for increasing attendance than providing a holistic ministry to people. Individuals have been crowded onto buses through contests and competition, with little to offer the riders after they arrive at the church. Reducing individuals to numbers is both demeaning and dehumanizing. One man reported that his sister, who was regularly picked up on Sundays by a bus ministry, had been baptized seven times at the same church. Packing in people in order to reach ecclesiocentric goals is a travesty to the sacrament of worship. Improper nurture and discipleship of the evangelized is a half-gospel that sometimes leaves misinterpretation and scars that last a lifetime. People are sometimes bussed in from such great distances that it is unrealistic to expect them to have any meaningful life in the church. It must always be remembered that individuals are always ends in themselves and never means to self-serving goals, no matter to what extent objectives are justified by ecclesiastical institutions.

Upscale economic congregations may be trying to cross impossible cultural barriers by bussing people to their churches. Such ministry may not be feasible for a church that is surrounded by a five-mile radius of upper-middle-class homes. A bus ministry would be frustrating to the workers and condescending to the disadvantaged. The cultural clash may be confusing and threatening to a child who would sense the disparity, but not know how to handle it. It would be better for churches to expend funds and energy planting and supporting churches homogeneous to their cultural context. Bus ministries are best effected by churches who attempt to reach people of similar socioeconomic backgrounds. David Moberg writes:

> Those who advocate the integration of heterogeneous people and groups within Christian congregations in effect argue for an assimilationist policy. This would compel minorities to reject their ethnic, racial, language, and cultural identities in order to become a part of the Christian group. Such ethnicide or "cultural circumcision" confuses the gospel with cultural values. It constitutes "religious cultural chauvinism," whether it occurs on a remote mission field or at home in America.[42]

CONCLUSION

This chapter has explored five intentional methodologies for evangelizing the lost. Most techniques are a variation of one or more of these methodologies. Many churches practice all of them to some extent. Other churches ignore almost all of them and realize no evangelistic fruit. None are more authentic than the rest, but will be dictated by the location of the church, traditions of the people, and the leadership's self-understanding of what God has called them to do. The goal of all evangelistic endeavor is the same as that expressed by Christ: "You did not choose Me, but I chose you, and appointed you, that you should go and bear fruit, and that your fruit should remain, that whatever you ask of the Father in My name, He may give to you" (John 15:16). Christ has appointed all Christians to bear evangelistic fruit, but the technique will vary according to the soil and customs of that particular location. The substance of the message is from God, but the structure is left to that sensitive and mysterious interface between faith and reason.

Methodologies do not work outside of the context of loving, Spirit-filled Christians. Structures are built on solid foundations of people nurtured in the disciplines of the Spirit. Growth accomplished by carnal church leadership seeking self-gratification will result in disillusionment rather than authentic discipleship. This is not to say that people don't find Christ when they are evangelized by individuals whose motives are not rooted in Christ. While God often blesses human ingenuity and human capability, they must be honed by His purifying love. Malachi prophesied, "For He is like a refiner's fire and like fullers' soap. And He will sit as a smelter and purifier of silver, and He will purify the sons of Levi and refine them like gold and silver, so that they may present to the Lord offerings in righteousness" (Mal. 3:2-3). Offerings are our humble means to glorify God and increase the work of His kingdom. May they come up into God's nostrils as a sweet smell and in no way defile His holy majesty. No fragrance is sweeter to God than individuals presented to Him by evangelizers who love both God and people.

VIII

structuring a church for evangelism

Numerical growth in the local church occurs in several different ways. The membership may be biologically prolific and replace dying members with a larger number of infants. Members may transfer to the church from other locations at a faster rate than they move out of the church's vicinity. It could be that the church is attractive enough for whatever reason to entice attendees at surrounding churches to make a switch. Unless a growing church examines its statistics, it will probably not be able to identify the type of growth that is taking place. For example, a church may be operating under the illusion that it is evangelistically successful when in reality it has received an infusion of warm bodies following a schism in a nearby church community.

DECLINE OF MAINLINE DENOMINATIONS

While I do not disregard the importance of assimilating any sudden appearance of people at the church's front door, our main concerns of this chapter are how to convert unbelievers and how to entice them to attend church. While the majority of local church leaders state that they want their church to be evangelistically successful, most of them demonstrate little intentional direction in carrying out the task and are extremely frustrated by past attempts to reach new people for Christ. Mainline denominations have been hemorrhaging for the last twenty years, including the United Methodist Church, the Presbyterian Church U.S.A., the Episcopal Church, the Evangelical Lutheran Church in America, the Disciples of Christ, the United Church of Christ, and the Lutheran Missouri Synod. Since 1970, Methodists, Presbyterians, and Episcopalians have collectively decreased by 4 million people. For all churches in the U.S. during the years 1970–1989, the aggregate total growth was between 12 and 13 million persons.[1] But two things need to be kept in mind. First, the U.S. population grew by 43 million during that same period of time.[2] Second, nearly one-half of the church growth mentioned above was in two denominations—the Southern Baptists and the Assemblies of God. Barna Associates states:

> Consider the fact that although Christian Churches spent in excess of one-quarter of a trillion dollars on ministry in America in the Eighties, we saw no growth in the proportion of adults who accepted Christ as their Savior. Put more directly, this means that we spent an average of $2,300 per non-Christian adult without generating any increase in our "market share."[3]

BUDGETING FOR EVANGELISM

An examination of a representative sample of church budgets would reveal that very little of the money expended by local churches is designated for outreach or evangelism. Most of it is spent on salaries, facilities, and denominational budgets. Granted, sufficient salaries and suitable sanctuaries are important for doing evangelism. The point is that few churches intentionally budget for reaching new people with the gospel. Normally less than 5 percent of a church's budget is designated for local evangelism. Howard Hanchey charges his own denomination, the Episcopal Church, with having a "maintenance mind-set" as opposed to a "mission mind-set." Hanchey documents the Episcopal Church's 33 percent decline in membership over the last twenty years and states, "The natural progression from mission to maintenance shows itself in two ways: a legitimate concern with expanding maintenance needs, such as repairing the roof or fixing the plumbing, and a healthy common life that turns into an unhealthy 'static triumphalism.'"[4] He goes on to define "static triumphalism" as the need to cling to what already is for the sake of safety and security. Such a mentality obscures present possibilities and opportunities.

The thesis of this chapter is that for evangelism to be effectively carried out in the United States, it needs to become a priority of the local church. There are several definitive steps that need to be taken.

ARTICULATING A VISION

The local church needs to articulate a vision for reaching new people for Christ. A vision consists of a goal, a desire to reach the goal, and the belief that the goal is attainable. The vision is embodied in a person who is the leader of the group. If the vision is held by subordinates, rather than the person who wields the most clout, it will fail and quite often create conflict within the church community. The greatest impediment to achieving a goal is lack of unity because the leader does not have sufficient authority to lead.

The influence to lead a congregation toward an evangelistic goal is proportionate to the degree of confidence that the congregation has in the leader (who almost without exception is the pastor). C. Peter Wagner observes unequivocally that the key person in a numerically growing church is the pastor. Wagner argues that the evangelistic pastor assumes responsibility for growth, works hard to achieve it, builds a knowledge inventory concerning church growth principles, and is willing to delegate ministry responsibilities to others. I have given a sociological and psychological profile of the numerically successful pastor, as well as key character qualities, in *What Really Matters in Ministry.*

Pastors may have dynamic leadership qualities and carefully articulate their vision, but their message will fall on deaf ears because of lack of confidence by the hearers. Confidence is predicated on the following pillars:

1. Compatibility is a certain fit between pastor and people and, in turn, between people and community that decreases or increases the probabil-

ity of evangelistic success. A recent seminary graduate may land a job in a setting where the people do not speak his or her language. The congregation may be concerned about tractors and fertilizer, while the last seven or eight years he or she has spoken only the language of academia or ecclesiology. It is possible for the pastor's culture and life experiences to be so far removed from his or her own congregation that forward movement will be exceedingly tedious. A Ph.D. in theology may feel that his or her talents are wasted in a blue collar community, while the congregation may feel that the pastor does not quite identify with their way of life no matter how hard he or she tries. Compatibility necessitates a meeting of the meanings, what David Buttrick refers to as "consciousness." While Buttrick is speaking of preaching as a metaphorical language, "a nexus of image, symbol, metaphors, and ritual,"[5] the same must be true of ministry as a whole. If there are not common images between pastor and people, there is a split consciousness, a serious fissure in compatibility.

2. *Confidence is also predicated upon perceived competence.* Can this pastor lead us to the promised land? Is enough expertise demonstrated to make us believe that he or she has the capabilities to lead us to the summit, rather than spin our wheels in the mud? Has the pastor announced a lofty goal without being able to accomplish daily, weekly, or even quarterly objectives that are the expected responsibilities of the position? Before announcing evangelistic hopes, a new pastor would do much better to paint the peeling front porch of the parsonage, conduct a vacation Bible school that hasn't been done in years, or demonstrate effectiveness in bringing in one or two new families by showing them constant attention. A few visible accomplishments in the beginning days of ministry will serve as a tremendous boost to the pastor's credibility in the eyes of the people.

3. *Confidence will not be won without political savvy.* The pastor will not be able to lead toward numerical goals without polling the leadership of the church. Polling is much more than conducting a questionnaire. It means identifying the thought processes and frames of references of those who have sacrificed over the years to make the church possible. Attempting to run roughshod over the opinion makers of the church will result in a no-win situation, with the pastor being the prime loser. The church will stay and the

pastor will move on to the next conflict. If the church senses that the pastor has goals other than those held by the church, the pastor will be assessed as self-seeking rather than church-serving. To lead and serve at the same time is a delicate task. C. Peter Wagner argues that the pastor must serve while at the same time accept the role of being the key person behind the growth of the church:

> Many pastors will spend their lives proving that they are servants, but will not accept the consequences of doing that well, namely the exaltation that God gives them as a leader and the power that goes along with it. Jesus washed the disciples' feet, but at no time during His earthly ministry was there any doubt in His mind or the disciples' minds who their leader was. Servanthood and leadership do not contradict each other in Christian work. They go together.[6]

One of the first steps of political savvy is discerning the degree of compatibility between the direction the church wants to go and the direction that the pastor wants to take it. An open-ended question should be raised by the pastoral candidate at the first meeting with the church leadership: "What do you want to see happen in this church over the next five years?" Quite often the laity will not be able to articulate evangelistic growth as a part of the church's plan. Most churches have a maintenance orientation rather than a progressive, long-range plan. But if the candidate perceives a definite recalcitrance among the church's board of directors to infuse the congregation with new people, he or she may need to politely ask to be excused from consideration.

If, however, openness to growth is perceived in the congregational leadership, the pastoral candidate should share dreams and aspirations with employers from the very beginning. But only after having gained the confidence of the laity will he or she be able to crystallize goals and invite people to follow in pursuit of those goals. The vision must first be shared with several confidants, such as an informal breakfast group or an ad hoc "futures" committee that will explore new avenues. As the vision evolves it will be shared with the board and finally the church. The vision should be supported by use of charts and statistics.

As the pastor articulates his or her case, an awareness is necessary of the mental blocks possessed by the membership that must be hurdled or completely broken down. Many long-time church members are satisfied with the social mix of the church and do not want it disturbed by new people. Many small churches are occupied by people who are related by blood and fear becoming a minority rather than the ruling majority. Some of the membership is so defeated and negative that they do not believe that anything significant can happen (or, if it does happen, the price is too great to bear). More people mean more problems and more expenditures for the existing members. Wagner offers the following accurate diagnosis:

> Churches which have remained small for some time are not simply miniature large churches. They have a different character altogether. The major difference lies in interpersonal relationships. In the small church there are no strangers. Everyone knows everyone else. The social situation is predictable and therefore comfortable. Preserving this value by maintaining the status quo becomes a very high priority in the lives of many church members.[7]

SELF-EXAMINATION

The second definitive step needs to be an increase of the knowledge inventory. "Know thyself" is more than a profound philosophical exhortation. It is a pragmatic must for a pastor and congregation. What kind of church is this? R. Daniel Reeves and Ronald Jensen claim, "Growing churches are able to match their resource capabilities with the spiritual and sociological realities and needs in the community."[8] Self-analysis is needed in order for a church to accurately assess its resource capabilities. The authors proceed to identify and define several typologies that enable the church to describe its identity. Most churches have never stopped to think about who they are. Churches would benefit from measuring themselves by Reeves and Jensen's categories:

Historical Typology

Stages of a church's growth include infancy, childhood, adolescence, young adulthood, and middle age. This typology serves to review pastoral tenure, facilities development, migration patterns that have affected the church, various crises that are a part of the church's history, and denominational loyalty.

Contextual Typologies

Geographical typology. What is the track record of growth with the various areas of the country and how are the regional characteristics related to the evangelistic enterprise? The uniqueness of the West Coast is that it boasts the fastest growing churches in the U.S. while at the same time having counties with the highest percentage of unchurched populations.

Urban/Rural typology. The surrounding environment affects the personality of the church. Downtown churches come in three varieties: midtown, inner-city, and inner-urban. Metroregional churches are large churches that serve a total metropolitan area because they are on the outskirts of a city and are serviced by major traffic arteries. Suburb or neighborhood churches come in several varieties: city suburb, metropolitan suburb, fringe suburb, fringe village, and fringe settlement churches. Independent city or small town churches are found in communities of 5,000 to 30,000 people that are not adjacent to larger metropolitan areas. Rural village churches are located in small towns that service large agricultural areas. Rural settlement churches are located in the middle of "nowhere," identified by a store and a gas station, with no other church in a five- to fifty-mile radius.

Community Image Typologies

These typologies tell us whether the church is well known within the town and if it is reputed as "the church to attend" if one is "somebody." Subordinate or secondary churches are those churches one attends if he or she isn't trying to be a "somebody." Exclusive churches are attended by people who want to be separated from others in the town in which they are located.

Philosophical Typologies

Philosophical typologies cluster around beliefs and congregational composition. Beliefs can be identified by examining the church's philosophy and by identifying the historical family with which the church aligns itself.

Philosophy typologies reflect the emphasis that is most evident in the church's lifestyle. Some major on soul winning. Others make the methodical teaching of Scripture their primary reason for existence. Some are highly relational, attempting to minister to people at the point of their need. Social action churches emphasize good deeds in terms of addressing social injustice and practicing mercy and kindness to the disadvantaged. Meanwhile, general practitioner churches try to give adequate attention to all of the above. Special purpose churches gear their ministry toward highly defined homogeneous groups such as single adults, college students, migrant workers, or recovering addicts. Forum churches are normally open-minded, pluralistic, and evangelistically nonaggressive. They are given to discovery and openness to various opinions rather than defending a doctrinal stance.

Philosophy typologies also examine the theological matrix of the church. Rather than simply tracing the church's individual history, this typology examines the influence of cultural/theological milieus that the church represents. The composite groupings carry labels such as fundamentalist, evangelical, holiness, Pentecostal, charismatic, mainline, Baptist, Catholic, cultic, and so on.

THE MEGACHURCH

One of the most phenomenal developments in church growth and evangelistic strategy today has been the frequent appearance of the megachurch. Megachurches may be the single greatest phenomenon of ecclesiasticism today. Before World War II, they were the exclusive domain of great preachers such as Henry Ward Beecher, Phillips Brooks, and George Truett. Today they are run by pastors who see themselves as CEOs who know how to get things done. In either case, megachurches are usually led by charismatic personalities who wield sufficient influence to cause people to adopt their vision for evangelizing the surrounding area. Lyle Schaller estimates that there are presently over 1,000 churches in America that average over 1,000 in attendance on Sunday morning. If there had been an official launching date for American megachurches, it would have been in the early 1970s. The prototype was pastored by a man who was an individualist, pastoring either an independent church or one within such a loose organizational system that he was allowed to be a maverick.

The sociological, psychological, and demographic dimensions of megachurches call for analysis. No one has done a better job of analyzing these dimensions than Lyle Schaller.[9] Among the reasons that Schaller gives for the proliferation of megachurches are the following:

1. *Denominational loyalties have broken down and people are no longer satisfied with attending the traditional church of their parents.* They are searching for a church of whatever denominational stripe that can meet a cluster of needs centered around family values. The larger a church is, the greater range of needs it can meet.

2. *There is an increasing mobility of society and a decreasing dependence on proximity for goods and services.* The neighborhood church is being replaced by churches located within sight of an interstate cloverleaf or at least with an easy access from a freeway. The improvement of roads has meant that the church that is ten or fifteen miles away is only ten or fifteen minutes away. People are willing to travel that distance to attend the church that they perceive best suits their situation.

3. *In an earlier chapter we noted the bleak economic future for many Americans; however, it can still be noted that upward mobility has brought for many suburbanites a high standard of living.* We are the best clothed and best housed generation that America has ever seen. The obsession for quality in technology, transportation, communication, and entertainment is addictive on both an individual level and a mass scale. George Barna highlights the concept of excellence as a current intrigue of the American people.

> For the past decade, we have stressed the importance of providing quality products and services. As consumers, we strive to locate companies that are dedicated to excellence as manifested through product quality and customer service. As employees, we are most interested in working for organizations whose performance is tops, and which esteem competence.[10]

The church has not been exempt from this quest. Of course, what God deems as excellent and what passes the quality control scrutiny of the American public may be far apart.

4. *The larger a church becomes, the more it increases its ability to become larger.* Advertising, programs, and multiplication of ministers

increase a church's visibility. Americans are categorized into consumer or target groups: marrieds, seniors, singles, young adults with children, etc. Never have Americans been so categorically labeled as they are today. When people are cognizant of their label, they are more intentionally directed to a group that fits the profile that matches their identity. They will shop around until they find the church with that particular profile. Churches that offer narrowly defined ministries are akin to specialty shops, as opposed to the one-stop shopping center in a mall-oriented culture. Schaller quotes a church staff member:

> Recently we began to expand our specialized ministries. We designed a mutual support group for adults who are children of an alcoholic parent or have an alcoholic relative. It grew rather slowly at first, but after about eight or nine months the floodgates opened. In two months we went from 30 to nearly 200.[11]

5. There has been a hemorrhaging of mainline churches over the last twenty years. People are looking for autonomous churches whose message and mission is not dictated by a denominational authority. As liberal churches increasingly adopted the implicit slogan "I'm as lost as you are; come join us so we can grope together," Americans looked for a more coherent and authoritative message. They began to question money spent on controversial causes that were not clear-cut biblical issues. By attending an independent church, there was an increasing satisfaction that money was being spent for community and local causes rather than denominational bureaucracy.

6. There are many other demographic causes for megachurches that could be mentioned, but the final cause is as much negative as it is positive. Schaller focuses on "the capability of the larger churches to offer a broad range of choices, not only in the times for worship, but also in how they can be engaged in doing ministry. The megachurch uses a smaller proportion of volunteers' time and energy in maintaining the institution."[12] In short, if a person attends a large church, it is less likely that he or she will be highly involved in the life of the institution. As a church grows, spectators increase and active volunteers proportionately decrease. In small churches, quite often everyone has a job—sometimes two or three.

Large churches lend themselves to autonomy and anonymity. People can step in and out of large worship celebrations in mammoth sanctuaries and hardly be identified, much less asked to do a job or take on a responsibility. This lack of accountability and privatization of religious experience is part of the socioreligious profile of the American public. As worship assemblies grow, devotion becomes more private than corporate. Many people desire to enter into sanctuaries without entering into the lives of others so there will be no further demands on their time and energy.

The strength of the megachurch is that it is able to offer quality programming and a wide range of choices. The church is able to attract the best in talent, music, teaching, counseling, and youth leadership. The facilities are on par with, if not better than, those that the attendees experience in their workplace and residence. The weakness is the consumer orientation that often expends all resources to reach people at the point of their felt need rather than being directed by means that are in keeping with God's holiness. Schaller states, "The down side of this, of course, is the tendency to depend more on the market than the mission. . . . To some, the popularity and success of the mega-church represents a dangerous concession to the rampant consumerism characteristic of contemporary American society."[13] A revival of numbers based simply on scratching people where they itch needs to be constantly red-flagged. The following assessment by *Newsweek* of young families returning to church is an alarm that needs to be heeded by anyone whose biblical concerns go beyond filling pews with warm bodies:

> Unlike earlier religious revivals, the aim this time (aside from born again traditionalists of all faiths) is support not salvation, help rather than holiness, a circle of spiritual equals rather than an authoritative church or guide. A group affirmation of self is at the top of the agenda, which is why some of the least demanding churches are now in greatest demand.[14]

OBSERVATION OF THE SURROUNDING COMMUNITY

The other half of the knowledge inventory is an exploration of the surrounding community. This has already been treated in the sociology chapter, discussion of church planting, and the typologies explained by Reeves and Jensen. But we have not sufficiently discussed the decisions that need to be made based on demographics. As a church examines its target area (e.g., a five-mile radius), it needs to ask several questions: Do we desire to reach these people for Christ? Do we have the means and personnel to evangelize the area? Does the present description of our church match the profile of the community? If the answer to these questions is no, then the church needs to move or disband. The only other option is to face death through atrophy.

The attendance at an inner-city church had dwindled from 500 to 250 over a five-year span. The church complex, which consisted of two large buildings covering almost a city block, were becoming increasingly difficult to financially maintain. The church decided it did not have the resources to reach the community in which it had been located for the past sixty years. Neither did it perceive that it could find the pastoral leadership that would be required to draw in suburbanites with sufficient resources to minister to the socioeconomic realities that surrounded the church. Because they were between pastors and thus did not want to be in a state of ambivalence when they decided on their new leader, the board unanimously voted to put the property up for sale and move to the outskirts of town. Having made their decision, they would then choose a person who would be willing to lead them in reaching a certain kind of person.

THE BABY BOOMERS

Yet many churches have moved to the suburbs and have remained small and struggling because they did not have a vision for reaching the people who were simultaneously relocating to the same area as the new church. One of the problems has to do with leadership. Many churches are directed by people who are over fifty and who think in different patterns and form different perspectives than those born after World War II (i.e., baby boomers). One must first recognize that there is a wide range of age among people born since 1945—almost half of a century. One must also remember that generalizations are often overly simplistic and even stereotyped. There is great diversity among baby boomers, but it would seem that at least the following can be assumed for most people born between 1945 and 1960. Boomers are more individualistic than their parents and distrust centralization of authority. They more readily favor a church that appears to be innovative by taking pragmatic measures to change the world around them. Those born after 1945 are far more educated than their parents. According to James Engel and Jerry Jones, authors of *Baby Boomers and the Future of World Missions:*

> More than 84% of all boomers have completed high school, and approximately half of them have finished at least one year of college. Over 25% have attended four or more years of college. They also believe in continuing education throughout life and are the backbone of the burgeoning community college system throughout the country.[15]

The statistics above hold several implications for evangelistic practice. Pastors must demonstrate educational and communication skills that are on par with those to whom they are ministering. Many who come to church want to leave with something that they have been taught and that they can implement in their daily lives. Because of the educational yearning, seminars on finances, marriage, and other relevant topics are excellent entrance points for boomers. Because of university training and having lived through the civil rights era, boomers are far more tolerant of other thought systems and will not tolerate a dogmatism that discredits others. This does not mean that the present generation cannot be taught dogma. It does mean that the church that takes the conceited position that it has a corner on truth will not be very attractive.

Engel and Jones highlight the entrepreneurial spirit of baby boomers:

> We are now seeing more companies being created than ever before in the history of our country. For example, we created 640,000 new companies in 1984. Compared to 93,000 per year during the industrial period of the 1950's. New businesses are being formed today at double the rate of ten years ago.[16]

If potential converts sense that the controlling motif of a congregation is tradition rather than a willingness to try new ministries, they will look for spiritual fulfillment elsewhere. Observing in the yellow pages that a church has its only worship service at the "sacred" hour of 11 A.M. is enough to turn off some boomers. Above all, the church must present itself as successful instead of projecting the image of a downtrodden pilgrim. The church must explicitly give attention to being successful in its corporate mission while enabling the newcomer to realize their full potential not only in the world of the sacred, but in everyday enterprises.

Entrepreneurial churches reach entrepreneurs by stressing a theology of vocation. God is interested in us just as much when we wear a hat on the construction job as he is when we remove our hats to enter a sanctuary. Because baby boomers have not followed in the vocational steps of their parents and are facing the economic realities of job shortages caused by more efficient technology, there is a tremendous emphasis placed on occupational security and job satisfaction. There is a much greater possibility that boomers will experience a mid-career change than did their forefathers. A "jobfinders" workshop may prove to be an efficient evangelistic tool.

The most critical concern for the present generation is in the area of family needs. "Boomers have a 500% greater likelihood of being single than their elders."[17] This means opportunities for evangelism in two specific areas. It is estimated that 50 percent of the adult population will be single by the year 2000. Never married, recently divorced, and single parents are looking for help, and the church needs to be poised for the mission. Second, families that have remained intact face the tension of trying to give adequate time to their individual family members while earning a living. It is difficult to balance relationships and avarice. An added tension for families is the insecurity of displacement. Very few upwardly mobile people remain in the community in which they were raised. They are looking for a warm fellowship that can provide stability and offer clues on how to maintain values that they feel are important. The value that is most often articulated is the nuclear family. *Newsweek* concluded that "the return to religion is fueled by the boomers' experience of becoming parents—and the realization that children need a place where they can learn solid values and make friends with peers who share them."[18] In one parent's words, "In this crazy world, any kind of positive influence you can give your children is worth the time."[19]

REACHING SECULAR SUBURBANITES

The church that reaches contemporary people does not need to manufacture a diluted "neo-theology." It will, however, be sensitive to traditional language that has little meaning for contemporary Americans. The relevant church will adopt a language that emphasizes the person of Jesus Christ first and the doctrine or theology of the church second. Christ is in control of the entire universe, but at the same time He is vitally interested in the present world of individuals. The church evidences this concern for the secular individual's personal world by expressing a clear theology of vocation. George Hunter indicts the church that ignores the "world of work," quoting Dorothy Sayers: "In nothing has the church so lost her hold on reality as in her failure to understand and respect the secular vocation. . . . How can anyone remain interested in a religion which seems to have no concern with nine-tenths of his life?"[20]

No one has done a better job in reaching the suburbanite family than Bill Hybels. Hybels is crouched and waiting for the person who has a condo, summer house, BMW, and other trinkets of success, but while adding zeros and toys is accumulating question marks about life. As dissatisfaction accompanies the binge for things, individuals crave for something more. For that reason Hybels is careful to envelop the gospel in contemporary idioms and focus biblical claims on everyday problems stemming from marriage, sex, adolescence, and the workplace. Relevancy is the key to drawing 15,000 people per week to his worship center in South Barrington, Illinois. When the worshipers arrive, they discover that esoteric liturgy and traditional church furniture have been removed. Instead, there is a fast-paced service orchestrated by soft rock, a drama group, and Bill Hybel's practical sermon. In the words of one observer, "It won't be predictable, at least if you expected it to look like a church: No robes, altars or stained glass. A 4,550 seat theater, complete with 12 big screen TV's showing close-ups of action on stage, just like at rock concerts."[21]

The high-tech service is not the only thing that draws people to Willow Creek. There are ninety activity groups that meet throughout the week, a daycare center that services 2,200 one- to ten-year-old children each week, and a club for older children that entices almost 500 kids a week to discuss such problems as peer pressure and family tension. And if there are those who think that Bill Hybels is all showbiz, slick marketing, and shallow spirituality, the operation deserves another look. There is a "New Believers" hour that takes place on Wednesday evening for those who desire in-depth Bible study and discipleship. This deeper commitment service attracts thousands.

One should not conclude that a growing church needs to be oriented toward a yuppie society. Such a notion would be fatal to evangelizing the majority of Americans. Seventy-five percent of American families, as of 1989, earned less than $50,000 per year. The median family income was approximately $29,000 per year.[22] There are huge throngs of people who do not drive BMWs and who do not shop out of Nieman Marcus catalogs. A church growth analyst need only drive to the opposite side of Chicago from Bill Hybels' ninety-acre campus to the industrial, smoke-filled towns of Gary and Hammond, Indiana. This is Jack Hyles' territory.

It is 10 A.M. as I drive into Hammond. Even though there are no stores open, I manage to find a service station attendant who tells me the location of the church. His deaf sister is a member of the church, but he doesn't go there because when he was small, he got lost in a crowd. If a person has "crowd phobia," Jack Hyles' church is definitely not the place to attend. The church advertises itself as the world's largest Sunday School with approximately 30,000 present on a given Sunday in its multifaceted facility and programs.

On this hot, humid Sunday morning, I went back to the future. The streets were rolled up and the only people in automobiles seemed to be going to church. After parking in the multilevel garage, I spoke to a young couple, both overweight adults, with two children. The man was dressed in a white shirt with no jacket. We ambled across the railroad tracks to the church about one block away, surrounded by older model cars. The men already in the sanctuary seemed to have all gone to the same barber. The scene was definitely from the 1950s. Everything that happens in the service is traditional. All the congregational songs and special music are traditional gospel singing. The first time we stood was for the reading of the Scripture (about thirty minutes into the service), read by a pastoral team member from Hebrews 12. The page from the *Scofield Bible* was announced, and the Scripture was read responsively.

The high point of this service was Jack Hyles' message. The sermon was topical, with little relationship to Hebrews 12 and only a couple of scriptural references. The title, "Staying in Your Game Plan," was supported by a plethora of illustrations derived from such subjects as Hoosier basketball, the Chicago Bears, hitchhiking home from the U.S. Army, the sacrifices of his mother to support her children, and putting a jigsaw puzzle together as a child. Hyles is a master communicator, retaining intimacy with the audience while at the same time exemplifying the authority of preaching. He volleys between the sublime and ridiculous, leaving his audience laughing one minute and dead serious the next. The message concludes with him asking, "Have you lost a piece to the puzzle?" Hyles affirms in conclusion, "There is a spot for you in God's great puzzle!"

First Baptist Church of Hammond, Indiana is a congregation that is led by a highly motivated pastor who considers his number one task in life to be soul-winning. He has been able to mobilize his laity and thousands of other pastors across the nation to fulfill the same goal. The church seems particularly adapted to reaching lower-class, ethnic minorities and those with particular needs, such as the deaf and unwed mothers. What it lacks in refinery, it makes up for in vision.

ARTICULATE AND IMPLEMENT A PLAN

Articulating a vision and describing a plan for evangelism are two different processes. The mice in Aesop's fable had a vision for hanging the bell on the cat so they could detect when their dreaded enemy was approaching. But they were hard put to come up with a plan for placing the bell on the cat, not to mention the difficulty of enlisting volunteers for the delicate and dangerous project. Most church bodies would draw a blank if called on to produce their plan for reaching the lost. They may claim a desire to evangelize and often preach on the Great Commission, but the idea remains extremely vague as to how evangelistic principles can be implemented in the corporate life of the church and the individual lives of the people. A good plan needs to be practical rather than theoretical, near rather than far, concrete rather than abstract, and quantifiably measurable rather than ephemerally nebulous. The evangelistic pastor will not perceive quality and quantity as polarities, but parallel rails of Christian endeavor.

A plan for evangelism has three essential elements: a mission statement, a philosophy behind the mission statement, and definite steps for implementing the mission statement.

A Mission Statement

A mission statement is more complicated than a slogan such as "Reaching Portland in the 90s" or "Healing Hurts and Building Dreams." However, slogans and mottoes are helpful in keeping the mission statement before the people. The mission statement represents the task cycle of the church. A task cycle has the following components:

Purpose: Why are we doing the task?

Product: The results we are trying to create.

Transformation: The methods or means used to change the state of something.

Functional Capability: Inputs, tools, and capabilities to engage in a transformation and produce a product.

A mission statement with the above components could be broken down into the following elements:

Purpose: To the glory of God.

Product: Fully functioning Christians, made holy in Christ.

Transformation: Turn non-Christians and nominal Christians into mature Christians through Bible teaching, evangelistic training, and overall equipping of the saints.

Functional Capability: A ministry of evangelism, gifts of the Spirit, teaching, and principles of evangelism (here we may even state what kind of principles, such as "Kennedy" or "Everyone Win One").[23]

A simple mission statement might look like the following:

> Portland First Church of the Nazarene will seek to transform non-Christians and nominal Christians into fully functioning and responsible members of God's kingdom made holy in Christ through teaching of the Word, celebration of the sacraments, instruction in stewardship, evangelistic training, and overall equipping of the saints for ministry. The leadership

of our church will constantly be searching for the best resources and methodology to ensure that Portland First Church of the Nazarene is evangelistically successful to the glory of God through the power of the Holy Spirit. God desires that we become a community of worshiping believers in love with Jesus Christ and one another. This love is to be shared with and demonstrated to the surrounding world in avenues of service.

A Philosophy behind the Mission Statement

Philosophies of ministry and evangelism normally evolve and are communicated to the congregation over a period of time. But many evangelistically successful pastors come to a church with a philosophy predicated upon convictions that have been honed over several years. They either introduce this philosophy to an existing church or plant a church that reflects their personal ecclesiology. This philosophy is unique enough to be reflected and identified in all aspects of the church's worship, education, evangelism, and recreation. It provides a unifying theme or pragmatic canopy under which all ministries are to be located. Rick Warren of Saddleback Community Church in Laguna Hills, California, a church that has grown from 0 to 4,000 in ten years, states that a guideline for starting a new ministry is that it must be in doctrinal and philosophical harmony with the church. "And it is more important that it be in philosophical harmony than in doctrinal harmony."[24]

And what is Rick Warren's philosophy of the church? "It is an organism rather than an organization." This particular statement provides a touchstone for every ministry that Warren's church establishes and every methodology that is implemented to reach people with the good news. The church is not an organization with boards, committees, and elections, but is a body of believers. The full-time staff functions as the "ad-ministers" of the church, enabling the rest of the church to become ministers. Becoming a member of the church is synonymous with being called to ministry.

Rick Warren is constantly teaching on the metaphor of the church as a body. Using Paul's analogy, the body functions as the basis of spiritual gifts, not elected offices. Pastor Warren made a covenant with his church. If they will do the ministry of the church, he will make sure that the body is well-fed. The feeding and leadership of the church should be in the hands of a few and the ministry of the church should be in the hands of many. If the ministry is in the hands of many, the more the church will grow spontaneously. The pastor is to act as a catalyst for the birth of ministries. By constantly encouraging lay ministers and the discovery of gifts, the church staff has built a gift-based structure that stimulates creativity. Warren's formula is that the increase of complexity is disproportionate to the increase of efficiency. Simple structures are more stable and more productive. Complex structures produce maintenance rather than ministry. Ministry produces evangelism. The challenge is to rediscover the church that operates as a gifted body so that ministry will be maximized and maintenance will be minimized.

Putting the Plan into Action

Bill Hybels is no doubt accurate when he indicts most churches for not having an evangelistic plan. The leadership at Willow Creek does not leave the working out of evangelism to individual interpretation. There is a corporate plan for the church to reach out into the community as individuals. The responsibility of the believer and the cycle through which the unbeliever must go in order to become a fully committed Christian is spelled out in detail. The goal is to transform "Harry" from a pagan concerned mostly with his own selfish pursuits into a reproducer of converts. There is a seven-step process by which a producer can produce reproducers. Hybels carefully articulates these steps to his entire congregation once a year:

1. *Build a relationship with a non-Christian person. Jesus was a friend of sinners.* He spent most of His time in the marketplace rather than in the temple or synagogue. Relationships can be built through recreation, sharing tasks, asking people for help, inviting people to social events, and organizations that provide common pursuits (e.g., Kiwanis, P.T.A.).

2. *Give a verbal witness.* After a person has earned the right through identification and befriending, it is appropriate to offer a solution to whatever question or problem the person may have. An entrance statement may sound like the following: "We talk about those things at Willow Creek Community Church." It is important to explain to the prospect that Willow Creek Community people will not try to corner the new attendee or in any way make him or

her feel awkward or out of place. The verbal witness is normally given to someone in the same subculture (such as campers, bikers, board members, housewives, and so forth). The more subcultures a church represents, the more evangelistically effective it will be.

3. Invite the person to the Sunday morning service. Better yet, bring them to the Sunday morning service. The service will be in terms that Harry can understand. Hybels challenges his people to imagine what it would be like to attend a Buddhist service where terms and rituals would be esoteric. At Hybels' church, Harry will attend a Sunday service in surroundings that are familiar and with people who have the same kinds of concerns and questions that he does. It is hoped that the overall impression received by the newcomer is that what is offered in the program is for now, the twenty-first century. Hybels writes:

> I've found that the unchurched person thinks most Christians, and especially pastors, are woefully out of touch with reality. "They don't have a clue as to what's going on in the world," he thinks. An unchurched person who does venture into a church assumes whatever is spoken will not be relevant to his life.[25]

Hybels explains that his quest for relevancy is behind his selecting 60 to 70 percent of his illustrations from newspapers, periodicals, TV, and other media.

4. Conversion. The worship service or sermon, possibly after several visits at Willow Creek, needs to be followed up by a theological discussion in terms that the person can understand. A lead-in question is necessary: "What did you think about the service? What did you think about the pastor's ideas in his sermon?" The conversation should eventually turn to Jesus Christ and how His life and message is relevant to the prospect's own situation. Every believer should be able to lead the repentant in a simple prayer of faith in Christ.

5. The New Community. It is now time for the new believer to put his or her roots down in Christ. The "new community," which meets on Wednesday evening, is Christianity 301–401, a time to hear expository messages and be nourished by the meat of discipleship. Those who gather on Wednesday evening normally total about a third of those who attend the Sunday service. All church members are expected to attend on Wednesday evening. And membership is not taken lightly at Willow Creek. "Each member shall sign a yearly statement of commitment to reaffirm his or her continued desire for membership."[26]

6. Small Groups. Every member is expected to be committed to a small group. Meeting at a specified time with a dozen other individuals allows opportunity for confession, mutual encouragement, the articulation of one's faith, and discussion of the Scriptures. Hybels calls the discipleship through small groups the backbone of Willow Creek's outreach ministry.

7. Service. Willow Creek emphasizes being involved in the life of the surrounding community through active social ministry. Church members are encouraged to let their light shine through food drives for the poor, inner-city projects in Chicago, and general service projects sponsored by the church or even the public sector. "Where are you intending to serve?" is an optimum discipleship question as one becomes a member at Willow Creek Community Church.

It is clear that in Hybels' plan, the evangelized go through a task cycle that is definitively and meticulously described. "Harry" is now ready to go out and look for "Larry" and experience the cycle being worked out in someone else's life. Hybels does not claim that his plan is "the divinely inspired plan" or the only plan. He does believe that it is God's plan given to the church's leadership and that it best fits Willow Creek's location and clientele.

The Characteristics of a Good Plan

It is inclusive. Inclusiveness does not mean a naïveté that believes that everyone will feel at home in the church. It does mean an attempt to erase arbitrary delineations and prejudices that would prevent people from attending. Inclusiveness also means that the pastor tries to produce an open, caring attitude among the members of the congregation that can be immediately sensed by outsiders. One pastor of a church that has doubled in size over the last ten years to a church of 1,250 on Sunday morning defined pastoral success as "accepting people where they are, expressing love to them with scriptural, personal convictions without condemnation of them."

The effectiveness of the plan can be measured. People who pastor growing churches do not deem numbers as the only criterion of success. A pastor may have gained fifty new families over the course of the year, yet lose a hundred families because of the shutdown of a nearby manufacturing plant. It still remains noteworthy that fifty new families were gained because of a significant plan. It is also important to evaluate whether the families are affiliating for the first time with a church rather than simply transferring from other churches. The church growth school has made us more acutely aware of the need to analyze evangelistic effectiveness. One may utilize a composite number to represent the current size of the church. If membership stands at 1,100 and the average attendance of the church for all Sundays during the past year was 900, the current size of the church is 1,000. If the church stood at 500 composite membership ten years ago, the decadal growth rate is 100 percent, which church growth analysts deem as healthy growth.

But a church growth check-up is more complicated than calculating numbers. The diagnosis must take into consideration surrounding demographics and other extension work the church may have engaged in, such as the planting of new churches. If the church above has planted another church within the last ten years and the new church has grown to 500, the decadal growth rate would be 200 percent.[27]

In order to figure what the decadal growth would be if the church continued to grow at the existing rate, one would need to multiply the number at the end of each projected year by the percentage which the church grew in the first year. For instance, if a church grew from 100 to 110 in 1990, it would have grown by 10 percent. If it grew by 10 percent each year it would have 261 members by 1999. The equation would look like the following:

1990 **1991** **1992** **1993** **1994**

100 x 10% =*110* x 10% =*121* x 10% =*133* x 10% =*146* x 10% =*161*

1995 **1996** **1997** **1998** **1999**

161 x 10% =*177* x 10% =*195* x 10% =*215* x 10% =*237* x 10% =*261.*

This church is currently experiencing a decadal growth rate of 161 percent. Decadal growth is the compounded growth rate for ten years. Charles Chaney and Ron Lewis enable us to understand a growth analysis as it relates to demographics by offering the following principles of assessment:

1. That your church has grown while the community has lost population. That is a sign of growth health.

2. That your church has declined while your community has grown. This is the sign of serious growth sickness.
3. That your church has grown at about the same rate as your community. That is a sign of mere maintenance ministries with no penetration of the unchurched community.
4. That your church has remained static in a declining population. That is a sign of some vigorous growth.
5. That your church has remained static in a growing population. That is also a sign of growth sickness.[28]

The plan is innovative in meeting people's needs. Effective evangelistic plans have built-in flexibility that always looks for new ways to serve people. Growing churches are able to package religion in agendas that have application to life situations. People identify with biblical characters only as they perceive that they have problems similar to theirs. It is not that David had conflict with the Amorites and the Amalakites that makes him interesting, but that he had conflict with his children and he fell to the temptation of lust. As a preacher, I don't need to primarily send people back to 1000 B.C., but I do need to place David in a setting to which people can relate.

Being innovative enough to relate the sacred to the contemporary in a concrete rather than abstract manner is the secret to effective evangelism. What is happening in the lives of people around our church needs to be an on-going topic of discussion. The more people perceive that the church is ministering to their needs, the more responsive they will be to evangelistic overtures. People who are moving to a new area need a welcome. People who are having a new child need congratulations. People who have achieved a worthwhile goal need recognition. People who have made a contribution to the life of the community need thanks. Chaney and Lewis write:

> Productive prospecting invokes finding and touching the lives of scores of people while realizing not all will be potential members for the church. Remember, the church is to take up the ministry of Jesus Christ to the world. That ministry is described by word and deed as a "servant ministry." We must keep asking, "Are we here to serve or to be served?"[29]

The laity are the evangelizers. Productive evangelistic plans provide tools and training to the lay membership so they can be effective witnesses within their spheres of influence. There are ongoing classes and materials available for those who want to discover gifts of the Spirit. The pastor and paid staff act, delegate, and preach as if they expect the laity to actively evangelize their friends and neighbors. Rick Warren states that his job is "to give ministry away." His willingness to give up control of ministry and trust in the abilities of his people has spawned forty-six different lay ministries. This attitude builds morale, fosters creativity, builds self-esteem, and leads to the spontaneous growth of the church. Lewis Drummond has observed that "the church should start with gifted people—not programs. Church structure should be built around people so there can be a channel through which the gifted ones can exercise their ministry. This was surely Paul's methodology."[30]

It is amazing how some pastors can stimulate such a high degree of sacrifice in the lives of their people. The willingness to model self-denial and equip their flock from the Scriptures have reproduced their efforts many times over. Jack Hyles calls it troutline fishing "because many hooks are spread throughout the urban area each week instead of one person fishing with a single rod and reel."[31] Pastors who are great evangelists are able to enable their people to catch the vision of what the Holy Spirit can do through them if they will only believe. They are consistently casting the "mantle" of the Lord upon others instead of desiring all of the events of the church to revolve around the pastor's office. The greatest authority that a pastor has is the right to commission men, women, and children for the work of ministry.

PROGRAMS THAT WORK

After a plan has been implemented, there is still the day-to-day task of creative program innovation. A program consists of an objective and a goal. The objective may consist of placing an usher at a specific exit in the church. The goal perhaps would be to greet newcomers who are brought by their friends through the exit because this particular entrance is not as congested as the main foyer. Another example would be a decision to send a string quartet dressed in tuxedos and evening gowns to a nearby college. If the quartet is in place on a summer evening, the objective has been accomplished. The goal could be to stimulate conversation with artistic students who never frequent a sanctuary for worship. Even though the overall vision of the church has been articulated, there still has to be program objectives and goals to carry out the vision. Though the church may have targeted a certain number in its quest for growth, program goals are not necessarily tied to specific numbers. "Chic" Shaver offers an illustration of a goal-oriented program:

> An analysis of the 1977 Sunday School records of my church showed that youth and children made up 39 percent of our attendance compared to a denominational average of 58 percent. Further we discovered that our adults were predominantly older. Finally it dawned on us that we needed to concentrate more on young adults which in turn would increase the children and youth. We took specific steps to strengthen family ministry:
>
> a. Redevelop nursery policies
> b. Organize a mother's club
> c. Show the James Dobson film series, Focus on the Family
> d. Start a men's breakfast
> e. Begin mother's day out
> f. Expand summer vacation Bible school
> g. Add another junior high class
> h. Add two new young adult classes
> i. Hire a youth minister[32]

Dr. Shaver's illustration is an example of the worth of an analysis aimed at locating areas of a church that need attention. Goal setting is more complicated than simply stating an arbitrary number that does not take into consideration existing strengths and weaknesses and the possibilities for correction. My dad was raised on an island where there are no longer any inhabitants. Until recent years a Methodist church was kept open by the remaining elderly residents. The objective was to keep the church physically maintained and the goal was to preserve a memory for returning visitors and former inhabitants. Even a superficial analysis would render the conclusion that church growth was out of the question. Ongoing objective analysis serves to keep the leadership of the church honest. Preserving a memory and keeping grass manicured around monuments are worthy causes as long as one is honest about objectives. But mementos and momentum are two different things.

If one's goal is to increase Sunday morning attendance by 10 percent over the next twelve months, one needs to accomplish some objectives that will help achieve that goal. The following are suggestions:

- Establish a committee that will assume responsibility.
- Demographically profile the surrounding community (within a two-mile radius).
- Sponsor two events that would draw outsiders: Halloween carnival and Valentine's banquet.
- Have a six-week course, a session each Wednesday evening, on follow-up evangelism.
- Out of the training session discover six people who will conscientiously follow up with prospects.
- Carefully examine the present facilities for obstacles to growth: entrances, parking, lighting, sound, heating, cooling, and Sunday School rooms.
- Promote a spring banquet to highlight achievements and recognize those who have been involved. Duncan McIntosh and Richard Rusbuldt write:

> There is much satisfaction for volunteers when specific targets are set and reached. This is a system of rewards. When an objective is reached it is cause for celebration. In many churches only dollar or money targets are established and nothing else is ever celebrated.[33]

Programs are as varied as churches. What fits one community does not suit another. Programs often call for the risk of experimentation since the Book of Acts is short on programs and the Scriptures do not give us specifics that would be applicable anywhere at any time. A church that attempts to run used school buses to an upper-middle-class neighborhood will be disillusioned. Programs are not transferable from one church to another with disregard to church personnel and surrounding demographics. For that reason evangelistic programs handed down to local churches by denominational headquarters often do not work. However, there are criteria by which programs may be evaluated. The following will serve as quality control checks by which effectiveness can be assessed:

Spirituality

Some church programs are both spiritually and evangelistically counterproductive. Athletic teams are a primary way to involve non-Christians in the life of the church. But if the air is filled with bickering and cursing during the heat of the contest, the witness becomes tainted. An event that doesn't represent Christ does not adequately represent the church.

When a layperson who was the member of a rapidly growing church with 3,000 in attendance was asked the secret of his church's success, he responded, "There is a prayer meeting held each morning at the church from 5:30 to 7 A.M. with approximately thirty in attendance. If the pastor is not out of town he is present at the prayer time."

Another church that has been evangelistically affected by prayer is Skyline Wesleyan in San Diego. Pastor John Maxwell meets with one hundred prayer partners once a month and before each worship service twenty men lay hands on their pastor and pray for him. While Maxwell preaches, there are a group of men in a room above the pulpit who are interceding for the service. Maxwell has prayed, "Lord, let there never be a Sunday when people are not saved at the church."[34] Skyline has grown from approximately 1,000 attenders to over 3,000 in the last ten years.

Visibility

A church may have a great product, but only a few people may know about it. Signs need to be placed at key locations. A brochure can be created that clearly represents the church's agenda. Space can be purchased in the yellow pages, and advertisements placed in the local media for special events. James Engel argues that radio is one of the most cost-effective ways to get the word out.[35] Whether a church should primarily use newspapers, billboards, radio, or TV depends upon the geographic area and clientele the church is trying to reach. A fifteen-minute announcement slot designated "The Church Corner" beamed from a Christian radio station will do little to reach the unsaved. Engel offers the following guideline:

> The basic goal of strategy is to select media vehicles that reach the target audience with a minimum of waste coverage

> (this is often referred to as selectivity). For this to be done, the audience must be specified with precision in such terms as age, geographic location, socioeconomic status, and so on. The next obvious step is to consult data on the audience of various candidate media (assuming such data are available) in these same demographic terms and select those that cover the target with least waste.[36]

The Church of the Nazarene has crafted the following announcement to be used by a local congregation as a radio announcement:

BACKGROUND: Blaring rock music.

VOICE 1: "Rock! Do your kids think this is the Rock of Ages?"

"Mighty music it may be, sung under the flare of light magnified a thousand-fold."

Background: Softer music.

VOICE 1: "But don't let your children confuse it with eternity. Long after today's pop chart heroes have passed from the airwaves, Jesus of Nazareth can live at the heart of their lives."

VOICE 2: "I'm Jeff Daniels, pastor of the Oakgrove Church of the Nazarene. Discover the power of Christ's teachings every Sunday at our Sunday School among friends that will treat them like family, a place that they will be listened to as well as taught. We want every Sunday to be a special time of joy and singing, hope and vision, adventure and growth. Join us. Welcome to the Oakgrove Church of the Nazarene. Our church can be your home."

Or, a church may attempt some advertising that is more subtle:

SETTING: Mother and daughter walking through the daughter's new home.

MOTHER: "Have you considered going to (fictitious name of an expensive furniture store) to furnish your living room?"

DAUGHTER: "Yes, I have already picked out a couch and chair that match the carpet."

MOTHER: "That's my girl. I always taught you to shop for the very best. That's the only way to be happy."

VOICE: "Can the right furniture really make a person happy? Are there not other values that bring more fulfillment than the acquisition of material possessions: love, honesty, acceptance, mutual understanding, and integrity? We talk about these things at First Presbyterian Church at the intersection of routes 77 and 95.

Service times at 8:45 and 11 A.M., Sunday. Call 225-3030 for more information."

The local church must be constantly thinking about how to increase its visibility to the non-Christian. Remember that the average consumer receives 6,000 commercial messages per day. Most of these people believe that the church is irrelevant to their everyday lives. The medium must seek to make the listener more intensely cognizant of a need and then offer a feasible suggestion for fulfillment. One must be able to touch dormant values that have been hypnotized by the false gods of American materialism. A church's visibility can be enhanced by a subtle undermining of society's already crumbling foundation through available means of communication. George Barna makes the following prediction:

> The 90's will see churches become more aggressive in marketing and advertising. In the early portion of the decade, telemarketing will be tried by thousands of churches. However, prospecting for new attenders will be done most commonly through direct mail advertising. Radio will become a more popular means of catching people's attention, since stations provide an opportunity to target a specific population niche more precisely than ever before. Newspaper advertising may also increase in use.[37]

Assimilation

It is one thing to entice people to attend a church—it is another thing to provide a setting that will make them feel at home. Most people attend several churches before they decide on a permanent residence. Good programs cover the pews with Velcro. *Fortune* magazine describes the growth success of Alan Houghton at the Church of the Heavenly Rest, an Episcopal parish in New York City. In nine years of ministry Houghton experienced a quadrupling of attendance, while the desperate financial situation greatly improved.

> Houghton's secret was to find a need the competition wasn't meeting. "In New York City, churches are like restaurants—there's one on every block," he says. "If you don't like the menu, you can walk down the street to eat somewhere else.

> We decided to try being a family parish in the middle of New York." He put a heavy emphasis on pastoral counseling, encouraged parents to park their infants' carriages in the aisles, and to counteract the forbidding architecture, he and his fellow priests greeted parishioners outside the building before services—"a deliberate attempt to say 'come on in.'"[38]

There is no one who has more accurately diagnosed how a church says not only "Come on in" but "You are welcome to stay" to investigating attenders than Lyle Schaller. *Assimilating New Members* is required reading for anyone interested in the retention rate among those who are shopping for a church home.[39] According to Schaller, many churches do not grow because they do not know how to minimize the "we-they" division. Those who have been in the church for years maintain the leadership positions, and there is a resistance to newcomers assuming significant authority within the church's administrative and ministry structures. The implicit message to a visitor is "You can stay, but don't expect to have a voice in the affairs of the church until you have earned the right over several months or years." The "old guard" is found in ecclesiastical as well as political structures. They have choked thousands of churches as well as secular businesses.

If a person who has been attending for several weeks does not discover a subgroup with which they can identify, they will not continue to attend. This may be a Sunday School class in which they really feel at home or the general impression that there is a group of people within the church that has the same kinds of problems that they do (e.g., potty training children). There are formal substructures within a church: choir, prayer groups, athletic teams, support groups, singles, elderly, married and so on. Churches that grow capitalize on specific interest and identity factors. Churches that are oblivious to these differences among people, and program as if everyone had the same proclivities, are as archaic as the company that exclusively manufactured buggy whips and failed to diversify. The attempt to specialize in ministries that appeal to various subgroups allows individuals to discover their niche within growing congregations. The more these niches or fellowship circles are multiplied, the more the church will grow. The bottom line is that evangelistic churches spell "welcome" in as many ways as possible.

Extramural

Most often churches assume that the heathen can be sung in, preached in, or hauled in to a sanctuary on Sunday morning. They don't realize that thousands of people may pass their property and see their church sign day after day, but the ecclesiastical structure does not register in the secular mind. People normally do not take note of that for which they are not consciously looking. The events of the church are held inside of the church for those who are safely in the fold. If one does not have parents to bring them or friends to invite them, the church seems to the secular mind to be a very exclusive club with esoteric practices.

For the last forty years evangelism beyond the walls of the church has been left to parachurch organizations such as Young Life and Campus Crusade, communities such as Koinonia Farms in Americus, Georgia, or unique churches such as the Salvation Army corps, which are located within the inner city. There are precious few churches willing to take risks by having events beyond the walls of the church. Most of the church's energy is expended in maintaining traditional programs, and the church's committed people are so busy attending services, sitting on committees, and doing volunteer work that they have little time for anything else. It is often difficult to envision the immediate return on sending a drama team to a city park, a singing group to a mall, or a Christian bookmobile to an area of the inner city. Such projects demand both time and energy, expenditures that are often evaluated as subtracting from the ongoing programs of the church.

Consider, for example, Esther Sanger, who founded Quincy Crisis Center in Quincy, Massachusetts. This outreach ministry, which is manned by 1,000 volunteers, ministers to "throw-away people like the homeless, hungry, alcoholics, drug users, AIDS victims, battered women, elderly, poor, and deserted mothers with babies."[40] After going back to school and finishing a Master of Arts in family counseling at age fifty-seven, Sanger started distributing her phone number as a twenty-four-hour crisis hotline in subways, on telephone poles, in all-night laundromats, and to people who lived on the streets, under bridges, in cemeteries, or on the beaches. She has enlisted both church and city agencies to feed, clothe, and shelter the thousands who have responded. The Quincy Crisis Center has distributed meals out of a van, sponsored a food pantry that delivers groceries to the needy, provided transportation for the elderly, and established a home for unwed mothers (which not only provides spiritual and emotional counseling, but teaches money management, parenting, nutrition, and career planning). Esther Sanger has herself discovered, and enabled others to discover, that evangelism needs to take on the form of servanthood after the manner of Christ.

The opportunities for the church to move into the public sector are legion if the people of God are willing to practice compassion in the marketplace. There are opportunities for off-site counseling centers, businessmen's luncheons, racket club Bible studies, and church teams sent to prisons or inner-city missions. The least a church can do is encourage its people to begin neighborhood Bible studies so that friends can be invited in for refreshments and a discussion of some relevant topics in the light of the Scriptures.

Quite often we are concerned about bringing sinners in before we send Christians out. That concept needs to be reversed by doing evangelism primarily outside of the inner sanctum. Such is the conviction of Phil Batten, a Nazarene minister, who sends a bus to the inner city of Cleveland, Ohio on a daily basis. The "Heaven Train" does not bring people to the church, but rather serves as an on-site sanctuary to 1,500 people per week, mostly children. Bible stories and verses are made more palatable by the use of "gospel magic," ventriloquism, and puppets. Of course, it all goes down better with a serving of hot dogs, chips, and pop. The ministry has been the impetus for the genesis of similar projects by other Churches of the Nazarene both within the U.S. and abroad.

People Programs

Programs must always be in terms of people. They must arise out of the resonation between people groups in the church and people groups in the community. For instance, a church with many singles is ideal for reaching singles. The people strengths of the people on the inside must be compatible with the people needs on the outside. Kennon Callahan succinctly states this working premise: "People win people. Programs do not reach people; people reach people."[41] Thus, the wise church will not do a plethora of programs for the sake of busyness, but will choose very carefully on the basis of a vision that is within the giftedness of the church and the conditions of the surrounding community that necessitate ministry. When programs move beyond these parameters, they become decreasingly effective. Thus, it is better to have a few workable program objectives, rather than many goals that are questionable because they are beyond the inherent vision of the congregation. Callahan states, "More often than not, mission simply grows itself up because a small number of people—three to five—have discovered similar longings to help with a specific human hurt and hope."[42]

Family Relationships

Erik Erikson suggests that love consists of a mutuality of devotion that overcomes the inherent antagonisms of divided function.[43] If there is truth in that definition, many of the antagonisms between persons result from a confusion of roles in the workplace and especially the home. The animosity that breaks up families is the single greatest blot on the American conscience. At no place is there a greater gap between the values Americans claim to cherish and the success rate of putting those values into practice. Families continue to fragment, children are indelibly scarred, and society becomes increasingly angry due to fractured psyches. George Barna writes:

> Americans typically identify their family life as their greatest source of happiness. Yet, we are increasingly likely to minimize the importance of keeping a marriage intact, to spend meaningful time with our children, and to desire to engage in family activities during our free time.[44]

This distance between the ideal self and actual performance causes most American parents to carry an overwhelming sense of guilt. The church that aims to repair this rip in the social fabric will in all likelihood be evangelistically oriented. Preaching, seminars, retreats, and materials that highlight family ministry address problems that many parents are seeking to solve. The success of Bill Gothard and James Dobson should be proof enough that parents will bring their children to churches that attempt to heal the hurts that haunt parents seeking to fulfill the unrealistic expectations of a hedonistic world. The church that counteracts the unrealistic charms of mythological TV and cinema personalities in a loving and aggressive manner will serve as a fortification for the battered nuclear family crying out for help. Churches that project themselves as docks where the ship of family can be repaired will serve as welcome havens for those seeking role clarification and a more determined commitment to weather the storm. Pastors who announce a sincere program to minister to individual family members, each as unique and deserving of special attention, will plant the gospel on fertile ground.

There are biblical principles for building strong foundations for the family. Bible stories abound with people who are attempting to relate in meaningful ways. The Scriptures are also clear about the consequences of living for self at the expense of others. The Scriptures tell us that "if possible, so far as it depends on you, be at peace with all" (Rom. 12:18). Principles of peace are attractive to people who are foundering because of the convulsions of a society without direction. There is a connection between healthy churches developing healthy families and healthy families strengthening healthy churches. People who do not realize that their soteriology or eschatology is deficient are highly cognizant that things ought to be better between them and their spouse and their children. The widest evangelistic door in the church's architecture has "family" written all over it.

CONCLUSION

All of the above calls for a dependence on the Holy Spirit in planning and fulfillment. The church that is evangelistically effective is able to seize the opportunities of the moment— opportunities that are unique to God's sovereign space-time allocation. The evangelistic church is firmly convinced that God calls corporately as well as individually. Many churches never catch the vision contained in the specific purpose that God had in mind when He called them into existence. Evangelistic preparation begins with a question: "Why did God plant our church in this community?"

When Jesus exhorted His disciples to "lift up their eyes and look at the fields," He was issuing something other than a generic command. Looking requires careful observation, assessment of the specific situation, and plans that would be at least as well thought through as those of a conscientious farmer. A farmer's very existence depends on careful preparation of fields and efficiency in gathering the harvest. Repeated failure at harvest will put a farmer out of business. We should be grateful that the analogy isn't perfect. True, God is as sovereign in harvesting corn as He is in reaping souls, but sovereign grace is never an excuse for shallow thinking in the offering of that grace. It means that both the individual and the church must continually attempt to grasp the "fullness of time" under the guidance of the Holy Spirit. Such guidance never ceases to address the methodologies of planning, planting, watering, and reaping. God-anointed evangelism calls for no less.

IX

proclamation as evangelism

Preaching is a prominent activity in the New Testament. The *King James Version* translates *euangelion* into some form of the verb "preach" 135 times. The noun "preacher" is used four times. Noah is referred to as a "preacher of righteousness" (2 Peter 2:5; 1 Tim. 2:7; 2 Tim. 1:11). Romans 10:14 pivots the evangelistic enterprise around the activity of preaching by asking the question "How shall they hear without a preacher?" Prerequisite to a person coming to salvation in Jesus Christ is the personal reception of a verbal communication concerning the Christ event. This does not mean that a person could not receive salvation through a private reading of the Scripture and the dynamic application of biblical truth by the Holy Spirit. But the normal course is that a person will be pointed to the Scripture by another through the dynamic of the Holy Spirit. Explanation and application of biblical truth are crucial aspects of the process of leading someone to Christ. The encounter between Philip and the Ethiopian eunuch (Acts 8) provides a case in point.

Other words are used in the New Testament for the above explanation and application. The frequent appearance (twenty-three times) of the word "persuade" in its various forms demonstrates the urgent, hortatory character of preaching. In a classic evangelistic text that places the motivation for evangelism within the framework of eschatology, Paul writes, "For we must all appear before the judgment seat of Christ, that each one may be recompensed for his deeds in the body, according to what he has done, whether good or bad. Therefore knowing the fear of the Lord, we persuade men" (2 Cor. 5:10-11). Rudolph Bultmann suggests this text refers to "authentic apostolic preaching."[1]

At other times Luke describes Paul's evangelistic activity as "reasoning," the presentation of a logical discourse that serves to bring about a positive response in the mind of the listeners. Gottleb Schrenk clarifies that *dialegoma* does not denote philosophical discourse, but rather a comprehensive declaration of the divine will, which calls for an obedient and percipient acceptance.[2]

DEFINING EVANGELISTIC PREACHING

One should not pretend that the activities referred to above are to be equated with the activity of preaching as we know it today. It has no doubt accumulated cultural nuances that would be surprising to a Paul or Peter miraculously transported to a Billy Graham crusade or Sunday morning worship service in a white clapboard church serenely situated on a Kentucky hillside. But I would suggest that the first and twenty-first century would find commonality in a working definition of evangelistic preaching as an audible, plausible, biblical discourse with a view to persuasion. This brief definition raises a critical issue. Is there any preaching that is not evangelistic? Probably not, if all preaching is aimed at leading to some decision by the hearers as they stand within the *ordo salutis.* All preaching is evangelistic if evangelism is defined as persuading persons to a certain course of action or thought.

PREACHING AND TEACHING

Preaching is offered by the speaker to the hearer as a change agent. Preaching that does not envision changing people is futile. Preaching has often been contrasted to teaching in that the latter seeks to impart knowledge rather than effect change. This demarcation would be difficult to prove even though the Scriptures suggest differentiation between the offices of evangelist and teacher (Eph. 4:11). A survey of the New Testament reveals that the former had an itinerant ministry that was likely to confront non-Christian elements in society (e.g., Paul), while the latter carried on a nurturing ministry at a settled location (e.g., Priscilla and Aquila). But one must keep in mind that much of Paul's energy *was* spent at particular locations (Ephesus and Corinth) and in the ministry of revisiting churches that he had previously founded.

The differentiation between proclamation and systematic instruction becomes a bit clearer if one examines the use of *katexeo* in the New Testament. Herman Beyer claims that Galatians 6:6 ("And let the one who is taught the word share all good things with him who teaches") "confirms the validity and necessity of a professional teaching ministry in the congregation."[3] Paul chooses a technical term for Christian instruction, a rare word hardly known at all in the religious vocabulary of Judaism. Catechism in the New Testament seems to be a definitive post-conversion exercise, as it was in the life of Apollos, who had received instruction *(katekemenos)* in the way of the Lord (Acts 18:25).

But on the whole, a simple demarcation between teaching and preaching breaks down in the New Testament. Jesus and his followers understood teaching in the same way that the Old Testament priests and prophets did. Teaching had a far greater purpose than simply an increase of knowledge inventory. Teaching provided a comprehension of God and his will—a comprehension that, if applied, would produce the fruit of ethical righteousness. Such application turned comprehension into wisdom. Wisdom is the goal of all teaching and preaching both in the Old and New Testament. Biblical wisdom is the God-given ability to see life from God's perspective. Karl Rinstorf writes, "The whole teaching of Jesus is with a view to the ordering of life with reference to God and one's neighbor. Thus his teaching constantly appeals to the will, calling for a practical decision either for the will of God or against it."[4]

The demarcation between preaching and teaching blurs even more when one considers that the primal evangelist, Jesus, more often taught than preached (Matt. 13:54; Mark 6:2; Luke 5:3; John 14:26). Also, the terms seem to be used quite interchangeably, as if one can preach and teach at the same time: "And Jesus went about all Galilee, teaching in their synagogues, and preaching the gospel of the kingdom, and healing all manner of sickness and all manner of disease among the people" (Matt. 4:23; cf. Matt. 9:35; 11:1). One may argue that teaching refers more to the systematic instruction of the Scripture, such as Christ's reference to the Old Testament law in the Sermon on the Mount, while preaching announces the new coming of the kingdom of God in Jesus Christ. But this is not altogether clear, because the most critical evangelistic exhortation that Jesus ever gave utilizes *didasko*—"Go therefore and make disciples of all the nations, baptizing them in the name of the Father and the Son and the Holy Spirit, *teaching* them to observe all that I commanded you; and lo, I am with you always, even to the end of the age" (Matt. 28:19-20).

ANALYSIS OF PETER'S POST-PENTECOST MESSAGE

The prototypical evangelistic message in the New Testament was preached by Peter on the Day of Pentecost (Acts 2). Considering its early date in the life of the church and the tremendous fruit that it bore, the occasion is worth close scrutiny. The following observations can be readily made:

1. *Peter had recently been filled with the Holy Spirit.* Had this not occurred, he probably would not have been so quick to be the most prominent person on this momentous occasion. The double witness of Christ's resurrection and the reception of the promised Paraclete seem to almost propel Peter into a leadership role. There is a confidence and clarity of mission like Peter had never evidenced before. Peter stood up and said to all that were gathered, "Pay attention!"

2. *Peter took a text.* He made a direct connection between the prophecy in Joel 2 and what was happening in Jerusalem (Acts 2:16-21). Contemporary events were explained in the light of Scripture. Peter also quoted three other well-known passages that supported a God-ordained design for not only what was currently happening, but the events of the previous several months. It was important for Peter to connect scriptural validity with experience.

3. *Both the Scriptures and the events pointed to the centrality of Christ:*

a. Through Him came salvation (v. 21).

b. God demonstrated His approval of Christ through signs and wonders (v. 22).

c. The ultimate sign and fulfillment of Old Testament prophecy was the resurrection from the dead (v. 24).

d. The ultimate victory of Christ (v. 34).

e. The present state of the crucified Jesus, now Lord and Christ (v. 36).

4. Peter made personal application both within and at the end of the message. Among his hearers were those who crucified Christ. If they had not personally swung the hammer and raised their voices, they had at least consented to His death: "You nailed to a cross by the hands of godless men and put Him to death" (v. 23). He returns to their individual responsibility in the corporate and universal guilt of all humankind: "Therefore let all the house of Israel know for certain that God has made Him both Lord and Christ—this Jesus whom you crucified" (v. 36). Peter believed that establishment of personal guilt is a motivation for action. The knowledge that one has had past influence in a negative situation suggests the potential for present initiative toward solution of that same situation.

5. Peter suggested both ways and means by which present initiative could be taken. Listeners needed to know that something could be done after the sermon was heard. "Repent, and let each of you be baptized in the name of Jesus Christ for the forgiveness of your sins; and you shall receive the gift of the Holy Spirit" (v. 38). Belief in Peter's message will result in action. Peter's message becomes a tertiary means and a positive response becomes a secondary means by which God conveys His justifying and sanctifying grace. The preaching, responding, and conveying are all due to God's loving prevenient grace, the *primary means.*

6. There was a personal word of assurance to the hearers that they were all included within the provision that Jesus proffered. "For the promise is for you and your children" (v. 39). The message was personalized to the extent that the hearers would have no doubt that they were within the scope of the invitation. Even before the conclusion, the inclusive nature of the beckoning was spelled out by the optimum evangelistic code phrase: "And it shall be, that everyone who calls on the name of the Lord shall be saved" (v. 21).

A PARADIGM FOR EVANGELISTIC PREACHING

The schemata outlined for the message of Peter is in agreement with a fourfold paradigm which Dennis Kinlaw describes for all preaching.[5] All listeners will hear from the preacher the answer to the following questions: Who are we? Where are we? Where do we need to go? How do we get there? Evangelistic preaching that does not address these four questions will ultimately fail. A look at the paradigm for the purpose of evangelistic preaching in America may prove to be helpful.

Who Are We?

Evangelistic preaching can never be prepared in isolation from a real live congregation. In fact, the preacher will envision that congregation at a particular time in a particular setting. He or she will envision as many individuals, age-groups, vocational groups, and economic groups as possible. It is not that the evangelist comes to attack a particular person or subgroup, but rather that he or she comes with the conviction that preaching is always dialogue and never monologue. A reading of the congregation must take place from the beginning of preparation until some point in time after the preaching event. The sermon is sandwiched between pre-assessment and post-assessment. The rigor of preparation is never done in a vacuum, but is surrounded by people's faces, voices, frowns, smiles, and sheer bewilderment.

Jesus used the second person pronoun "you" in the Sermon on the Mount twenty-seven times! Jesus knew what His listeners were thinking as He spoke. He was able to think within their frame of reference— religiously, morally, vocationally, and socially. He addressed their human tendencies toward pride, avarice, revenge, anxiety, and judgmental attitudes. The listener should inwardly exclaim, "This guy knows me! Has he been reading my mail or going through my file cabinets?" Identification with one's audience is one of the first laws of preaching. Christ had not been snooping around anyone's home, but He had spiritual X-ray vision. Immediately when He finished His sermon, the results were in: "The multitudes were amazed at His teaching; for He was teaching them as one having authority, and not as their scribes" (Matt. 7:28-29).

Not only must there be an understanding of who the congregation is, but there must be at least partial identification with its needs and aspirations. A sermon that totally disagrees with the listener's ideology will only increase dissonance. The speaker better make sure that his or her listeners agree with at least 95 percent of what is being said. It will be difficult enough to persuade listeners on the remaining 5 percent. Ideally, the 95 percent of agreement will lend enough credibility to one's message to change the 5 percent of the listeners' lifestyle that is out of alignment with biblical standards. But such identification does not guarantee success, as exemplified in the sermon of Stephen in Acts 7. Most of the sermon consisted of Hebrew history, which could not be disputed by his Jewish audience. It was Stephen's statement of application that really got him a quick exit to a shower of stones. "You men who are stiff-necked and uncircumcised in heart and ears are always resisting the Holy Spirit; you are doing just as your fathers did" (Acts 7:51). He broke the first rule of preaching: Don't attack someone else's parents. And its corollary: Don't attack someone else's children. Of course, there is always the possibility of fallout. John Wesley stayed away from preaching in churchyards where there were too many stones lying around.

If a person is to be reached with the gospel, the evangelist must be acquainted with the cultural parameters that define the target audience. In *How Does America Hear the Gospel?* William Dyrness argues that Americans are primarily defined by "three complexes of values, American materialist bias, their temperamental optimism and their individualism."[6] A pragmatic utilitarian faith was sought by seventeenth-century Puritans, as well as by the twentieth-century middle class. The Puritans certainly held a higher view of God's sovereignty than present-day Americans, but the covenant that John Winthrop enunciated while still on the *Arabella* traded obedience to God for His favors of protection and provision in the New England wilderness.

Dyrness observes (and I think correctly) that Americans identify themselves via their material goods more than any one thing. Tear down the hedge of goodies and gadgets that surround Americans, and the outside vacuum will be so great for most people that there will be an unbearable psychological and spiritual implosion. The breathless immediacy and expediency that fuel the work ethic needed for the materialistic enterprise have led to a deep sickness in the American people. Much of that sickness is evidenced in failed relationships.

Dyrness' conclusion is that we are at least partially defined by the limitations of our culture and that the gospel must be at least initially addressed in these terms. People need to understand what shapes them before they can be grasped by what they need to be shaped. The gospel needs to be presented in terms of shared hopes and stresses, but every hearer needs to realize that his or her aspirations and exigencies are overshadowed and even displaced by a far greater value—the death by crucifixion as exemplified by Christ. "For if we died with Him, we shall also live with Him" (2 Tim. 2:11). In the wake of American perennial optimism and material greed is a jettison of broken lives and mangled psyches. "As we become sensitive to these needs, they may become for all of us metaphors of our great need for the grace of God, and the means by which we will understand something more of that central transaction between humanity and God on the cross."[7]

Where Are We?

The question of who people are is vitally related to where they are. Haddon Robinson writes, "Life changing preaching does not talk to the people about the Bible. Instead, it talks to the people about themselves—their questions, hurts, fears, and struggles—from the Bible."[8] These existential questions are normally the chief motivation that drives people to church and causes them to give a preliminary hearing to the gospel. If the preaching is irrelevant to their needs, they will probably go to another church next Sunday or possibly not go at all. The perceived immediate crisis that one asks the church to solve may be referred to as a felt need. Felt needs represent what is of immediate importance to a person or groups of people, such as marriage, family, agriculture, or vocations. Felt needs vary with cultures, while real needs are universal. People in California normally aren't concerned about the corn crop in Iowa, but both Californians and Iowans need to know that God offers forgiveness through Jesus Christ.

Dialogical preaching is well aware of where people live. The evangelistic preacher is attuned to the socioeconomic makeup of the audience. But such classifications at times tend toward group stereotyping. Not only are there exceptions to the group, but every preacher needs to address the myriad individuals in regard to their unique experience in the group. Fred Craddock stresses the use of empathetic imagination, which he describes as "the capacity to achieve a large measure of understanding of another person without having had that person's experience."[9] Craddock suggests the simple exercise of heading a blank piece of paper with the title "What is it like to be?" The preacher would then visualize specific persons: a homeless man, a person who has just been fired, or a pregnant teenager. "For the next fifteen minutes scribble on the page every thought, recollection, feeling, experience, name, place, sound, smell, or taste that comes to mind."[10] Such an experience would serve to place the gospel on the frequency of those who need to hear it most.

For the reasons above, Bill Hybels, senior pastor of Willow Creek Community Church, confesses that he lives "with a sanctified terror of boring people or making the relevant Scriptures irrelevant."[11] Sermon titles and topics need to address the ways in which people daily live. Hybels claims that 60 to 70 percent of his illustrations come from current events. "Why? Because when I can use a contemporary illustration, I build credibility. The unchurched person says, 'He's in the same world I'm in! He's aware that Sean Connery and Roger Moore no longer play 007.'"[12] Hybels suggests that people need to hear something other than "pray more, love more, serve more, or give more."[13] All of that may be true, but people need to know that the pastor is refracting life through the same lens that they are. They will give heed to the Book of Isaiah only if it focuses on the Persian Gulf, or at least the gulf between them and their spouse, children, or parents.

Focusing evangelistic preaching on felt needs is tricky business. Much preaching stops there and never focuses on real needs. Unless the transition is made from perceived needs to the deep spiritual issues of life, preaching will be no more eternally effective than a lecture in a secular university. Hybels warns that preaching will miss the mark if the main goal of our ministry is to help people lead happy, well-adjusted lives and be more helpful to each other. "We want to develop fully devoted followers of Jesus Christ. They should think Christianly, act Christianly, relate Christianly."[14]

The primacy of crisis solving is the error that Dyrness accuses

Robert Schuller of making. Schuller claims that "the need for dignity, self-worth, self-respect, and self-esteem is the deepest of all human needs."[15] Dyrness argues that one should not fault Schuller for using alienation, despair, loneliness, and all of the other causes or results of low self-esteem as evangelistic segues into the gospel. But is our deepest human need low self-esteem or a lack of realizing God's design for our lives? Schuller argues that some people are already so surrounded by negativism they do not need to have their low self-esteem further amplified by being told that they are sinners. What Schuller needs to recognize is that "sinner" is not an arbitrary label, but rather a diagnosis rendered by spiritual physicians. Even if we fully agree with Schuller that people do not need to be told that they are bad because they are already carrying sufficient guilt, they still need to have their estrangement from God identified as sin. Confession of sin and reconciliation with God are the only means to restored self-esteem. Self-esteem outside of those avenues is carnal pride.

The problem with much Christian "felt need" preaching is that it looks for immediate solutions to immediate problems and then stops there, rather than looking for the design and purpose that God wants to implement out of the crisis. Unless the crisis is superseded by solid Christian commitment for the glory of God, preaching cannot be called evangelistic. Unless evangelistic preaching points to the glorious possibility of grace, above and beyond coping with tension, it will fail to become truly evangelistic.

The bottom line is that relevant communication asks the right questions. That is the first principle of Theodore Baehr's *Getting the Word Out*. Christian proclamation asks questions of its audience in order to find out what questions the audience is asking. "How does my audience perceive the subject matter of my communication? What image does my subject matter conjure up in the mind of a typical member of my audience? What does my audience think are the positive attributes of my subject matter?"[16] Such questions will prevent the preacher from starting in a field with which his or her audience is unfamiliar. A discourse may be highly theological without using strange terms and esoteric imagery. Baehr states, "Talking down to your audience is wrong, but visualizing your audience as someone who has no knowledge of your field of expertise but is bright, human, curious, and responsive is an excellent way to make sure that you and your guests explain yourselves on your program in the clearest and most interesting way possible."[17] While Baehr is speaking primarily of television programming, the same could certainly be said of the relationship between the evangelist and the audience.

One of the toughest questions that the church faces in Western civilization is how to reach people who are relatively happy. James Engel argues that people are not unhappy simply because they do not know Jesus Christ as their personal Savior. Happiness is a relative frame of mind predicated upon degrees of satisfaction between what is and what ought to be. The family that lived in Plato's cave were happy because they were unaware of an outside world that offered something better. Had someone told them of a better habitat, reception of the message would have created desire. Desire would have become crisis if their efforts to move from the cave were thwarted. Frustration may have led to alternate methods of pursuing fulfillment. The person would be identified on the "3" or "2" level of Engel's scale (see below)—"Problem recognition and intention to act."

Stages in the "Passage" Through the Life Cycle

1. *Pulling Up Roots.* **18–22. A transition from parent's beliefs to the establishment of new strictly personal beliefs. Often characterized by an identity crisis.**
2. *Building the Dream.* **22–30. "Forming the dream" and working one's aspirations through occupational and marital choices. Much importance placed on "doing what we should."**
3. *Living Out the Dream.* **30–35. Putting down roots, living out one's aspirations and making them become a reality.**
4. *Midlife Transition.* **35–45. Reassessment of the dream and the values which have been internalized. A final casting aside of inappropriate role models. Equilibrium will be restored either through a renewal or a resignation to the realities of life.**
5. *Middle Adulthood.* **45–59. Reduced personal striving and more emphasis on living consistently with a clarified code of values placing more importance on personal relationships and individual fulfillment.**
6. *Late Adult Transition.* **60–65 and beyond. Diminished active occupational life and eventual retirement. Retirement can either lead to renewal or resignation.**

The essence of Engel's scale is that people are not standing around just waiting to receive Christ. Both lack of knowledge concerning the implications of the gospel and relative satisfaction with the way life is presently going act as blinders, hindering the search for deeper meaning. It will normally not be very fruitful to share Jesus with someone who is absorbed by material pursuit (not having yet experienced disillusionment) and who only has a vague awareness that God exists. Generally a person will work their way through the scale by degrees, rather than transversing by a great leap. Engel suggests that attacking the status quo and shedding new light will stimulate the knowledge search. The burden of proof is on the Christian to demonstrate to the world that his or her life is somehow different and better than that offered by the world. Engel writes:

> Individuality, achievement, economic success, doing my thing . . . all these represent common values of the world. Would unbelievers see different values if they closely examined most of our churches, both corporately and individually? Or would they see a group of humans who have let cultural values contaminate their spiritual life?[18]

A person will serve only as the opinion maker in the life of another if he or she is deemed trustworthy in the eyes of the customer. The customer is going to ask, "Who am I going to believe out of all the conflicting voices that are making unique claims about their product?" Any sign of ulterior motives, moral lapses, and self-promotion will be suspect. The "beyond reproof" and "without blemish" authority of the preacher is designated as ethos. No one has ever defined its essence more accurately and succinctly than Aristotle.

> Persuasion is achieved by the speaker's personal character when the speech is so spoken as to make us think him credible. We believe good ideas more fully and more readily than others: this is true generally whatever the question is, and absolutely true when exact certainty is impossible and opinions are divided. This kind of persuasion, like the other, should be achieved by what the speaker says, not by what peo-

> ple think of his character before he begins to speak. It is not true, as some writers assume in their treatises on rhetoric, that the personal goodness revealed by the speaker contributes nothing to his power of persuasion; on the contrary, his character may almost be called the most effective means of persuasion he possesses.[19]

Daniel Bauman helpfully differentiates between antecedent ethos and manifest ethos. The former has to do with the reputation that precedes the speaker—pedigree, degrees, life experiences of which the audience may already be aware, and whatever else may be mentioned in the introduction. Billy Graham brings a high degree of antecedent ethos to a given speaking situation. Antecedent ethos is translated into manifest ethos by the expertise, trustworthiness, and personal dynamism of the speaker.[20] The onus is on the speaker to demonstrate to the listeners why they should listen.

Personal dynamism is also associated with the other twin pillar of credibility, pathos. Pathos is the excitement, emotion, and enthusiasm that the speaker displays for both the topic and the audience. Pathos lifts the message above the mundane and perfunctory. Enthusiasm is the antidote to self-doubt and serves to increase audience receptivity even if the logic is not entirely flawless and plausible. Syllogisms outside of a personality bathed in conviction will never be sufficient to change people. Phillips Brooks succinctly defined preaching as communicating divine truth through human personality. Personality will either speak like the pedantic, secondhand truths of an operational manual or cry out the firsthand inspiration of the transcendent poet. It is this vision for preaching that Walter Brueggeman has borrowed from the ruminations of Walt Whitman.

> After the seas are all cross'd, (as they seem already cross'd)
> After the great captains and engineers have accomplish'd their work.
> After the noble inventors, after the scientists, the chemist, the geologist, ethnologist,
> Finally shall come the poet worthy of that name,
> The true son of God shall come singing his songs.[21]

Where Do I Need to Go?

The credibility of the speaker, the conviction of the Holy Spirit, and the listener's dissatisfaction with the status quo prompts the question "Where do I go from here?" It should not be taken for granted that Christianity is represented in the listener's mind as a clearly unique option. Who are Christians? The people who fight against the Muslims in Lebanon, the Catholics who make up the Irish Republican Army? Everyone who lives in the West except Hindus and Muslims, who have been displaced? The crowds who follow Kenneth Copeland and Jerry Falwell on TV? The people who voted for Pat Robertson? Those who espouse the "American way of life"? Those who live in Christian ghettos with the privileged passcards that allow them to access Christian bookstores, Christian dating services, Christian nightclubs, and Christian yellow pages? "Christian" signposts are so numerous that without a biblical theology and Spirit-led discernment, not only confusion but outright deception is sure to ensue. The indictment by Walter Brueggeman merits close scrutiny by the would-be evangelist:

> When we embrace ideology uncritically, it is assumed that the Bible squares easily with capitalist ideology, or narcissistic psychology, or revolutionary politics, or conformist morality, or romantic liberalism. . . . Preaching among us happens in this context in which truth is greatly reduced. That means the gospel may have been twisted, pressed, tailored, and gerrymandered until it is comfortable with technological reasons that leaves us unbothered, and with ideology that leaves us with uncriticized absolutes.[22]

Whether a person is engaged in one-on-one witnessing or preaching to thousands, it cannot be assumed that Christianity represents common denominators in the minds of the listeners. The following attempt at evangelism by the young Randall Balmer indicates the importance of semantical nuances in the evangelistic foray:

> In Bay City, Michigan, on a rainy day during my childhood, I finally mustered the courage to "witness" to Stanley Strelecki, my next-door neighbor and playmate. Though not yet in my teens, hundreds of hours of sermons, Sunday school lessons, revival meetings, and Bible study had prepared me for this moment.

> "Stanley," I began, my voice quavering. "Are you a Christian?" There. The opening gambit, everyone said, was the toughest. After that initial exchange, I had been promised, witnessing would get easier.
>
> "Yes," he answered.
>
> None of the coaching, none of the role-playing in church youth meetings or pep talks at Bible camp, had prepared me for that response. I was ready with reasoned arguments about the existence of God, the sinfulness of humanity, and every person's need to accept Christ as his or her savior. But how do you deal with someone who lies about his spiritual condition? Stanley, I knew, was a Roman Catholic, not a Christian, a plight in some respects worse than outright paganism, I had been told, because it lulled followers into a deadly complacency. But Christian? Certainly no Catholic, no matter how benighted, would dare call himself a Christian.
>
> "Are you sure?" I asked meekly, beating a hasty retreat. He was sure. Once the rain cleared, we resumed playing catch and fantasizing about our futures in professional baseball.[23]

Balmer goes on to describe firsthand the evangelical kaleidoscope that exists throughout the United States. The individual parts all claim to be the real McCoy, if not the only way into the kingdom: the dispensationalists at Dallas Theological Seminary, a bizarre "bible prophet" in Phoenix, a holiness camp meeting in southern Florida, and an Indian mission run by Episcopalians on the plains of North Dakota. They are adept at carving their niche, bolstering the fidelity of their followers, and arguing a hermeneutic delivered to them by the Apostle Peter, if not God Himself. Knocking over straw men and drawing sharp demarcations in the sands of theological rift are self-serving communication techniques.

Every evangelist has the task of pointing the way to the Christ described in the Scriptures and revealed by the ongoing dynamic of the Holy Spirit. All evangelistic preaching is ultimately bragging about Jesus, but I cannot presume that my boasts, no matter how well-intentioned, have not been skewed by the traditions of the fathers. Because the message passes through human instrumentality, there must always be the suspicion of subjectivity. We must be willing to acknowledge the possibility that our individualistic perceptions may lie between the truth and our interpretation of the truth.

Weeding our arbitrary distinctions and doctrinal schemes from the incarnate Word will be an endless task. As we prayerfully approach the text, we must pray that God will enable us to receive the Scriptures afresh, in spite of the preconceived notions that would block us from digging into the mind of the author and above all the intentions of the Holy Spirit. Proclamation boxed in airtight doctrinal schemes sometimes communicates smug certitude rather than confident assurance. We do not claim to fully comprehend the historical and eternal Christ or to be fully liberated from all the warped images and cultural anthropomorphisms through which we view God. The preacher should strive to exalt Jesus and only Jesus above the smog of petty ecclesiastical debate and self-serving agendas, so that hearers will be confronted by Christ and Christ alone. The end result should be a revelation such as that which transformed George Fox:

> But as I had forsaken all the priests so I left the Separate preachers also, and those called the most experienced people: for I saw there was none among them all that could speak to my condition. And when all my hopes in them and in all men were gone, so that I had nothing outwardly to help me, nor could tell what to do, then, Oh! then, I heard a voice which said, "There is one, even Christ Jesus, that can speak to thy condition; and when I heard it my heart did leap for joy."[24]

Fox's testimony represents one of the great paradoxes of preaching: how to bring people into immediacy through mediation, how to be a visible instrument and point people beyond that instrument. Fox's despair and ensuing personal revelation did not discredit the vocation of preaching. He gave the rest of his life to that vocation and often reflected after a preaching situation, "I spoke to their condition." Yet it was not Fox who ultimately spoke, it was an inner light sent from a transcendent source.

The Jesus whom the preacher presents stands at every heart's door, yet He is in no way to be made synonymous with His creatures or any other part of His creation. He is both the Christ who walked with humankind and the Christ who is revealed in the Book of Revelation. Even though He became flesh, He was still transcendent above the greed, racism, and religiosity of His day. He dismantled the vigorous legalism of the ecclesiastics with the radical hermeneutic of the new kingdom: "Ye have heard but I say unto you." Christ was not out to restructure the old world, but to offer a new world, a new perspective on life. When Jesus left the gravitational pull of earth, little had changed—hardly enough to merit a brief notation in secular history. But a few inner worlds had been so radically transformed that they would shape the next 2,000 years of history. At every preachment there is the possibility that Christ will create a new inner world that will transform the outer world. It is this possibility of so displacing the worldview of contemporary persons that causes Brueggeman to define preaching as a "poetic construct of an alternate world."[25]

The Jesus who we preach transcends modern culture, American culture, and ecclesiastical culture. Modern culture is defined by relativism, hedonism, materialism, and autonomous individualism. American culture is defined by patriotism, imperialism, manifest destiny, and democracy. Ecclesiasticism is defined by rules, doctrine, organization, and moralisms. The answer to the human agony is found in none of these artifices. It is certainly not found in ourselves. All forms of self-discovery are ultimately like a bank account that is in the red and a fuel tank whose needle is below the empty mark. Faith in psychology, technique, principles, and education to fundamentally change people is a reductionism of the highest order.

Another irony of preaching is that it is bragging about Jesus. How can one brag about the "lily of the valley" and the "bright morning star"? What more can be said? My five-year-old daughter, while sitting in the second pew at a very liturgical 11 P.M. Christmas Eve service, when the Lucan narrative of the Christmas story was begun, exclaimed in a voice that could surely be heard several rows back, "I've heard this before!" Her boredom was similar to the ho-hum attitude of every preacher and every congregation who once again try to grasp who this Jesus is that we are supposed to follow. Can the Holy Spirit transmit a fresh love letter, a perspective that is charged with relevancy to a unique situation that the worship participant may be experiencing? Could someone leave saying, "I saw something about Christ which I have never seen before?" Perhaps so, if the preacher believes that the revelation of Christ is inexhaustible and that the Holy Spirit bears fresh witness to Christ daily.

How Do We Get There?

The ultimate question of the evangelist is "What will you do with Jesus?" To the unconverted, the question will be asked in terms of an initial commitment. To the backslider, the question will be asked in terms of recommitment. In addressing those who are growing in grace, Christ needs to be applied to the areas of marriage, finances, and vocation. G. Campbell Morgan stated, "We must not be led astray from the essential work of the Christian ministry by imagining we have some gift that does not include within it something of the evangelistic necessity or, urging the claim of Christ upon individuals."[26]

But how does one find Christ? The message cannot be left open-ended. There needs to be a sharp focus on the ultimate purpose driven home by the speaker's conviction. The speaker has left no doubt in the listener's mind that if Christ is sought, He will make a radical difference in the listener's life. The preacher has expected the listener to go away forever changed because the spoken word has been translated by the Holy Spirit into the living Word. The idea that the Holy Spirit would break in upon both preacher and all other worship participants is too much of a burden for many pulpiteers. The willingness to be a "God-speaker" brings accusations of playing God or perhaps demagoguery. Nevertheless, the evangelist must humbly perceive himself or herself as a change agent in the lives of those seeking for reality in a world that is no friend of grace. James Daane wrote, "The cool, nonchalant even cavalier manner in which many Protestant ministers occupy the pulpit is a travesty on its sacred and mysterious function."[27]

Telling people how to come to Christ is marked by clarity and confidence. There can be no ambiguity in the concluding invitation. This is the time for the preacher to be free from notes and converse intimately with the congregation. The two or three minutes of instruction will serve as stepping-stones to the Savior. The evangelist will speak out of experience, but at the same time not give the impression that he or she has arrived at some plane of infallibility. This is the point where the evangelist's genuine concern for the well-being of the listener needs to be evident. Those invited to a strange world will follow only after sensing that the speaker "really does care for me." In Fred Craddock's words:

> Empathy and understanding do not make the preacher "soft

> on sin" or lead to the loss of a person's prophetic indignation. Rather, the understanding preacher has come to see who the real enemy is and where the real battle lines are to be drawn. The scalpel replaces the ax and surgery replaces bruising.[28]

For those who are outside of the kingdom of God, it must be made clear that the only way in is through repentance and complete trust in the atoning work of Christ. Theology must be expressed nontheologically through metaphors, object lessons, and simple illustrations as to what it means to put one's trust in Christ. The invitation may include direction to perform a physical act or assume a particular posture that accents and affirms a decision that has been made. Bodily action serves to dramatize decisions and solidify the intentions of psychosomatic creatures.

Requests for a physical response both honor the immediate conviction of the Holy Spirit and recognize the limitations of the human spirit, which in this life depends on physical symbols to convey the spiritual: the partaking of bread and wine at an altar, coming forward to an altar at an invitation, recording a commitment on a piece of paper, praying audible prayers in unison with a counselor, and so forth. Not all of the above are ordinances instituted by Christ, but nevertheless have a sacramental value. A sacrament is an ordinary channel by which God conveys His prevenient, justifying, and sanctifying grace. The Lord's Supper at the end of a message would be a perfect time to invite a sinner to the redeeming love of Christ. The elements received in good faith by the repentant serve as a converting ordinance, a door through which people pass into the kingdom of God.

Whatever request is made by the evangelist should be repeated at least twice, if not three times, in very simple terms. It may be that the physical symbolism in a pastoral situation needs to be varied so that the people do not begin to trust in the means rather than the end. Billy Graham has maintained the same invitational procedure for decades. Changed tactics may lead to confusion for both novice counselors and the unchurched who may be responding. The effective evangelist describes a very clear path and assures the congregation that Christ is willing to meet them more than halfway. David Mains designates clear invitational instructions as "building bridges to action." Mains writes, "I have found through years of lay-preacher dialogue that if I can't tell my listeners what to do, if I can't reconstruct good bridges for people, they probably won't figure out applications for themselves."[29]

Practical suggestions for the invitation include the following:

1. *The purpose of the message needs to be defined before the message.* John Broadus argued that a sermon can serve different functions: evangelistic, theological, ethical, devotional, inspiriting, and actional. The actual content and concluding invitation will be determined and planned according to the overall purpose. Broadus writes,

> An evangelistic sermon will naturally appeal to emotion more extensively than a didactic sermon; a devotional sermon will be more explanatory and persuasive than argumentative; a theological sermon of the apologetic type will be largely argumentative while the simple instructional type will be in the main, explanatory; inspiriting sermons will be strengthened by illustrative examples.[30]

Broadus did not argue for clear demarcation and mutual exclusiveness between purposes. But a constant invitation to initial salvation by singing "Just as I Am," no matter what the topic, will prove to be trite and innocuous. However, it is perfectly acceptable to issue an invitation to a new aspect of living in Christ at the end of every message. Preaching that does not call for decision falls short of New Testament proclamation. John Henry Jowett wrote, "In all our preaching we must preach for verdicts. We must present our case, we must seek a verdict, and we must ask for immediate execution of the verdict."[31]

2. *The invitation must be bathed in prayer with utter dependency on the Holy Spirit.* Clever argument and moral suasion may prompt people to act, but only the Holy Spirit can bring individuals to Christ. The preacher provides a second witness to the witness of the Holy Spirit. The truth of both the written and living Word is established in the mind of the hearer. Dennis Kinlaw writes:

> We never arrive in someone's life before the Holy Spirit. We never touch someone before God touches him. When God leads us to somebody, He has been there before us. We never preach to someone in whose life God has not already been at work. That prior work of the Spirit of grace makes the effectiveness of our witness possible. I call this "the Law of the Second Witness."[32]

3. Be optimistic concerning the power of truth, the ability of God to do what He has promised, and the receptiveness of the people to receive God's promises. The Holy Spirit is breaking up the fallow ground and assuring the listener that God is able to turn barren lives into fruitful branches connected to the living Vine. Encouraging the divine potential within every human life, no matter how downtrodden, is far more productive than scolding, conjoling, degrading, and belittling. The challenge is to give someone the opportunity to invite the Christ, who has been feebly yet faithfully described, into their everyday lives. Brueggeman says it well:

> In their yet to be formed condition, seminarians' largely preach sermons filled with 'ought' and 'must' and 'should.' I have found myself growing in resistance to such sermons that purport to speak God's command. I have found myself discovering that mostly I do not need more advice, but strength. I do not need new information, but courage, freedom, and authorization to act on what I already have been given in the gospel.[33]

The preacher must remember that people do not fail God because they do not know what God wants them to do. Most people to whom we preach will have already had enough light to come to Christ, though that will certainly not be true of everyone. People do not reject Christ because there is some innate propensity to disobedience and reprobation that has predetermined their fate. The evangelist needs implicitly or explicitly to underline his or her invitation with the rhetorical question "Who wouldn't come to Christ if they really believed that the eternal, all-powerful God is pulling for them, is on their side, and is pledging His sufficiency to them in the following absolute terms: 'And God is able to make all grace abound to you, that always having all sufficiency in everything, you may have an abundance for every good deed' (2 Cor. 9:8)?"

THE SUPREME MOTIVE FOR EVANGELISTIC PREACHING

The Scripture gives two terse definitions of God: God is love; God is holy. There is a double movement in each definition. Not only do holiness and love define God, but God defines holiness and love.

The preacher should present a God succinctly and profoundly defined by "holy love." If the appeal of the evangelist is underlined by a lesser agenda than God's character, it is amiss. A holy God has revealed Himself through a loving sacrificial act. John wrote, "In this is love, not that we loved God, but that He loved us and sent His Son to be the propitiation for our sins" (1 John 4:10).

The proclaimer will constantly battle other agendas that would preempt God's cosmic plan to transform sinners into loving people separated unto Himself. Church growth, political revolution, institutional recruitment, crisis solution, and all personal agendas are inferior motives when appealing to people for decisions. They may serve as doors through which people enter, but the preacher always needs to envision himself carrying people over the threshold to encounter a Christ radiant with loving holiness. God's astounding commitment to enter into an eternal relationship of holy fidelity with a lost world erases naive sentimentality and narcissism.

The passion and earnestness that the preacher experiences and exhibits does not come from being in an emotional frenzy. It is imparted by the Holy Spirit as the preacher understands the heart of God. Preaching is not simply interpretation of Scripture; it is the Holy Spirit breathing God's emotion into the heart of the proclaimer as the words are being uttered. Every statement is emotionally charged by the Spirit-anointed preacher.

Evangelistic preaching is bathed in the passion of Christ. Emotions will be fired up as the preacher prepares by reviewing Christ's pathos. Thus, whatever emotion the evangelist expresses will not be perceived as a dramatic distortion, but as a barometer of the temperament of both the idea and moment. In Stevenson and Diel's words, "True emotion does not call direct attention to itself; rather, because it is appropriate to each idea as it is being expressed it calls attention to the idea and powerfully reinforces that idea."[34]

FREE MORAL AGENCY

The appeal should not only be in keeping with the character of God, but faithful to the design of the creature by the creator. The tension between God's sovereignty and human freedom is perhaps creation's grandest paradox. Rather than trying to unravel a mystery, it would be helpful to state what we do understand. All creaturely existence is limited by contingencies. God is all-powerful and can work toward His good pleasure. God has given sufficient freedom to persons whereby they can demonstrate their love to God through voluntary obedience rather than external coercion. Any outside infringement on a response motivated by love mitigates human potential and subtracts from God's pleasure. God's pleasure is enhanced when people respond out of inherent desire rather than extrinsic forces.

Let's assume that a person responds at least physically and verbally to a gospel appeal. If the appeal leaves a bad aftertaste, taints of regret, and shadows of embarrassment, then the person has probably been manipulated rather than lovingly drawn to the Savior. Any form of invitation that leaves the person saying, "I had no idea where they were going to take me" or "How did I get into this predicament?" has robbed the individual of his or her personal freedom. If the invited respond because of peer pressure, awkwardness, or ostracism, they have not freely come to Christ. Worse yet, they have been driven from God because Christ was falsely represented. Christ desires people who will seek Him with all their heart, much as a thirsty person desires water. An individual with a parched mouth does not have to be conjoled by technique, exaggerated predictions, and endless appeals that batter the listener rather than offer a solution to life's most basic need.

In the communication process, the audience is always sovereign. God has willed that the ultimate choice belongs to created existence. God has made the primary move through a Lamb slain from the foundation of the earth. The next move is up to the individuals who make up humankind. The case in point is Christ's encounter with the rich young ruler (Matt. 19). Christ was quite clear as He lovingly communicated with this mideastern sheik regarding the costs of following the Savior. When Jesus implied that this young man's assets were so frozen that God could not get to them, he sadly turned away. God could have forced His way into the man's vaults, but He respected the individual's right to hold onto his possessions rather than release them for eternal good. Christ did nothing extraordinary to prevent rejection, which is so difficult for many evangelists to swallow. James Engel writes, "Jesus exemplified an ethical standard that many contemporary evangelists violate (we hope in innocence rather than willfully): 'Any persuasive effort which restricts another's freedom to choose for or against Jesus Christ is wrong.'"[35]

ISAIAH'S MODEL

Isaiah 55 offers a prime example of the paradigm for preaching that we have explored in this chapter. Isaiah identifies the people to whom he is speaking. They are people who are figuratively without food and money to purchase the basic necessities of life. Their dominant characteristic is their dire need. The evangelist seeks to articulate the needs of those to whom he is called, needs of which they may or may not be cognizant. Their immediate response may be, "I did not know that I was poor, blind, naked, and hungry."

Where are those people? They are frantically scurrying about, earning enough money to buy things that do not ultimately satisfy. They are caught in a vicious cycle of gluttony and starvation. They are suffering from spiritual anorexia brought on by gorging without vital nourishment. The search for satisfaction continues until life becomes a dead end at the end of a one-way street. It is only when the realization of futility sweeps over a person stymied with the frustration of creatureliness that they are ready to listen. "Incline your ear and come to Me. Listen, that you may live; and I will make an everlasting covenant with you, according to the faithful mercies shown to David" (Isa. 55:3).

Where does the listener need to go? "Seek the Lord while He may be found; call upon Him while He is near" (Isa. 55:6). In the midst of God's "everlasting lovingkindness" (Isa. 54:8), there is an urgency in the message. God's love is forever, but humankind's opportunities are limited. It may be that even in our eternal lostness God does and will love us. But one is reminded of the words of Christ concerning the Jews: "If you had known in this day, even you, the things which make for peace! But now they have been hidden from your eyes" (Luke 19:42). Jesus wept because blindness could exist in the midst of such blazing light, and His own people had squandered the most crucial opportunity that had ever been given a generation of humanity. The urgency in any preacher's voice must come from the sense that this particular opportunity will never be repeated.

How do we find the Christ? By seeking Him and calling upon Him. It is not repentance without reformation. "Let the wicked forsake his way, and the unrighteous man his thoughts" (Isa. 55:7). God's response is one of compassion, not scorn or rebuke. Repentance is not for the purpose of placating a capricious God or propositioning a manipulative one. God in His infinite mercy and unfathomable compassion has provided a chariot of mercy to transport weary passengers into a world of blessing rather than cursing.

> For you will go out with joy, and be led forth with peace; the mountains and the hills will break forth into shouts of joy before you, and all the trees of the field will clap their hands. . . . Instead of the nettle the myrtle will come up; and it will be a memorial to the Lord, for an everlasting sign which will not be cut off (Isa. 55:12–13).

Such a world would be mystifying to the uninitiated. No wonder it is ruled by one whose thoughts are not our thoughts and whose ways are not our ways. "For as the heavens are higher than the earth, so are My ways higher than your ways, and My thoughts than your thoughts" (Isa. 55:9). Whether people choose to dwell on the parched hills surrounding the Dead Sea or the plush green valleys of Jezreel and Megiddo will be up to them. Whichever, God states, "So shall My word be which goes forth from My mouth; it shall not return to Me empty, without accomplishing what I desire, and without succeeding in the matter for which I sent it" (Isa. 55:11). God will continue to offer through the mouths of men and women an alternate world, whatever their present circumstance.

CONCLUSION

This chapter has not argued for a biblically specific office or role that designates certain preachers as "evangelists." The role, however, has been generally accepted by American evangelicals since the early eighteenth century, when George Whitefield came storming into New England.[36] America's first celebrity, as Harry Stout calls him, defined a pastoral care office that was distinct from the settled parish professional. The itinerant's business was the salvation of souls, while the pastor's enterprise concerned routinization of preaching to and caring for the same people year after year. Trying to biblically validate one as opposed to the other is futile. The church of Paul's time was quite different from the sociopolitical institution that was the center of New England life and that could expect at least tacit compliance to Christianity. In contrast, the New Testament church was an ever expanding movement that left us with preaching models that are overtly and intentionally evangelistic. There was little New Testament indication of what forms preaching would take in the twenty-first-century church.

God's forms have varied as the church has taken on various shapes and sizes throughout the centuries. God's gifts are both sovereignly bestowed and temporally defined. If the church needs traveling evangelists with a contemporary, yet prophetical, message, God will see that they are available. Yet it cannot be argued, either biblically or historically, that evangelistic preaching is left to a distinct coterie of individuals who have a corner on the enterprise. All preaching is in some sense evangelistic. All preachers need to do some preaching that is essentially and specifically evangelistic. Such preaching will not only deal with the new birth, but sanctification themes that lead believers to new spiritual heights and understandings. Anything less will produce a church that is stagnant or, worse yet, ultimately lost.

X

the evangelism of worship

John and Mary and their three children, ages two, seven, and ten, have just attended First Suburban Church in Anytown, U.S.A., for the first time. John passes the church every morning on his way to work. He had noticed the intriguing sermon topics posted on a modern marquis next to the highway. The words "This church can be your home" seemed inviting enough. One day while in casual conversation about golf with a work acquaintance named Bob, John discovered that Bob played weekly with three or four buddies from First Suburban, where he attended. In fact, Bob invited John to participate in a golf tournament sponsored by First Suburban. The guys were friendly and made John feel accepted. Though Bob had previously invited John to church, no one said anything about religion at the tournament, except for the invocation prayed at the beginning.

John and Mary had both attended mainline churches as youngsters, though their families were not particularly devout. They had often discussed religion and the possibility of finding a church to attend, but somehow had not carried out those intentions during their twelve years of marriage. Kyle, the oldest son, had recently begun asking some serious theological questions. One of his best friends went to church; one day Kyle asked his dad why they didn't go to church. Stress at work, the desire to provide a value structure for the family, the friendship of the guys at the golf tournament, and Kyle's question all combined to place the family in church that first Sunday. But the question remained: Were they going to return to First Suburban or perhaps look for another church? Kyle gave a positive report on children's church, which had been conducted during the adult worship service. The parents were impressed by the greeters, who had personally escorted the members of the family to their respective places in Sunday School and the nursery. "Special attention" seemed to be the motif of the morning, all the way from the car door openers to the greeters.

But the family discussion going home did not so much center on the sequence of events as it did on the worship service. The choir sounded great, and the pastor's message on the biblical meaning of work had been especially meaningful for John. One sentence had uniquely stuck in his mind: "The microcosm of your workplace can take on cosmic proportions if you take Jesus Christ to work with you." And the music sounded different at this church from what they remembered church music to be like. The bass guitar, snare drums, and several trumpets gave the service a contemporary sound that was appealing. The rhythm of the service was upbeat, yet there was a reverence and enthusiasm among the people that did not belie it was a worship service. The comments passed between John and Mary on the way home were quite positive. They were confident that they would attend next Sunday.

WORSHIP: AN END IN ITSELF

If evangelism is the door of the church, worship is its interior. Worship is not a means by which the church can evangelize the world. Rather, evangelism is a means of bringing people into the experience of worshiping a holy God. We do not experience worship in order to become better witnesses for Christ. We become a better witness for Jesus Christ in order to experience God's holiness through worship. If we truly worship God, we will become better witnesses to the power and grace of God. It is in worship that we best reflect the image of a holy God. Ultimately, we do not meet together to solve the political crisis, the economic crisis, or even the family crisis. Our agenda is simply to meet with God and experience His presence. It is an agenda that is worthy of all the time and energy of which God Himself is worthy. Worship is an end in itself.

WORSHIP: GOD'S SHOWCASE OF CELEBRATION

It is in glorifying and enjoying God that we are at our best as evangelists. It is not difficult to ascertain whether people are enjoying God in worship. It is evident in the exuberance of singing, the glow of countenances, and the enthusiasm of body language. The newcomer can immediately detect whether these people whom he or she has never met before are in worship because of perfunctory obligation or whether Sunday morning worship is the highlight of the week. Anticipation, as with any other mood, is contagious. The moods of both the people and the Holy Spirit must be prayed for and planned for. Churches that grow have a philosophy of worship which, if not explicitly stated in written form, has been at least communicated by the leadership.

Worship is the church's showcase and, most importantly, God's showcase. It is the ultimate product that the church has to offer. Pastors who realize this truth strive for creativity and freshness, without sacrificing biblical authority and the well-worn traditions of the church. The question is not how to maintain a tradition, but how biblical principles of worship can become meaningful and renewed for contemporary persons. The church that accomplishes this will have to give worship high priority. The pastor who cannot lead the people in worship, even though he or she may be able to counsel, administrate, and even preach, has missed the most important priestly function. Worship needs leadership! If worship is the ultimate of all that people do, then in no place is the leadership and authority of the pastor more evident than in worship. Duke University chaplain William Willimon said, "For in the leadership of worship, the community function of the priest is revealed most clearly, the source of the priest's officialness is affirmed most strongly and a pastor's self understanding will be laid bare for all to see."[1]

AUTHORITY FOR LIVING

It is through worship that people will discover authority for living. People seek authority. It is through worship that people are put in contact with a transcendent God who offers the strength to face another day at the office or the grace to cope with diapers and dishpans at home. The world drains and drags, but worship fills and uplifts. It is through worship that forgiveness, healing, and acceptance are mediated. For that reason, the benediction is the climax of the service. For many, especially the pastor, the benediction signifies a dismissal ritualized by a bland prayer that implicitly communicates, "It's finally over." Benediction means "blessing," and it is the pastor who has the authority to bless the people. This concluding act needs to be transformed into a climactic charge from the worship leader to the people for all to go out into the kitchen, gymnasium, factories, offices, and classrooms of the community as change agents for the ushering in of the kingdom of God. Worship transforms the menial tasks and mundane drudgeries into appointed ambassadorships for the King of kings. The blessing of worship commissions everyone to claim their God-given places and job descriptions as important persons in God's overall plan to redeem the world.

UNDERSTANDING OF LIFE

Life is increasingly perplexing for moderns. The monolithic worldview of our ancestors has been bludgeoned by sociology, psychology, and the rapid multiplication of technology. Modernity is defined as a diversified urban society characterized by high technology, specialization of labor, impersonal bureaucracy, and the emaciation of a worldview *(weltanschaaung)* that revolves around the supernatural. The current success and consumer orientations are attempted antidotes to the depersonalization and secularism of a society that has lost the God who crowned humankind with glory and honor. The trade-off has been a tarnished, lackluster appearance that, for the unredeemed, grows dimmer rather than brighter. Thoreau was not entirely wrong when he charged that "the mass of men lead lives of quiet desperation."

Worship must cast light on the perplexities of everyday existence and provide coherent understanding. Coherency means that life has rhyme and reason. God does not throw dice—events that surround our personhood are not left up to chance. Every worship service must leave the participant with the knowledge that "God causes all things to work together for good to those who love God, to those who are called according to His purpose" (Rom. 8:28). Worship transforms groping into God-directed living. The unregenerate individual who enters a worship service must be made to see the big picture and, more importantly, enabled to perceive that he or she is a critical part of the big picture. Albert F. Bayly wrote the following words:

> Lord, whose love through humble service
> Bore the weight of human need
> Who upon the cross forsaken
> Offered mercy's perfect deed
> We your servants bring the worship
> Not of voice alone, but heart
> Consecrating to your purpose
> Every gift that you impart.[2]

This hymn lets people know that they are not only part of the big picture, but that they can be on God's team. Evangelistic worship says to the outsider, "God wants you, you are of value, and we want to enable you in making a contribution to an eternal cause with temporal consequences." The church offers self-actualization through Christ's simple invitation: "Come, follow Me." No cause serves more to exalt human existence and to enable persons to transcend the triviality that engrosses most of humanity. The menial tasks that are endured are transformed into responsibilities that are endearing to a God who has said, "Whether, then, you eat or drink or whatever you do, do all to the glory of God" (1 Cor. 10:31).

Evangelistic worship says to individuals, "You do not have to create your own meaning and chart your own direction; rather, you can be a part of the divine drama. You can cast your lot with the triune Godhead. God has a plan for your life and you can choose to be a part of that plan." In no place is this better communicated than in worship. The gathered people say with loud exclamation, "God is in control!" Nothing happens outside of His providence.

Worship writer Robert Webber writes:

> Now when I move into the sanctuary and prepare to worship, I enter into a time of rest, a time of relationship, a time to celebrate the truths that give direction to my life. My whole body, soul, and spirit became engaged in rehearsing the work of Christ which gives shape and form to my life. It is the source of my values, the energy that holds my family together, and the purpose of my work. Worship connects me with the past, gives meaning to the present, and inspires hope for the future as my soul and spirit become blended again into the drama of Christ's life, death and resurrection.[3]

Webber continues by discussing the difference between a comedic and tragic script. The tragic script is nihilistic and fatalistic, represented by Albert Camus' *The Plague* and Samuel Beckett's *Waiting for Godot*. The plot lacks resolution and ends with a question mark rather than an exclamation point. In contrast, the comedic script resolves the tension and ironies that have plagued the participants. Hope is justified and justice is triumphant. Good triumphs over evil because Christ has triumphed over Satan. "All's well that ends well" is transformed from a glib cliché into an eschatological assurance worth staking our lives on. Though the difficulties of life cannot be erased, the tragedy of existence can be conquered through Christ when He is the focal point of the worshiping community. Every worship service should broadcast to all true seekers the final score: "Jesus is going to win!" In a world where chaos reigns and where the most directed moments that some people spend are in rush hour on the freeway, it is no small achievement to instill within people the belief that everything is going to turn out all right in the end.

ALIVE IN WORSHIP

For a generation attempting to grab all the gusto, dead, slovenly worship will be less than satisfying. It is no wonder that charismatics have been on the leading edge of evangelism among American churches. The hand clapping, arm waving, and foot stomping to joyful praise songs lead the casual observer to believe that worship calls for total immersion of the self, mind, body, and soul. Much worship in Protestant churches calls for little immersion in anything, much less complete devotion to the Lord of the universe. True worship is passionate. Without passion, there is cold orthodoxy rather than life. At times there is neither orthodoxy or life.

It should not be understood that those who go by the name of "charismatic" have a corner on the worship market—everyone who is a member of the body of Christ is charismatic. They are possessors of joy, grace, and gifts of the Holy Spirit. As I have previously stated, "The word *charis* has special importance within the New Testament economy, it is used 151 times in the Greek New Testament."[4] The church cannot exude life without being in touch with the supernatural. It is the Holy Spirit who enables the members to minister to one another and to lift a voice of one accord in worship. Newcomers to our worship services must be impressed that this is a spiritual exercise that exceeds human endeavor. People are seeking for answers that human institutions cannot provide. They will come to the church that believes in the miraculous (i.e., that God intervenes in special ways). If worship does not lift people out of the ordinary, it has missed the life that flows from Calvary as mediated by the present dynamic actions of the Holy Spirit.

When God is at its center, worship is alive, but not necessarily spectacular and never ostentatious. People who lead in worship or are special facilitators (e.g., greeters, ushers, choir, orchestra, and platform personnel) need to ask God to enable them to transcend the agendas that detract from Spirit-filled worship. The "upfronters," as Ann Ortlund designates them, need to have complete concentration and undivided attention on the business at hand. The fact that they are lost in worship will be the most significant catalyst in enticing others to do the same. They will communicate with their eyes, expressions, and body language that they are not only participating but would rather be in God's house than any other place. After all, if the leadership would rather be somewhere else, certainly that will be communicated to the visitor. There is no quicker way to undercut evangelism.

While worship elicits emotion, it is not to be equated with emotionalism. Life is a drama full of emotions: sadness, laughter, amazement, and love. The absence of those emotions in a worship service renders the experience as bland and disappointing. Worship must be felt. A movie, play, or novel that is not felt by the reader or viewers is not worth the time of engagement. A good worship service engages the participant by exhibiting a wide range of emotion: the humor of an anecdote, the celebration of a birth, the sadness of a human tragedy, and the anger of righteous indignation. The absence of these emotions makes the worship service appear empty to the newcomer. What is on the inside is entirely separated from the concrete realities of existence. While the old dichotomy between the rational and the emotional is superfluous, the point is that worship cannot be filled with abstractions. Every worship service is a marriage between Christ and His bride. We are celebrating love at its deepest level. If the bride goes to sleep during the ceremony, why should anyone attend? It's more profitable to stay home in bed.

INCLUSIVENESS

Every worship service practices ritual. Some kneel for prayer, some stand for singing, some respond with prescribed forms of confession, repentance, and praise, while others pray extemporaneously at an altar railing. Quite often rites are so inherited and traditional that those enforcing them forget the truth that the symbolism represents. The lighting of candles may mean something entirely different to a child, or even an acolyte, than it does to the priest who plans the service. We are quite often like the sentry who was posted by Catherine the Great of Russia to guard the first flower of spring on the palace grounds. After more than a hundred years of a soldier being posted at the same spot, almost everyone forgot why he was there! If the why of a ritual is lost, the meaning of that moment in worship is lost on those who are participating.

William Willimon states, "Psychology often exercises the prophetic function of telling me that everything I do is not done simply because I love God and the church."[5] Rites of worship may be done out of denominational pride, cultural bias, intellectual ostentation, or the clannishness of socioeconomic status. Congregations in denominations of recent origin, which view their group as complete within itself, may not understand what it is to be part of the church universal (catholic). Such an attitude fails to see the importance of reciting the Apostles' Creed or singing the Gloria Patri.

As the church moved westward in the nineteenth century, there was a mitigation of symbolism and ritual in order to accommodate the migrant Americans who had little religious rootage. Worship services were simple: without vestments, processionals, or books to orchestrate responsive readings and unison prayers. James White states, "The frontier tradition in Protestant worship came about as a response to a practical pastoral problem: how to minister to a largely unchurched population scattered over enormous distances of thinly settled country."[6]

What resulted from the above was a simple order of worship that could be easily grasped by the common uneducated person: songs, prayer, offering, and a sermon with an altar call at the end. The purpose of worship was not so much to glorify God as it was to gather in the heathen and get them saved—certainly that would glorify God. But where did that leave the saints who needed ongoing nurturing through symbolism and creeds that would draw them into the vitality of God's sanctifying grace? Thus the church was faced with a dilemma that has never been satisfactorily resolved: how to minister to saints and sinners alike in the same worship service. How does the leadership satisfy the old guard in the worship service and at the same time not exclude those who are visiting the church for the first time?

The answer to the above problem is not to do away with higher symbolic worship. In order for worship to become inclusive, we do not have to do away with all mystery. God is able to meet both saint and sinner alike through the sacraments. Robert Webber states it cogently:

> God works through life, through people, and through physical, tangible, and material reality to communicate his healing presence in our lives. The point is that God does not meet us outside of life in an esoteric manner. Rather, he meets us through life incidents and particularly through the sacraments of the church. Sacrament then, is a way of encountering the mystery.[7]

There is no reason why the novice cannot encounter the mystery of God through the sacraments and other forms of worship if the leadership will take time to ask and answer the following questions:

1. *Does the context of the worship service indicate warmth, openness, and acceptance to newcomers?* If there is esoterica in the worship service, it will be far more palatable if the pretext is a warm welcome with significant affirmation by smiling faces. The optimum context for any ritual is "You may not understand how or why we do this but we are sure glad you are here to do it with us."

2. *Are some forms of worship badges of belonging rather than invitations of grace?* It should be made clear that any means of grace such as song, creed, or ordinance can be an entrance point for the person willing to put his or her faith in Christ. While most free churches do not practice closed Communion, the introduction to the Eucharist at times leads participants to believe that only those who have passed muster through careful introspection may partake. We need to be aware that the ordinances are primarily God's signs to us and not our signs to God. Webber states, "Rather than sending me into myself in search of this or that sin to confess, the Eucharist makes me aware that I never have been and never will be worthy. But more than that, the Eucharist tells me that I am acceptable to God because of Jesus Christ."[8] Everything that is done in the worship service needs to signify acceptance. This does not mean that everyone present is spiritually healthy. It does mean that God is ever present to convey grace to the lowest and hungriest seeker through the acts of worship.

3. *Are the forms freshly anointed forms?* The question is not whether the church is formal or informal. Every church has forms (i.e., acts or rites of worship). Has the worship leader asked God to envelop the form in recreativity so the act of worship will become vital and relevant to the congregants? Anything can become perfunctory, whether we do it infrequently or frequently. Is there some new insight, introduction, or analogy that one can give the congregation that will make a stale tradition become alive, relevant, and meaningful? Does the worship team pray together that God will use everything done in the worship service to penetrate unbelieving minds?

The evangelistic character of worship demands careful planning. It means filtering out as much technical language as possible. It is certainly possible to celebrate Jesus' death and resurrection without using the word "soteriology" and affirm the ultimate triumph of the church without stumbling over "eschatology."

Maintaining theological depth does not mean eliminating the question "How does this sound to the uninitiated?" or "How does one erase insider language without vitiating the forms of worship?" Such questions, though difficult to answer, may yield a great harvest, if continually asked.

If the worship leader is constantly praying and planning that God will give new forms by which God's grace can be conveyed, both the newcomer and the old-timer will join in the process of discovery. David Mains challenges pastors to be imaginative when he states, "Don't be afraid of thinking up new ways to worship God through the senses. Your creativity is the limit, so long as the ideas are purposeful and within congregational acceptance." Among his illustrations are using fresh baked bread for Communion, the opening of perfume in a sanctuary as we speak of the aroma of Christ, and the passing out of nails at the church door as the congregation prepares to reflect on the death of Christ. If carefully planned, and not done repetitiously, these symbols can enable all to gain a perspective they have not previously known. For the unredeemed, such vivid expressions of Christian truth will likely never be forgotten.

SAYING WELCOME TO OUTSIDERS

It must be remembered that symbols and rituals do not provide inclusiveness for people—people demonstrate inclusiveness to other people. No matter how strange or familiar is the pattern of worship, people will not return unless they are affirmed. Nothing will substitute for a vivacious and warm greeting team. No matter how small the church is, persons should not be allowed to enter alone. People should not be given instructions about where to go; rather, they need to be taken. To point a newcomer out by asking him or her to stand during the worship service tends to embarrass and sometimes even alienate the individual. A warm reception, before and after the service, is much more effective in making a person feel at home. As the church grows, people need to be strategically placed throughout the sanctuary so that visitors will not slip away unnoticed. The entire welcome team needs training and should not be taken for granted.

Patrick Keifert, in his book *Welcoming the Stranger,* argues that many worship services focus on an ideology of intimacy. The church serves as a place where people can escape from the friendless public square. The shared values of religion, to which the church is friendly and the world unfriendly, provide a collective subjectivity of intimacy. It is this intimacy that often fences out the stranger. Keifert argues that ritual which focuses vertically on God, rather than horizontally, is a means for including the stranger. A newcomer is not faced with having to penetrate clannishness that implicitly states, "You have to prove yourself first." The classical and historical rites of worship offer to the public immediate participation. A worship service then becomes a community of the gospel, rather than a family with privatized ground rules and insider language. Focusing on God does not mean that the church ceases to be friendly.

But being friendly is not being family! The difference between these two kinds of relationships is critical. Every service must open congregational space so that people may join in at their own pace; every worship ritual must tell every worshiper that the place and the ritual are open to all. It must pronounce clearly that the conditions of participation are set by the gospel itself, not by the unwritten rules of a family of insiders.[9]

THE LANGUAGE OF WORSHIP

The language of worship must reflect the concrete realities of everyday life. This principle does not eliminate the singing of stately hymns, creedal affirmations, or the praying of a printed collect. The problem with much worship is that it is not only irrelevant, but trite. Instead of beginning the service with a pallid "Good morning," worship leaders should try calling the people to worship as did the ruler of the ancient synagogue:

> LEADER: Bless ye the Lord, the One who is to be blessed.
> PEOPLE: Blessed be the Lord forever.

Or, the leader could try affirmations that were possibly used in the worship of the first-century church:

> LEADER: The Lord is risen.
> PEOPLE: He is risen indeed.

Or:

> LEADER: Holy, Holy, Holy is the Lord God.
> PEOPLE: The whole earth is filled with His glory.

Or:

> LEADER: Lift up your heads, O ye gates.
> PEOPLE: And the King of Glory shall come in.

Using phrases that are biblical does not rule out the use of contemporary language that causes worship to cut across paths that are familiar to the unchurched. Consider the following lines from Marilee Zdenek that may be used for an invocation:

> It's a brand new day, Jesus,
> a shining Sunday that's just been born
> and has only twenty-four hours to live it up,
>
> This day is a special one for me
> for no reason except that I choose to make it
> special and the choice is mine.
>
> Today I want to tune into my feelings and accept
> them, to wake the joy that lies sleeping beneath
> a blanket of everydayness
> and say, "It's time to get up and celebrate—
> this is the Lord's day—and mine!"
>
> I want to worship you, Lord, with all the stops out
> to sing a hymn like I mean it for a change,
> to dance with tambourines and drums and
> shouts of joy, like you told us to in the olden days,
>
> I want to dance like David and pray like Paul
> and find out what hallelujah really means,
>
> Help me to shake loose from my hang-ups
> and feel the freedom to be spontaneous and alive.
>
> Today I want to go to church, unafraid to laugh
> or cry or show the human feelings that I hold inside.
>
> And when the hour has ended, please make the meaning
> of it last.[10]

A good time to attempt creative and contemporary language is on the special days of the year. If the Christian calendar cues worship, it can be theocentric and relevant at the same time. There is no more critical time for the language of earth to become the language of heaven than on special days when the church is likely to host infrequent attenders. Relevance does not mean that we have to be manipulated by a secular calendar. James White states, "Our de facto calendar stresses human agency; that of the early church centered upon what God had done and continues to do through the Holy Spirit."[11] Mother's Day does not have to replace Pentecost Sunday, and such days as Ascension Sunday can be utilized to share the practical message of transcendence over the nagging strains of life. The following serves as a bold poetic call to worship on Easter Sunday that will arrest attention:

> The Reception Committee of Heaven invites you this morning to join the angelic hosts of the universe in celebrating the resurrection of Jesus and His return home. The Holy Spirit will emcee the program. Activities expected will be joyous singing, grateful praise, warm fellowship and above all a heartfelt worship. Acceptable attire will be a radiant smile, a glowing countenance and modesty adorned with humility. Highlighting the ceremonies will be crowning Jesus King of Kings and Lord of Lords. Don't miss the event of the ages. This invitation is personal but all are invited. The Spirit and the Bride say "Come."
>
> **Time:** Now
>
> **Place:** Anywhere
>
> **Admission Charge:** Paid by the blood of Christ
>
> **Sponsor:** The Godhead
>
> **Menu:** The Bread of Life and the Water of Life

Affirmations of belief or ascriptions of praise that are taken from the *Book of Common Prayer* serve as good examples of language that confronts us with the kingdom of God. But if we use only those sources, seekers may get the impression that the kingdom of God does not interface with the kingdom of earth. The most powerful evangelistic petition that the Christian can pray is the words of our Lord: "Thy kingdom come, thy will be done on earth as it is in heaven." The language of worship needs to reflect a cosmology that is not totally foreign to someone who hungers for a religion that will at least mitigate the friction that they experience between themselves and the environment. Good worship leading, as well as good preaching, calls for the celebrant to reflect theologically on the world in which he or she lives. Such reflection calls for theological imagination to impregnate worship forms. Note the following affirmations of faith by John Killinger:

> I believe in the beauty of spring that is known in windy skies, blossoming fruit trees, waving jonquils, and sweet-smelling grass. I believe in the warmth of a friendship that is communicated in gentle eyes, a loving smile, a fond touch of the hand, and an arm laid on the shoulder.
>
> I believe in the power of Christ, whose presence is felt in every season of the year but especially now, when life wells up everywhere and folks feel a quickening in their souls because spring and summer is on the way.
>
> I believe Christ is responsible for both spring and friendship, and that the excitement I feel today is related to the fact that He was dead, but is alive forevermore, not only in our memories but in the truest kind of actuality.
>
> I worship him by coming here, and say Hallelujah! Christ is alive and in this very place![12]

An immersion in poetry and prose with powerful, concrete images would serve to articulate "the poetic construct of another world" in terms that even the theological novice can grasp. Remember that worship in the Old Testament was filled with sights and sounds acting out a drama that would rival today's cinema. Much worship today is so sanitized and abstract that it seems vacuous to the uninitiated. There is always a wealth of concrete images to be found in the Psalms that can cause a worship service to come alive with relevancy. Consider the words of Psalm 66:1-7:

> Shout joyfully to God, all the earth;
> Sing the glory of His name;
> Make His praise glorious.
> Say to God, "How awesome are Your works!
> Because of the greatness of Your power

> Your enemies will give feigned obedience to You.
> All the earth will worship You,
> And will sing praises to You;
> They will sing praises to Your name."
> Come and see the works of God,
> Who is awesome in His deeds
> toward the sons of men.
> He turned the sea into dry land;
> They passed through the river on foot;
> There let us rejoice in Him!
> He rules by His might forever;
> His eyes keep watch on the nations;
> Let not the rebellious exalt themselves.

Such must have been the thoughts of James Whitcomb Riley when he wrote the following words that I used as a call to worship on a crisp Sunday morning in October.

> I don't know how to tell it—but ef sich a thing could be
> As the angels wantin' boardin', and they'd call around on me—
> I want to 'commodate 'em—all the whole-indurin flock—
> When the frost is on the punkin and the fodder's in the shock![13]

Accommodating both humans and angels is the task of evangelistic worship.

THE COMMUNITY GATHERS

As the community of believers comes together, they celebrate their oneness in Christ. As individuals minister to one another within the gathered body, they offer empirical evidence to the surrounding world that there is a power sufficient to free individuals to live beyond themselves. Jesus spoke to His disciples about the importance of this witness when He stated, "By this all men will know that you are My disciples, if you have love for one another" (John 13:35). When Pentecost arrived, there also came economic revolution, as exemplified by the account in Acts 2:45: "And they began selling their property and possessions and were sharing them with all, as anyone might have need." Charles Van Engen is correct when he states, "As never before the Church of Jesus Christ must discover what it means to be a fellowship of love."[14]

Though the liberality of the early church was not limited to ministry among the *ekklesia,* we are led to believe that the primitive Christians made sure that their own were taken care of. One of the most indicative statements concerning the church's commitment to the welfare of all believers is found in Acts 4:34-35: "For there was not a needy person among them, for all who were owners of land or houses would sell them and bring the proceeds of the sales and lay them at the apostles' feet, and they would be distributed to each as any had need." It was this principle that Paul had in mind when he wrote, "So then, while we have opportunity, let us do good to all people, and especially to those who are of the household of the faith" (Gal. 6:10).

One of the grandest opportunities that the church has to do good and thus be a witness is during the corporate celebration. It is then that the Holy Spirit can do some of His most effective evangelistic work. The celebrant who enters the worship service should pray that God will lead him or her to someone who needs a word of encouragement or even physical assistance. People who sit in the same place every Sunday, similar to the season baseball seat that they have purchased, quite possibly are not interested in absorbing someone else's problems, especially someone that they do not know very well. Members should not attend worship for mutual back-scratching; rather, they should be there to allow the love of God to flow freely.

A church can be so harmonious that the wholeness of relationships is immediately sensed by those on the outside looking in. Smugness, tight-lipness, protective facades, defensive veneers, and hypocritical posturing are all evangelistic turnoffs. When the unbeliever observes the mingling of laughter and tears, the laying on of hands, and the bearing of one another's burdens, they conclude, "These people really care about one another." Outsiders can discern when the insiders like one another.

The church presents a dynamic evangelistic witness when it makes public ministry that is happening within the body. One church utilizes a "minute on ministry" to publicize acts of mercy, healing, and the many forms of reaching out to others. Quakers often designate a time of open worship in the service when the celebrants, by acknowledging in some way that they have been ministered to or have been given the opportunity to reach out to someone else, celebrate interlife within the body. At worship services of The Church on the Way, the congregation is divided up into small groups for twelve to fifteen minutes of prayer and sharing. Pastor Jack Hayford states, "The unchurched like this part of the service, realizing the personal nature of the time. The unsaved must feel the concern of the local body for their hurt and their loneliness."[15] Horace T. Allen, Jr., who serves as a professor of worship at Boston University's School of Theology, writes:

> Therein lies much of a Christian community's power to woo a world back from its dry, dusty, dreary deserts of power-plays, competition, vice, and violence. It will not suffice any longer simply to tell the world of its vacuity; we must demonstrate the fullness of life by the character and the style of our common life.[16]

It was in 1970 that Ray Stedman began "the body life service" at the Peninsula Bible Church in Palo Alto, California. His call to worship communicated, "This is the body of Christ. We need each other. You have spiritual gifts that I need, and I have some that you need. Let's share with each other." The invitation provided the catalyst for confession, testimonies of victory, requests for prayer, immediate intercession for a person in need, the distribution of consumer goods, and even the permission to take as much as ten dollars out of the offering plate if an attender was in dire financial need. *Christianity Today* commented on the evangelistic success:

> The numbers increased by leaps and bounds. For over a year now it has been going on with no sign of a let-up. Every service is different. Love, joy and a sense of acceptance prevail so strongly that awed visitors frequently remark about a spiritual atmosphere they can almost scoop up in their hands. Koinonia has come![17]

THE FREEDOM OF WORSHIP

No time or place is appropriate for manipulating people, much less the house of God. The commercialism of worship so angered Jesus that He drove the money changers from the temple with a scourge of cords. The salvation of Christ is a free gift that Isaiah universally offers: "Ho! Every one who thirsts, come to the waters; and you who have no money come, buy and eat. Come buy wine and milk without money and without cost" (Isa. 55:1). Bill Hybels describes his Sunday morning service as "no strings attached." First-time visitors are not asked to give anything, say anything, or sign anything. In fact, if someone is a visitor they are publicly reminded during the offertory that they are perfectly free to not participate in giving. People will not return to a worship service that attempts to immediately mold them into a certain type of person. Our evangelism often attempts to make demands too soon.

The church's legalism has been one of the primary obstructions to evangelism. Even those who in the past lived permissive lifestyles often clothe themselves in rigidity after having received saving grace. Because of mental blocks or lack of security, legalists soon forget the long-suffering and kindness that reached them when they were trapped in sin. Today's hedonists are not interested in trading the trap of sin for the trap of legalism. Legalism has exchanged romance with the Savior for a relationship of prescription. For some, professing a Christian relationship with God is about as personal as following the orders of a pharmacist. We, at times, confuse the process of transforming people in Jesus Christ with conforming them to our likeness. If newcomers suspect the latter, they will be offended by the condescension and paternalism.

A visitor should be impressed that he or she doesn't have to act in a particular way at a worship service. The constant emphasis on the liberty that the Holy Spirit gives will enable the new participant to enter in at points where he or she is comfortable. Remember, we have all been programmed by the customs and rituals that are embedded in our subconscious. Comfort is a process that is achieved by gradual doing and the breaking down of biases. Not everyone would feel comfortable getting on their knees during the prayer time.

Much charismatic worship has excelled in allowing people to express themselves openly without infringing on others, while at the same time maintaining order. This is no small accomplishment. If the Holy Spirit prompts people to exercise gifts in ways that seem understandable to the outsider, without coercing the newcomer to participate, seed will often be planted. We forget that the Holy Spirit is the evangelist who utilizes obedient and willing vessels. Paul illustrates this evangelistic principle when he writes, "But if all prophesy, and an unbeliever or an ungifted man enters, he is convicted by all, he is called to account by all; the secrets of his heart are disclosed; and so he will fall on his face and worship God, declaring that God is certainly among you" (1 Cor. 14:24-25).

THE CHRIST STORY

Evangelistic worship rehearses the Christian drama. It is that drama which overshadows and consumes all other dramas. All of life is interpreted by the death and resurrection of Jesus Christ. Every service celebrates that gift of all gifts, the atoning work of our Lord. All Christian truth converges into the affirmation of Paul: "For I determined to know nothing among you except Jesus Christ, and Him crucified" (1 Cor. 2:2). The cue for worship on this temporal stage is taken from the eternal setting of the twenty-four elders and the thousands of angels around the throne of God who sing, "Worthy is the Lamb that was slain to receive power and riches and wisdom and might and honor and glory and blessing" (Rev. 5:12). The test for fittedness in the New Jerusalem is fittedness for worship within the community of earthly saints.

In one of the best known evangelistic encounters of our Lord's earthly pilgrimages, He gives His concise theology of worship: "God is Spirit, and those who worship Him must worship in spirit and truth" (John 4:24). Whether Christ was referring to "spirit" as inward affection beyond physical acts or as the Holy Spirit, one thing is absolutely clear—true worship consists of passionate adoration of Jesus Christ. Jesus later made it clear that the role of the Holy Spirit is to bear witness to the Son of God: "When the Helper comes, whom I will send to you from the Father, that is the Spirit of truth who proceeds from the Father, He will bear witness of Me, and you will bear witness also, because you have been with Me from the beginning" (John 15:26-27).

Evangelistic worshipers are friends of Jesus bragging about their best friend. The Holy Spirit's ultimate objective in a worship service is to reveal the reality of God in Jesus Christ.

REPENTANCE AND REFORMATION

Evangelistic worship does not gloss over the gap between human sinfulness and God's holiness. The congregation's response echoes the response of Isaiah in the temple, "Woe is me, for I am ruined! Because I am a man of unclean lips, and I live among a people of unclean lips; for my eyes have seen the King, the Lord of hosts" (Isa. 6:5). God's holiness as revealed in Jesus Christ calls for a prostration of spirit, if not total body. No one is left faultless in the light of Christ's glory, pastor included. Thus it is always proper for the minister to pray that God's seraphim will purge every tongue with coals from the altar of Yahweh. At this point, the gathering of God's people becomes unique among all other kinds of gatherings. Unfortunately, the overwhelming presence of God's holiness is not experienced often enough by the gathered community. At this point, the leadership of the church needs to take responsibility for the atmosphere of the worship service. Willimon states, "A minister is a priest who leads us before the Holy. But the minister is also a person among other persons who usually becomes uncomfortable when the Holy breaks in."[17]

Revivals that have had evangelistic harvests have begun with confession of sin. If the celebration leader wears a religious halo that displays in neon colors, "Everything is all right, I never sin," the Holy Spirit will be blocked from probing the inner consciousness of worshipers. The worship leader leads the congregation in praying, "Forgive us our transgressions as we forgive those who transgress against us." But confession is incomplete if it is not resolved in the miracle of transformation. Much congregational confession is perfunctory, offering little hope that Christ can and does give the power to live above sin. The intercession of Christ and the cleansing blood that flows from Calvary has failed if those repenting are not able to successfully crush the temptation of the enemy. More correctly, ministers have failed if they do not enable worshipers to understand the importance of Hebrews 7:25 ("He is able also to save forever those who draw near to God through Him, since He always lives to make intercession for them"). Evangelistic worship constantly offers a Christ who can change the nature of persons from self-seeking to self-surrendering. The only door through which Christ may be invited is repentance. Evangelism by any other route is enlistment, not transformation. C.S. Lewis wrote:

> It is the difference between paint, which is merely laid on the surface, and a dye or stain which soaks, right through. He never talked vague, idealistic gas. When He said, "Be perfect," He meant it. He meant that we must go in for the full treatment. It is hard; but the sort of compromise we are all hankering after is harder—in fact, it is impossible.[18]

EVANGELISM AND THE SACRAMENTS

God has given us corporate signs by which we can understand His love through Christ. For the most part, the church has readily accepted two as specifically ordained by Christ: baptism and the Lord's Supper. There are, however, many other acts of corporate worship, such as the washing of feet, kneeling at an altar, placing money in the offering plate, and the marriage ceremony, which all have sacramental value. Every sacrament—the ordinary channels by which God conveys His grace—should be interpreted in the context of Christ's atoning work. In the bread and wine is the presence of Christ, which can be experienced anew just as fresh food and water is both nourishing and refreshing to the physically hungry. Remember, the first time that Jesus mentioned the sacrament was just after feeding the 5,000, when He said: "Truly, truly, I say to you, unless you eat the flesh of the Son of Man and drink His blood, you have no life in yourselves" (John 6:53).

Evangelistic worship offers life through the sacraments—these are physical signs on the stage of Christ's drama. They are more than decoration. Without them, it is difficult to perceive what Christ did 2,000 years ago and what He continues to do at the Father's right hand. We do not condemn those who claim an immediacy of Spirit and would refer to the ordinances as unnecessary props. But most of us need tangible means to experience God's incarnate love. The Incarnation is not a fact that lost meaning at the ascension of Christ. God meets us in quite tangible and physical ways, simulating the physical interaction that Jesus had with His followers while on earth. As it has been said, "Jesus was God's audiovisual." Individuals, both inside and outside of the church, need audiovisuals—visible images of the invisible God.

We may be thankful for the new use of drama as a worship form. Some churches employ short sketches, while others concentrate on larger productions, especially Passion plays. In a day of graphic images in both art and cinema, Americans do not excel in abstractions. Evangelistic worship should not allow attenders to let their minds run aimlessly, attempting to create meaning with their own props. No, our purpose is to give them alternative objects that allow profane minds to see beyond the toys that have occupied them throughout the week. The transition is as great as transforming a nursery into a sanctuary prepared for a wedding ceremony. Nothing is left to chance.

The visible vessels of grace enhancing worship of our loving Lord are no less important than the tokens of love that are displayed and exchanged at a wedding. (One should take the opportunity to attend a Quaker wedding celebrated in a Sunday morning worship service.) Just as those signs of marriage are a powerful witness to the world of love, trust, and fidelity, so we offer God's signs to searching individuals that Christ is the polestar of all existence. In our breaking, eating, drinking, giving, sharing, touching, anointing, dunking, pouring, and washing, we physically and spiritually carry out Christ's words: "Do this in remembrance of Me." One is hard put to defend the proposition that those words would apply to only two ordinances, or to argue that there is only one prescribed way to celebrate a particular sacrament. Concerning the Lord's Supper, Horace T. Allen, Jr., writes:

> A table may be spread, beautifully with fine wine and a great loaf of bread (not pre-cut). Shining silver may be used, or strong pottery. These aesthetic preoccupations are not an idolatrous "gilding of the city" but the open acknowledgment that human life especially in the presence of "the desert out there" desperately needs the grace of beauty, freedom and glory.[19]

Unfortunately, evangelicals have not paid close enough attention to the initiation rites, nurture, and discipleship practiced by the early church. Baptism in the early centuries was not performed immediately after a profession of faith. It was the culmination of several months, or even years, of discipleship training and catechetical teaching. Preparation not only ordered the experience of the novice, but elaborate community ritual brought the local church into covenant with the new Christian. Pentecost Sunday became the high day for receiving new converts dressed in white robes, hence the designation "Whitsunday." The early church was deeply convinced that elaborate rituals of purification and denunciation representing the signs and seals of the Holy Spirit were crucial for the formation of Christian character. Note the preparation of baptismal candidates as described by Hippolytus in the third century:

> Those who are to be baptized should be instructed to bathe and wash themselves on the Thursday. And if a woman is in her period, let her be put aside, and receive baptism another day. Those who are to receive baptism shall fast on the Friday. On the Saturday those who are to receive baptism shall be gathered in one place at the bishop's decision. They shall all be told to pray and kneel. And he shall lay his hand on them and exorcize all alien spirits, that they may flee out of them and never return into them. And when he has finished exorcizing them, he shall breathe on their faces; and when he has signed their foreheads, ears, and noses, he shall raise them up.[20]

PLANNED FOR QUALITY

The Holy Spirit does not meet people as a greeter at the front door when they show up for worship. The Holy Spirit does not abide in sanctuaries built with hands, no matter how ornate or theologically decorated they may be. The Holy Spirit abides within persons—on Saturday as well as Sunday. And unless the Holy Spirit is preparing the person to worship before they arrive at the designated place of gathering, it will be highly unlikely that the individual will have a genuine worship experience. This is especially true for the upfronters (worship leaders). The Holy Spirit doesn't just happen to show up, with little mental or spiritual preparation on the part of the worshiper.

There are three rules for worship—Prepare! Prepare! Prepare! There is a specific reason why the Hebrews began the Sabbath at 6 P.M. on Friday. There is no other way to be prepared for the next morning. But the upfronters cannot afford to wait until Saturday night to begin to prepare. The chief upfronter plans and prays all week that God will enable him or her to enable the people to connect with the Holy One of Israel. He or she enlists others in this cause in order that the worship service has a quality that is fitting for a King. Ortlund writes:

> Yes, it's fair to put the burden on the up-fronters.
> They've got to care.
> They've got to cry.
> They've got to bang on the gates of heaven.
> They've got to pound the Throne.
> They've got to accept on their backs the
> Burden of the Lord.[21]

It is possible to be so caught up in detail and form that one misses the life of the Spirit. Thankfully, this is not frequently the case. Polarizing preparation and spontaneity is a false antithesis. The preparation of prayer and planning invites God to break in upon the service in whatever manner He chooses. The pastor who walks in the Spirit prepares for worship no less than he prepares for the sermon. He is then better organized, less confused, and less frustrated than the pastor who doesn't walk in the Spirit. The holiness of God and the Spirit of Pentecost are not equated with off-the-cuff, slovenly, impulsive, less-than-our-best efforts in preparing to worship.

Evangelistic worship is concerned with both what God sees and with what sinners think. There is a correlation, since there is "more joy in heaven over one sinner who repents than over ninety-nine righteous persons who need no repentance" (Luke 15:7). Worship needs to so enrapture the church that the sheep on the outside of the fold mumble under their breath, "I'm sure missing out on something there." Every detail, even if the church is meeting in a storefront, needs to be given sight and sound appeal. One pastor has breakfast with his soundman every Sunday morning because he believes that he is a critical part of making the worship service happen. Every person who participates in leadership is integral to the evangelistic appeal—no one should participate without rehearsal. One planter pastor rehearses his worship on Wednesday evening with insiders, not only so that it will bring greater glory to God, but in order that the worship service will have greater appeal to outsiders.

The celebrants of worship should give no less attention to the details of timing, tempo, transition, and lines than does the director of a Broadway stage production on opening night. The *Wall Street Journal* said this about Ed Young's state-of-the-art church in Houston: "Every week, Mr. Young and his staff review and critique game films of Sunday's service for pacing and liveliness. . . . Attention to quality control produces a church in which computers regulate mood lighting during services; a corps of parking attendants empty a 2,500-car lot in 30 minutes flat, and shuttle buses whisk late comers to and from outlying parking decks."[22] While it is true that few churches can offer the aesthetics of Second Baptist's $34,000,000 complex with its marble floors and bubbling fountain, every church can present a carefully orchestrated service. The question is not so much whether the service is orchestrated, but whether the orchestration is directed by the Holy Spirit. Committed celebrants plan and pray that every cord will be plucked for the sanctification of the saints and the salvation of sinners for the glory of God. Neither saint nor sinner is served by the discord of less than our best in the great drama of worship.

CONCLUSION

Evangelistic worship is not a particular kind of worship. The adjective "evangelistic" does not call for a radical accommodationism to modernity, much less a faddishness uprooted from the liturgical soil of the historical catholic faith. But it does seek to make meaningful to moderns the mystery of sacrament and ritual in ways that offer interpretation of the peculiarities of the present day. Both the religiously initiated and uninitiated face life's complexities on a daily basis. The insiders who prepare worship face the delicate balance of offering wellsprings that are satisfying both to the mature believer and the thirsty seeker. Admittedly, some services will be more palatable to one than the other.

One must keep in mind the differences between a worship service and a discipleship group that emphasizes esoteric spiritual exercises. A worship service is far more generic than a spiritual formation session. A worship service is neither totally for the unbeliever nor the believer. In fact, it is for God, who is approachable by either—at whatever stage of grace they have received. Worship, possibly not on any one Sunday, keeps the full gamut of grace in mind. The church seeks to provide understanding of its worship to the uninitiated. It must keep in mind that grace is sovereign. It is God who administers the mysteries of grace through the mysteries of sacrament.

Worship is rational, and yet transrational. It is the confidence that God makes Himself known above and beyond the categories of human analysis. Thus the wonder, enthrallment, and passion of worship will be far more evangelistic than the pragmatism of technique, no matter how comprehensible the latter may be to pagans. Even hedonists can detect the difference between dead formality and passionate sacrifice. The ethos of sacrifice is committed to the proposition that a designated time and place of corporate worship is nonoptional. Optioned-out pagans are searching for such clear-mindedness; being face-to-face with ultimate reality clears everyone's mind—saint and sinner alike. Such is worship in Spirit and truth.

XI

lifestyle evangelism

Every area of expertise spawns "buzz words," inside language, and technical jargon. The areas of practical theology are no exception. Seminary preaching students in the sixties and seventies were to be "transparent" and "confessional" in their preaching. Today, they are taught to tell stories, utilize narrative, and be implicit rather than confrontational. A generation ago, evangelicals taught the importance of prayer and Scripture reading as a critical means of grace for those who would engage in ministry. Today, those practices, along with a focus on the spiritual exercises of the mystics and monastics and a heightened view of the sacraments, are known as "spiritual formation."

Heading into the third millennium, if there is a code phrase for evangelism, it is "lifestyle evangelism." *The Random House Dictionary of the English Language* defines lifestyle as "the habits, attitudes, tastes, moral standards, economic level, etc., that together constitute the mode of things of an individual or group."[1] This definition enables us to clear up common misconceptions concerning lifestyle evangelism. First, lifestyle consists primarily of being and secondarily of doing. The proposed definition lists characteristics (e.g., habits, attitudes, and tastes) that identify individuals or groups. It is admitted that actions are the outflow of character identity. A rich lifestyle results in Mr. Jones driving a BMW, but next year he may be driving a Lexus. Mr. Jones is a person of financial means with rich tastes. The car that he drives is indicative of his rich tastes. Or he may be a person of penury and still drive a new car while his children go hungry. In that case, he would be known at least by some as a profligate or, worse yet, a child abuser.

Lifestyle evangelism is not a technique or methodology. It is the actions, words, and pursuits that flow from a value structure. A lecture concerning the advantages of driving a Ford rather than a Mercedes is not likely to change Mr. Jones' automotive tastes, but a change in value structure may lead Mr. Jones to consider spending his money differently. For the same reason, constantly nagging congregations about techniques and methodology that will benefit the church numerically will normally fall on deaf ears. Yet most lifestyle evangelism essays trail off into technique—how the people on the inside of the church can have house parties, go fishing with their neighbor, or conduct Bible studies in order to be evangelistically effective.

Lifestyle is not technique; it is the aura that we emanate to the world around us that identifies who we are. Lifestyle evangelism rests as much on the surrounding world's perception of Christianity as it does on the actual identity of individuals who call themselves Christians. Christians are not specifically known as people who take their neighbors fishing for chinook on the Columbia River, but perhaps they should generally be known as persons who take time to be actively engaged with their neighbors because they love people.

Secondly, most exposés of lifestyle evangelism begin by criticizing the programs and methodologies of the church for not being evangelistically effective. Thus, intentional evangelism is divorced from lifestyle evangelism, as if the latter is a new direction in which the church needs to go. A case in point would be a diatribe against follow-up house visitation that utilizes a systematic presentation of the plan of salvation. We have already noted the limitations of such a program. But the main limitation is that spending time and energy calling on people is not part of the value structure of the average Christian because their affections do not produce that particular activity. Lifestyle is to programs as blood is to the human life system.

Effective evangelistic systems are energized, motivated, defined, and encompassed by a lifestyle that evidences God's ultimate concern for humanity. Evangelistic programming divorced from appropriate lifestyle is hypocritical. Imagine the would-be evangelist presenting the gospel over the phone to his neighbor in broken segments because the only time he can allot is between innings of the baseball game or during the commercial breaks of the basketball game he is watching on TV. Eternal matters are hardly congruent with such a presentation.

The direction of the church need not do away with intentional evangelism, but it should define programs that are contextualized by lifestyles that are in keeping with the values of the gospel. The church needs to do an identity check before it can find its role as a reforming and evangelistic influence in the world. David Watson writes:

> Those who are called to such a task make it a priority to have a spiritually disciplined walk with Christ. This being so, they seek to know God for God's own sake. They delight in those spiritual practices which take them into the presence of God. They know the power of prayer. They drink from the wellspring of the scriptures. They feed on the liturgies and sacraments of the church. They build one another up through Christian conference, intentionally questing for the will of God in the company of like-minded Christian colleagues. And most important of all, they take the time to contemplate and meditate on God's truth. As Robin Maas has put it, they keep their appointments with God and thus learn more of the mind of God.[2]

Lifestyle evangelism is as old as Abel offering an acceptable sacrifice to God. The act was met by the defiance of his brother and the murderous rejection of revealed religion. Lifestyle evangelism is certainly as old as Noah, who gathered his family into the ark. Though they may have questioned his sanity, the immediate family members found it difficult to argue with his commitment and loving concern. The saints through the ages would be somewhat confounded, if not completely dumbstruck, by the addressing of lifestyle evangelism as a separate entity or a particular cog in the evangelistic wheel. For Peter and Paul, lifestyle evangelism came with the territory or, more accurately, invaded the territory. Evangelism was lifestyle and lifestyle was evangelism.

The thesis of this chapter is that lifestyle evangelism finds its focus in the character and ministry of Jesus. It means adopting Christ's frame of reference and exhibiting principles of righteousness that are the building blocks of everyday spontaneous action. But this frame of reference also includes the carefully thought out plans of a newly planted church whose very survival is predicated on evangelistic effectiveness. Jesus incarnationally fulfilled the answer to Micah's question: "And what does the Lord require of you but to do justice, to love kindness, and to walk humbly with your God?" (Micah 6:8) Evangelism that disregards effective kingdom principles because the church has not individually or corporately incarnated the reign of Christ will be heard by the world as only a sounding brass and a tinkling cymbal.

The rest of this chapter will outline five components that define the lifestyle of the Christian. While this list is not exhaustive, the following elements are essential for an evangelistic witness to the world.

CLARITY OF COMMITMENT

Jesus Christ came to do the will of His Heavenly Father and thus glorify the Father. This inner quality was an obedient mind-set that flowed from love and was evidenced in commitment. Jesus first evidenced this as a twelve-year-old when He was inadvertently left behind by His parents as they returned to Nazareth from the Feast of the Passover. After a frustrating search, they found their son in dialogue with some rabbis at the temple. Jesus' parents were dumbfounded by His response: "Why is it that you were looking for Me? Did you not know that I had to be in My Father's house?" (Luke 2:49).

The relational ethic of representing the Father on earth became the categorical imperative of the three years of Jesus' ministry. While the inner law of love for the Father was misunderstood by His family, the disciples, and certainly the Jewish community, they could not deny that Jesus was committed to a course that went against the grain of conventional wisdom. Even His closest friends were at times mystified. Consider Peter's attempt to talk Jesus out of going to Jerusalem and falling into the hands of the Jewish and Roman authorities. To this quite feasible argument Jesus adamantly, if not vehemently, responded, "Get behind Me, Satan! You are a stumbling-block to Me; for you are not setting your mind on God's interests, but man's" (Matt. 16:23).

Though the world could not understand the controlling factor of Jesus' interests (i.e., the Father's business), no one could question His commitment. One does not have to argue for the validity of the commitment to be impressed by the commitment. Commitment in and of itself is attractive to people who are searching for meaning. Admittedly, some commitments/causes are more attractive than others. The same singular commitment was found in Paul before and after his Damascus road conversion. But the cause radically changed, a cause to which he constantly referred. For this cause or reason (i.e., the great love of Christ), Paul endured hardship to take the gospel to the Gentiles (Eph. 3:1). The cause was contagious. A message was nonverbally communicated: "There is a direction that will provide meaning and coherency to your world."

The above message is delivered in the face of a world that has adopted the lottery as one of its primary metaphors. This metaphor graphically represents fate by rotating a hopper of numbered Ping-Pong balls which at the conclusion of the rotation will be aligned in a series of numbers. There will always be individuals who tire of trusting or hoping in chance formation and who will, in turn, search for intelligent alignment. The Christian mind refrains from the lottery not because there is some type of prescriptive ethic forbidding it, but because the lottery is diametrically opposed to a commitment aligned with the Mastermind that orders the universe.

One of the primary reasons for evangelistic ineffectiveness is lack of commitment. Too many of us fall in the category of the seed sown among thorns. "This is the man who hears the word, and the worry of the world and the deceitfulness of wealth choke the word, and it becomes unfruitful" (Matt. 13:22). It is a continual fight to keep the ultimate from becoming the penultimate.

The problem of evangelism is not so much that the church is competing with the world's commitments. Rather, it is that the church is competing with its own distractions. God has a lot of competition within the church. Singularity of purpose will not be recovered by moralizing or scolding, but by constantly lifting up images and metaphors that represent the exalted reign of Christ. This is contrasted to the trivial pursuits that warp our direction and defuse our energy. The pursuit after apparent goods will have to be exchanged for the supreme good. The church itself will have to experience a supernatural conversion that saves the organism from constantly calculating how apparent goods can bring gratification to finite selves. William Temple writes:

> For obligation is not a calculation of the interests of the organism and of the way to serve these; it is an appreciation of value, so distinct as to demand the sacrifice of all other interests for its sake. The mind which has achieved that is detached from the whole might of nature.[3]

TRANSCENDENCE

Norris Rochester is an electrical engineer employed by Endless Conduit International. ECI has just designed a new product that is going to earn them millions. Norris is not only one of the chief design engineers, but during the past several months he has traveled the planet accepting huge orders for this marketing gem. Sales went gangbusters for a year until an electrical supply house in southern India complained that the electrical device, which is ECI's bread and butter, will not carry the necessary voltage in a newly constructed hydroelectric plant; the device will have to be removed. If the Indian engineers are correct, this one project alone will cost ECI $750,000 and will probably encourage other ECI customers to make the same claim. Not only is ECI's reputation at stake, but so are millions of dollars in revenue. Norris was asked by the company to do a careful quality control check by running a series of tests on this device. To his and inside management's chagrin, the tests validated the claim of the company in southern India. Management asked Norris to "polish up" his report, which he refused to do. He was removed from the project, demoted, and at the present time fears for his job.

The small milltown is located in central Oregon, where things have been going from bad to worse during the last couple of years. For the past twenty years, a plywood plant, paper mill, and lumber mill have employed over half of the working adults. Two years ago the plywood plant closed; this past week, the lumber mill announced that it would close production at the first of the year. Denise Thornton has taken her three small children to Anybody's Church for the last several months. In fact, during the fall revival she went forward at the evangelist's altar call and professed Christ as her personal Savior. Her husband, Dan, who is employed at the lumber mill and hasn't attended church in years, came with his wife for the first time on the first Sunday in December. As he sat at the back of the sanctuary, which was almost full with seventy-five people, he heard the pastor give an invitation for "testimonies." One of the first people to stand up was Nick, whom Dan casually knew because they work at the same mill. Nick has a quiet manner, but in very clear tones he briefly shared how he knew God was going to take care of him and his family. His words penetrated Dan's anxiety about his future and left him with a troubling awareness brought on by the contrast between his fears and Nick's apparent security. He left wondering if he should make an appointment with the pastor.

Evil comes in many forms: ecological imbalance, economic imbalance, ethical imbalance, and, ultimately, the imbalance of the human heart. From Sir Thomas Moore dropping the bribe overboard in *A Man for All Seasons* to the family who stands on Sunday morning and glowingly praises God for how the Holy Spirit has brought comfort at the death of a loved one, men and women have triumphed over life's inequities. We do not claim that only Christians demonstrate a resilience of the human spirit that overcomes the most severe of circumstances. But it is only the Christian community that demonstrates the resurrection power of Jesus Christ that transcends the evil that has descended from the fall of Adam.

It is not that Christians have a simplistic answer to the problems of pain. It is certainly not that the Christian community has adopted a false dualism that claims that the seemingly pleasurable is from God, while discomfort is from Satan. What may rob us of our immediate fulfillment may be the real goods of life. A faith that is a bulwark stemming the tide of misfortune is one of the most meaningful testimonies that Christianity produces. It stands as an evangelistic beacon throughout the centuries, provided by those who, in spite of the loss of creature comforts, demonstrate a triumph of spirit.

The testimony of transcendence is especially forceful when those in need are able to forget themselves and place the needs of others before their own. Transcendence is not merely a coping technique; sheer coping is primarily a concern for the self. Transcendence is other than compensation for failure, because failure is the frustration of one's own ends not being accomplished. Rather, it is a value that realizes that those who are most "successful" are at times the most miserable. For example, a man whose every step had been marked by "success," and who had just made 10 million dollars by placing his newly founded company on the New York Stock Exchange, drove his BMW to the top of a mountain and put a bullet in his brain. Such action is confounding to those who are driven by the world's philosophy. But those who transcend with or without earthly goods have explored the theological truth of Paul's affirmation in 2 Corinthians: "For you know the grace of our Lord Jesus Christ, that though He was rich, yet for your sake He became poor, so that you through His poverty might become rich" (8:9).

At Oxford University on Martyr's Square, there stands a statue of three of the main players in the English Reformation: Thomas Cranmer, Nicholas Ridley, and Hugh Latimer. Approximately one hundred yards from that spot, they were burned at the stake for standing by their convictions and transcending the fleeting political and religious disputes of the moment. Cranmer served as Archbishop of Canterbury, the ecclesiastical head of the Anglican Church under Henry VIII—who had appointed himself as Supreme Head of the Church in 1532. Nicholas Ridley, a very capable preacher and theologian, served as Bishop of London during the early years of the English Reformation. Hugh Latimer was eventually appointed Bishop of Worchester, but was best known as the preacher to the court of Henry VIII. As a theologian and proclaimer of the gospel, Latimer was unsurpassed in all of the English Reformation. The first time he appeared to preach before the king at the majestic St. George's Chapel, Latimer paused after reading the Scripture and stood silent, turning his head as if listening for a message. While remaining in such a posture, he loudly exclaimed: "Latimer! Latimer! Latimer! Be careful what you say! Henry, the King, is here!" Upon further reflection, he even more loudly exclaimed: "Latimer! Latimer! Latimer! Be careful what you say! The King of Kings is here!"[4]

Latimer mightily championed the cause of the Reformation. After the reign of Edward IV and a subsequent short, ten-day reign of Lady Jane Grey, Latimer, along with the other leaders in the Protestant religious cause, was imprisoned by the new queen—"Bloody" Mary, who inadvertently furthered the cause of the Protestant Reformation more than any other person. After remaining imprisoned at Oxford for eighteen months and refusing to recant their evangelical faith throughout long theological disputations, Ridley and Latimer were burned back to back at the stake on October 16, 1555.

On the night before his martyr's execution, a full-length white shroud was delivered to Latimer. In an emotion-packed scene, he was heard to say before being led to his violent execution: "It is my wedding garment. I must begin my journey shortly. I would be clad in white for the happy event." After Ridley and Latimer were chained to the stake, wood laid, reeds stacked, and the fire kindled, Latimer was heard to speak those immortal words of testimony: "Be of good comfort, Master Ridley, and play the man. We shall this day light such a candle by God's grace in England as I trust shall never be put out."[5]

Thus, Christianity has been lighting candles down through the centuries and the darker the day, the brighter the light. From the spread of Christianity throughout the world of the apostles to the revival that has produced millions of converts in communist mainland China in the late twentieth century, oppression has almost invariably meant increased possession of faith, both qualitatively and quantitatively. Thus, Christianity in America has been presented with its most ironic problem—how to grow and abound in the age of plenty and prosperity. We have somehow never learned the transcendence expressed by Paul: "I know how to get along with humble means, and I also know how to live in prosperity; in any and every circumstance I have learned the secret of being filled and going hungry, both of having abundance and suffering need" (Phil. 4:12).

SYMPHONIC EXISTENCE

A zeal for life is created by the harmonic relationship between the creature and the surrounding creation. Such harmony serves to dispel cantankerousness, censoriousness, and plain meanness of spirit. Passionate people evidence magnanimous spirits that encompass the moment with all of its people problems and opportunities. It is the optimistic bias toward life that is so essential to effectiveness in life's pursuits, whether they be secular or profane. To embrace every moment as good is more than simply getting through the moment—it is to say with God after every created day "it was good." To affirm this is to be of the same mind as the Father of Lights, in whom there is no feebleness and from whom comes every good gift.

God's created order is a friendly place for the trusting person. "To the pure, all things are pure" (Titus 1:15). There is an affinity with the task of the day because the task has been given from God to better His created order, which has been tarnished by sin. "Whatever your hand finds to do, do it with all your might" (Ecc. 9:10). Such relish for the mundane is an anomaly to the world, but an anomaly which at least in some quarters does not go unnoticed. While a famed athlete fumes and stews that he is receiving insufficient playing time or salary, and sums up his situation by saying, "All of the joy has gone out of the game," an orderly walks his rounds of changing bed pans with a smile on his face and an encouraging word to each of the patients. When a CEO of a large corporation arrives home in his Mercedes and enters his multimillion dollar home, he is sullen and caustic toward his wife and children. On the other hand, a concrete worker, who has been on his knees all day with a trowel, greets his family with love and concern.

Admittedly, the above contrasts may be overly simplified and even stereotyped. All athletes are not unhappy, and all wealthy people are not stingy and petty. But for those who do know their God, there is an intensity of purpose and ardor of spirit that is not lost on those with whom they have daily contact. It is not that the Christian is always gleeful, hilarious, or confident that events are going to be so ordered that the day's benediction will be "a good time was had by all." Rather, the Christian is well aware of the words of the preacher: "There is an appointed time for everything. And there is a time for every event under heaven. . . . A time to weep and a time to laugh; a time to mourn and a time to dance" (Ecc. 3:1, 4).

The ups and downs are the major and minor keys of life's oratorio. The oratorio tells the story of an existence lived before God in wonder and praise. It is the life of a schoolteacher in an obscure village who relishes her students as entrusted gifts. It is the cripple at the squeaky organ in the inner-city church who feels that it is her job to encourage as many people as she can. It is the cook at the small café by a steel mill who somehow always rises above the heat and greets customers with a cheerful disposition. Somehow, all is right when all isn't right. Sand and grit in the craw of life is replaced with a cosmic emotion that elicits wonder and security. The code phrase for such joyous declaration is "I belong," which is sufficient cause for "singing and making melody with your heart to the Lord" (Eph. 5:19).

The refrain of this evangelistic symphony is "Life is more; it is more than mundane existence; it is more than planning for the future; it is more than catering to myself." This is not the evangelism of indictment but invitation, not of addition but of belonging, not of preachment but demonstration. It is the kind of evangelism that Malcolm Muggeridge graphically describes in his book *Jesus Rediscovered,* as he gives his own personal testimony of discovering Christ.

> And You? I never caught even a glimpse of You in any paradise—unless You were an old, colored shoe-shine man on a windy corner in Chicago one February morning, smiling from ear to ear; or a little man with a lame leg in the Immigration Department in New York, whose smiling patience as he listened to one Puerto Rican after another seemed to reach from there to eternity. Oh, and whoever painted the front of the little church in the woods at Kliasma near Moscow—painted it in blues as bright as the sky and whites that outshone the snow? That might have been You. Or again at Kiev, at an Easter service when the collectivization famine was in full swing, and Bernard Shaw and newspaper correspondents were telling the world of the bursting granaries and apple-cheeked dairymaids in the Ukraine. What a congregation that was, packed in tight, squeezed together like sardines! I myself was pressed against a stone pillar, and scarce-

> ly able to breathe. Not that I wanted to, particularly. So many gray, hungry faces, all luminous like an El Greco painting; and all singing. How they sang—about how there was no help except in You, nowhere to turn except to You; nothing, nothing, that could possibly bring any comfort except You. I could have touched You then, You were so near—not up at the altar, of course, where the bearded priests, crowned and bowing and chanting, swung their censures—one of the gray faces, the grayest and most luminous of all."[6]

SIMPLICITY

The pastor has made an appeal from the pulpit. The appeal may be for people to join an evangelistic team on Thursday evening, or to start a home Bible study in their neighborhood. Classes and training were offered to enable them to get started and provide the ongoing equipping and encouragement. Proportionate to the large congregation of evangelical and Bible-believing Christians, very few people responded. In regard to the dozen individuals who did begin participation in the Thursday evening evangelism sessions, the attrition rate was high and attendance sporadic. The pastor began to doubt his leadership abilities and teaching skills. Perhaps these people didn't have the "gift" of evangelism anyway. Perhaps the church should depend on lifestyle evangelism and not try to force round people into square holes. Remember the ecclesiastical adage: "If it doesn't fly, prepare for a soft landing."

The problem with the alternate plan, lifestyle evangelism, is that it is the foremost reason why the church is not successful at evangelism. "Christians" do not possess the values, agendas, and orientation so essential to doing intentional or unintentional evangelism. Our privatized, individualistic, materialistic, hectic schedules effectively isolate us from many activities that call for a radically different orientation toward people and their eternal destiny. The fact is, people who are failing at relationships because of their quest for things, who are alienated from their neighbors because of their twelve-hour workdays, who are stressed out because of being dictated to by the world's definition of blessedness, should not talk about doing evangelism, much less attempt it. Jack Bernard, in a perceptive article that calls for the Christian to enter a new culture, states, "Before we ever start asking questions about how to communicate the gospel, we need to deal with a much more important question, 'What kind of people ought we to be in order to be bearers of the words of life?' "[7]

Before one can penetrate the culture with an alternate worldview, one must be able not only to identify the culture, but make sure there is a differentiation between the penetrator and the penetrated. Thomas Oden defines the axial assumptions of modernity, the age and milieu in which Americans live, as "contempt for pre-modern wisdom, absolutized moral relativism, the adolescent refusal of parenting, idealization of autonomous individualism, and scientific empiricism as the final court of appeal in truth questions."[8] The practical results of these philosophical underpinnings have been narcissistic hedonism, minimal commitment to covenant responsibility, rampant consumerism, and a privatization of values that implicitly states, "You mind your own business, and I'll mind mine." There is a perception that we are free from external standards imposed by others, when we are really enslaved to the prevailing culture's criteria of what it means to be a person of significance in today's fast-paced society.

We have some vague notion that we are trapped on a treadmill that seems to be turning faster and faster. Commercialism tells us that we can control its rotation by purchasing computers, cellular phones, dictation devices, answering machines, calendar portfolios, elaborate filing systems, and endless credit and identification cards that will perform infinitely elaborate and detailed services. These only serve to grease the axle of the treadmill. We are going nowhere fast, because we have not adequately defined where we need to go. Hence, it is difficult to entice people to go with us.

Vernard Eller defines the simple life as the "believer's inner relationship to God finding expression in his outward relationship to 'things.' "[9] The simple life is not a matter of volition, rules, prescriptions, egalitarianism, or even voluntary poverty. It is a total reorientation of the self-life to the center of all existence. We cannot map out a course of evangelism unless the polestar of our own lives has been examined and reconsidered. If pagans visit our churches, they are looking for people with a different polestar and the freedom of navigation that reference to that polestar brings. Unfortunately, seekers discover that the people housed in the edifice called a church are trapped in the very same anxieties and trivial pursuits that they are. The church has traded its eternal center for more temporal affairs, which is a frontal assault on the uniqueness of new creatures who are bound for the eschaton. Such blurred identity and amorphous description were not always true of those who call themselves Christians.

Richard Foster designates simplicity as the most outward expression of the Christian disciplines. Indeed, it probably more quintessentially represents what is popularly understood as lifestyle evangelism than any other one criterion. It is the sine qua non that enables the pagan world to hear a clear trumpet call by the would-be evangelist. But the hedge of possessions obtained by restlessness and greed mutes the call or, at least, throws it off-pitch. Consider a recent poultry plant fire and the twenty-two employees who were consumed in that fire. Subsequent investigation revealed low wages, neglected safety precautions, slavish hours, and management that neglected the welfare of their workers in order to line their pocketbooks. No doubt, some individuals in the ownership and management team were professing Christians. All of us need to hear the words of Amos:

> Therefore, because you impose heavy rent on the poor and exact a tribute of grain from them, though you have built houses of well-hewn stone, yet you will not live in them; you have planted pleasant vineyards, yet you will not drink their wine (Amos 5:11).

Is there any escape from this unquenchable thirst to consume, quite often at the expense and exploitation of others? Richard Foster suggests that we think of the misery that comes into our lives from the enormous greed that entraps us, that we practice a silence and solitude before God that dims the world's noise, and that we refuse to live beyond our means. People need to be motivated by a joy that doesn't take themselves too seriously and radically enables them to reschedule their priorities so that they have time to spend with their neighbors. Probably those who are the most effective evangelistically are families that have so radically restructured their existence that they have turned their large house, located next to a university, into a haven for students, or who have bought and renovated a structure that will serve as a hospice for

AIDS patients, or transformed their gentleman's farm into a halfway house for unwed mothers. The list is endless as to how resources can be transformed into evangelistic tools.

Simplicity means that we make changes that enlarge our circumference of resources, rather than diminish them. Widening one's circle of alternatives for being evangelistically effective may not necessarily mean moving to the inner city to start a mission for the homeless or a medical clinic for the destitute. But it will certainly mean heeding Foster's accurate advice that one should

> stress the quality of the life above the quantity of life. Refuse to be seduced into defining life in terms of having rather than being. Cultivate solitude and silence. Learn to listen to God's speech in his wondrous, terrible, gentle, loving, all embracing silence. Develop close friendships and enjoy long evenings of serious and hilarious conversation. Such times are far more rewarding than the plastic entertainment that the commercial world tries to foist upon us.[10]

To be released from possessions to persons, from stress to simplicity, from consternation to contentment, is not a matter of resolution. Rather, it is what theologians have referred to as the expulsive power of a higher affection. It is holy obedience rooted in the eternal love of Jesus Christ. The expulsive power of holy love roots out the minor for the major, the temporal for the eternal, and the relative for the absolute. Holy love is able to visualize the greater cause; thus, "No soldier in active service entangles himself in the affairs of everyday life, so that he may please the one who enlisted him as a soldier" (2 Tim. 2:4).

That's it! We are too entangled in the affairs of this life to do the work of evangelism. There is a conflict of priorities, and only one thing will solve the conflict—pleasing Him! Archbishop William Temple stated, "The spiritually minded man does not differ from the materially minded man chiefly in thinking about different things, but in thinking about the same things differently."[11] If we are going to begin to think differently about the souls of people, we will have to first think about things differently. That must have been what Jesus meant when He prayed for His disciples, "They are not of the world, even as I am not of the world. Sanctify them in the truth; Your word is truth. As You sent Me into the world, I also have sent them into the world" (John 17:16-18).

If anyone knows about how to relate to both things and people under the canopy of pleasing God, it is Mother Teresa. She and the Sisters of Charity have ministered to 54,000 dying people from the streets of a metropolis whose squalid conditions are possibly the most despicable in the world. Claiming to be only a "pencil in the hand of God," she believes the poor are God's greatest gift to her because as she ministers to their needs, she is able to be with Jesus twenty-four hours a day. We try to pray through our work by doing it with Jesus, for Jesus, to Jesus—that helps us put our whole heart and soul into it. The dying, the crippled, the mentally ill, the unwanted, the unloved—they are Jesus in disguise.[12]

Is it any wonder that the world is so attracted to her? They have never encountered anyone so radically free to be an evangel of mercy, healing, and hope. Her serene confidence and single-minded direction is founded squarely on her philosophy of simplicity, which she reveals in the following statement:

> Take our congregation: we have very little, so we have nothing to be preoccupied with. The more you have, the more you are occupied, the less you give. But the less you have, the more free you are. Poverty for us is a freedom. It is not a mortification, a penance. It is joyful freedom. There is no television here, no this, no that. . . . I find the rich much poorer. Sometimes they are more lonely inside. They are never satisfied. They always need something more.[13]

INCLUSIVENESS

Imagine the idyllic community, a small farm town in Iowa, a fishing village on the coast of North Carolina, or a borough of houses nestled in a valley filled with apple orchards along the Snake River in eastern Washington. It may take imagination to produce that town because it is far less likely to exist today than it was fifty years ago. In the center of this town from yesteryear was a store that sold nearly anything anyone would need. In the evening the men of the community, who had put in a hard day of mostly physical labor, would gather around the store's pot-bellied stove and swap stories. It was both a closed and close society that offered identity, security, and a sense of belonging. Everyone was known by their first name, and except for the most intimate details, everyone knew each other's business. And why not? Almost everyone in the town was in the same business.

For these people, the city was a place where those who enjoyed the best in life only visited. Life consisted of country as opposed to urban, self-employment rather than working for someone else, quiet contrasted with noise, serenity contrasted with stress, and pastoral images that were the antithesis of the colossals of the metropolis. Unfortunately, those times have become a blurred memory for all of us. The Iowa farmer has gone high-tech; the apple orchard farmer had to sell his acreage and now commutes to a plant that manufactures parts for Boeing; the fisherman commutes to a larger community that has larger ports and boats, and is gone all week from his family. But not only has the vocational mode changed, the *sitz in leben* has been invaded by a world that does not share the values of the preceding generation. Disequilibrium is intensified by the fact that these parents will exert far less vocational influence on their children than their parents had on them.

The real question is "Will today's fathers be able to sufficiently dispel the images of a world gone berserk in order for their children to possess the underpinnings that support life's most basic structures?" The news is filled with gang slayings, mass murders, child molestations, riots, and rapes. In other words, society with all of its intensity, rage, and alienation is much less able to offer the character building blocks it once did. Our children have been betrayed. It is now a parental duty to teach children mistrust and suspicion, because we never know when one is going to be strangled, or taken advantage of in more subtle ways. One teenager just killed another one because the victim would not hand over his stylish coat. The result of this malaise of estrangement is an increasing fear of people one does not know. The only solution for most people is to maintain distance from others. Contrast our contemporary situation with the Deuteronomic law:

> For the Lord your God is the God of gods and the Lord of lords, the great, the mighty, and the awesome God who does not show partiality nor take a bribe. He executes justice for the

> orphan and the widow, and shows His love for the alien by giving him food and clothing. So show your love for the alien, for you were aliens in the land of Egypt (Deut. 10:17-19).

This command is not lost on the writer to the Hebrews: "Do not neglect to show hospitality to strangers, for by this some have entertained angels without knowing it" (Heb. 13:2). The rationale is twofold. First, all people are God's creation and His most prized possession. Second, the full realization of personhood treasures other personhoods. William Temple's expression of this truth is unsurpassed:

> Your being is personal, live as a person in fellow membership with all others, who being personal, are your fellow members in the community of persons. Strive to grow in fullness of personality, in width and depth of fellowship; and seek to draw the energy for this from that to which you and all things owe their origin, the Personal Love which is Creator and Sustainer of the world.[14]

All of us who are now part of the kingdom were at one time disenfranchised. By the grace of God we were "cut a deal," made fellow heirs with Jesus Christ even though we had no resources with which to buy into the kingdom. God has given us the task of offering the same deal to others. To invite others in doesn't mean less of the kingdom for us, it means an even greater share. This concept (God's love flowing through us) should lead us to embrace as many people as possible. Our inclusive spirit serves as the door through which they may enter. But alas, we are not standing at the door waving people in, much less running to greet them as the father of the prodigal son in Christ's parable. We have instead usurped Jesus' task of separating the sheep and the goats even before the Great Shepherd returns.

We who are filling the pews consider ourselves to be safely in the fold, while lost lambs are left to fend for themselves. And if these lost lambs do return, they will probably be so bruised, dirty, and bleeding from the world that we described that they wouldn't fit in any way, especially when greeted by those of us who are flabbergasted that they finally showed up at all! If the celebration of the church is in any way mooted, it should be because there are family members absent from the banquet table. David Watson is correct in his indictment that many Christians act as if the gangplank to the ship of Zion has already been taken up and the elect are on a pleasure cruise to Paradise. The parochial and exclusive demeanor that many church members adopt is an affront to the inclusive nature of God's righteousness. Many churchly activities are amphetamines being gulped down by the insiders with no regard for those prodigals piled up at the door. Watson writes:

> For if persons are to be tried in an eternal court for neglecting to respond to the gospel as it is regularly proclaimed and demonstrated by the average North American congregation, any competent defense lawyer would immediately, and successfully appeal. Which is, of course, precisely what Christ does for us in eternity.[15]

If the church is going to be evangelistically effective, there must be a wide-open stance that affirms and embraces outsiders. If the isolated and alienated are the strangers in our land, Christians must go out of their way to break down the walls of estrangement. Friendliness, openness, ready conversation, initiating fellowship, and entering into another's world are all vital evangelistic activities. Intrusiveness is always a liability, but a visit into most evangelical churches will demonstrate that the insiders are not prone to unwarranted invasions of privacy. It is quite possible to stand in the foyer of many churches for several minutes, while being passed by dozens of Christians, and never be identified as a unique person who is visiting a foreign territory for the first time. This can be baffling to the person who is searching for belonging and acceptance in a world that depersonalizes him or her most of the time. True Christianity affirms identity, allows people to discover their identity, and provides security of identity in Jesus Christ. Such security allows personhood to promote the commonwealth of values without the threat that individual identity will be compromised. The "called-out" ones suddenly take an intense interest in the welfare of the whole.

The posture of lifestyle evangelism must be the desire to extend the kingdom through warmth and love to all people without classifying them. We must go out of our way to nonjudgmentally learn their story. The Christian must hunger to explore the thread of commonality that binds the I to the Thou. The evangelist prays for divine wisdom that will serve as the guiding light for engaging others in sincere dialogue. We must offer ourselves in relationship before we test to see whether another's paradigm of rationality is going to match ours. Christians get caught in the trap of believing that they have been elected to protect their own theological paradigm, rather than enabling others to explore the theology of God's universal grace. This defensive posture puts the Christian ill at ease around nonbelievers, rather than providing expression that immediately communicates, "You are a long lost friend of the kingdom. Did we grow up in the same neighborhood?"

Oscar Thompson argues that one of our problems of inclusion is that we attempt to include those who are distant before we concern ourselves with those in proximate circles. If one tries to evangelistically leap "concentric circles" where there are broken relationships, the result will be barrenness. Reconciliation must take place between the would-be evangelizer and those who are immediate, such as family, relatives, and close friends. It then proceeds to those who are more remote (e.g., business acquaintances and those who we have not even met). Evangelism is predicated upon loving relationships that begin closest to us. This practice cannot be extended to strangers unless it is the habitation of an intentional, Spirit-filled, daily attitude that is continually practiced. The evangelist has to make a decision that wherever there is discord, he or she will be an instrument of peace. Peace is what kingdom advancement is really about.

The first step is to pray that God will lead us naturally into the lives of others. Joseph Aldrich encourages us to visualize the Spirit of God hovering over others.[16] This begins by praying individually for our neighbors and praying for those people whom we will meet for the first time today. This prayer includes not only intercession, but the petition that God will open the lives of the estranged and the willingness on the part of the believer to enter at the right moment. For those of us who are awkward in making new acquaintances, we may find some help in reading Becky Pippert's *Out of the Saltshaker and into the World* or watching the film series of the same name. The belief that life becomes meaningful by face-to-face encounters can lead to countless explorations into the rich mosaic of human consciousness. It is the belief that not only do I have something to offer, but that every individual is a treasure in God's cosmic revelation. The encounter is both spontaneous and disciplined. Pippert writes:

> We have choices in how we communicate. We should want to make any conversation count in representing Jesus Christ. But that brings us back to Jesus' own example. Jesus directed his conversations, for instance, with the woman at the well. He did not manipulate her, yet he did not allow red herrings to get him off the track. He was not molded by her presuppositions. Her alternatives did not keep Jesus from his.[17]

Pippert suggests three conversational models that serve as evangelistic forays. "Model A" consists of investigating, stimulating, and relating. Investigating simply means initiating dialogue with a casual comment or question such as "How are you?" or "Are you as tired as I am?" Stimulation occurs when there is audible theological reflection to what the person has said. "Yes, it seems I'm tired all the time" may be responded to with a second question: "I wonder if God ever gets tired?" or "Wouldn't it be nice to have wings, so we wouldn't have to ride these airplanes?" The third step, relating, consists of conversation in the following manner: "Come to think of it, God did at one time get tired—when Jesus came to earth. His nature is to understand our tiredness. That's one of the reasons we celebrate Christmas."

Pippert is indebted to Donald C. Smith, a former staff member of InterVarsity, for "Model B": concentric circles. Again, the conversation begins with a general interest question, such as "Are you in college?" It then proceeds to a specific interest inquiry: "Where do you go to school?" or "What is your major?" Next comes the philosophical or abstract response: "I'm curious, why would you want to major in mathematics? It seems difficult to me. How would you apply that to life?" At this point, there is a good probability that there will be opportunity for theological rumination. "Is there any end to mathematical exploration? Where would it eventually lead someone? To God? It seems to me that mathematics supports an order to the universe. Where do you think that order comes from—God?"

Pippert's third model, "Model C," consists of relationships, beliefs, and epistemology. Relationships begin with the kinds of general inquiry questions of the first two models, such as "Where are you from?" or "Do you still have family back there?" The answer may well open up the opportunity for sorting through beliefs: "Isn't Kansas where they are having all of the conflict over abortion?" or "Isn't Oregon where they are fighting about the spotted owl?" If a specific question doesn't come to mind, the evangelist may want to ask a more general question: "Have you ever wondered what your life would have been like if you had been born outside of the U.S.?" Or, "I have often been amazed that I wasn't born somewhere else. Have you?" All of the statements should lead to a conversation about ethics or providence. The epistemological question simply asks, "Why do you believe that?" It explores the source and certitude of that belief. Any of these conversations may lead to a fruitful discussion about God and even a sharing of the plan of salvation. The foregoing discussion is the closest that we have come to talking about technique or methodology in this chapter.

DIETRICH BONHOEFFER

If and how to be a Christian were the questions with which Dietrich Bonhoeffer intensely and painfully grappled during Hitler's rise to power and the subsequent world conflict. He as much as any other person represented the five characteristics that have been delineated in this chapter. As a lecturer in systematic theology at the University of Berlin, pastor to a German congregation in London, and the head of a new seminary for the Confessing Church at Finkewald, he increasingly became the leading spokesman against the Nazi regime. Even though he could have escaped the retaliation by choosing to remain in the U.S. in 1939, he decided to return, knowing that to be a redemptive agent in the church's recovery he would have to share in its suffering. Bonhoeffer continued his work in the resistance movement throughout the early forties, but after having been implicated in a plot to assassinate Hitler, he was imprisoned in Berlin on April 5, 1943. He was executed by hanging at Flossenburg (Bavaria) on April 9, 1945 at the age of thirty-nine.

Bonhoeffer's biography portrays him as a jovial person who loved people. His most joyous moments were around the piano with family and friends, laughing, joking, and singing—all while hoisting a stein of beer. But equally joyful were his contemplative times before God in which he hammered out the ethics that were to be personally determinative in perhaps the most tumultuous and demonic epoch that the world had yet to experience. As the family fortunes and possessions shrank (Bonhoeffer's father was a professor of psychiatry), the courage, spirit, and theological pursuit of Dietrich Bonhoeffer burned brighter and brighter. A full humanity hammered out on the anvil of an increased persecution brought together the ordinary and the extraordinary. Bonhoeffer wrote, "The cross is the differential of the Christian religion, the power which enables the Christian to transcend the world and to view the victory."[18] People who have discovered that differential believe themselves to be people of destiny. While on board a ship in 1939, Bonhoeffer penned:

> God chooses the sinner to be His servant, so that His grace may become perfectly evident. The sinner shall do God's work, and show forth His grace. When God forgives a man, He gives him work to do. But this work can be sustained only in discipleship. Large programmes only lead to the places where we stand ourselves; but we ought only to be found where God is. We can be no longer anywhere else than where He is.[19]

This man was in love with life, yet when he was increasingly deprived of its necessities, he wrote, "Desires of which we cling closely can easily prevent us from being what we ought to be and can be; and on the other hand, desires repeatedly denied for the sake of present duty make us richer, lack of desire is poverty."[20] A fellow prisoner, a British officer named Payne Best, was later to write:

> Bonhoeffer was all humility and sweetness. He always seemed to diffuse an atmosphere of happiness, of joy in every smallest event in life, and of deep gratitude for the mere fact that he was alive. . . . He was one of the very few men I have ever met to whom his God was real and ever close to him.[21]

The closing paragraph from Mary Bosanquet's account of this twentieth-century martyr succinctly and most accurately expresses lifestyle evangelism:

> In Eberhard Bethge's phrase: "Secret discipline without

> worldliness becomes pure ghetto; worldliness without the secret discipline pure boulevard." Bonhoeffer's life was lived far from the boulevard and progressively further from the ghetto; it was lived with God and for God, with men and for men, ever more fearlessly exposed by the multifarious world, and it is by his life as much as by his words that he spoke and can speak today.[22]

CONCLUSION

Lifestyle evangelism conjures up every virtue that promotes the temporal welfare of personhood as encompassed by the eternal purposes of God. Yet it is something far greater than a list of virtues. It is an edifice that is built upon the *summum bonum*—the highest good—the love of God. The entrance sign is inviting, not so much because the exterior is perfect (and it never is), but because it is the dwelling place of Jesus Christ. Good things within do not define or even verify His presence, but to be sure it is His presence that distinguishes all that is right and good about life. Prevenient grace has provided a sufficient foretaste for "whosoever will" to become a permanent resident in God's house, a spiritual kingdom made without hands.

Lifestyle is the heart and soul of evangelism—an evangelism that earnestly seeks the wisdom of God with the full intention of acting out that wisdom. Lifestyle evangelism makes sure that it seeks Him before it attempts to do something for Him. Doing and going for Him is in vain unless He dwells within. Lifestyle evangelism is Christ in the soul of persons. It is Christ evidenced in the life of the believer. That essentially was the promise of Pentecost: "In that day you will know that I am in My Father, and you in Me, and I in you" (John 14:20). If there is a single axiom for evangelism, it is this: Divinely wrought internal change results in an external difference in both being and doing. Such is the work of the kingdom.

XII

evangelism in a technological age

William Fore defines communication as the "process in which relationships are established, maintained, modified, or terminated through the increase or reduction of meaning."[1] It is a constitutional given that everyone searches for meaning. The problem for Christian communication is that Americans search for meaning in such diverse ways. There are thousands of associations in America, ranging from owners of Airstream trailers to owners of AK-47 machine guns touting white supremacy. Nearly the only common denominator in both the corporate and atomistic quest for meaning is that individuals generally reach for objects or ideas that they believe will benefit them in some immediate and practical way—emotionally, physically, or monetarily.

A critical question for evangelism standing on the brink of the third millennium is whether mass media reflect values that are in place or provide a fulcrum sufficient for the overturning of values that lead to misguided quests and disillusioned hopes. For all communication there has to be a certain amount of agreement with perceptions that are already valued in order for people to listen and receive stimulation from new ideas and perspectives. For the past fifty years, there has been a growing number of Christian communicators who believe that stimulation can best be accomplished through mass appeal, primarily via radio and television. In the last ten years this methodology has been seriously questioned.

First of all, the stars of Christian television shot themselves in the foot with bullets of greed for power, lust for sex, and other sins that have plagued the human heart long before the electronic church came into existence. Second, there is a growing coterie of sociologists who through thoughtful and provocative analysis have not only questioned the effectiveness of "solid state" evangelism, but have suggested profound incongruities between the electronic medium and the Christian message. Quentin J. Schultze writes:

> If evangelism has suffered at the hands of its own media, it has not been because of scandal or corruption, but rather because of a misplaced hope in the techniques and technologies of American culture and society. . . . In spite of all of the evangelical media in existence today, giving away the faith has probably never been more difficult.[2]

CHRISTIAN RADIO

The Christian use of radio was not fraught with such complexity when Presbyterian Donald Barnhouse and Lutheran Walter Maier took to the airwaves in the late 1920s. Both became popular, but were subsequently overshadowed by Charles Fuller, who began his "Old Fashioned Revival Hour" over the Mutual Broadcasting System in 1937. During World War II Fuller's voice could be heard over a thousand radio stations.[3] According to Schultze, "Fuller paid about $1.6 million for time on Mutual alone in 1944, and his weekly audience was estimated by popular media at 20 million."[4] Radio evangelism has been characterized by a wide range of personalities. Bob Schuller's accusatory preaching and political meddling earned him 500 articles in the *Los Angeles Times* between 1927 and 1933. And then there was the far more sedate medical doctor M.R. DeHaan, who gave in-depth Bible exposition in his "Radio Bible Class," which aired on 600 stations. The radio dial provided consumers with an index to their favorite brand of religion. Technology and religion had been irrevocably wed together.

The willingness of an ever increasing plethora of religious organizations to purchase air time and the increasing number of stations to buy syndicated programs created a monetary monster. A lack of theological sophistication, which would have separated the hucksters from the real McCoys, and the escalation of money solicitation over the airwaves increased the embarrassment of secular networks. These networks began to question their relationship to religious broadcasting. There was more and more pressure from both the secular media and religious press to ban commercial religious programs. Some networks, such as NBC, never allowed paid time slots at all, and in 1944 Mutual Broadcasting restricted religious programming to Sunday morning.

The above confusion and charges that small fundamentalist groups who did not receive free time from the large communication conglomerates were being discriminated against led to the founding of the National Religious Broadcasters (NRB) by the National Association of Evangelicals in 1944. NRB envisioned itself as the arm of salvation in religious broadcasting. Dennis Voskuil recalls that "NRB quickly attempted to disassociate itself from radio racketeers by adopting a code of ethics regarding program content, technical broadcast quality, and financial disclosure."[5] Even more critical to its "reason to be," NRB lobbied and cried out against the dissenting liberal voice of Protestant mainline churches and their attempts to preempt paid religious broadcasting. Evangelicals were now united to fill the airwaves with gospel preaching and music and waft via radio frequency to every land that "Jesus saves."

By the 1970s evangelicals no longer needed to do battle with the pagan media giants. They were now strong enough and were producing sufficiently suitable broadcast material to build Christian radio stations by the hundreds. Schultze documents that the stations that devoted at least twenty hours per week to religious broadcasting grew from 111 stations in 1973 to 449 stations in 1979. The increasing popularity of the FM band and the "growing up" of gospel music provided both inexpensive outlets and an entertainment medium. By the 1980s popular preachers such as Chuck Swindoll and Charles Stanley were entering millions of homes and automobiles, while the talk format of such programs as James Dobson's "Focus on the Family" enjoyed growing receptivity. The religious no longer had to glean a theological tidbit among the tares of heathen programming, but could tune into a constant diet of their favorite preachers and musicians. The resulting religious glut proved to be both bane and blessing. While it succeeded in not being tarnished by secular programming and not having to appeal to pagan sponsors, it completely removed the sacred from the profane, establishing what Schultze calls a "religious ghetto."[6] The evangelistic message had been muted for those who most needed to hear it. Schultze writes:

> The barrage of "successful" preaching and teaching programs deepened the roots of the evangelical radio ghetto. By pleasing the very small audience attracted to those kinds of broadcasts, stations virtually guaranteed that they would never attract a wider group of listeners. All evidence indicated that few evangelicals would listen for long to large blocks of syndicated programming. In 1980 only about 20 percent of the religious radio audience tuned in for three or more hours weekly.[7]

TELEVISION

No communication medium has affected the way Americans think and act as has television. People are persuaded to drive certain cars, vote for particular candidates, and trust specific brokerage houses—all with appropriate jingles and background music, not to speak of handsome men and beautiful women. Television watching fills leisure time more than any other pleasure pursuit. As Neil Postman so capably argues, we have gone from a nation that relied on exposition, logic, and rhetoric for its information base to a nation that makes decisions predicated on emotional images. Postman states that the most significant American cultural fact of the second half of the twentieth century is the decline of the age of typography and the ascendancy of the age of television. "Our politics, religion, news, athletics, education, and commerce have been transformed into congenial adjuncts of show business, largely without protest or even much popular notice. The result is that we are a people on the verge of amusing ourselves to death."[8]

Indeed, things have changed, as they always do. Instead of horses we have fiber optics; in the place of hot camp meeting tabernacles infested by flies we have plush air-conditioned studios; rather than pacing preachers with expansive lungs and thick vocal cords in front of a sounding board there are talk show formats with both video and sound monitors. Bringing the preacher of your choice into the living room has replaced huddling with family and neighbors in a clapboard church listening to a not-so-polished preacher dressed in a black suit that matched his older model automobile. But quality was not so much on the minds of the religious progenitors of TV as was quantity. The automatic American assumption is that God is always in agreement with mass distribution. Billy Graham stated:

> Television is the most powerful tool of communication ever devised by man. Each of my prime time "specials" is now carried by nearly 300 stations across the U.S. and Canada, so that in a single telecast I preach to millions more than Christ did in his lifetime.[9]

By the 1980s, getting the good news out was so linked with TV that a new word was coined: "televangelism." But televangelism did not originate with the slick sets of Jim Bakker and Pat Robertson. In the 1950s, almost all of the mainline denominations attempted to utilize television as a gospel medium. None were more successful than Monsignor Fulton J. Sheen, who with his down-to-earth, practical style attracted millions of viewers in "Life Is Worth Living." Fore states, "For 30 years network audiences for the mainline programs ranged as high as 15 million viewers per week. All three faith groups maintained weekly radio programs as well."[10]

But for the most part, the message of the mainline preachers did not carry the punch of the ascending evangelical new birth popularity, and it certainly couldn't keep pace with the more sensational charismatic agenda of the Pentecostals. Billy Graham preached a verdict to people, and the result of hundreds coming forward could be filmed in panoramic technicolor while the camera focused on the anguish and joy of individual faces. However, even the results wrought by the preaching of America's most popular evangelist were sedate compared to the close-ups of people being healed by Oral Roberts. "Immediatism" was the wedding ring that tied the knot of the marriage between television and evangelical religion. But immediate results were not the only reason that mainliners left their churches and tuned in to evangelical preachers. The latter preached coherent messages with smiles and "biblical" formulas for success and antidotes for loneliness, despair, and anxiety. After William Fore wrote an article for *TV Guide* in 1980 ("Why T.V. Evangelists Can't Be Pastors"), he received a deluge of letters that accused the local church of being "dry, unfriendly, cold, not filled with the Spirit, unbiblical, works of Satan, dead, or dying." Fore writes:

> These letters drove home to me the sobering fact that the electronic church is a formidable threat to mainline churches today, not because it threatens to reduce income or attendance, but because it has revealed a critical failure on the part of most mainline churches to deal with many of the people in their own neighborhoods.[11]

Television was able to enter the neighborhood as no medium before it, and secular entertainment was not going to steal the show. In the 1960s, Oral Roberts left the rented arenas and auditoriums and went to a studio set. Cameras and the latest technology were able to not only zoom in on his son Richard as the featured soloist, but also offer a close view of the latest building on the university campus or medical center. As Jeffrey K. Hadden has pointed out, "Special projects can elicit donations far in excess of what is needed; the surplus can pay the bills for air time and general operations."[12] Even more innovative was Rex Humbard. He was the first person to build a church with television broadcasting as a central purpose. His popular message and family-style format, which beamed from his spectacular 220-foot domed-roof Cathedral of Tomorrow, made him an early favorite among TV preachers. Rex, Oral, and Billy were only a foretaste of things to come. Up until now watching religious television had been only seeing through a glass darkly.

In 1959 Pat Robertson bought a defunct UHF station in Portsmouth, Virginia and turned it into the multimillion dollar CBN ministries, with twenty-four-hours-a-day programming. The Yale Law School graduate created a talk show called the "700

Club," which mixed the banalities of popular guests with serious discussion of politics and national issues, "feeding some 5,500 cable systems nationwide via satellite on a 24-hour-a-day basis."[13] Hadden reports that the $230 million CBN empire has become the nation's third largest cable television network with its 1,500 employees managing a production that is broadcast to forty-three countries in various languages per week. In 1985 a Nielsen survey indicated that 425,500 households were tuned into the "700 Club" at least 15 minutes per day, and 16,300,000 viewers watched the program sometime within the period of a month. It is no wonder that Robertson was able to make a serious bid for the presidency of the U.S.

While CBN and its offshoot, PTL (featuring Jim and Tammy Bakker), have used dialogue formats modeled after Johnny Carson and Merv Griffin, no one has utilized television for straightforward evangelistic preaching more effectively than Jimmy Swaggart. Swaggart's honky-tonk music and shoot-from-the-hip preaching appealed mostly to a lower-middle-class socioeconomic structure, which wanted life painted in black-and-white dichotomies that were free of ambiguities. Swaggart built a $30 million ministry center in Baton Rouge, acquired a half dozen radio stations, and sold 12 million gospel music albums. Hadden writes, "Swaggart's southern drawl, loud exhortations about sin, and three-piece suits have made him the archetypal televangelist."[14] Before his shameful fall in 1988, Swaggart reached over two-and-a-half million households per day and had a TV congregation that extended around the globe.[15]

The irony of the description of the archetypal televangelist is that the most watched TV preacher does not fit the archetype at all. Robert Schuller's well-constructed, alliterated sermons, carefully modulated voice, and orchestrated worship services in the 4,000-seat Crystal Cathedral lend an aesthetic appeal that makes him the perfect choice for recreation room worship when one misses church on Sunday morning. Schuller's "Hour of Power" emphasizes positive thinking and pragmatic principles for daily living. His charisma, clear communication techniques, sermons with limited biblical content, and earned doctorate allow for a wide sociological appeal that crosses socioeconomic barriers. As a member of a mainline denomination, Reformed Church in America,

Schuller clearly demonstrates that television preachers should not be stereotyped or monolithically described. Hadden's description is apt:

> Robert Schuller is Swaggart's antimatter counterpart. He is cool, rational, and optimistic where Swaggart is sweaty, emotional, and premillenially pessimistic. Schuller preaches "Possibility Thinking" which is an unapologetic play on Norman Vincent Peale's "Positive Thinking." Swaggart preaches hellfire and brimstone and is trying to save all the souls he can before the battle of Armageddon.[16]

THE QUESTION OF EFFECTIVENESS

How effective is television as a tool of evangelism? The numbers question continues to plague the industry, and has yet to be adequately answered. Early estimates by the National Religious Broadcasters that claimed that religious broadcasting reached as high as 130 million viewers were greatly exaggerated. In 1984 the Annenberg School of Communications issued a report that estimated that the religious television audience was 13.3 million people. A Gallup Poll conducted at the same time suggested that the total number of people who watched at least some religious broadcasting during the course of a month may be closer to 70 million. In 1985 Pat Robertson commissioned the A.C. Nielsen Company to research his listening audience, a study that demonstrated that the previous Gallup Poll was not far from wrong. The following summary paragraph from Jeffrey Hadden leads him to answer the question "Is Anybody Listening?" with an unqualified yes.

> The cumulated monthly audience-cume, in the trade-for the top ten religious programs was 67.7 million households; the unduplicated cume, 34.1 million households. On a monthly basis, then, the duplicated cume is inflated by 98 percent. Since Nielsen estimates a total of 85.9 million T.V. households in America, the unduplicated figure indicates that, on average, 40 percent of all American households watch at least one segment of religious television each month. The unduplicated figure for an average week is 21 percent.[17]

A more critical question for evangelism is not "How many are watching?" but "Who is watching?" Polls and surveys seem to indicate that, for the most part, people who watch Christian television are already Christian. William Fore claims that "fully 77% of the heavy viewers of religious T.V. are church members and almost all of them attend church at least once a month."[18] He quotes the Annenberg School of Communication: "Viewers of religious programs are by and large also the believers, the church goers, the contributors. Their viewing . . . appears to be an expression; a confirmation of a set of religious beliefs and not a substitute for them."[19] In short, people do not come to church any more than they would because of TV, and possibly not as much. Again we quote from Fore:

> As far back as 1978 a study by the Institute for American Church Growth indicated that mass evangelism is not an effective method of increasing church membership. Another revealed that most people come to church as a result of someone personally known to them or because of strong pastoral leadership. Still other studies have shown that more than 80 out of 100 people who have joined the church in recent years come because of the word of a friend or relative. Far fewer than one out of 100 have come as a result of electronic evangelism.[20]

But the conclusion should not be made that people are not converted through watching religious TV. At least it can serve as a contributing factor to move someone toward the threshold of the kingdom, or it can be an affirmation for someone who is new in the faith. Stewart M. Hoover interviewed twenty families who regularly watch the "700 Club" and discovered three common denominators among them. Watching of the "700 Club" was intensified by personal crisis: suicides in the families, bankruptcies, a car accident that resulted in the death of a spouse, alcoholism, and marital problems. Another salient theme is that there was disillusionment either with the church with which they had been historically associated or with the one that they presently attended. The parachurch (i.e., in the form of religious TV) gave them the strength to stay and fight or the impetus to search for another church. But probably what the "700 Club" most provided for these church attenders was the assurance that they were part of something bigger than their local church and denomination. In their perception, Pat Robertson was serving to spread a belief system on a national and international level, a belief system which they espoused in their local neighborhood and towns. It was their belief that the "700 Club" could provide a more efficient, professional, and sophisticated technology to do what the local church could do in only an emaciated fashion.

> They see it as transcending the local and the particular, introducing their world view into the public stage where it can receive the respect and hearing it deserves. The program enhances the credibility of their beliefs and affirmations, which were previously marginal in American social and intellectual life.[21]

A CRITIQUE OF TELEVANGELISM

While some believe that television enhances the credibility of evangelical religion, there are also plenty of detractors. Both theologians and sociologists of communication charge that mass distribution has tainted the message rather than being faithful to a biblical theology of salvation. The electronic church consistently personifies a utilitarian pragmatism by highlighting individuals who have been in crisis, but after having turned to God took on a glorious aura of success. Fore charges the electronic church with being Manichean, separating all of life into a dualism of black and white, Christians and Communists, capitalists and socialists, theists and humanists. That which we interpret as good is from God and that which is interpreted as evil is from Satan. And, of course, TV preachers seem to claim the ability to discern what is coming from God and what is being delivered by Satan. For the most part, it does not dawn on cathode theologians that much evil is simply the result of wrong individual choices or the social implications of living in a fallen world.

This naïveté substantiates Fore's charge of Pelagianism, a theological error of which Americans are especially fond. The chief tenet of TV doctrine is possibility thinking, which either denies or disregards the doctrine of original sin and adopts as its slogan "Where there's a will there is a way." In addition to the theological deficiency,

TV evangelists frequently reflect the values of society as a whole (e.g., materialism, power, security, and utilitarian self-interest that makes the individual primary and the community secondary). Fore charges that "most of the distortions of general television are found within religious television, except that sexism, authoritarianism, and emphasis on simple and crass answers to problems are even more blatant."[22]

No communication methodology has more validated Marshall McLuhan's theory that the "message is the medium and the medium is the message" than television. Clifford Christians charges, "While claiming to save the world through mass communication, evangelicals have merely adopted the techniques of the secular culture they so deplore. . . . Hoping to convert others, they are reshaped themselves by the marketing ethos and stimulators-response mentality of the commercial broadcasting industry."[23] Christian television has failed to be redemptive, not only because it has failed to understand culture, but because it has chosen America's most enculturated medium to proclaim a message that is diametrically opposed to the American ethos. A central Christian value, "Be not conformed to this world," has been lost in religious TV's mad dash to the evangelistic goal line. Christians points out that in the paradigm of television no meaningful transcendent vision exists beyond the time and space accessible to the senses. Life is located only within the universe we see and hear, and not in some referent beyond immediate experience. In this secular version of the world, the supernatural—realities higher and deeper beyond the immediate—is excluded. Visual media such as television, cinema, and photography encourage a sensate worldview.[24]

Television as a medium is not able to deal with the nuances of the gospel and the paradoxes of theology, much less the transcendence of a Holy God. Instead, it emphasizes personalities, sensory impressions, the God of the seen as opposed to the God of the unseen, and immediate possibilities rather than self-denial. Reading the Scriptures through the illumination of the Holy Spirit or even listening to anointed preaching with an open mind develops a sanctified imagination that grasps for the mysteries and abstractions that are inherent to God-talk. Television, on the other hand, precludes such imagination with concrete images and larger-than-life personalities who serve more as icons than conveyors of grace. Quite often the charismatic personalities and elaborate sets magnified by TV close-ups are ends in themselves rather than divine symbols. Robert Wuthnow writes, "The contrast between the religious devotion that comes from these highly structured settings and the lonely prophet in the wilderness contemplating the mysteries of the Great Commandment is profound.[25]

Postman suggests that even though a microcomputer may be able to disseminate a greater amount of information to a fourth-grader than a conscientious schoolteacher can, there is something indispensably lost in the translation. The same can be said for the flesh-and-blood personalities who have confronted millions of individuals over the centuries with the claims of the gospel. An essential ingredient is lost if they are replaced by a larger-than-life celebrity projected from a studio far away.

It behooves evangelists to give at least as much attention to the purity of the transmission as they do to efficiency. Purity has to do with the uniqueness of preaching the gospel, as opposed to the generalities of selling cars and soap. The latter needs no prerequisites, no perplexity, no exposition—only powerful images backed by a rhythmic beat more attuned to primal urges than sanctification of those urges. Such an atmosphere is far different than the sacred space represented in the average church or even by a tent pitched in an oak grove. Postman doubts the possibilities of decontaminating television of its profane uses to the extent that it can properly represent the otherworldliness of the Christian message. A secular-needs orientation immersed in the American culture undermines the stringent demands of biblical Christianity. Postman writes:

> There is no great religious leader from the Buddha to Moses to Jesus to Mohammed to Luther—who offered people what they want. Only what they need. But television is not well suited to offering people what they need. It is "user friendly." It is too easy to turn off. It is at its most alluring when it speaks the language of dynamic visual imagery. It does not accommodate complex language or stringent demands. As a consequence, what is preached on television is not anything like the Sermon on the Mount. Religious programs are filled with good cheer. They celebrate affluence. Their featured players become celebrities. Though their messages are trivial, the shows have high ratings, or rather, because their messages

> are trivial, the shows have high ratings. I believe I am not mistaken in saying that Christianity is a demanding and serious religion. When it is delivered as easy and amusing, it is another kind of religion.[26]

A SANE AND REALISTIC APPROACH TO THE ELECTRONIC DISTRIBUTION OF THE GOSPEL

Is the discourse above sufficient reason for issuing a recall on the 1,400 radio stations and over 250 television stations in the U.S. that dedicate themselves primarily to religious broadcasting? The answer is that while they may be due some serious program overhauling, it cannot be argued that they do no good in equipping, encouraging, and edifying the Christian community. Broadcasting the gospel overseas via radio seems to be generally positive as a missionary effort. Only God is able to fully evaluate the increments of grace that are distributed in mass quantities to seeking souls over the airwaves. While it is true that television and radio demonstrate little direct influence in issuing converting grace, electronic evangelism holds the potential of serving as a contributing force in the discipling of people who are either in a pre- or post-conversion religious experience. There will always be the liability that haunts all mass evangelism—an instantaneous mentality that often skirts the intricacies of Christian nurture. In the meantime it will serve as a supplement, for better or worse, to the myriad forms of evangelistic endeavor that have been practiced down through the centuries.

The word "supplement" suggests that electronic evangelism will never serve as a replacement for meticulous and laborious activities that have gone into making saints since the days that Jesus issued those troublesome words from a hillside: "For the gate is small, and the way is narrow that leads to life, and few are those who find it" (Matt. 7:14). It is a mistaken notion to believe that electronic media is the ultimate evangelistic tool, the final link in God's plan to convert the world and usher in the millennium. Televangelism is fraught with so many difficulties that we are not even sure whether it can serve on an ongoing basis as a catalyst for ushering people into the kingdom, much less ushering in the kingdom itself.

It is still understood by most non-Christians that the gathered people who meet at specific times and places, whom the Bible designates as the *ecclesia,* is the primary source for spiritual food. Non-Christians who flip on the TV are normally looking for a diversion, rather than a head-on confrontation with the truth about themselves and ultimate reality that can only be found in an infinite God. Win Arn, a church growth analyst, argues that although TV has a legitimate role in pre-evangelism, the "high tech of television can never replace the high touch of congregations filled with loving people."[27] In attempting to answer the question "Is TV Appropriate for Mass Evangelism?" Arn responded:

> Each year, about 2 million religious television and radio programs are beamed over some 7,000 stations. The programs have made little impact on non-Christians. More than 70 percent of Americans either have no religious affiliation or are Christian in name only. Religious television doesn't seem to significantly impact this group. In a survey we conducted of 40,000 church-related Christians, only .01 percent said they attended church as a result of mass evangelism, including religious radio and television. However, more than 85 percent said they came to Christ and to church primarily because of a friend, relative, or associate.[28]

In a scholarly and provocative article, Thomas E. Boomershine has traced the history of religious communication: decalogue on stone, oral tradition, earliest writing, Josiah's scroll, and invention of the printing press. Boomershine's contention is that each time a group or institution has not responded to a new communication technology and the pattern and meanings that form around that technology, they have been marginalized or emaciated to the point of ineffectiveness. He unequivocally identifies the church's response to the culture of the electronic media by utilizing its primary languages of image and narrative as its most important decision concerning future development. Boomershine indicts the Christian community by stating that it is "negligent and cowardly for the church only to bemoan what the electronic church is doing and do nothing to form a more faithful communication of the gospel to a world in desperate need of the true knowledge of God."[29]

REDEMPTIVE SUGGESTIONS

At the present time there is nothing to indicate that electronic media are going to serve as a McCormick's reaper in the vast harvest of souls. If it is to serve even as a serious scythe in the evangelistic enterprise, it must go through the following reformation.

First, the message must be seriously examined in the light of Scripture. While no one comes to Christ out of disinterested benevolence, there still has to be a confrontation of the utilitarian, selfist theology that shapes much of TV's doctrine. A producer will need to at least partially eliminate the simplistic formulas that tie Christian commitment to subsequent prosperity. Pursuing the American dream and following Christ are divergent paths, and listeners need to hear that Christ may not be at all comfortable in the theological house that Ben Franklin built. One of the ways that this can be accomplished is to switch from lavish sets loaded with Christian media stars to critical issue pursuits that would seek answers with a Christian worldview. Bill Moyers' "Journal" suggests a construct that would allow inductive investigation and escape much of the triviality of current Christian TV. Rather than being subverted by American culture, TV needs to offer serious reflection on many of the things that constantly preoccupy Americans: sports, sex, work, and parenting.

Second, electronic media must seek to erase the sharp and often superficial dichotomies between the sacred and the profane. Our real problems in America are not humanism, secularism, communism, and all the other "isms." Christians and non-Christians alike are often enmeshed in the same problems of carnality, pride, avarice, and hedonism. Christian TV has not been able to free Americans from the evils inherent in capitalism, the Protestant work ethic, and the ideals of the American experiment, which, in spite of our best intentions, have gone awry. The tension that Richard Niebuhr depicted in his seminal work *Christ and Culture* and the ambiguities that Reinhold Niebuhr described in *The Ironies of American History* have fully escaped TV. In listening to much of Christian TV, one would think that compliance with the dream of our deistic forefathers is synonymous with Christianity, while divergence from it is anti-Christian. Oh well, Quakers and Mennonites have not played well in the electric church. Religious television has been far more concerned with returning to an American primitivism and nationalism than a primitive Christianity. It is not fully appreciated that Christians need to pay more attention to what Jesus thought than what Thomas Jefferson and James Madison thought.

Third, the sooner Christian television can divorce itself from right-wing politics, the better. Once a TV personality aligns himself or herself with a partisan doctrine, in spite of nonpartisan disclaimers, or, worse yet, becomes a candidate for political office, he or she ceases to be a Christian prophet. Political aspirations call for posturing, nuancing, calculating, scheming, and waffling—very unlike the prophetical and evangelistic announcements of John the Baptizer. The very fact that Pat Robertson was ruffled when the press referred to him as a "televangelist" is a case in point for the identity crisis that characterizes media Christianity. An evangelist is free to believe that God really does change the course of hurricanes. The political aspirant for America's highest office does not have that freedom, at least if he hopes to one day live at 1600 Pennsylvania Avenue. A true evangelist cannot remain faithful to the biblical call and speak out of both sides of his mouth. Don Cox writes:

> While all evangelicals have a responsibility to speak out on issues of importance such as abortion, protection of the family, and moral values that cross into the political realm, we must be careful to keep those items separate from the task of evangelism. I think that the stereotyping of evangelical ministries with the "New Right" has hurt our ability to evangelize all people.[30]

Fourth, in order to maintain evangelistic integrity, televangelists must arrive at financial integrity. Financial statements and salary amounts must be open to the general public. Financial compensation and fringe benefits should be commensurate with other religious professionals. Salaries such as the one Billy Graham draws can be on the top end of the scale without being ridiculous (i.e., without being five or ten times the amount of a well-paid pastor). The association between giving and an ipso facto blessing must be severed. Electronic religion, which is a costly business, would possibly do better to turn to product sponsorship rather than a constant barrage of financial appeals substantiated by projects that are not really at the heart of the ministry. The need for a large constant cash flow presents the electronic church with its greatest dilemma: how to sell the self-denial religion of the lowly Galilean to a consumer-oriented society. Attaining financial integrity is a mandate for televangelists to examine themselves for ethical contradictions that fall short of the standard of holiness to which God has called all of His church, especially those who preach His name among the lost. Never were the lost given such an opportunity to scrutinize the glaring inconsistencies that are magnified by TV close-ups of "God's spokesmen."

Fifth, if electronic media are going to serve as a responsible component in the wide range of evangelistic methodologies, there must be accountability to the local church. Individualism and privatization mark television partially because there is little relationship between TV's programs and goals and the corporate life of believers. Fund-raising, counseling, and decision-making are done without input from the church on either local or denominational levels. It is my opinion that most church leaders believe that the local fellowship that they attend would not change one iota if all religious programming immediately ceased. The electronic church needs to send "advance" people into the ecclesiastical community to find out how both can mutually benefit from each other's ministry.

Every evangelistic contact televangelism makes needs to be forwarded to a local congregation for follow-up. Any suspicion that one is in competition with the other needs to be completely erased by more careful organization and communication. The local church cannot wash its hands in the detergent of default. Very few congregations have wrestled with their relationship to the electronic church, much less made overtures to get involved. The electronic church will have to confess that it has ultimately failed if it does not increase its audience's affection for and commitment to a local body of believers. A new generation of Christian TV producers must do everything in their power to invalidate the indictment made by Robert Wuthnow:

> If anything should draw people out of the secret recesses of their homes and force them to live (as clergy liked to say) "in community," it was the church. The Bible itself commanded believers not to forsake the assembly. It was in the

> midst of the assembled faithful that the miracle of kerygma happened. Now television was replacing this community with a miracle of its own—the miracle of sitting motionless and alone before a preacher who was thousands of miles away and who could not listen nor love—only speak.[31]

Finally, quality must come before quantity in both message and results. Fidelity to the message must come before extent of distribution, and since Islam has the most adherents of any religion besides Christianity, success can never be predicated upon numbers. As Quentin Schultze reminds us, "In a nation where the *National Enquirer* is the best selling paper, success is indeed a curious blessing."[32] A TV minister may not be a church historian or theologian, but he or she is called to rightly divide the Word of Truth. God needs more than an advertisement. He desires presentation by men and women who have sought to know Him intimately and come to grips with His polarities: love and justice, mercy and holiness, sovereignty and free grace.

Educational institutions must explore the interface between sound evangelistic content and present media technologies. They must then construct a theological edifice to house a communication revolution. Ken Curtis believes this calls for graduate programs that are able to conduct sustained analysis of Christian programming as well as prepare Christians for a media industry calling for actors, writers, and producers. In arguing for more Christian drama and citing an award-winning piece on the life of C.S. Lewis titled *Shadowlands,* Curtis writes:

> The world does notice Christian efforts in the media arts when those efforts are marked by excellence, creativity and craftsmanship. While the secular industry is resistant to propagandistic religious programming, these and similar efforts have demonstrated that it is not opposed to religious themes in general. If the quality (from the idea to the story, to the script, to the screen) is excellent, it will have its market.[33]

CONCLUSION

If the Lord tarries, "no eye has seen nor ear heard" what wireless computer systems will yet produce. The revolution in computerized communication systems is staggering to all but the most technical minds. Only those who believe that technology is antithetical to spirituality will prevent the sanctification of today's scientific discoveries for the advancement of kingdom enterprises. Christians always face the dialectic that there is a delicate balance between the sacred and profane, while at the same time striving to make all of life sacred. Communication systems attempt to harness the latest understanding of scientific reality for the sake of efficiency. While efficiency is not the ultimate goal of evangelization, sound theology does not avoid the scientific world in which we live. No matter how deep the probe or advanced the insight, God is always there ahead of the most astute mind. Is it possible that evangelism could utilize communication electronics no less than did George Washington Carver claim the peanut? Sanctified means to accomplish holy purposes are not limited to the way things have always been done.

It is still left to some technotheologue to explore the uses of cellular evangelism. Internet, E-mail, and the information highway, to name a few, are new evangelistic frontiers. It is doubtful, however, that gadgets and gizmos will revolutionize proclamation of the good news. Even as I write this chapter, the U.S. presidential candidates are traveling by bus and train, pressing the flesh, and kissing babies at whistle stops. Some things never change. If any single conclusion may be drawn from the above, it is this: evangelism must not abandon the airwaves to the "prince of the power of the air."

The totality of Christian gifts and talents must be brought to bear upon the totality of the enterprise. Certainly that includes those who specialize in the most contemporary of communication endeavors.

conclusion: the third millennium trajectory of evangelism

The planetary system as we now understand it is relatively predictable. For instance, we can foretell an eclipse that results from the earth, moon, and sun's alignment on a particular date. Or, we can send telescopic satellites hurtling toward Saturn, because we can predict their relative orbit from year to year. Notice that I have hedged with the word "relative." There is some evidence that the sun's circumference is growing, while the moon is moving farther from our planet. Astrologists forecast that in 8 billion years, the sun will be 2,000 times brighter, turning the earth's oceans into boiling cauldrons. Obviously, there is no danger that we will be sucked into a giant helium fireball before the turn of the century. Neither are we trying to impose a scientific interpretation on apocalyptic literature. It is still too soon to separate theory from fact. The fact that we can be relatively sure of is that things change.

Less predictable than the planets and stars are those pieces of metal, rock, and frozen gas hurtling through the galaxies of space. An asteroid made up of stone and metal missed the earth by just 700,000 miles on March 23, 1992. The impact would have probably wiped out civilization. But don't rest easy, we're not out of the woods (asteroid field) yet. If a comet with a diameter of six miles across slammed into the earth, it would eliminate two-thirds of all life. Presently, there is just such an object hurtling toward Earth that threatens life as we now know it. An astronomer recently gave it a one-in-ten-thousand chance of hitting Earth on August 14, 2126. My great, great, great, great, great grandchildren could be in for a real surprise. There is no need to be fatalistic, but it is never too early to add another cosmological liability to the growing list (which includes a return of another glacier age in 2,000 years).

Looking ahead is tricky business, but not as speculative as one might think. Evangelism is a more predictable enterprise than is the detection of doomsday projectiles and the pendulum swing of the earth's geological clock. For the latter, prediction is a mixture of scientific calculation and educated conjecture. Between the two, there is an enormous latitude for error. Even scientists find themselves talking in terms of fate and luck. But in the theist's vocabulary, there are no such words. Both evangelism and astronomy are under the watchful eye of the sovereign God. Everything revolves around Him. While He is not predictable in terms of specific events, circumstances will not evolve out of arbitrary caprice. All that takes place in the future will be ordered by grace and justice, which flows from His holy character. He is the "Sun" of Righteousness who provides a reference point for all of life's actions and responses. A relationship with God offers an open and closed system at the same time. Life is open to the full potential of grace for each individual—nothing extraneous to God's power can intrude or destroy the personal relationship He offers and desires with His creation. Evangelism, in reference to the polestar of all existence, is predetermined to succeed. The course has been set by the One who said, "Behold, I am making all things new" (Rev. 21:5).

The "all things new" leads us to believe that God's idea of redemption is much bigger than ours. God wants to redeem the arts, the sciences, and the literature of our day and age. The trouble is that there just aren't enough Michelangelos, Blaise Pascals, and C.S. Lewises to go around. Part of that is the church's fault. We have been unable to bridge satisfactorily the gap between the Renaissance and the Reformation. Evangelism's trajectory can no longer be reckoned by isolationistic soul-winning camps who narrowly define salvation as activities with an overtly Christian label. Evangelism's domain is exploring the outer limits of the universe while plunging the depths and intricacies of the unconscious mind. Evangelism's probe knows no off-limits. It is to be a part of life, wherever life is found.

Treating evangelism as a methodology that has limited spheres of influence that are appropriate to a narrow field of study will be devastating to the building of the kingdom. Instead, evangelism needs to be perceived as interdisciplinary, with its thumb on the pulse of every endeavor in which persons participate. But evangelism has often operated with a tunnel vision that offers a truncated view of life. For instance, Nathan Hatch's indictment that evangelicalism has been unable to seriously engage the life of the mind needs to be carefully weighed. "Instead of engaging those who deny theistic assumptions, evangelicals spend most of their intellectual energies in intramural discussion."[1]

One might assume that trajectories are largely determined by the force of the catapult or the lift power of the launch. Thus we envision evangelistic success as being defined by the commitment and sacrifice of the people who fill our church pews. And when they miss a church function we wonder why they aren't as "committed" as their parents and grandparents were in the good ol' days. Actually, they are more committed—committed to a plethora of activities that were not a part of our parents' and grandparents' world. The competing commitments are so myriad that the choices are perplexing. Yes, it may be that the church can offer a value structure that would clarify choices and alleviate self-imposed stress. But the church, no matter how much it calls for institutional service, will not eliminate Little League baseball, computer classes at the community college, the annual school play, service organizations such as the Kiwanis or the Saddle Club. Evangelism commitments have often been spelled in terms of sacrifice for the church rather than forays into the world. Evangelistic effectiveness does not rest as much on commitment to an evangelism class or course as it does on the redemption of commitments that are already in place.

Evangelism is the kingdom of God invading, engaging, and embracing the world and its constituency. The conquest is not without its risks. One can easily be blindsided by the threats of accommodationism and compromise that lurk in uncharted territories. But the venture will have to face those perils rather than play it safe, all the while trusting the infinite mind of God to keep evangelism's trajectory on course. If evangelism steers clear of bioethics, space technology, information processing, communication theory, environmental conservation, public education, governmental processes, and the entertainment industry, evangelism will hardly register as a blip on society's radar screen. Salt will become so diluted and light so diffused that it will go undetected in the mainstream of society. It was never God's intention for the kingdom to be unwittingly marginalized.

Evangelism at its best is not defined as an activity but as a force for good, invading and beating back the powers of evil. It is the light where darkness prevails; it is the right where wrong dominates; it is the teacher where ignorance blinds; it is the truth when falsehood misleads; it is the liberty when self enslaves; it is life in the face of death; it is consolation in the midst of sorrow; it is bread in the emptiness of hunger; it is forgiveness in the grip of condemnation; it is the victor in the hour of defeat; it is peace in the rage of turmoil; it is the healer in the agony of affliction; it is the deliverer from the tyranny of oppression; it is the savior when all else in life has failed.

Evangelism is the personification of the victorious Christ in life's every deed and word. Its trajectory will be determined by the Author of all life. He is the Supreme Reference. Our task is to stamp His signature on existence wherever it is encountered. More properly expressed, our task is to uncover His inscription that is already etched on every facet of the universe. The trajectory of evangelism is the radiance of Christ's glory, which will burst into the third millennium with the same unbounded power and glory with which it began the first millennium. Christ invites us to come along. Whether He returns immediately or tarries for another hundred years, the trip's going to be awesome. *Hang on!*

notes

CHAPTER ONE

1. Gerhard Kittel, ed., *Theological Dictionary of the New Testament,* vol. 2 (Grand Rapids: Eerdmans, 1964), 730.
2. Ibid., 720.
3. Lewis A. Drummond, *The Word of the Cross: A Contemporary Theology of Evangelism* (Nashville: Broadman, 1992), 138.
4. William Packard, *Evangelism in America: From Tents to T.V.* (New York: Paragon House, 1988), 21.
5. Michael Green, *Evangelism through the Local Church* (Nashville: Thomas Nelson, 1992), 34.
6. David Barrett, *Evangelize! A Historical Survey of the Concept* (Birmingham: New Hope, 1987), 14.
7. Ibid., 16.
8. Ibid., 23.
9. Ibid., 30.
10. Ibid., 28.
11. Ibid., 37.
12. Ibid., 44.
13. Ibid., 45.
14. Ibid., 43.
15. Ibid., 45.
16. Donald G. Bloesch, *Essentials of Evangelical Theology,* vol. 2 (San Francisco: Harper and Row, 1978), 159.
17. J.I. Packer, *Evangelism and the Sovereignty of God* (Downers Grove, Ill.: InterVarsity, 1961), 41.
18. William J. Abraham, *The Logic of Evangelism* (Grand Rapids: Eerdmans, 1989), 65.

19. Mark A. Noll, Nathan O. Hatch, George M. Marsden, eds. *Christianity in America: A Handbook* (Grand Rapids: Eerdmans, 1983), 73.
20. *The Complete Works of John Wesley*, 3d ed. (Kansas City: Beacon Hill, 1978), 3:373.
21. Abraham, *The Logic of Evangelism*, 51.
22. Charles R. Taber, "God vs. Idols: A Model of Conversion," *Journal of the Academy for Evangelism in Theological Education* 3 (1987-88): 22–32.
23. William Hinson, *A Place to Dig In* (Nashville: Abingdon, 1987), 173.
24. Abraham, *The Logic of Evangelism*, 95.
25. C. Peter Wagner, *On the Crest of the Wave: Becoming a World Christian* (Ventura, Calif.: Regal, 1983), 51–69.
26. Robert E. Coleman, *Evangelism on the Cutting Edge* (Old Tappan, N.J.: Fleming H. Revell, 1986), 137.
27. Patrick R. Keifert, *Welcoming the Stranger* (Minneapolis: Fortress, 1992), 72.

CHAPTER TWO

1. Edward R. Hardy, ed., *The Library of Christian Classics: Christology of the Later Fathers* (Philadelphia: Westminster, 1954), 373.
2. Arland Hultgren, *Christ and His Benefits* (Philadelphia: Fortress, 1987), 16.
3. Ralph Earle, *Word Meanings in the New Testament* (Grand Rapids: Baker, 1989), 136.
4. Wayne McCown, "Such a Great Salvation," *Wesleyan Theological Journal* 1 (1981): 172–73.
5. William A. Dyrness, *Let the Earth Rejoice* (Westchester, Ill.: Crossway, 1983), 190.
6. Hultgren, *Christ and His Benefits*, 195.
7. H. Ray Dunning, *Grace, Faith & Holiness* (Kansas City: Beacon Hill, 1988), 382.
8. John Wesley, *Sermons: An Anthology*, eds. Albert C. Outler and Richard P. Heitzenrater (Nashville: Abingdon, 1991), 330.
9. Thomas Oden, *Systematic Theology*, vol. 2, *The Word of Life* (San Francisco: Harper and Row, 1989), 393.
10. Paul A. Mickey, *Essentials of Wesleyan Theology: A Contemporary Affirmation* (Grand Rapids: Zondervan, 1980), 129.
11. Ibid., 129.
12. Dyrness, *Let the Earth Rejoice*, 48.
13. Walter Brueggemann, *Biblical Perspectives on Evangelism* (Nashville: Abingdon, 1993), 26.
14. Charles R. Wilson, "Christology," *A Contemporary Wesleyan Theology*, Vol. 1 (Grand Rapids: Zondervan, 1983), 338.
15. Oden, *Systematic Theology*, Vol. II, 366.
16. Donald G. Bloesch, *Essentials of Evangelical Theology*, Vol. II (San Francisco: Harper and Row, 1978), 133.
17. Dyrness, *Let the Earth Rejoice*, 188.

18. *Works of John Wesley,* 2: 396.
19. *Works of John Wesley,* 11: 417.
20. Colin Williams, *John Wesley's Theology Today* (Nashville: Abingdon, 1960), 65.
21. John Wesley, *Sermons: An Anthology,* 118.
22. Ibid., 119.
23. Paul M. Bassett and William M. Greathouse, *Exploring Christian Holiness,* vol. 2, *Historical Development* (Kansas City: Beacon Hill, 1985), 159.
24. Ibid., 167.
25. Bloesch, *Essentials of Evangelical Theology,* vol. 1, 98.
26. John Wesley, *A Plain Account of Christian Perfection* (Kansas City: Beacon Hill, reprint, 1971), 51.
27. Wesley, *Complete Works,* 380.
28. Ibid., 412.
29. Robert Wall, "Glorification in the Pauline Letters," in *Wesleyan Theological Perspective,* vol. 1 (Anderson, Ind.: Warner, 1981), 164–65.

CHAPTER THREE

1. Tom Sine, *Wild Hope* (Dallas: Word, 1991), 211.
2. Scott M. Peck, *People of the Lie: The Hope for Healing Human Evil* (New York: Simon and Schuster, 1983).
3. Samuel Chadwick, *The Path of Prayer* (New York: Abingdon, 1931), 81.
4. Gilbert Tennent, "An Unconverted Ministry," in *American Christianity: An Historical Interpretation with Representative Documents,* vol. 1, ed. H. Shelton Smith, Robert T. Handy and Lefferts A. Loetscher (New York: Scribners, 1963), 325–26.
5. William Booth, "Who Cares," in *Twenty Centuries of Great Preaching: An Encyclopedia of Preaching,* vol. 2 (Waco, Texas: Word, 1971), 227.
6. David Bosch, *Witness to the World: The Christian Mission in Theological Perspective* (Atlanta: John Knox, 1980), 40.
7. Tom Nees, "The Answer to AIDS: Obedience," *Preacher's Magazine* 65 (Spring 1990): 16.
8. *The Complete Works of John Wesley,* vol. 8, Addresses, Essays, Letters (Kansas City: Beacon Hill, 1978).
9. Larry Ingram, "Evangelism as Frame Intrusion: Observations on Witnessing in Public Places," *Journal for the Scientific Study of Religion* 28, no. 1 (March 1989): 20.
10. John R. Stott, *The Lausanne Covenant: An Exposition and Commentary* (Minneapolis: World Wide Pubs., 1975), 30.
11. Bosch, *Witness to the World,* 19.
12. Herbert J. Kane, "The Work of Evangelism" in *Perspectives on the World Christian Movement* (Pasadena, Calif.: William Carey Library, 1981), 566.
13. Dallas Willard, *Spirit of the Disciplines* (San Francisco: Harper and Row, 1988), 218.

14. Reinhold Niebuhr, *The Nature and Destiny of Man: A Christian Perspective*, vol. 2 (New York: Scribner's, 1964), 111.
15. Bosch, *Witness to the World*, 207.
16. James F. Engel, *Contemporary Christian Communications: Its Theory and Practice* (Nashville: Thomas Nelson, 1975), 104.
17. George Sweazy, *The Church as Evangelist* (New York: Harper and Row, 1969), 55.
18. Abraham, *The Logic of Evangelism*, 200.
19. Chadwick, *The Path of Prayer*, 18.
20. Ronald C. White, Jr., and Howard Hopkins, *The Social Gospel: Religion and Reform in Changing America* (Philadelphia: Temple UP, 1976), 42.
21. John L. Peters, *Christian Perfection and American Methodism* (Grand Rapids: Zondervan/Francis Asbury, 1985), 198.
22. Wayne Detzler, "Biblical Integrity and Revival" in *Evangelism on the Cutting Edge* (Old Tappan, N.J.: Fleming H. Revell, 1986), 46.
23. Donald G. Bloesch, *Essentials of Evangelical Theology*, vol. 2 (San Francisco: Harper and Row, 1978), 162.
24. John Wesley, *The Journal of John Wesley*, Vol. 8 (London: The Epworth Press, 1938), 20.
25. Gerhard Kittel, *Theological Dictionary of the New Testament*, vol. 2 (Grand Rapids: Eerdmans, 1964), 697.
26. Bosch, *Witness to the World*, 236.
27. Stott, *Lausanne Covenant*, 60.
28. Albert Schweitzer, *Out of My Life and Thought* (New York: Henry Holt and Company, 1933), 110–11.
29. Robert E. Coleman, *Nothing to Do But Save Souls: John Wesley's Charge to His Preachers* (Grand Rapids: Zondervan/Francis Asbury, 1990), 49.
30. John Stott, *Christian Mission in the Modern World* (Downers Grove, Ill.: InterVarsity, 1975), 170.
31. See Robert E. Coleman, *The Master Plan of Evangelism* (Huntingdon Valley, Pa.: Christian Outreach, 1963).
32. See Robert E. Coleman, *They Meet the Master* (Fort Lauderdale, Fla.: Christian Outreach, 1973).
33. Sine, *Wild Hope*, 270.
34. David Bosch, *Transforming Mission* (New York: Ortus, 1991), 246.
35. Donald A. McGavran, *Effective Evangelism: A Theological Mandate* (Nutley, N.J.: Presbyterian and Reformed, 1988), 11.
36. Harry S. Stout, *The Divine Dramatist* (Grand Rapids: Eerdmans, 1991), 36.
37. Wesley, *Journal*, Vol. 4, 325.
38. Wesley, *Complete Works*, Vol. 8, 113.

CHAPTER FOUR

1. See R. Laurence Moore, *Selling God: American Religion in the Marketplace of*

Culture (New York: Oxford Univ. Press, 1994).

2. Mark A. Noll, Nathan O. Hatch, and George M. Mardsen, eds., *Christianity in America: A Handbook* (Grand Rapids: Eerdmans, 1983), 10.

3. Ibid., 12.

4. Charles W. Ferguson, *Organizing to Beat the Devil* (New York: Doubleday, 1971), 123.

5. J. Edwin Orr, *The Fervent Prayer* (Chicago: Moody, 1975), 139.

6. Sydney E. Ahlstrom, *A Religious History of the American People,* vol. 1 (New York: Image Books, 1975), 539.

7. William L. Lumpkin, *Baptist Foundations in the South* (Nashville: Broadman, 1961), 20.

8. Ibid., 56.

9. Ferguson, *Organizing to Beat the Devil,* vii.

10. Fredrick A. Norwood, *The Story of American Methodism: History of the United Methodists and Their Relations* (Nashville: Abingdon, 1974), 146.

11. Ezra Tipple, *Francis Asbury: The Prophet of the Long Road* (New York: The Methodist Book Concern, 1916), 172.

12. Ivan Howard, "Controversies in Methodism Over Methods of Education of Ministers Up to 1865" (Ph.D. diss., Univ. of Iowa, 1965), 11.

13. Ibid., 12.

14. William G. McLoughlin, *Revivals, Awakenings, and Reform: An Essay on Religion and Social Change in America, 1607-1977* (Chicago: Univ. of Chicago Press, 1978), 8.

15. Ibid., 8.

16. Perry Miller, *Jonathan Edwards* (Westport, Conn.: Greenwood, 1949), 148.

17. Jonathan Edwards, *A Treatise Concerning Religious Affection* (New York: American Tract Society, 1850).

18. Robert W. Jensen, *America's Theologian: A Recommendation of Jonathan Edwards* (New York: Oxford Univ. Press, 1988), 76.

19. Robert Handy, *A Christian America: Protestant Hopes and Historical Realities* (New York: Oxford Univ. Press, 1984), 26.

20. McLoughlin, *Revivals, Awakenings, and Reform,* 132.

21. Ahlstrom, *Religious History of the American People,* vol. 1, 435.

22. Ferguson, *Organizing to Beat the Devil,* 136.

23. Mendel Taylor, *Exploring Evangelism: History, Methods, Theology* (Kansas City: Nazarene Publishing House, 1964), 417.

24. Ferguson, *Organizing to Beat the Devil,* 187–88.

25. H. Shelton Smith, Robert T. Handy, and Lefferts A. Loetscher, *American Christianity: An Historical Interpretation with Representative Documents,* vol. 2 (New York: Scribner's, 1963), 12.

26. Ibid., 22.

27. Taylor, *Exploring Evangelism,* 448.

28. McLoughlin, *Revivals, Awakenings, and Reform,* 125.

29. Timothy Smith, *Revivalism and Social Reform* (New York: Abingdon, 1957), 64.

30. Ibid., 67.
31. Orr, *The Fervent Prayer*, 9.
32. William McDonald and John Searles, *The Life of Reverend John S. Inskip* (Boston: McDonald and Gill, 1885), 201–2.
33. Melvin Dieter, *Revivalism and Holiness* (Ann Arbor, Mich.: Xerox Univ. Microfilms, 1973), 118.
34. Ibid., 199.
35. John L. Peters, *Christian Perfection and American Methodism* (Grand Rapids: Zondervan/Francis Asbury, 1985), 111.
36. Harry Stout, *The Divine Dramatist* (Grand Rapids, Mich.: William B. Eerdmans, 1991), 211.
37. Winthrop S. Hudson, *Religion in America: An Historical Account of the Development of American Religious Life* (New York: Scribner's, 1981), 231.
38. Ibid., 234.
39. Ibid.
40. "Colorful Sayings from Colorful Moody," *Christian History* 9/25, n.d., 9.
41. Bernard Weisberger, *They Gathered at the River* (Boston: Little, Brown, 1958), 210.
42. "Colorful Sayings from Colorful Moody," 10.
43. Weisberger, *They Gathered at the River*, 199.
44. Ibid., 258.
45. Ahlstrom, *A Religious History of the American People*, 206.
46. Ibid., 206–7.
47. Marshall Frady, *Billy Graham: A Parable of American Righteousness* (Boston: Little, Brown, 1979), 286.
48. Ibid., 279.
49. Ibid.
50. William Martin, *A Prophet With Honor* (New York: William Morrow, 1991), 75.
51. David Edwin Harrell, Jr., *Oral Roberts: An American Life* (San Francisco: Harper and Row, 1985), 91.
52. Ibid., 67.
53. Ibid., 180.
54. Ibid., 147.
55. John Wimber and Kevin Springer, *Power Evangelism* (San Francisco: Harper and Row, 1986), 109.
56. Abraham, *The Logic of Evangelism.*
57. Wimber, *Power Evangelism*, 31.
58. Arthur M. Schlesinger, "A Critical Period in American Religion," in *Religion in American History* (Englewood Cliffs, N.J.: Prentice-Hall, Inc., 1978), 307.
59. Ibid., 310.
60. Agnes Rush Burr, *Russell H. Conwell and His Work: One Man's Interpretation of Life* (Philadelphia: John C. Winston, 1926), 214.
61. Ibid., 212.

62. Ibid., 438.
63. Ibid., 224.
64. Ibid., 225.
65. Ibid., 421.
66. Powhatan James, *George W. Truett: A Biography* (New York: Macmillan, 1939), 155.
67. Ibid., 163.
68. Ibid., 73.
69. Ibid., 248.
70. Elizabeth O'Conner, *Call to Commitment: The Story of the Church of the Saviour, Washington, D.C.* (New York: Harper and Row, 1963), 20.
71. Ibid., 112–13.
72. Ibid., 105.
73. Ibid., 102–3.
74. Ibid., 93.
75. Ibid., 158.
76. Ibid., 294.
77. Ibid., 94.
78. Nathan O. Hatch, "Evangelicalism as a Democratic Movement," in *Evangelicalism and Modern America* (Grand Rapids: Eerdmans, 1984), 81.
79. J. Alan Youngren, "Parachurch Proliferation: The Frontier Spirit Caught in Traffic," *Christianity Today*, 6 November 1989, 39.
80. Joel D. Heck, *Make Disciples: Evangelism Programs of the Eighties* (St. Louis: Concordia, 1984), 57.
81. James Hefley, *God Goes to High School* (Waco, Texas: Word, 1970), 117.
82. Emile Cailliet, *Young Life* (New York: Harper and Row, 1963), 37.
83. Bill Bright, *Come Help Change the World* (Old Tappan, N.J.: Fleming H. Revell, 1970), 77.
84. Ibid., 19.
85. Smith, *Revivalism and Social Reform*, 81.
86. See Gilbert Barnes, *The Antislavery Impulse, 1830-1834* (New York: D. Appleton Century, 1933).
87. Edward H. McKinley, *Marching to Glory: The History of the Salvation Army in the United States of America, 1880-1980* (San Francisco: Harper and Row, 1980), 1.
88. Norris Magnusun, *Salvation in the Slums: Evangelical Social Work, 1865-1920* (Metuchen, N.J.: Scarecrow, 1977), 161.
89. Ibid., 170.
90. Ibid., 172.
91. Ibid., 56.
92. Ibid.
93. Ibid., 10.
94. Ibid., 25.
95. Ibid., 5.

96. Ibid., 91.
97. Ibid., 14.
98. Ibid., 17.
99. Smith, *American Christianity*, 114.
100. Leslie R. Marston, *From Age to Age a Living Witness* (Winona Lake, Ind.: Light and Life, 1960), 39.
101. Ibid., 405.
102. John V. Smith, *The Quest for Holiness and Unity* (Anderson, Ind.: Warner, 1980), 65.
103. Ibid., 165.
104. Ibid., 168.
105. Ibid., 180.
106. Magnusun, *Salvation in the Slums*, 130.
107. Ibid., 31.
108. Smith, *Revivalism and Social Reform*, 154.

CHAPTER FIVE

1. R.S. Peters, ed., *Brett's History of Psychology* (Cambridge: M.I.T. Press, 1965), 755.
2. Aurelius Augustinus, *On Education*, trans. George Howie (South Bend, Ind.: Gateway, 1969), 99.
3. Richard Baxter, *The Reformed Pastor: Classics of Faith & Devotion* (Portland, Ore.: Multnomah, 1982), 56.
4. Ibid., 98.
5. Jonathan Edwards, *A Treatise Concerning Religious Affection* (New York: American Tract Society, 1850), 35.
6. Ibid., 122.
7. Thomas C. Upham, *Mental Philosophy* (New York: Harper and Brothers, 1883), 352–53.
8. Sigmund Freud, *Civilization and Its Discontents* (New York: W.W. Norton, 1963), 71.
9. E. Brooks Holifield, *A History of Pastoral Care in America: From Salvation to Self-Realization* (Nashville: Abingdon, 1983), 324.
10. Carl Jung, *Collected Works*, vol. 9, Part 2 (London: Routledge and Kegan Paul, 1958), 275.
11. Edward C. Whitmont, *The Symbolic Quest: Basic Concepts of Analytical Psychology* (Princeton, N.J.: Princeton Univ. Press, 1969), 165.
12. Ibid., 13.
13. Ibid., 143.
14. Victor Frankl, *The Doctor and the Soul* (New York: Knopf, 1955), 74.
15. Whitmont, *The Symbolic Quest*, 153.
16. Ibid., 154.
17. Erik H. Erikson, *Identity, Youth and Crisis* (New York: W.W. Norton, 1968),

106.
18. Ibid., 136.
19. Erik H. Erikson, *Childhood and Society* (New York: W.W. Norton, 1950), 267.
20. Erik H. Erikson, *Young Man Luther: A Study in Psychoanalysis and History* (New York: W.W. Norton, 1962), 179.
21. Erikson, *Identity, Youth and Crisis,* 128–29.
22. Daniel Levinson, *The Seasons of a Man's Life* (New York: Ballantine, 1978), 49.
23. Ibid., 60.
24. Ibid., 215.
25. James F. Engel, *Contemporary Christian Communications: Its Theory and Practice* (Nashville: Thomas Nelson, 1975), 125.
26. Ibid., 125.
27. Ibid., 126.
28. James W. Fowler, *Stages of Faith: The Psychology of Human Development and the Quest for Meaning* (San Francisco: Harper and Row, 1981), 50.
29. Ibid., 51.
30. Ibid., 52.
31. Ibid., 167.
32. Ibid., 202.
33. Ibid., 14.
34. Ibid., 192.
35. Lesslie Newbigin, *Foolishness to the Greeks: The Gospel and Western Culture* (Grand Rapids: Eerdmans, 1986), 63.
36. Ibid., 14.
37. Ibid., 20.
38. Robert Ornstein and Paul Ehrlich, *New World, New Mind: Moving Toward Conscious Evolution* (New York: Simon and Schuster, 1989), 62.
39. Newbigin, *Foolishness to the Greeks,* 37.
40. Thomas C. Oden, *Structure and Awareness* (Nashville: Abingdon, 1969), 87.
41. See Thomas C. Oden, *Game Free* (New York: Harper and Row, 1974).
42. See Thomas C. Oden, *TAG, The Transactional Awareness Game* (New York: Harper and Row, 1976).
43. Frank Lake, *Clinical Theology* (London: Darton, Longman and Todd, 1966), 1111.
44. Ibid., 262.
45. Engel, *Contemporary Christian Communications,* 78.
46. Rollo May, *Love and Will* (New York: W.W. Norton, 1969), 319.

CHAPTER SIX

1. Allan Bloom, *The Closing of the American Mind* (New York: Simon and Schuster, 1987), 354.
2. Ibid., 260.

3. Paul E. Johnson, *A Shopkeeper's Millennium: Society and Revivals in Rochester, New York* (New York: Hill and Wang, 1978), 135.
4. Ibid., 35.
5. James D. Hunter, *American Evangelicalism: Conservative Religion and the Quandary of Modernity* (New Brunswick, N.J.: Rutgers Univ. Press, 1983), 130.
6. Richard Perkins, *Looking Both Ways: Exploring the Interface between Christianity and Sociology* (Grand Rapids: Baker, 1987), 170.
7. George Gallup, *The Unchurched in America* (Princeton, N.J.: Princeton Religion Research Center, 1988).
8. See Peter L. Berger, *A Rumor of Angels* (New York: Doubleday, 1969).
9. John Naisbitt and Patricia Aburdene, *Megatrends 2000: Ten New Directions for the 1990's* (New York: William Morrow, 1990), 131–57.
10. Hunter, *American Evangelicalism,* 125.
11. Gallup, *The Unchurched in America,* 47.
12. George G. Hunter, *How to Reach Secular People* (Nashville: Abingdon, 1992), 41.
13. Ibid., 52.
14. Timothy Smith, "Lay Initiative in the Religious Life of American Immigrants, 1880-1950," in *Religion in American History,* ed. John Mulder and John Wilson (Englewood Cliffs, N.J.: Prentice-Hall, 1978), 359–60.
15. Howard G. Chua-Eoan, "Stranger in Paradise," *Time* 19 April 1990, 29.
16. Ibid., 33.
17. John T. Seamands, *Harvest of Humanity* (Wheaton, Ill.: Victor, 1988), 193.
18. C. Peter Wagner, "A Vision for Evangelizing the Real America," *International Bulletin of Missionary Research* 10, no. 2 (April 1986): 60.
19. Ibid., 64.
20. See Raymond Bakke, "Refugees and World Evangelization," in *The Refugees among Us* (Monrovia, Calif.: MARC, 1983).
21. Ralph Winter, "The New Macedonia: A Revolutionary New Era in Missions Begins," in *Perspectives on the World Christian Movement* (Pasadena, Calif.: William Carey Library, 1981), 297.
22. Roger S. Greenway and Timothy M. Monsma, *Cities: Missions' New Frontier* (Grand Rapids: Baker, 1989), 45.
23. Naisbitt, *Megatrends 2000,* 305.
24. Thomas C. Oden, *Pastoral Theology: Essentials for Ministry* (San Francisco: Harper and Row, 1983), 279.
25. Greenway, *Cities,* 79.
26. Margaret Poloma and Brian Pendleton, "Religious Experience, Evangelism, and Institutional Growth within the Assemblies of God," *Journal for the Scientific Study of Religion* 28, no. 4 (December 1989): 428.
27. Wade Roof and William McKinney, *American Mainline Religion: Its Changing Shape and Future* (New Brunswick, N.J.: Rutgers Univ. Press, 1987), 234.
28. Dean Kelly, *Why Conservative Churches Are Growing* (New York: Harper and Row, 1972), 15.

29. Ibid., 102.
30. Leonard Sweet, "The 1960's: The Crisis of Liberal Christianity and the Public Emergence of Evangelicalism," in *Evangelicalism and Modern America* (Grand Rapids: Eerdmans, 1984), 32.
31. Roof and McKinney, *American Mainline Religion*, 60.
32. Sweet, "The 1960's," 45.
33. Roof and McKinney, *American Mainline Religion*, 229.
34. Naisbitt, *Megatrends 2000*, 293.
35. Ibid., 293–94.
36. See Terry Muck, *Alien Gods on American Turf* (Wheaton, Ill.: Victor Books, 1990).
37. Robert N. Bellah, et al., *Habits of the Heart: Individualism and Commitment in American Life* (New York: Harper and Row, 1985), 84.
38. Jonathan Alter and Pat Wingert, "The Return of Shame," *Newsweek* (6 February 1995): 22.
39. Bellah, *Habits of the Heart*, 235.
40. Ibid., 239.
41. Ibid., 246.
42. Bloom, *Closing of the American Mind*, 25.
43. Ibid., 78.
44. Ibid., 118.
45. See article "James Dobson," in *The Oregonian*, 9 June 1990.
46. M. Scott Peck, *People of the Lie: The Hope for Healing Human Evil* (New York: Simon and Schuster, 1983), 264.
47. Carl L. Bostrom, *Ministry: Why Retire?* (Indianapolis: The National Center on Ministry with the Aging, 1983), x.
48. T.R. Cole, "Aging, Meaning, and Well-being: Musings of a Cultural Historian," *International Journal of Aging and Human Development* 19 (1984): 329.
49. James Field, "Pastoral Care for the Elderly," unpublished paper (1990): 19.
50. Timothy P. Weber, *Living in the Shadow of the Second Coming* (Grand Rapids: Zondervan, 1983), 5.
51. Ibid., 223.
52. Robert Ornstein and Paul Ehrlich, *New World New Mind: Moving toward Conscious Evolution* (New York: Simon and Schuster, 1989), 2.
53. Ibid., 7.
54. Larry Reibstein, "That Sinking Feeling," *Newsweek*, 4 November 1990, 19.
55. Donald Barlett and James Steel, "America, What Went Wrong," *Philadelphia Inquirer*, 1991.
56. Ibid.
57. See Robert T. Handy, *A Christian America: Protestant Hopes and Historical Realities* (New York: Oxford Univ. Press, 1984).
58. See George Barna, *The User Friendly Church* (Ventura, Calif.: Regal, 1991).
59. *Seattle Times*, 8 August 1992. n.p.

CHAPTER SEVEN

1. E. Brooks Holifield, *A History of Pastoral Care in America: From Salvation to Self-Realization* (Nashville: Abingdon, 1983), 318.
2. Charles Leerhsen, et al., "Unite and Conquer," *Newsweek* (5 February 1990): 50–55.
3. Neal McBride, "What's the Big Deal about Small Groups?" *Discipleship Journal* 59 (1990): 18–20.
4. Joseph C. Aldrich, *Life-Style Evangelism: Crossing Traditional Boundaries to Reach the Unbelieving World* (Portland, Ore.: Multnomah, 1981), 190–91.
5. See Dale E. Galloway, *20/20 Vision: How to Create a Successful Church* (Wheaton, Ill.: Tyndale, 1986).
6. Richard Peace, *Small Group Evangelism: A Training Program for Reaching Out with the Gospel* (Downers Grove, Ill.: InterVarsity, 1985), 67.
7. Ibid., 68.
8. Ibid., 85.
9. Galloway, *20/20 Vision*, 142.
10. Carl F. George, *Prepare Your Church for the Future* (Tarrytown, N.Y.: Fleming H. Revell, 1991), 74.
11. David Allan Hubbard and Clinton W. McLemore, "Evangelical Churches," in *Ministry in America: A Report and Analysis, Based on an In-Depth Survey of 47 Denominations in the United States and Canada, with Interpretation by 18 Experts* (San Francisco: Harper and Row, 1980), 356.
12. Darius Salter, *What Really Matters in Ministry: Profiling Pastoral Success in Flourishing Churches* (Grand Rapids: Baker, 1990), 34.
13. Harold Rogers, *Harry Denman: A Biography* (Nashville: Upper Room, 1977), 58.
14. Dawson Trotman, *Born to Reproduce* (Colorado Springs: NavPress, 1987), 22–23.
15. Bill Bright, *Come Help Change the World* (Old Tappan, N.J.: Fleming H. Revell, 1970), 46.
16. James D. Kennedy, *Evangelism Explosion* (Wheaton, Ill.: Tyndale, 1983), 26–27.
17. Ibid., 31.
18. Ibid., 34.
19. Ibid., 97–98.
20. Ibid., 104.
21. Holifield, *History of Pastoral Care*, 211.
22. Hunter, *American Evangelicalism*, 83.
23. Kennedy, *Evangelism Explosion*, 112.
24. Salter, *What Really Matters in Ministry*, 47.
25. Wesley L. Duewel, *Mighty Prevailing Prayer* (Grand Rapids: Zondervan/Francis Asbury, 1990), 201.
26. Lewis A. Drummond, *The Awakening That Must Come* (Nashville: Broadman, 1978), 105.
27. James D. Kennedy, "Learning How to Witness," in *The Pastor Evangelist*, ed.

Robert S. Greenway (Philadelphia: Presbyterian and Reformed, 1987), 99.
28. Engel, *Contemporary Christian Communications*, 133–34.
29. Dallas Willard, *Spirit of the Disciplines* (San Francisco: Harper and Row, 1988), 70.
30. Harry L. Reeder III, "Revitalizing a Dying Church," in *The Pastor-Evangelist*, ed. Roger S. Greenway (Philadelphia: Presbyterian and Reformed, 1984), 178.
31. Kenneth B. Bedell, ed., *Yearbook of American & Canadian Churches 1996* (Nashville: Abingdon, 1996), 243–55.
32. Elmer Towns, *Getting a Church Started* (Lynchburg, Va.: Elmer L. Towns, 1982), 69–111.
33. Joseph James, *On the Front Lines* (Winona Lake, Ind.: Light and Life, 1988), 28.
34. "How to Select Church Planters." (Pasadena, Calif.: Charles E. Fuller Institute, n.d.), 5–9.
35. Towns, *Getting a Church Started*, 29.
36. Kennedy, *Evangelism Explosion*, 158.
37. James, *On the Front Lines*, 4.
38. Earl Parvin, *Missions USA* (Chicago: Moody, 1985), 279.
39. Paul Wilkes, "The Hands That Shape Our World," in *The Atlantic Monthly* (December 1990): 75–76.
40. Jack Hyles, *Church Bus Handbook* (Hammond, Ind.: Hyles-Anderson, 1970), 11–12.
41. Dean M. Kelly, *Why Conservative Churches Are Growing* (New York: Harper and Row, 1977), 164.
42. David O. Moberg, *Wholistic Christianity* (Elgin, Ill.: Brethren, 1985), 126.

CHAPTER EIGHT

1. Bedell, *Yearbook of Churches*, 243–55.
2. "Statistical Abstract of the United States" (United States Department of Commerce, 1991), 13.
3. Barna Research Group, *The Church Today: Insightful Statistics and Commentary* (Glendale, Calif.: 1990), 26.
4. Howard Hanchey, *Church Growth and the Power of Evangelism* (Cambridge: Cowley, 1990), 20.
5. David Buttrick, *Homiletic* (Philadelphia: Fortress, 1987), 125.
6. C. Peter Wagner, *Leading Your Church to Growth* (Ventura, Calif.: Regal, 1984), 83.
7. Ibid., 17.
8. R. Daniel Reeves and Ron Jensen, *Always Advancing: Modern Strategies for Church Growth* (San Bernardino, Calif.: Here's Life, 1984), 30.
9. Lyle E. Schaller, "Megachurch!" *Christianity Today*, 5 March 1990, 20.
10. George Barna, *The Frog in the Kettle: What Christians Need to Know about Life in the Year 2000* (Ventura, Calif.: Regal, 1990), 35.

11. Schaller, "Megachurch!" 21.
12. Ibid., 21.
13. Ibid., 22.
14. Kenneth L. Woodward, "A Time to Seek," *Newsweek*, 17 December 1990, 56.
15. James Engel and Jerry Jones, *Baby Boomers and the Future of World Missions* (Orange, Calif.: Management Development Associates, 1989), 13.
16. Ibid., 13.
17. Ibid., 14.
18. Woodward, "A Time to Seek," 50.
19. Ibid., 51.
20. Hunter, *How to Reach Secular People*, 96.
21. Cindy L. Yorks, "Gimme That New-Time Religion," *USA Weekend* (April 1990): 14.
22. "Statistical Abstract," 449.
23. Mission statement taxonomy is from the James River Corporation.
24. Rick Warren, *How to Turn an Audience into an Army*, excerpts read by author, Laguna Hills, Calif.: Saddleback Community Church.
25. Bill Hybels, Stuart Briscoe, and Haddon Robinson, *Mastering Contemporary Preaching* (Portland, Ore.: Multnomah, 1989), 36.
26. Bill Hybels, *Structure of Ministry* (South Barrington, Ill.: Willow Creek Community Church, n.d.), 19.
27. Current composite size of 1,500 - Original size of 500 = Gain of 1,000. Therefore, the Original size of 500 is doubled by the gain of 1,000 new members. This translates into a decadal growth rate of 200 percent.
28. Charles L. Chaney and Ron S. Lewis, *Design for Church Growth* (Nashville: Broadman, 1977), 95.
29. Ibid., 127.
30. Lewis A. Drummond, *The Word of the Cross: A Contemporary Theology of Evangelism* (Nashville: Broadman, 1992), 311.
31. Chaney and Lewis, *Design for Church Growth*, 173.
32. Charles Shaver, "How to Develop an Evangelistic Congregation," *Preacher's Magazine*, September-November 1984, 13.
33. Duncan McIntosh and Richard E. Rusbuldt, *Planning Growth in Your Church* (Valley Forge, Pa.: Judson, 1983), 80.
34. Elmer Towns, *10 of Today's Most Innovative Churches* (Ventura, Calif.: Regal, 1990), 24.
35. Engel, *Contemporary Christian Communications*, 150–59.
36. Ibid., 168.
37. Barna, *Frog in the Kettle*, 143.
38. Thomas A. Stewart, "Turning Around the Lord's Business," *Fortune*, 25 September 1989, 117.
39. See Lyle E. Schaller, *Creative Leadership Series: Assimilating New Members* (Nashville: Abingdon, 1978).
40. "Esther Sanger Called Mother Teresa," *Grow* (Summer 1990): 1–4.

41. Kennon Callahan, *Twelve Keys to an Effective Church* (San Francisco: Harper & Row, 1983), 64.
42. Ibid., 5.
43. Erikson, *Identity, Youth and Crisis*, 137.
44. Barna, *Frog in the Kettle*, 159.

CHAPTER NINE

1. Gerhard Kittel, ed., *Theological Dictionary of the New Testament*, vol. 6 (Grand Rapids: Eerdmans, 1964), 2.
2. Kittel, *Theological Dictionary*, vol. 2: 94.
3. Kittel, *Theological Dictionary*, vol. 3: 639.
4. Kittel, *Theological Dictionary*, vol. 2: 140.
5. Dennis Kinlaw, "Preaching Holiness," as delivered at the Christian Holiness Association Convention, Kansas City, Mo., 1982.
6. William A. Dyrness, *How Does America Hear the Gospel?* (Grand Rapids: Eerdmans, 1989), 19.
7. Ibid., 148.
8. Haddon Robinson, "Blending Bible Content and Life Application" in *Mastering Contemporary Preaching* (Portland, Ore.: Multnomah, 1989), 65.
9. Fred Craddock, *Preaching* (Nashville: Abingdon, 1985), 95.
10. Ibid., 97.
11. Hybels, "Keeping Ourselves on Target," in *Mastering Contemporary Preaching*, 154.
12. Ibid., 36.
13. Ibid.
14. Ibid., 166.
15. Dyrness, *How Does America Hear the Gospel?* 124.
16. Theodore Baehr, *Getting the Word Out: How to Communicate the Gospel in Today's World* (San Francisco: Harper and Row, 1986), 102.
17. Ibid., 270.
18. Engel, *Contemporary Christian Communications*, 128.
19. J. Daniel Baumann, *An Introduction to Contemporary Preaching* (Grand Rapids: Baker, 1972), 42.
20. Ibid., 43.
21. Walter Brueggemann, *Finally Comes the Poet: Daring Speech for Proclamation* (Minneapolis: Fortress, 1989), viii.
22. Ibid., 2.
23. Randall Balmer, *Mine Eyes Have Seen the Glory: A Journey into the Evangelical Subculture in America* (New York: Oxford Univ. Press, 1989), 3–4.
24. George Fox, *The Journal of George Fox* (New York: E.P. Dutton, 1924), 11.
25. Brueggeman, *Finally Comes the Poet*, 6.
26. R. Alan Streett, *The Effective Invitation* (Old Tappan, N.J.: Fleming H. Revell, 1984), 36.

27. James Daane, *Preaching with Confidence* (Grand Rapids: Eerdmans, 1980), 9.
28. Craddock, *Preaching*, 98.
29. David Mains, "Building Bridges to Action," in *Preaching to Convince* (Waco, Texas: Word, 1986), 133.
30. John Broadus, *On the Preparation and Delivery of Sermons* (New York: Harper and Brothers, 1944), 156.
31. Streett, *The Effective Invitation*, 38.
32. Dennis Kinlaw, *Preaching in the Spirit* (Grand Rapids: Zondervan, 1985), 84.
33. Brueggeman, *Finally Comes the Poet*, 284.
34. Dwight Stevenson and Charles Diel, *Reaching People from the Pulpit* (Grand Rapids: Baker, 1978), 77.
35. Engel, *Contemporary Christian Communications*, 59.
36. Harry S. Stout, *The Divine Dramatist* (Grand Rapids: Eerdmans, 1991), 13.

CHAPTER TEN

1. William H. Willimon, *Worship as Pastoral Care* (Nashville: Abingdon, 1979), 209.
2. Alfred F. Bayly, "Lord, Whose Love in Humble Service," *Hymns for Praise and Worship* (Nappanee, Ind.: Evangel, 1984), 504.
3. Robert E. Webber, *Worship Is a Verb* (Waco, Texas: Word Books, 1985), 29.
4. Darius Salter, *What Really Matters in Ministry: Profiling Pastoral Success in Flourishing Churches* (Grand Rapids: Baker, 1990), 67.
5. Willimon, *Worship as Pastoral Care*, 30.
6. James F. White, *Protestant Worship: Traditions in Transition* (Louisville: Westminster/John Knox, 1989), 173.
7. Robert Webber, *Evangelicals on the Canterbury Trail: Why Evangelicals Are Attracted to the Liturgical Church* (Waco, Texas: Word, 1985), 45.
8. Ibid., 51.
9. Patrick R. Keifert, *Welcoming the Stranger* (Minneapolis: Fortress, 1992), 134.
10. Marilee Zdenek and Marge Champion, *God Is a Verb* (Waco, Texas: Word, 1979), 91.
11. James F. White, *Introduction to Christian Worship* (Nashville: Abingdon, 1980), 62.
12. John Killinger, "Reviving the Rights of Worship," *Leadership* (Fall 1989): 83.
13. James Whitcomb Riley, "When the Frost is on the Pumpkin," in *Childcraft*, vol. 2 (Chicago: Field Enterprises, 1954), 68–69.
14. Charles Van Engen, "Faith, Love, and Hope," in *The Good News of the Kingdom*, ed. Charles Van Engen (Maryknoll, N.Y.: Orbis, 1993), 256.
15. Elmer Towns, *10 of Today's Most Innovative Churches* (Ventura, Calif.: Regal, 1990), 66.
16. Horace T. Allen, Jr., "Worship as Art, Evangelization and Mission," *Reformed Liturgy and Music* (Summer 1989): 111.
17. Ray Stedman, *Body Life* (Glendale, Calif.: Regal, 1972), 143.

18. Willimon, *Worship as Pastoral Care,* 98.
19. C.S. Lewis, *Mere Christianity* (New York: Macmillan, 1952), 169.
20. Allen, "Worship as Art," 111.
21. James F. White, *Documents of Christian Worship* (Louisville: John Knox, 1992), 153.
22. Anne Ortlund, *Up with Worship* (Ventura, Calif.: Regal, 1982), 63.
23. See R. Gustav Niebuhr, "Megachurches Strive to Be All Things to All Parishioners," *Wall Street Journal,* 13 May 1991.

CHAPTER ELEVEN

1. *The Random House Dictionary of the English Language* (New York: Random House, 1987), 1111.
2. David Watson, *God Does Not Foreclose* (Nashville: Abingdon, 1990), 21.
3. William Temple, *Nature, Man, and God* (London: Macmillan, 1934), 467.
4. Clara Stuart, *Latimer: Apostle to the English* (Grand Rapids: Zondervan, 1986), 62.
5. Ibid., 339.
6. Malcolm Muggeridge, *Jesus Rediscovered* (New York: Doubleday and Company, Inc., 1969), 49–50.
7. Jack Bernard, "I Found Jesus in My Wallet," *World Christian Magazine* (April 1990): 24.
8. Thomas Oden, *After Modernity. . .What? Agenda for Theology* (Grand Rapids: Zondervan, 1990), 50.
9. Vernard Eller, *The Simple Life* (Grand Rapids: Eerdmans, 1973), 11.
10. Richard Foster, *Freedom of Simplicity* (San Francisco: Harper and Row, 1981), 123.
11. Temple, *Nature, Man, and God,* 468.
12. Edward Desmond, "A Pencil in the Hand of God," *Time,* 4 December 1989, 11.
13. Ibid., 11.
14. Temple, *Nature, Man, and God,* 196.
15. Watson, *God Does Not Foreclose,* 90.
16. Joseph C. Aldrich, *Life-Style Evangelism: Crossing Traditional Boundaries to Reach the Unbelieving World* (Portland, Ore.: Multnomah, 1981), 20.
17. Rebecca Pippert, *Out of the Saltshaker and into the World: Evangelism as a Way of Life* (Downers Grove, Ill.: InterVarsity, 1979), 128.
18. Mary Bosanquet, *The Life and Death of Dietrich Bonhoeffer* (New York: Harper and Row, 1968), 189.
19. Ibid., 209.
20. Ibid., 254.
21. Ibid., 272.
22. Ibid., 280.

CHAPTER TWELVE

1. William F. Fore, *Television and Religion: The Shaping of Faith, Values and Culture* (Minneapolis: Augsburg, 1987), 39.
2. Quentin Schultze, "Keeping the Faith: American Evangelicals and the Media," in *American Evangelicals and the Mass Media,* ed. Quentin Schultze (Grand Rapids: Zondervan, 1990), 42–43.
3. Ibid., 83.
4. Ibid., 22.
5. Dennis Voskuil, "The Power of the Air: Evangelicals and the Rise of Religious Broadcasting," in *American Evangelicals and the Mass Media,* ed. Quentin Schultze (Grand Rapids: Zondervan, 1990), 85.
6. Schultze, *American Evangelicals,* 176.
7. Ibid., 178.
8. Neil Postman, *Amusing Ourselves to Death* (New York: Viking, 1985), 4.
9. Ibid., 118.
10. Fore, *Television and Religion,* 80.
11. Ibid., 101.
12. Jeffery K. Hadden and Anson Shupe, *Televangelism: Power & Politics on God's Frontier* (New York: Henry Holt, 1988), 122.
13. Ibid., 83.
14. Ibid., 124.
15. Ibid., 156.
16. Ibid., 124.
17. Ibid., 156.
18. Fore, *Television and Religion,* 105.
19. Ibid., 105.
20. Ibid., 112.
21. Stuart M. Hoover, "The Meaning of Religious Television: The '700 Club' in the Lives of Its Viewers in American Evangelicals and the Mass Media," in *American Evangelicals and the Mass Media,* ed. Quentin Schultze (Grand Rapids: Zondervan, 1990), 240.
22. Fore, *Television and Religion,* 109.
23. Clifford G. Christians, "Redemptive Media as the Evangelical's Cultural Task," in *American Evangelicals and the Mass Media,* ed. Quentin Schultze (Grand Rapids: Zondervan, 1990), 332.
24. Ibid., 342.
25. Robert Wuthnow, "Religion and Television: The Public and Private," in *American Evangelicals and the Mass Media,* ed. Quentin Schultze (Grand Rapids: Zondervan, 1990), 208.
26. Postman, *Amusing Ourselves to Death,* 121.
27. Win Arn and Paul Crouch, "Is TV Appropriate for Mass Evangelism?" *Christianity Today,* 16 October 1987, 50.
28. Ibid.

29. Thomas E. Boomershine, "Doing Theology in the Electronic Age: The Meeting of Orality and Electricity," *Journal of Theology* (1991): 14.
30. Don Cox, "Evangelism and the Mass Media," in *Evangelism in the Twenty First Century, ed. Thom S. Rainer*(Wheaton, Ill.: Harold Shaw, 1989), 72.
31. Wuthnow, "Religion and Television," 201.
32. Schultze, "Keeping the Faith," 43.
33. Ken Curtis, "What Now? Practical Guidelines for Media Involvement," in *The Agony of Deceit: What Some T.V. Preachers Are Really Teaching,* ed. Michael Scott Horton (Chicago: Moody, 1990), 229.

CONCLUSION

1. Nathan O. Hatch and Michael S. Hamilton, "Can Evangelism Survive Its Success?" *Christianity Today,* 5 October 1992, 30.

index